UNDERSTANDING AND USING MICROCOMPUTERS

UNDERSTANDING AND USING MICROCOMPUTERS

Steven M. Zimmerman
College of Business and Management Studies,
University of South Alabama

Leo M. Conrad
Computer Education Research Institute Inc.

West Publishing Company
St. Paul   New York   Los Angeles   San Francisco

COPYRIGHT © 1986 By WEST PUBLISHING COMPANY
COPYRIGHT © 1988 By WEST PUBLISHING COMPANY
50 W. Kellogg Boulevard
P.O. Box 64526
St. Paul, MN 55164–1003

Library of Congress Cataloging-in-Publication Data

Zimmerman, Steven M.
    Understanding and using microcomputers.
    (The Microcomputing series)
    Includes bibliographies and index.
    1. Business—Data processing.   2. Microcomputers—
Programming.   I. Conrad, Leo M.   II. Title.   III. Series.
HF5548.2.Z58   1988   650'.028'5416   87–19044
ISBN 0–314–60096–5

Copy Editor: Barbara Bergstrom
Text Design: Linda Beauvais
Cover Design: Artform Inc.
Artwork: Alice B. Thiede, Carto-graphics

Registered Trademarks

Ability is a trademark of Xanaro Technologies, Inc., **Amiga** is a trademark of Commodore Business Machines, Inc., **Anadex** is a trademark of Anadex, Inc., **Apple I, Apple II, Apple II+, IIc, Apple DOS, Apple Macintosh, Apple Macintosh DOS,** and **Appleworks** are trademarks of Apple Computer, Inc., **AT&T 6300** is a trademark of American Telephone & Telegraph, **Atlantic Research Corporation XT** is a trademark of Atlantic Research Corporation, **Basic 386** is a trademark of Advanced Logic Research, **Boardroom Graphics** is a trademark of Analytical Software, **Business Graphics** is a trademark of Business and Professional Software, Inc., **Business Graphic System** is a trademark of Peachtree Software, Inc., **CPM, Concurrent CPM, MPM-86,** and **CPM-86** are trademarks of Digital Research, Inc., **Commodore DOS** is a trademark of Commodore Business Machines, Inc., **Centronics** is a trademark of Centronics Data Computer Corporation, **Chart Master** and **Sign Master** are trademarks of Decision Resources Corporation, **Compaq Deskpro 386 Model 40** and **Compaq Portable II** are trademarks of Compaq Computer Corporation, **Compuserve** is a trademark of H & R Block Company, **Context MBA** and **Corporate MBA** are trademarks of Context Management Systems, **Crosstalk XVI** is a trademark of Microstuf, Inc., **Data Capture** and **Data Capture PC** are trademarks of Southeastern Software, **Data General Model 2** is a trademark of Data General Corporation, **DataStar, ReportStar, InfoStar, MailMerge,** and **WordStar** are trademarks of Micropro International Corporation, **Davong Multilink** is a trademark of Davong Systems, **dBase II, dBase III, dBase III Plus, Framework,** and **Framework II** are trademarks of Ashton-Tate, **Desqview** is a trademark of Quarterdeck Office Systems, **Display Write** is a trademark of International Business Machines, Inc., **Dow Jones News/Retrieval Service** is a trademark of Dow Jones & Company, **Easinet** is a trademark of Esprit Systems, Inc., **EasyLink** and **Telex** are trademarks of Western Union, **Electric Pencil** is copyrighted by Michael Schrayer, **Enable** is a trademark of The Software Group, **Encore!** is a trademark of Ferox Microsystems, Inc., **Energraphics** is a trademark of Enertronics Research, Inc., **Epson FX-80, HX-20, JX-80, QX-10,** and **Epson Printers** are trademarks of Epson America, **Ethernet** is a trademark of Xerox Corporation, **F.A.S.T.** is a trademark of Dean Witter Company, **Fancy Font** is a trademark of Softcraft, Inc., **Fontastic** is a trademark of IHS Systems, **4-Point** is a trademark of IMSI, **FX700P** is a trademark of Casio Computer Corporation, **GEM Desktop** is a trademark of Digital Research Inc., **Giraph** is a trademark of Compu Vision International, **Graph Talk** is a trademark of Redding Group, Inc., **GraphPlan** is a trademark of Chang Laboratories, **Graphwriter** is a trademark of Graphic Communications, Inc., **IBM PC, XT, AT, PC Jr., PC Network, PS/2 Models 30, 50, 60, 80, OS/2, IBM Convertible, 360, 3270,** and **Personal Decision** are trademarks of International Business Machines, Inc., **Inset** is a trademark of APG Software, **Intel 4004, 8008, 8080, 8086, 8087, 8088, 80186, 80286, 80287, 80386** are trademarks of Intel Corporation, **Jazz, Lotus 1-2-3,** and **Symphony** are trademarks of Lotus Development Corporation, **Kaypro II** and **Kaypro 386 Model A** are trademarks of Kaypro Computer Corporation, **KnowledgeMan** is a trademark of Micro Data Base Systems, Inc./Consumer Products, **Koala Pad** is a trademark of Koala Technologies Corporation, **Leading Edge Model D** is a trademark of Leading Edge Products, Inc., **MS DOS, Microsoft Windows, Microsoft**

(continued on page 371)

To our students

CONTENTS IN BRIEF

Contents in Brief

CONTENTS

CHAPTER 3   OPERATING SYSTEMS

CHAPTER 4   WORD PROCESSING

CHAPTER 5   ELECTRONIC SPREADSHEETS

CHAPTER 6   DATABASE

CHAPTER 7   GRAPHICS

CHAPTER 8   MICROCOMPUTER COMMUNICATION

CHAPTER 9   COMMUNICATIONS WITH CENTRAL COMPUTERS

CHAPTER 10   LOCAL AREA NETWORKS

CHAPTER 11   THE INTEGRATION OF OPERATIONS AND DATA FILES

CHAPTER 12   HOW TO SELECT SOFTWARE AND MICROCOMPUTERS

PUBLISHER'S NOTE

This book is part of THE MICROCOMPUTING SERIES. As such it is an endeavor unique both to West Educational Publishing and to the College Publishing Industry as a whole.

We are "breaking this new ground" because in talking with educators across the country, we found several different needs not easily met by just one publication. Those needs are:

1. To teach the principles or concepts of microcomputer use independent of running specific software programs,
2. To teach the skills of specific application software programs, and
3. To create a microcomputer curriculum flexible enough to handle changes in technology or courses with a minimum of change in the teaching materials used.

THE MICROCOMPUTING SERIES is an innovative attempt to meet those needs by closely integrating a machine independent overview of microcomputers (the core text) with a series of inexpensive, software specific, "hands-on" workbooks. Although each text in the series can be used independently, they become especially effective when used together to provide both an understanding of how microcomputers work as well as experience using popular software packages.

We hope THE MICROCOMPUTING SERIES fits your needs and the needs of your students, and that you will adopt one or more of its components for use in your classes. We are also interested in hearing your reaction and suggestions concerning our series and encourage you to share your ideas with us through:

West Publishing Company
College Division
50 W. Kellogg Blvd.
P.O. Box 64526
St. Paul, MN 55164

ABOUT THE AUTHORS

Steven M. Zimmerman and Leo M. Conrad have written together twelve books, one major software product, and over 100 articles in the area of micro-computers. Included in their writings have been texts on quality control, spreadsheets, and business applications on the IBM PC and the Apple IIe.

Steven M. Zimmerman

B.S. Lehigh University
M.S. Columbia University
Ph.D. University of Arkansas

Professor: University of South Alabama. Teaching undergraduate and gradu-ate courses in business microcomputer applications, industrial management, quality control, operations research, applied statistics and other quantitative analysis procedures in business; 1971–present.

Contributing Editor: H&E Computronics Inc. 1982, 1983.
Vice President and Consultant A&Z Management: Service Inc. 1978–present.
Associate Professor: West Virginia University. 1969–1971.
Instructor: University of Arkansas. 1968, 1969.
President: Mike-O-Neal Motel. 1963–1980.
Assistant Professor: Newark College of Engineering. 1961–1969.
Instructor: Hofstra University. 1961.
Industrial Engineer: Grumman Aircraft Engineering Corp. 1957–1961.

Leo M. Conrad

B.S. Tulane University
B.A. Columbia Pacific University
M.B.A. Columbia Pacific University
M.A. Columbia Pacific University

President: Computer Education Research Institute, Inc. 1986–present
President: Imagineering Concepts, a consulting firm in microcomputers, public relations and management. 1956–present.
President: American Society of Technical Writers. 1985–present.
Instructor: Continuing Education. University of South Alabama. 1983.
Instructor: South West State Technical College. 1978–1979.

PREFACE

The first edition of *Understanding and Using Microcomputers* was published just as the microcomputer revolution brought forth the creation of a new introductory microcomputer user course. That course, which includes hardware, operating systems, word processing, spreadsheets, data base, graphics, communications, and integrated programs, is now part of the curriculum at most schools.

Our goal with this second edition has been to keep up with the continuing evolution of that course by meeting the needs of a changing student population and changing hardware and software capabilities. These exciting and dramatic changes are reflected in additions to this new edition, which include:

Coverage of New Hardware:
  Personal System/2
  Microcomputers using the Intel 80386 microprocessor
  Better graphics and color displays
Coverage of New Software:
  Chart graphics
  Graphics editors
  Desktop publishing software:
    Font programs
    Graphics and text integrators
    Page layout programs
Coverage of New Topics:
  Artificial Intelligence
  Decision Support Services
  Growth of shareware market
  Selecting computers and software for the home
Thorough Updating
  A thorough updating of all time dependent information, including illustrations, comparison charts, etc.

NEW HARDWARE COVERAGE

The introduction of the IBM Personal System/2 microcomputers represent a departure from past technology. We have detailed these changes and some of its consequences.

The development of the Intel 80386 microprocessor means the power of microcomputers have taken another quantum leap. Microcomputer hardware may now use up to 4 gigabytes of RAM and better service the multi-user and multi-tasking needs of users.

The number of pixels on screens have grown to over 2048 by 2048. The IBM PS/2 displays 640 by 480 pixels in 64 colors. Screens and video pc boards may be obtained for many specialized purposes including desk top publishing. Screens that display two pages of text and graphics side by side are available.

NEW SOFTWARE COVERAGE

Users have graphic programs available that may be used to create many different types of charts, with a large variety of display options. Our text helps users learn what is available and what can be accomplished.

Many graphics editors are now available to enhance standard charts, create freehand images, move and combine images from image libraries, and to add color. Programs and hardware that make it possible to perform electronic publishing at a reasonable cost are available. These programs include font generators, graphics and text integrators, and page layout programs. Users have a variety of programs at a variety of costs from less than $100 to approximately $12,000 to select from for these tasks.

Students and users on limited budgets have many good programs available as shareware and freeware programs. These programs may be obtained and investigated before being paid for. They provide a wealth of capabilities to users with limited budgets.

The field of microcomputing is constantly changing. We have updated the time dependent information in our text to reflect the most current changes in hardware, software, and techniques of use.

GOALS OF THIS TEXT

The book and its teaching support package are designed to make learning and teaching about microcomputers easier for both student and teacher. This book is designed so that the beginning student will learn about microcomputers and their use as personal productivity tools. This textbook is written so an individual with no computer background can read and understand it.

The objectives of this text are:

1. To illustrate how and why microcomputers are used in the "real world."
2. To develop personal microcomputing skills so the student may increase his or her own learning productivity in other courses by learning to:
    a. Use word processing programs.
    b. Use spreadsheet programs.
    c. Use data base programs.
    d. Use graphics programs.
    e. Use communication programs.
    f. Use integrated and overlay programs.
    g. Select hardware and software.

3. To provide the foundation for a series of books which can be used for the entire microcomputing curriculum.

4. To clearly explain the features that are found in general application software so the student may be better able to select hardware and software. These concepts are then applied to a variety of microcomputers and programs.

5. To integrate each of these components into one complete and flexible education experience which will provide students with the skills needed for our present technology as well as the broader concepts of understanding needed for adapting to future environments.

Highlights of this text include:

1. Chapter Outlines and Goals: The reader is able to look ahead to see the intent of each chapter.

2. "Micros in Action.": Examples of how the application program being studied are used by an actual organization.

3. "User Windows.": Hints on how individuals and companies should use the application program being studied.

4. Margin definitions: Each new key term is defined in the margin. Additional terms may be defined in the text.

5. Hardware Requirements: For each type of software package, the needs of each application program is identified so the user is better able to set up a system.

6. Hardware and Software Comparison Charts: Selected systems and software packages are compared at the end of each chapter to demonstrate the variety available and to help in the evaluation process.

7. Key Terms: At the end of each chapter the key microcomputer terms are listed. They are critical to the understanding of the chapter material.

8. Chapter Summaries: List the important topics and concepts covered.

9. Review Questions: These questions help the students to focus the important issues in the chapter.

10. Discussion and Application Questions: These questions are used to direct the students' outside activities.

11. Laboratory Assignments: Laboratory assignments are used to direct the students' activities in the microcomputer laboratory.

12. Problems: In the spreadsheet and database chapters, problems have been included for assignment and/or practice in the use of these programs.

13. Text Glossary: All margin definitions plus additional terms defined in the text are organized into an end of text glossary.

14. Appendices: For technical material needed in special situations. Appendix A: The History of Microcomputers Time Line; Appendix B: Types of Index Organization; Appendix C: Cases; Appendix D: The Importance of Software Documentation.

15. Cases: Three teaching cases are including as a capstone activity.

16. Supplements:

    a. Instructors manual with test bank.

    b. Test bank files are also available on a 5¼″ disk in MS/PC DOS format as ASCII files to qualified adopters.

    c. Overhead transparency masters.

THE MICROCOMPUTING SERIES

The textbook may be used alone. It also may be used as part of The Microcomputing Series, a complete learning package consisting of:

1. A core text, Understanding and Using Microcomputers. This text is a foundation text. It is neither machine nor software specific. It presents basic microcomputer concepts in a general framework for the student to build on.
2. A series of software specific (MS/PC-DOS) workbooks which you can "mix and match" to meet the needs of your current microcomputer environment as well as your future one, whatever it may be. We are very fortunate to be working with a team of experienced and talented educators in the preparation of this series. For a complete listing of the titles and authors, please refer to the publishers' note earlier in this book.

Steven M. Zimmerman
Leo M. Conrad

ACKNOWLEDGEMENTS

Many individuals helped in the effort to create this book. Among those helping were an outstanding team of educators who reviewed several drafts of the manuscript. We thank them for their time, their ideas and their commitment. They are:

Reviewers of The First Edition Before Publication

Bev Bilshausen, College of Dupage; Lloyd Brooks, Memphis State University; Carol Clark, St. Louis Community College-Florissant Valley; David Cooper, University of Connecticut; Ilene Dlugoss, Cuyahoga Community College; Ben Guild, Wright State University; Don Lyndahl, Milwaukee Area Technical College; Robert Nau, Tulane University; Gregory Parsons, University of South Maine; Floyd Ploeger, Southwestern Texas State University; Tim Robinson, Ramapo College; Arthur Strunk, Queensborough Community College; Jack VanLuik, Mt. Hood Community College; Karen Watterson, Shoreline Community College.

Adopters Who Have Reviewed The First Edition After Publication

Jack Gilman, Florida International University; Russell Hari, Chemeketa Community College; R. Wayne Headrick, Texas A & M University; Cynthia Kachik, Santa Fe Community College; Jeanette Muzio, University of Florida; Norman McNeal, Sauk Valley College; Paul Saunders, Royal Business School; Ralph Shafer, George Washington University; Jimmy K. Tang, San Diego Community College; George Upchurch, Carson-Newman College; Karla Vogel, University of New Hampshire-Manchester; Michael R. Williams, Kirkwood Community College.

Reviewers Of The Second Edition Before Publication

George Bright, University of Houston; Elaine Daly, Oakton Community College; Cynthia J. Kachik, Santa Fe Community College; Norman McNeal, Sauk Valley College; Chris Moyer, Wright State University; Michael R. Williams, Kirkwood Community College.

The "Micros in Action" feature would not have been possible without: Doug Houston and Carol A. Zimmerman of Doug Houston Real Estate; Bart Johnson of Scott Paper Company; Aubrey Diehl of Schneider Fleming Insurance; Jean King of Jean King and Associates; John Hanley of Burnett-Wilson Inc., General Contractors; Frank Knippenberg of Dean Witter; Robert Moore of Gleem Paint Center; Andres Aviles, Paul Reeves, and Stanley M. Zimmerman of International Software Consultants; and Bryan Nearn of Flautt and Mann Properties, Inc.

Among the many individuals who helped at various critical points in the project were: Warren Beatty of the University of South Alabama, Kirt Burdick of Teledyne, Andy Lightborne of the University of South Alabama, Eileen Mathis of Scott Paper Company, Gene Shockley of Burroughs Computers, John Coleman Smith of Automation Technology, and William Walker, of the University of South Alabama. Thanks to the many companies in the microcomputer field that provided us with technical support and encouragement.

The West Publishing team of professionals including Tim Reedy, Sharon Walrath, and Richard Wohl among others made the task of completing the original manuscript possible. The second edition was overseen by Bill Gabler, Barbara Bergstrom, Stacy Lenzen, and Richard Wohl. Their help and cooperation added many improvements to the text.

Steven M. Zimmerman
Leo M. Conrad

Understanding and Using Microcomputers

1

GOALS

Upon completion of this chapter you will be able to:

Understand how the microcomputer is used.

Define a microcomputer from several points of view.

Discuss the history of computers and microcomputers.

Identify some of the social, moral, and legal issues involved with using microcomputers.

OUTLINE

Chapter Goals

What Are the Functions of Microcomputers?

Word Processing
Spreadsheets
File and Data Base Management
Graphics
Communication
Integrated Programs
Specialized Application Programs
Artificial Intelligence
Decision Support Systems

What Are the Costs of Microcomputers?

What Are the Parts of Microcomputers?

Inside the CPU Box
Input Devices
Output Devices
On-Line Data Storage Devices

The Different Sizes of Microcomputers

Desktop
Transportable
Laptop
Pocket

Historical Development of Computers, Systems, and Software

The Hierarchy of Hardware, Operating System, and Software

Disk Operating Systems

Computer Languages

Legal and Ethical Issues

Ownership of Programs
Ownership of Data
Data Security
Misuse of Data

Summary

Key Terms

Review Questions

Selected References

MICROCOMPUTERS

The microcomputer is an important tool because it may be used to increase personal and business productivity. It is an economical and efficient way of accomplishing tasks.

These tasks include: producing professional documents (word processing programs); making analyses (electronic spreadsheet programs); maintaining lists of customers, clients, and inventories (data base programs); producing presentations (business graphics programs); communicating with other computers (communication and networking); the integration or combining of several of these tasks together (integrated programs); and performing specialized functions such as accounting (specialized **application programs**). There are three levels of application programs:

Application program:
A program designed to perform a specific function.

1. General application programs: word processors, spreadsheets, data base, graphics, and communications
2. Specialized application programs: general ledger, tax forms, statistical analysis, inventory control, quality control
3. Custom application programs: created by a programmer for a specific purpose in a specific organization

Software:
Programs, instructions that tell the microcomputer how to perform.

The microcomputer, combined with **software** (instructions that tell the microcomputer how to perform, also called programs), is often credited with being "powerful," meaning it has many capabilities to accomplish a variety of objectives.

The microcomputer is a recent arrival on the scene. We will outline the history of computers and microcomputers. We will also examine the history and future trends of software developed for microcomputers because accomplishing objectives depends on software.

Operating system:
The program that directs the flow of data among the parts of the microcomputer, the user, and the application program, often called the disk operating system (DOS or OS).

The microcomputer is a valuable productivity tool, because programs called **"operating systems"** have been developed to make them relatively easy for the user to control. The operating system is the controller, similar to a police officer directing traffic flow. The operating system directs the flow of data and instructions among the parts of the microcomputer, the user, and application programs.

Along with the rapid changes and increases in capabilities that have occurred in microcomputers, there are a number of business, legal, moral, and social issues that have developed. We will examine these issues.

The microcomputer as a personal computer is a device used by individuals to increase personal productivity in solving problems as well as a productivity tool.

A user of a large central computer system is expected to have some knowledge of how the computer works, how to use the operating system, and often how to program the computer. The microcomputer user expects the microcomputer and its programs to be designed to solve problems. The microcomputer and its programs and **documentation** are expected to be **user friendly**.

Documentation:
Narrative supplied with programs to help the user operate the software.

User friendly:
Microcomputers and programs that are easy to use.

WHAT ARE THE FUNCTIONS OF MICROCOMPUTERS?

The microcomputer helps solve problems. The microcomputer is a tool to use in solving problems. There are several general classifications of programs available for the microcomputer that are particularly valuable to the user.

1. Word processing
2. Spreadsheet
3. File management and data base management
4. Graphics
5. Communication with other microcomputers
6. Communication with central computers
7. Local area networks
8. Combinations of the above

This list of programs forms the outline of this textbook. It is a list of what we believe is important for you to learn about microcomputers.

Word Processing

A **word processing program** is designed to produce professional documents more quickly and accurately than a typewriter. Its capabilities include:

1. Creating and editing text
2. Printing text
3. Storing and retrieving text

Creating text is typing, editing, and retyping. Printing is producing a **hard copy** in the form specified by the edited material. Storing is saving the text for future use.

Word processing is the production of letters, reports, memos, and other documents (see Figure 1–1). It also includes the use of spelling, grammar, footnoting, indexing, and document assembly capabilities usually found in separate programs. Document assembly programs are often used in legal offices for the creation of individual wills and other legal documents from prerecorded paragraphs.

Spreadsheets

Spreadsheet programs are used for calculation (formula oriented) and presentation of data under the control of the end user. The screen is divided into columns (vertical division) and rows (horizontal division). The intersection of a column and a row is called a cell.

Figure 1–2 illustrates a manual accounting spreadsheet for posting. Figure 1–3 is the form found on the back of the report you receive from your monthly bank statement. This form is designed to help you balance your checkbook. It, too, is a good application of a spreadsheet. The spreadsheet program helps the end user solve common everyday business problems and tasks.

The spreadsheet program user must know how to solve the business problem, but needs only a minimum of microcomputer knowledge to use the program. Any problem that can be solved with pencil, paper, and calculator may be solved using a spreadsheet program.

File and Data Base Management

File management programs are simple filing programs. **Data base management** may include complete application programs with an objective such as an

---

Word processing program:
A program designed to aid an individual in the creation, editing, printing, storing, and retrieving of text.

Hard copy:
Text printed on paper.

Spreadsheet programs:
Programs that are used for calculation (formula oriented) and presentation.

File management programs:
Programs designed to store, update, and retrieve data. These programs are limited to managing simple files with narrow objectives.

Data base management programs:
Programs designed to store, update, and retrieve data. These programs are not limited to any particular type of application.

FIGURE 1–1
Microcomputer and Printer with Form

FIGURE 1–2 A Manual Accounting Spreadsheet

(a)   General Journal   Page 1

Date 19XX		Description	Post. Ref.	Debit	Credit
	1	CASH	11	15000	
		OWNERS EQUITY, STACEY CAPITAL	31		15000
		STACEY CONTRIBUTED FUNDS TO THE			
		BUSINESS			
	2	TRUCK	15	4000	
		CASH	11		4000
	2	EQUIPMENT	17	1800	
		CASH	11		1000
		ACCOUNT PAYABLE	21		800
		EQUIPMENT FOR BUS $1000 DOWN			
		BALANCE DUE IN 30 DAYS			

IMPORTANT Please examine this statement immediately. We will assume that the balances it shows are correct unless you notify us of any disagreement within 60 days.

BALANCING YOUR CHECKING AND SAVINGS ACCOUNT

Before you start, please be sure you enter ***In your checkbook or savings register*** any interest earned, automatic transactions or bank charges includig those shown on this statement.

A. Enter deposits not shown on this statement.

date of deposit	amount
Total A	

B. Enter all checks, withdrawals and bank charges not shown on this statement.

outstanding check number	amount
Total B	

Follow instructions below to compare transactions recorded on your statement with those in your checkbook.

NEW BALANCE shown on other side

PLUS Total A ________

EQUALS ________

MINUS Total B ________

EQUALS your current checkbook balance ________

FIGURE 1–3
Checkbook Balancing Form

inventory system or **programming languages** in which many different applications can be created. The objective, the skills available, the cost of the programs, and the microcomputer available determine which option is better.

Programming language: A language used by programmers to create, store, recall, and edit instructions to computers.

File and data base management programs are designed to store, update, and retrieve information. The entering, recording, recalling, sorting, and using of stored **data** should be controlled by managerial guidelines so that the objectives of the end user may be accomplished.

Data: Facts that have been collected, organized, and stored.

Data bases include customer mailing lists, inventory lists, employee records, student records and grades, credit information, etc. Microcomputers, with the addition of data base programs, can be used to manage and maintain business data bases.

Data base: A collection of data stored in your microcomputer that is used for a variety of purposes.

Graphics

Graphics may be divided into several classifications:

1. Standard graphics
   a. Analytical
   b. Presentation
2. Engineering/scientific graphics

Standard analytical graphics programs have the capability of producing bar charts, pie charts, and line type graphs (see Figure 1–4). Business graphics are often used to impress a customer or a supervisor more easily than lists, words, or tables. The data from spreadsheet or data base programs may often be used to prepare graphic presentations without the need to re-enter the data.

Standard graphics programs: Programs that have the capability of producing bar charts, pie charts, and line type graphs.

FIGURE 1–4
Bar Chart on Screen

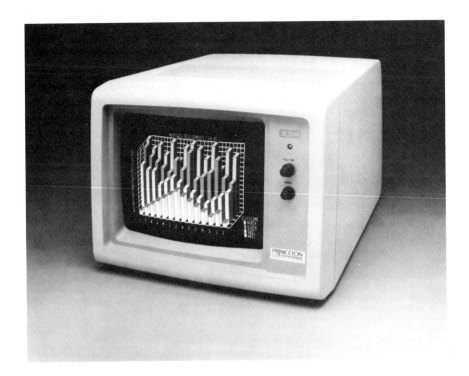

Business presentation graphics are graphics that combine art and photography (on the screen) with data for sales and other presentations. The graphics capabilities of the microcomputer include the handling of television pictures and combining them with microcomputer output. Marketing managers will be interested in these capabilities for their potential in advertising. Figures 1–5 and 1–6 are examples of what is currently available.

Engineering/scientific graphics include CAD, computer aided design, CAE, computer aided engineering, CADD, computer aided design and drafting among other similar applications. Figures 1–7 and 1–8 are examples of engineering graphics in use.

Other graphics include line charts such as organization charts, flow charts, control charts, and statistical analysis charts.

Communication

Communication program:
A program that allows computers to communicate with each other.

Communication programs make it possible for microcomputers to communicate with most computers. They can act as a dumb terminal, i.e., communicate only under the control of an operator using the keyboard, or as a smart terminal that can transfer data files between two computers. The capability to communicate requires a modem (device to connect the computer to a telephone) or a null-modem (device that makes the computer behave as if it is connected to a telephone). Cables and software complete the communication needs.

Integrated Programs

Integrated programs:
Programs that combine the capabilities of two or more general or specific application programs.

Integrated programs have different combinations of capabilities available at the same time for selected tasks. There are programs available which combine

FIGURE 1–5
Digitized Picture and Microcomputer Output

the features of one or more general programs. Integrated programs often include electronic spreadsheets and the capability to perform graphics. Some programs combine word processing, spreadsheet, data base, graphic, and communication capabilities.

FIGURE 1–6
Presentation Graphics

FIGURE 1–7
Engineering with a Touch Screen

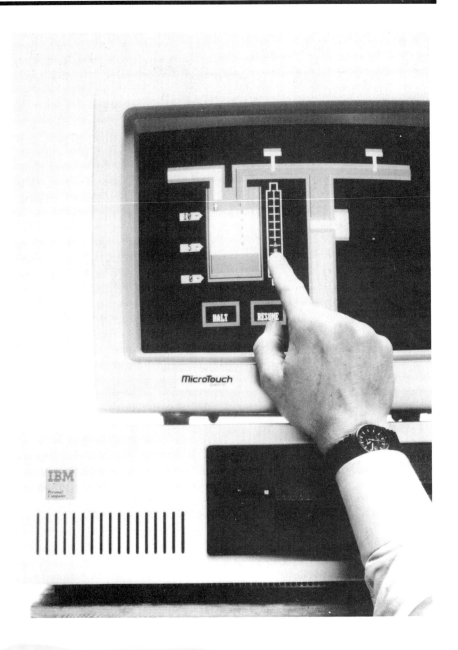

Specialized Application Programs

Specialized application programs will help those who have a need to solve a specific problem. The specialized application program is an alternate tool you may use to solve your problems. Examples include statistical, accounting, inventory, payroll, real estate evaluation, or project management programs as well as others. Figure 1–9 shows a profit and loss statement produced by an application program on a microcomputer and printer.

A common approach to creating special programs is to design them for a vertical market. A vertical market is a narrow market limited to a specific professional area. Examples of vertical markets are:

FIGURE 1–8
Engineering Graphics Hewlett-Packard System

1. Accountants
2. Medical doctors
3. Veterinarians
4. Building contractors

Artificial Intelligence

Intelligence is the ability to learn, to understand, and to deal with new situations. Intelligence is associated with human beings. Artificial intelligence (AI) is the art and science of making computers behave in a manner resembling intelligent human behavior. Computers that have artificial intelligence are considered by some to be fifth-generation machines. Artificial intelligence is used to create programs for end users. The end user is often not aware of the use of AI in the program.

One application of AI is the design and development of expert systems. An expert system contains the decision-making rules of experts that have been captured and stored in a computer. Expert systems may be developed for a situation where a data base exists, the decisions are based on the facts stored in the data base, and the decision process is relatively simple.

Decision Support Systems

An integrated management information and planning system is a decision support system (DSS). Decision support systems provide management with the ability to query its computer systems for information in a variety of ways, to analyze information, and to predict the impact of decisions before they are made.

FIGURE 1–9

Profit and Loss Statement

```
                         January 3, 1987

                 West Brook Real Estate
                    4151 Bay Lane Road
                   Mobile,Alabama 36605

          P r o f i t   and   L o s s   S t a t e m e n t

   Revenue
   Number Account      Current Period        Year to date
                       Amount    Percent     Amount    Percent
   ------------------------------------------------------------
   6010 Rent Inc       1,760.00     32        4,810.00     28
   6020 Evaluation         0.00      0        4,116.39     24
   6025 Mgt Serv.      2,701.75     49        2,701.75     16
   6030 Capital          571.98     10        2,262.50     13
   6040 Interest         364.37      7        1,708.19     10
   6050 Consultant        0.00      0        1,000.00      6
   6900 Misc. Co         124.00      2          496.00      3
                       ----------             -----------
                       $5,522.10             $17,094.83
                       ==========             ============

   Expenses

   Number Account      Current Period        Year to date
                       Amount    Percent     Amount    Percent
   ------------------------------------------------------------
   9100 Maintena         837.47     27        2,139.95     16
   9200 Supplies          68.48      2        2,530.32     18
   9300 Deprecia       1,286.37     42        5,145.48     37
   9400 Interest         577.52     19        2,336.62     17
   9500 Operatio         134.90      4          141.06      1
   9501 Advertiz           0.00      0           36.30      0
   9510 Utilitie           0.00      0          150.00      1
   9520 Insuranc           0.00      0          117.17      1
   9530 Taxes Re           0.00      0          435.95      3
   9532 Other Ta           0.00      0            0.00      0
   9540 Professi         133.40      4          240.73      2
   9550 Travel (          0.00      0            0.00      0
   9560 Local Au          52.70      2          246.33      2
   9570 Medical            0.00      0          239.67      2
                       ----------             -----------
                       $3,090.84             $13,759.58
                       ==========             ============

   Profit              $2,431.26             $3,335.25
```

The programmer that creates a decision support system uses AI and computer behavioral, financial, economic, statistical, and mathematical models, among other tools. DSS is the integrated set of tools that help management make better decisions.

WHAT ARE THE COSTS OF MICROCOMPUTERS?

The microcomputer purchase price is less than $15,000. The cost of a microcomputer includes its purchase price, maintenance cost, and operational costs. These costs vary depending upon the location of the purchaser, the time in the life cycle of a microcomputer it is purchased, the source from which it is purchased, the support included in the purchase price, and whether the purchase was cash or credit.

If a microcomputer is purchased when the model is first introduced to the market, you must expect to pay full list price. After the initial sales period the price usually drops and some discounting is available.

From a purchase price point of view, microcomputers are defined as computers selling for less than $15,000. We estimate that the average professional paid less than $15,000 for a "full-featured" microcomputer system between the late 1970s until today. Few units, except for ones with "extra capabilities," sell for more. Figures 1–10 and 1–11 are examples of typical microcomputer systems.

Starter systems have sold for as little as $50. These units, however, often mushroom in price to over $1,500 when their capabilities are expanded.

A "full-featured" system is one that includes most of the accessories available, a printer, and memory capacities equal to the standard of the time. Figure 1–12 illustrates a full-featured system.

"Extra capabilities" refers to state of the art developments when they are first introduced. The extra capability feature of one year is often a standard feature the next year.

The purchase price is not the only cost consideration for microcomputers. Most microcomputer systems are reliable and have minimal maintenance costs. However, business professionals may protect themselves with maintenance contracts that cover repairs on **hardware.** These annual contracts cost between 10 and 20 percent of the purchase price and are available from local computer dealers. Most problems may be avoided with periodic cleaning and careful use.

Hardware:
The part of the microcomputer you can see and feel.

The cost of operating a microcomputer system also includes salaries, ribbons, and paper. The benefits obtained in terms of increased productivity mean that you can expect the cost of operating a microcomputer to be less than performing the same functions some other way. In chapter 12 you will learn about business evaluation methods called break-even and payback analysis.

FIGURE 1–10
IBM Personal System/2 Model 30

FIGURE 1–11
Compaq Systems

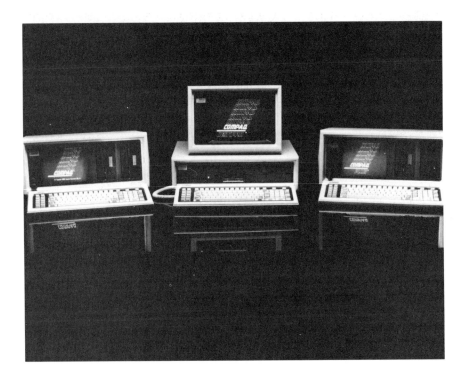

These techniques compare the cost of two alternate methods of doing a task, and aid you in determining which is best for your needs.

WHAT ARE THE PARTS OF MICROCOMPUTERS?

The microcomputer hardware is the part of the microcomputer you can see and feel. The microcomputer hardware consists of:

1. The computer case (CPU box) contains as a minimum:
    a. A microprocessor
    b. Cards with circuits to control data storage devices
    c. Circuits to communicate with external devices
    d. Chips containing the computer's internal memory
        RAM, Random access memory
        ROM, Read only memory
2. Input devices that connect you to the computer, such as a keyboard, voice recognition unit, bar code readers, etc.
3. Output devices that show you what the computer has done or is doing, such as a cathode ray tube (CRT, screens, monitors), telephone modems, printers, and plotters.
4. On-line memory devices:
    a. floppy disk drives
    b. hard disk drives, fixed or removable
    c. tape recorders

FIGURE 1–12
Hewlett-Packard's UNIX System

Inside the CPU Box

The core of the microcomputer is the **microprocessor.** It contains the central processing unit (CPU) of your computer as well as other circuits. Usually the capabilities of microcomputers are contained on **cards** or **boards** with special circuits such as ones that control data storage devices or that communicate with devices such as monitors and printers. The memory of the microcomputer, read only memory (**ROM**) and random access memory (**RAM**), is also in the box.

Input Devices

The primary method of input from a human to the microcomputer is through a keyboard. There are many designs for keyboards, but most are similar to that of the typewriter (see Figure 1–13).

Microprocessor:
An integrated circuit on a silicon chip usually less than two inches long and a half-inch wide, that consists of the arithmetic, logic, control, and memory units. The remaining hardware supports this chip.

Cards, boards:
Flat pieces of material with printed circuits and electronic components to add special capabilities to the microcomputer. Often called PC (Printed Circuit) boards.

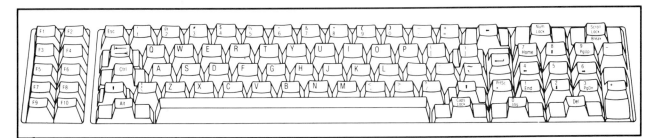

FIGURE 1–13   The Microcomputer's Keyboard

ROM:

Read only memory. Memory with instructions (programs) needed when operating the microcomputer. The user cannot write data into ROM. Sometimes called firmware.

RAM:

Random access memory. Memory used for data and program storage by the user. The user can write and read data in RAM.

I/O:

Input and output devices or methods.

Output Devices

The primary method of output from the microcomputer to humans is the CRT (cathode ray tube), also called a screen, monitor, or VDT (video display tube). It looks like a television set (see Figure 1–14). Input and output devices are often called I/O devices.

On-Line Data Storage Devices

On-line storage devices are devices that store (record) computer data and programs, but are not electronically an "internal" part of the computer. On-line storage devices are sometimes referred to as secondary storage devices. In many microcomputers these devices are mounted in the same case as the other parts of the computer, but they are electronically connected through special controller boards only. The methods of recording computer information include floppy disk drives, hard disk drives, and large format magnetic tape (see Figures 1–15 and 1–16).

THE DIFFERENT SIZES OF MICROCOMPUTERS

The wide variety of sizes, shapes, capabilities, and design among microcomputers makes it easy for the business professional to find a system that fits a particular need. A microcomputer may be one of four sizes; desktop unit, transportable, laptop computer, or pocket computer.

FIGURE 1–14
CRT

FIGURE 1–15
Hard Disk Drive System with Tape
Backup

FIGURE 1–16
Two Floppy Disk and Hard Disk
System

Desktop

A **desktop microcomputer** is one that fits on a desk (see Figure 1–17). It may be a "full-featured" unit having all the parts usually found in a microcomputer at any given time. Desktop units may have large monitors, external on-line storage devices, as well as other **peripherals.**

Desktop units have the greatest capabilities because they have the most internal room to expand to satisfy many needs, by using add-on boards or cards containing additional circuits.

Transportable

The **transportable microcomputer,** sometimes called **portable microcomputer,** is similar to the desktop microcomputer in its capabilities. The transportable is a self-contained package (see Figure 1–18). The parts generally packaged include a monitor, disk drives (both floppy and hard disk), keyboard, and the microprocessor, including external connections for printer and communications. Some units include printers while others include built-in modems for communication over telephone lines.

The transportable is useful for professionals who have to travel, for giving sales and educational presentations because it often can be connected to external monitors for group viewing of the contents of the screen, and for users who want a microcomputer that takes up less room, that is, has a smaller **footprint** on the desk.

Desktop microcomputer:
A microcomputer that has the greatest capabilities, most expansion room, and requires a part of a desk for its work area.

Peripheral:
A device such as a printer, bar code reader, or modem connected to a microcomputer to give it special capabilities.

Transportable microcomputers:
Microcomputers that are packaged with most of the features of a desktop, including a monitor.

Portable microcomputers:
Often refers to transportable, and at other times to all computers smaller than transportable.

Footprint:
The amount of space taken on a desk by a microcomputer.

FIGURE 1–17
AT & T 6300 Desktop System

FIGURE 1–18
Hewlett-Packard's Transportable on the Move

Laptop

Laptop computers have "full size" keyboards and are currently the smallest units upon which word processing can be performed (see Figures 1–19 and 1–20). Traveling professionals may use laptop computers in airports and on some airplanes. Outside sales people find it convenient to use microcomputers for direct sales support when making house calls.

Laptop microcomputer: A microcomputer that fits in a briefcase and/or may be used on an individual's lap.

USER WINDOW

COMPUTERS SAVE TIME

The salesman used a battery-powered laptop microcomputer to type his sales report in the airport. When he returned to his office, the text was transferred to the desktop computer and he was able to return home in time for dinner. By typing his report at the airport he saved an hour.

FIGURE 1–19

Epson HX–20 Laptop Computer

FIGURE 1–20

Traveling with Radio Shack's
Model 100

Pocket

The smaller the computer, the more specialized it tends to be. The **pocket computer** has the most limited memory and capabilities, and it tends to be a calculation and data storage device only. There are some pocket computers with expanded memory that are useful in many business applications where physical size is critical.

HISTORICAL DEVELOPMENT OF COMPUTERS, SYSTEMS, AND SOFTWARE

The history of microcomputers may be divided into five phases:

- Phase 1—Pre-microprocessor: Before the development of the Intel 4004 chip.
- Phase 2—Hardware and Operating System Development: Computer clubs and basic hardware led to the creation and development of the microcomputer hardware and operating system.
- Phase 3—Software Development: The development of commercial programs needed by the business professional.
- Phase 4—Professional Use: The use of the microcomputer by professionals without computer training or background.
- Phase 5—Connectivity: The use of the microcomputer as part of a system.

Appendix E is a detailed time line of the history of microcomputers.

Phase 1 included the development of computer and electronic theory and the manufacturing capabilities to produce smaller computers. The development of the Intel 4004 microprocessor identifies the end of this phase. Figure 1–21 illustrates the size reduction of circuits.

USER WINDOW

GROWTH BEYOND EXPECTATION

Most business professionals felt as Thomas J. Watson, Sr., president of IBM, did in the late 1940s: at the most eight or ten computers would be needed in the United States to satisfy all business and scientific needs. IBM entered the computer business only after Thomas J. Watson, Jr., took control of the company from his father. Since then, over eleven million microcomputers alone have been sold.

Phase 2, hardware and operating system development, covers the period when computer clubs and hobbyists called hackers were responsible for the creation and design of microcomputer hardware and the operating systems needed to make the microcomputers work.

Phase 3, software, saw the development of general, specialized, and custom application programs. The software hobbyists first developed programs

FIGURE 1–21
The Size of Memory Circuits

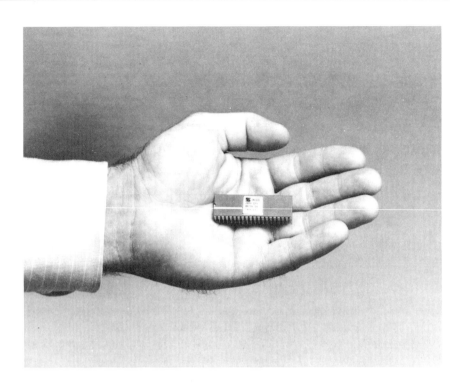

for their own use. Many of these programs became the first commercial programs.

Programs were generally produced only for selected microcomputers. The rule "Find the software, then purchase the hardware" had to be followed carefully.

Among the first programs to become commercially available in the late 1970s were accounting programs such as general ledger, accounts payable, and accounts receivable. Payroll programs came later.

Michael Shrayer developed "Electric Pencil" in 1975 for the Altair and later adapted it for the Radio Shack Model I microcomputer and other microcomputers. Electric Pencil was the first word processor available for microcomputers. Word processing resulted in a big increase in the use of microcomputers because it is so much easier, quicker, and less expensive to use than typing.

VisiCalc was the first spreadsheet program to be developed (1979). Its existence created a market for microcomputers that had not previously existed. The market developed because VisiCalc could be used by the business professional to solve selected business problems more efficiently than any other method available.

There are many different brands of spreadsheet programs such as Super-Calc (originally, a spreadsheet program that is now an integrated program), Multiplan, and Lotus 1–2–3 (also an integrated program). They are all similar to the original VisiCalc. The capabilities of newer versions of integrated spreadsheet programs have expanded to include graphics, communications, data base functions, and others.

In Phase 4 the end user came to dominate microcomputer use. The hardware and operating system concepts were developed in Phase 2; the basic software, word processing, spreadsheets, and data base programs were created in Phase 3. The introduction of microcomputers with packaged programs, like the Osborne 1, and the introduction of the IBM PC in 1981 marked the beginning of Phase 4. You are part of it.

A current trend in Phase 5 is to integrate the operations of all computer facilities in an organization. Microcomputers are being connected to mini and mainframe computers as workstations. Programs are being written that look, feel, and work the same on all sizes of equipment, from micro to mainframe. Data is being transferred up and down between computers of different sizes.

THE HIERARCHY OF HARDWARE, OPERATING SYSTEM, AND SOFTWARE

Hardware is the foundation upon which operating systems are developed. Hardware and operating systems form the basis on which applications program are designed. The hardware of a microcomputer was needed before an operating system could be developed. An operating system is the program that makes the parts of a microcomputer system work as a system. After operating systems became available, utilities and programming languages were developed. Application programs were then developed, because it was much easier to develop applications using the operating system, utilities, and programming languages. An overview of the **hierarchy** of hardware and software is shown in Figure 1–22.

Hierarchy:
Classification or grading of a group or set from high to low.

You have now learned about the development of the many hardware parts of a microcomputer. Disk operating systems underwent concurrent development.

FIGURE 1–22
The Hierarchy of Hardware, Operating System, and Software

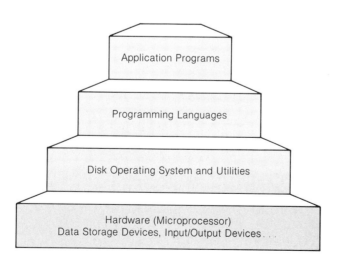

DISK OPERATING SYSTEMS

The disk operating system is the program used to make all the parts (hardware and software) of the microcomputer work together. Computer users, usually through programs, send instructions to the disk operating system, which then directs the hardware how to carry out the given instructions (see Figure 1–23). The disk operating system is what makes your computer hardware, printer, monitor, keyboard, disk drives, tape recorder, and software work together as a system.

Each part of the microcomputer system must react with split-second timing to accomplish different tasks. A good operating system makes the task of getting useful results from a microcomputer look easy.

The more popular operating systems found in microcomputers include:

1. Apple-DOS, Apple Disk Operating System used on Apple computers.

2. Apple-Macintosh DOS, Apple Disk Operating System used on the Apple Macintosh.

3. CP/M, Control Program/Microcomputer—operating system used for business applications.

4. MS–DOS/PC DOS, Microsoft Disk Operating System/Personal Computer Disk Operating System used on the IBM PC, XT, AT, and compatibles.

FIGURE 1–23
The Disk Operating System Directs the Flow of Traffic

5. OS/2, Operating System 2 for multi-user operation on the IBM Personal System/2 microcomputers and compatibles.

6. TRS–DOS, Tandy Radio Shack–Disk Operating System used in various forms on many Radio Shack microcomputers.

7. UNIX. The multi-user operating system developed by Bell Laboratories. Versions of UNIX include Venix and Xenix.

A family of microcomputers is defined by the operating system used. Application programs created to work on one member of a microcomputer family will often operate on most microcomputers using the same operating system.

COMPUTER LANGUAGES

Computer languages have been developed to fit different user needs. To program (give instructions to) a microcomputer, a computer language is used. The objective in designing a computer language is to create a limited language that human beings can relate to, and that a computer can understand so that a set of machine language instructions may be generated. Humans speak English, French, and other similar languages. Microcomputers speak with on and off switches, a binary number language. The computer language bridges the gap between human and **machine language.** Computer languages are often classified as **assembly languages, low level languages,** and **high level languages.**

The most popular microcomputer language is **BASIC,** Beginners All-purpose Symbolic Instruction Code. The original version was developed at Dartmouth College by John Kemeny and Thomas Kurtz as a teaching language. The version of BASIC on today's microcomputers has many capabilities beyond the original language. BASIC's popularity can be traced to its relative ease of learning and its added capabilities.

Standards defining the acceptable statements in BASIC and other languages are maintained by ANSI, American National Standards Institute. The standard is not complete because of the rapid changes in hardware, capabilities, and software in the microcomputer industry. There are many "dialects" of BASIC which vary greatly.

Instructions written in a computer language may be converted to machine language using a compiler or an interpreter. A compiler is a translator program that takes the near English code and translates it into a set of machine language codes all at one time. If there are any **syntax** errors, such as misspelling a word, the compiler will not be able to complete its task. All such errors must be eliminated at this step.

An interpreter is a program that translates a line of near English code into machine language, executes the line of code, translates the next line, etc. This type of translator is slower, but easier for the development of new applications because it helps with error elimination.

Some of the languages available on microcomputers are shown in Table 1–1.

Machine language:
A formal system of signs and symbols including rules for their use that convey instructions to a computer.

Assembly language:
A language that is close to machine language and may be easily converted using a special program called an assembler.

Low level language:
A computer language near machine language.

High level language:
A computer language near English.

BASIC:
Beginners All-purpose Symbolic Instruction Code.

Code:
The use of symbols or numbers to represent letters, numbers, or special meanings.

Syntax:
The manner in which the code must be put together for the computer to understand, including spelling.

TABLE 1–1
Microcomputer Languages

Language	Application	Compiled	Interpreted
ASSEMBLY*	Used to create machine language programs.		
BASIC	Found on most microcomputers.	X	X
C	Structured programming language; Can perform many tasks that would normally require the use of assembly-machine programs.	X	
COBOL	COmmon Business Oriented Language; For business programs such as accounting.	X	
FORTH	FOuRTH generation language; Business, scientific, process control, robotics. Contains a resident assembly language.	X	
FORTRAN	FORmula TRANslator; Engineering and science applications.	X	
LOGO	Education; Uses graphics for programming.	X	
PASCAL	Simple and structured for general applications.	X	X

*Assembly is almost always available on microcomputers. It is generally the language used to create high-level language compilers and interpreters.

LEGAL AND ETHICAL ISSUES

Legal and ethical questions abound. Currently the legal and ethical issues of the most concern to the microcomputer user include:

1. Ownership of programs
2. Ownership of data
3. Data security
4. Misuse of data

Ownership of Programs

It is easy to copy programs for backup and other purposes. However, when a program is sold, you purchase the right to use it on a single computer or in a single location. You do not purchase the right to re-sell it or give it to your friends (see licensed agreement, Figure 1–24).

It is estimated that as much as 80 percent of the software being used in corporations and by individuals was not purchased legally. The software has been copied in violation of the licensing agreement. There are no accepted solutions to this problem, and now that you are entering the world of computers, it has become your problem.

Whatever the legal resolution of unlicensed software copying is, you should do everything in your power to act within the law. You would not like to lose your job and destroy your career by stealing a piece of software.

Ownership of Data

Software belongs to the developer and designer. Data belongs to the individual or institution that collects it. To enter a data base without the consent of the owner, or to view, copy, or damage the information in any manner, is neither moral nor legal in most instances. State and federal laws addressing the unauthorized entry of individuals to data bases are under development.

FIGURE 1–24
Software Agreement

Rawhide Software
1163 Napoleon Road
Bowling Green, Ohio 43402

RAWHIDE ™ LICENSE AGREEMENT

READ BEFORE OPENING: CAREFULLY READ THE FOLLOWING LICENSE BEFORE YOU OPEN THE SEALED PACKAGE. OPENING THE SEALED PACKAGE CONSTITUTES YOUR ACCEPTANCE OF ALL TERMS OF THIS LICENSE. IF YOU DO NOT AGREE WITH THEM, PROMPTLY RETURN THE SEALED PACKAGE UNOPENED TO RAWHIDE SOFTWARE AT THE ABOVE ADDRESS OR TO WEST PUBLISHING COMPANY ("West"), 50 WEST KELLOGG BOULEVARD, ST. PAUL, MINNESOTA 55101, AND YOU WILL HAVE NO FURTHER LIABILITY.

　　1.　**License.** Rawhide Software ("Rawhide") grants you a non-exclusive, non-transferable limited license to use, copy and permit others to use the copyrighted software contained on the diskette in the sealed package, together with the accompanying copyrighted user documentation (collectively, "Software"). All use must be in accordance with the terms of this License. Title to and ownership of the Software remains in Rawhide.

　　2.　**Limitations.**

　　a.　You may use the Software solely for educational and instructional purposes in connection with a college-level course for which a West text is the approved textbook (the "Course").

　　b.　You may permit enrollees in the Course to use the Software.

　　c.　You may copy the Software for use in connection with the Course but you may make only that number of copies which is reasonably necessary for such use.

　　d.　When you copy the Software, you must also reproduce the machine-readable copyright notice on each copy and affix a reproduction of the copyright notice contained on the enclosed diskette on each copy.

YOU MAY NOT USE, COPY, MODIFY, DISTRIBUTE OR TRANSFER THE SOFTWARE, IN WHOLE OR IN PART, EXCEPT AS EXPRESSLY PERMITTED IN THIS LICENSE.

　　3.　**Term and Termination.** This License is effective when you open the sealed package and remains in effect until terminated. You may terminate this License at any time by ceasing all use of the Software and destroying the Software and all copies you have made. It will also terminate automatically if you fail to comply with the terms of this License. Rawhide may terminate this License one year after its effective date by giving you notice of termination. You agree to cease all use of the Software and to destroy the Software and all copies upon termination.

　　4.　**No Warranty.** NEITHER RAWHIDE NOR WEST WARRANTS THE PERFORMANCE OF OR RESULTS THAT MAY BE OBTAINED BY USE OF THE SOFTWARE. THE SOFTWARE IS PROVIDED "AS IS" WITHOUT WARRANTY OF ANY KIND, EXPRESS OR IMPLIED, INCLUDING THE WARRANTIES OF MERCHANTABILITY OR FITNESS FOR A PARTICULAR PURPOSE.

　　5.　**Limitation of Liability.** Neither Rawhide nor West shall be liable to you for any damages, including direct, incidental, special, consequential or any other type of damages, arising out of this License or the use or inability to use the Software.

　　6.　**Proprietary Rights.** You acknowledge that the Rawhide ™ name, the names of the Rawhide programs and the Software (including all support materials) are copyrighted, trademarked or owned by Rawhide as trade secrets and/or proprietary information and that all such matter shall remain the exclusive property of Rawhide.

　　7.　**Governing Law.** This Agreement will be governed by the laws of the State of Minnesota.

YOU ACKNOWLEDGE THAT YOU HAVE READ THIS LICENSE AND AGREE TO ALL ITS TERMS. YOU ALSO AGREE THAT THIS LICENSE IS THE ENTIRE AND EXCLUSIVE AGREEMENT BETWEEN YOU, RAWHIDE AND/OR WEST AND SUPERCEDES ANY PRIOR UNDERSTANDING OR AGREEMENT, ORAL OR WRITTEN, RELATING TO THE SUBJECT MATTER OF THIS AGREEMENT.

Data Security

Data security systems and procedures are difficult to create and maintain. It is said, "Whenever a better security system is created, someone will come up with a method of breaking the system." Many individuals earn their living creating and maintaining data security systems.

Misuse of Data

Data is a valuable asset of a business or an individual. Data may represent power to earn money and control the activities of individuals. Data may also harm individuals when used wrongly, by error or by intent. Government data bases have long been a concern of individuals who worry about possible invasion of privacy.

Increasing capabilities of microcomputers mean that individuals and businesses are able to maintain their own data bases. Many problems will be created by the proliferation of electronic data bases.

As a manager or user of a data base you have a responsibility to use the data in a professional manner. The laws on how these data bases can be used and the responsibility of the owners are just now being written. You will be judged by their standards once they are implemented. You have the opportunity and obligation to participate in the development of these standards.

SUMMARY

The microcomputer has been defined from several points of view. Some of the social, moral, and legal issues associated with the use of microcomputers have been reviewed.

Microcomputers have various aspects that include:

1. The microcomputer is a useful tool.
2. The microcomputer purchase price is less than $15,000.
3. The microcomputer hardware is the part of the microcomputer you can see and feel. The parts are
   a. The CPU box: microprocessor, PC-boards, memory
   b. Input devices
   c. Output devices
   d. On-line memory devices
4. The different sizes of microcomputers make it easy for the users to find a system that fits a particular need.
5. The five phases of microcomputer history are
   - Phase 1—Pre-microprocessor
   - Phase 2—Hardware and operating system development
   - Phase 3—Software development
   - Phase 4—Professional use
   - Phase 5—Connectivity
6. Hardware is the foundation upon which operating systems are developed.
7. Hardware and operating systems form the foundation upon which application programs are designed.
8. The disk operating system is the program used to make all the parts of the microcomputer hardware and software work together.
9. Computer languages have been developed to fit different user needs.
10. Some legal and ethical questions of microcomputer use:
    a. Ownership of programs
    b. Ownership of data
    c. Data security
    d. Misuse of data.

Application programs
BASIC
Standard business graphics programs
Code
Communication programs
Data
Data base
Data base management programs
End user
File management program

Hard copy
Hardware
I/O
Machine language
Microprocessor
Operating systems
Programming language
Software
Spreadsheet programs
Word processing program

1. Why is the microcomputer a useful tool? *increase productivity*

2. What are the three levels of application programs? *General, special & custom*

3. What is the function of programs, that is, software? *Give instructions to Computer*

4. Why is the microcomputer a personal computer? *small, inexpensive & easy to use*

5. What does a word processing program do? *aids in creating, editing, printing etc of text*

6. Give some examples of the output of a word processing program. *letters, menus, reports*

7. What are data base programs designed to do? *file data so it can be retrieved efficiently*

8. What is the difference between data and facts? *data is a collection of facts*

9. Give some examples of the output of a data base management system. *Mailing lists, inventory lists*

10. What do analytical graphics programs do? *produce bar, pie & line graph charts*

11. What are the limits of microcomputer communications? *the speed of transmission, or modem*

12. Why would a user select a specialized application program? *solve a specific problem*

13. What is artificial intelligence? *ability to learn, understand & deal with new situations*

14. For whom are expert systems intended? *special customers*

15. What makes up a DSS? *floppy or hard disk*

16. What does a DSS do? *stores data for future reference*

17. Identify the costs associated with the purchase of a microcomputer. *Purchase, maintenance & operating*

18. What is a "full-featured" microcomputer system? *includes most of accessories available*

19. Why should a user consider the purchase of a microcomputer maintenance contract? *To minimize expensive downtime.*

20. What are the physical parts of a microcomputer? *CPU, monitor, keyboard, printer*

21. What is the relationship between the microprocessor and the CPU? *the microprocessor is the CPU*

22. What is a microprocessor? *IC that has arithmetic, logic, memory & control functions*

23. What is RAM and ROM? *Random access memory / Read only memory*
24. What is a PC board? *printed circuit board with electronic components*
25. What is the primary method of input to a microcomputer? *keyboard*
26. What is the primary method of output from a microcomputer? *monitor*
27. What are some methods of recording computer information? *disks & tapes*
28. What is a peripheral? *device connected to the CPU*
29. What is a laptop computer? *small portable computer to be used on lap*
30. What are the five phases in the history of microcomputers? *1, 2, 3, 4 & 5 Pg. 21*
31. What was the first word processing program? *electric Pencil*
32. What was the first electronic spreadsheet program? *VisiCalc*
33. What events signaled the beginning of Phase 4? *IBM PC in 1981*
34. What is the hierarchy of a microcomputer system? *Pg 23*
35. What does the disk operating system do? *Makes all parts work together*
36. What is the importance of families of microcomputers based on operating systems? *Commonality of programs.*
37. What is the objective of a computer language? *one that humans can relate to easily*
38. What is a compiler and what is an interpreter? *translates program language to machine language*
39. Identify some legal and ethical issues in microcomputer use.
40. What is the estimated amount of illegal software being used? *80%*
41. Who owns software? Who owns data? *seller / user*
42. What is the responsibility of the manager/user of a data base? *Use data in professional manner*

SELECTED REFERENCES

Dologite, D. G. *Using Small Business Computers.* 2d ed. Prentice-Hall, 1988.

Freiberger, Paul, and Michael Swaine. *Fire in the Valley.* Osborne McGraw-Hill, 1984.

Hicks, James O., Jr. *Information Systems in Business: An Introduction.* West Publishing Company, 1986.

Hines, Douglas V. *Office Automation,* John Wiley & Sons, Inc., 1985.

Hopper, Grace Murray, and Steven L. Mandell. *Understanding Computers,* 2d ed. West Publishing Company, 1987.

Huff, Kathryn. *Developing and Using Microcomputer Systems.* West Publishing Company, 1987.

Leigh, William E., and Michael E. Doherty. *Decision Support and Expert Systems.* South-Western Publishing Co., 1986.

Potter, George B. *Data Processing—An Introduction.* Business Publication Inc., 1984.

2

GOALS

Upon completion of this chapter you will be able to:

Identify the important features of hardware.

Review the significance of compatibility.

Identify and name the parts of a microcomputer.

List some of the systems currently available.

Explain how each part of the microcomputer fits into the overall system.

OUTLINE

HARDWARE OF MICROCOMPUTERS

Configuration:
The matching of hardware, software, and operative system settings so that all the parts work with and communicate with all the other parts of a system.

Compatibility:
Capability of microcomputers to work together as a system and to exchange physical parts.

Microcomputers come in different sizes and shapes. They have many parts that are joined together to form a system. Hardware is that part of the microcomputer you can see and feel. It is difficult to determine the function of microcomputer hardware from its outside appearance. Knowledge of the importance, parts, the available microcomputer hardware, typical **configuration,** and **compatibility** with other brands of microcomputers is a step in the process of learning how to evaluate and select the appropriate hardware for a specific need.

The microcomputer (see Figure 2–1) is a collection of parts that form a system. In this chapter you will learn how the parts of the system work together.

WHY YOU MUST LEARN ABOUT MICROCOMPUTER HARDWARE

The professional must learn about hardware in order to select the best combination of capabilities and cost to match needs. The microcomputer is an answer to problems. A microcomputer system consists of application software built upon a hardware foundation. The remaining chapters of this book are devoted to software; this chapter studies the hardware foundation.

In order to purchase a system intelligently, the user must know his or her needs, the capabilities of a typical system, and its cost. The professional must also know what can be added and how the system can be expanded to satisfy current and future needs.

One decision users must make is the selection and justification of microcomputer hardware and software. This book is designed to help you learn about microcomputer hardware, operating systems, and available programs. It

FIGURE 2–1
Microcomputer in Use

HARDWARE OF MICROCOMPUTERS

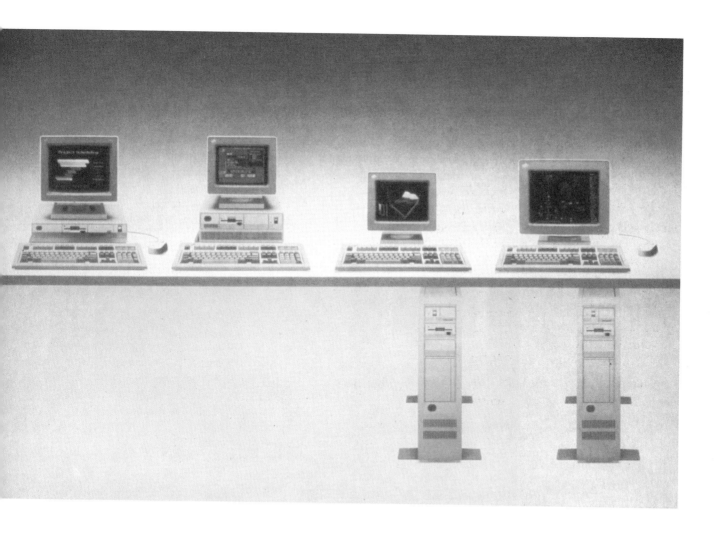

Configuration:
The matching of hardware, software, and operative system settings so that all the parts work with and communicate with all the other parts of a system.

Compatibility:
Capability of microcomputers to work together as a system and to exchange physical parts.

Microcomputers come in different sizes and shapes. They have many parts that are joined together to form a system. Hardware is that part of the microcomputer you can see and feel. It is difficult to determine the function of microcomputer hardware from its outside appearance. Knowledge of the importance, parts, the available microcomputer hardware, typical **configuration,** and **compatibility** with other brands of microcomputers is a step in the process of learning how to evaluate and select the appropriate hardware for a specific need.

The microcomputer (see Figure 2–1) is a collection of parts that form a system. In this chapter you will learn how the parts of the system work together.

WHY YOU MUST LEARN ABOUT MICROCOMPUTER HARDWARE

The professional must learn about hardware in order to select the best combination of capabilities and cost to match needs. The microcomputer is an answer to problems. A microcomputer system consists of application software built upon a hardware foundation. The remaining chapters of this book are devoted to software; this chapter studies the hardware foundation.

In order to purchase a system intelligently, the user must know his or her needs, the capabilities of a typical system, and its cost. The professional must also know what can be added and how the system can be expanded to satisfy current and future needs.

One decision users must make is the selection and justification of microcomputer hardware and software. This book is designed to help you learn about microcomputer hardware, operating systems, and available programs. It

FIGURE 2–1

Microcomputer in Use

will be your responsibility as a user to study your company's needs. The microcomputer salesperson can help you match hardware and software with your problems.

USER WINDOW

ASK QUESTIONS

It is best to ask questions before you spend your money.

Late one evening a business associate called. He announced that he was about to purchase a second word processor for his office. His partner had an old Apple Macintosh, and he wanted to exchange files and data with his partner. He had been told to purchase an IBM PC and wanted to know how difficult it would be to exchange files and data between the two machines.

Our answer was "very difficult." We recommended a Macintosh if he wanted to share data files.

A simple question before buying saved frustration and dollars.

HARDWARE: THE PARTS OF A COMPUTER

The parts of a microcomputer include:

- In the CPU Box
  a. Microprocessor (on Motherboard)
  b. ROM and RAM
  c. Cards—PC Boards (Expansion)
  d. DIP Switches
- Input Devices—Keyboard, Voice Recognition Units
- Output Devices—Monitor (CRT, Screen), Printer
- On-Line Storage Devices and Media.

Each manufacturer uses a design philosophy, called design architecture or just architecture. Many designs use the concept of a motherboard. A **motherboard** is a printed circuit board containing the microprocessor, some computer memory, and selected controller circuits to direct the signals that are received from external connectors, and often the ability to be expanded. Figure 2–2 shows a printed circuit board and Figure 2–3 examines the inside of a microcomputer.

The concept of design architecture may be illustrated by comparing the Apple IIe and the IBM PC. Both of these microcomputers have a number of slots into which are inserted cards with special capabilities. The Apple looks at slot number one for the printer controller card; the IBM PC seeks a printer card in whatever slot it may be. The Apple IIe looks for slots; the IBM PC looks for function.

Another part of microcomputer design architecture determines how the microcomputer is packaged. The microcomputer may be in one container or come in a number of parts. The main unit that is called the CPU box contains the microprocessor (CPU), memory (ROM and RAM), expansion cards, and

Motherboard:
A printed circuit board or card containing the microprocessor, computer memory, and selected controller circuits to direct the signals that are received from external connectors.

FIGURE 2–2
Printed Circuit (PC) Boards

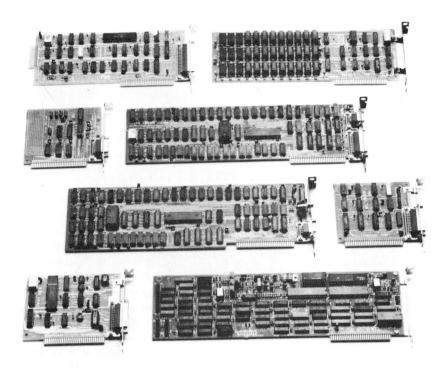

FIGURE 2–3
Inside a Microcomputer

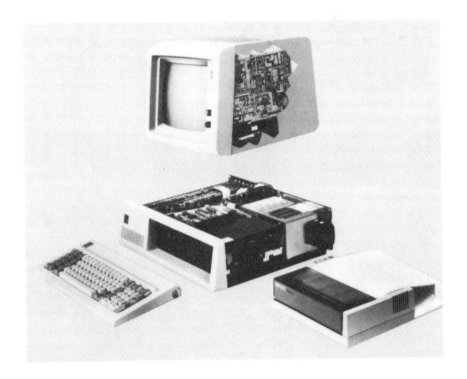

configuration switches (DIP switches). We have not been able to identify a better name than CPU box. We are still looking for options. Input, output, and on-line storage devices may or may not be in the CPU box depending on the design architecture. Figure 2–4 shows an overall diagram of a microcomputer system.

In the CPU Box

The CPU box usually contains a microprocessor mounted on a printed circuit board, ROM and RAM, other printed circuit boards, and DIP switches.

Microprocessors (on Motherboard) The microprocessor is commonly found on the motherboard inside the CPU box. A microprocessor is a single chip that is the central processing unit of the microcomputer. It contains an arithmetic and logic unit, a control unit, and registers. With the addition of a power supply, memory, and other circuitry, the microprocessor becomes a complete microcomputer. Figure 2–5 illustrates the size of a microprocessor.

Binary digits called **bits** are combined to create characters, bytes. In communications word size refers to the number of bits per character transferred. Microprocessors handle words in groups of 8, 16, 24, or 32. Some of the more popular microprocessors, the number of bits used per word size, and the operating systems that are available for them are found in Table 2–1. Microcomputers commonly process 8, 16, and 32 bits at one time. A 16 bit microcomputer may process two eight-bit **bytes** (characters) at one time. The overall speed of a microcomputer is a function of the number of bits per word, or **word size**.

To be useful in many applications a microprocessor needs a minimum word size of eight bits. The word size determines:

- Potential speed
- Maximum RAM that may be used directly
- Sophistication of programs

Bit:
A binary digit. The microcomputer uses a binary number system consisting of 0 and 1. A bit is a 0 or a 1.

Byte:
A sequence of eight binary digits taken as a unit.

Word size:
The number of bits a microprocessor can handle at a time. In communications it is the number of bits per character.

FIGURE 2–4

Diagram of a Microcomputer System

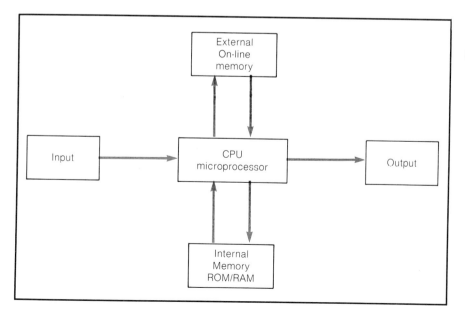

TABLE 2–1   Microprocessors

Microprocessors	Address Bus Width	Internal RAM	Word Size (Arithmetic/logic unit and external data width)	Operating System
Intel 4004			4	none
Intel 8008			8	none
Intel 8080	16	64K	8	CP/M
Zilog Z80	16	64K	8	CP/M, TRS–DOS*
Motorola 6800	16	64K	8	Commodore DOS
MOS Technology 6502	16	64K	8	Apple, Commodore DOS
Intel 8088	20	640K	16/8	MS–DOS, PC DOS
Intel 8086	20	640K	16	MS–DOS, PC DOS
Intel 80286	24	16Megabytes	16	MS–DOS, PC DOS, OS/2
Motorola 68000	24	16Megabytes	16	Apple Macintosh DOS
Motorola 68020	32	4Gigabytes	32	Apple Macintosh DOS
Intel 80386	32	4Gigabytes	32	MS–DOS, PC DOS, OS/2
Motorola 68030	32	4Gigabytes	32	Apple Macintosh DOS

*Radio Shack uses the trade name TRS–DOS for the operating system on all its computers except the models that use MS–DOS, no matter what chip is used.

Address bus width: Number of bits for internal addressing memory. This value determines the maximum amount of internal memory a computer may directly address. MS/PC DOS limits some systems to 640K.

Arithmetic/logic unit width: Maximum number of bits manipulated during one instruction.

External Data-bus width: The number of bits transferred in one clock cycle.

The microprocessor, combined with an operating system, determines the maximum file size and the programs available to solve problems. You will learn more about operating systems and how they perform their tasks in the next chapter.

FIGURE 2–5
The Size of the Z80
Microprocessor

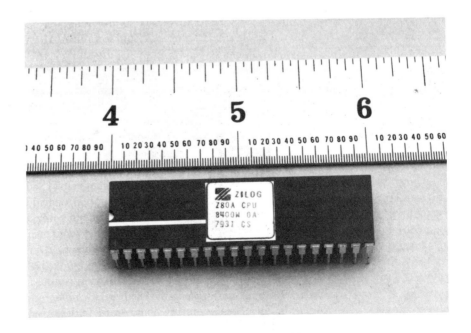

ROM and RAM Microcomputers contain both ROM and RAM internal memory. ROM, read only memory, contains instructions for the microcomputer. RAM, random access memory, is available for the user to store programs and data.

The amount of ROM needed depends on the manner in which the microcomputer is to be used. In transportables and desktop microcomputers, ROM may be used for getting the system started and for containing special-purpose programs. ROM (see Table 2–2) contains a program called a "boot strap" program, that is used to load the operating system into the RAM of the microcomputer from external devices where it is stored. Loading the operating system from an on-line storage device is often called booting.

Microcomputers use ROM, PROM (programmable read only memory), and EPROM (erasable programmable read only memory) to store selected application programs. Laptop microcomputers use these chips to store word processing, data base, and communications programs. A popular method of supplying insurance sales professionals with programs for pocket and other portable microcomputers is through the use of EPROMs.

The problems that may be solved depend on the application programs available. The programs available are a function of the amount of RAM and the programming skill of the program's creator. The amount of RAM needed by specific programs will be examined in later chapters.

Measuring RAM and ROM Before proceeding further we need a measure of RAM. Microcomputer memory, RAM and ROM, is measured in K (see Table 2–3), or kilobytes, units of 1024 bytes. Most eight-bit microcomputers contain 64K, 65,536 bytes (2 raised to the 16th power, or 64 times 1024). The eight bits are called a byte. Some eight-bit microcomputers can use over 64K, but only with the use of special programming procedures. Sixteen-bit computers can use over half a million bytes of memory.

Generally, only pocket microcomputers and starter systems have less than 2K of RAM. Programs using such limited memory may do many tasks in small increments. They use small amounts of data at a time. Despite these limitations, many applications are found for these machines. Real estate sales professionals use them for calculating mortgage information, while insurance sales professionals use them in lieu of rate books.

Pocket microcomputers often contain RAM that maintains its memory when the machine is turned off. CMOS, complimentary metal oxide semiconductor, is used because it requires little power. Bubble memory, a thin

Types of Microcomputer	Start System	Operating System	Word Processing	Spreadsheet	Communication	Custom (*)
Pocket	x	x		x	x	x
Laptop	x	x	x	x	x	x
Transportable	x					
Desktop	x					

*Application programs supplied on PROMs or EPROMs.

TABLE 2–2
Use of ROM

TABLE 2–3
Measuring Memory

Power of	Bytes	Kilobytes (K)
2^6	1	0
2^{10}	1024	1
2^{16}	65536	64

magnetic recording film, is used because it requires no power. This means the microcomputer contains its programs and data when turned off. When the sales professional walks in to give a presentation, perform an analysis, or make a sales presentation, the microcomputer is ready. An on-line storage device is not required for the storage of programs and data using bubble memory.

Microcomputers with 48K to 64K were the business standard for several years. These machines could do word processing, electronic spreadsheets, data base maintenance, graphics, and communication. Each application was generally created as a stand-alone (not integrated) program. Most business applications, such as general ledger programs, were available for these machines.

With the introduction of the IBM PC, available RAM expanded from 64K to 640K. At first the only programs available were expanded versions of the ones used in 64K microcomputers. Soon, integrated programs started to appear. Integrated programs now combine word processing, spreadsheets, data base, graphics, and communication. Programs that allow multi-tasking, operating more than one program at a time, and multi-users, two or more people sharing the same microprocessor, were developed.

Many professionals need only the programs and other capabilities available in microcomputers with 64K of memory. These individuals are benefiting from the expanded memory capabilities in newer systems by a drop in the price of the 64K machines. In addition, as programmers gain experience, they are able to create programs that fit within the 64K limit and do many of the same things that programs do with the larger amounts of memory. On the other hand, some microcomputers can now use over 16MB, sixteen million bytes, of RAM.

When selecting a microcomputer, you must determine the maximum amount of RAM needed by the specific program you plan to use. Some programs will often not be able to take advantage of extra memory in your computer. Generally, electronic spreadsheet, data base, and engineering/scientific graphics programs require the most RAM.

PC-boards:
Printed circuit boards that are used to expand the capabilities of microcomputers.

Serial communication port:
Connection to communicate, sending one bit after another in series.

Parallel communication port:
Connection to communicate over a number of "parallel" wires at the same time.

Physical compatibility:
The capability to exchange physical parts with other microcomputers.

Cards, PC–Boards (Expansion) The capabilities of the microcomputer may be expanded with internal cards or boards called printed circuit boards (**PC-boards**). Some boards or computers may be expanded with chips.

Many microcomputers have slots for adding additional circuits on microcomputer boards (cards) for expanded capabilities. PC–boards are available to add memory, to connect to telephones, for **serial** and **parallel communication** (out of specified ports,) to use voice recognition units, to use bar code readers, to operate laboratory equipment, as well as for other special needs. Some cards are referred to as multifunction cards because they add a number of of functions rather than one. Many manufacturers produce microcomputers that accept the same physical cards as the IBM PC. Microcomputers which accept the same physical parts are **physically compatible**.

The outside of a microcomputer is a neat looking box (see Figure 2–6). Looking at a desktop unit with its top removed, you will see a collection of computer chips, printed circuit boards, disk drives, power supply, cooling fan, and some empty slots for additional cards.

Even the smallest microcomputer may be expanded through the purchase of special cartridges and chips.

DIP Switches DIP, Dual Inline Package, refers to a housing commonly used to hold a chip. A **DIP switch** is usually a series of toggle switches mounted in a DIP approximately the same size as a chip.

DIP switches must be set to tell the microcomputer the amount of memory installed, the peripheral devices connected, and the communication procedures used between devices in most microcomputers. Setting the DIP switches (configuring the parts of the microcomputer system) is usually done by the seller of microcomputers.

DIP switches are found in many microcomputers, printers, and other peripherals. DIP switches are not used in the IBM Personal System/2. Instead, the configuration is set using software and the battery-powered memory that is used to remember the settings when the computer is powered down.

DIP switch:
A series of toggle switches mounted into a DIP, that are mounted on a pc-board. The switches are used for system configuration.

Input Devices

The most common **input device** for microcomputers is the keyboard. Most keyboards look like typewriters with the addition of a numeric keypad and function keys. There are differences among the keyboards produced by different manufacturers. Some are better used for word processing, while others are better for programming.

Input device:
A device connected to the microcomputer through which data and instructions are entered.

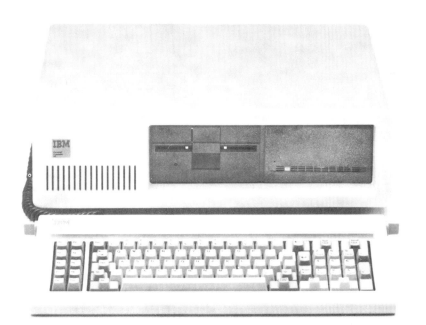

FIGURE 2–6
The IBM XT

The most common keyboard is call QWERTY. It is named for the order in which the letters are arranged in the top row. The arrangement of keys on QWERTY keyboards was designed to slow down the user. The Dvorak keyboard layout is designed to assign the most used letters to the stronger fingers. Both QWERTY and Dvorak keyboards are available for microcomputers.

Microcomputers may be operated with voice recognition devices (see Figure 2–7). Current technology involves two types of voice recognition. The microcomputer can learn to recognize general voice instructions or distinguish individual voices. Individual voice recognition may be used for security and identification. The microcomputer can learn to make selections from a list of choices. It is possible to dictate letters and complete documents.

Devices such as the "bar code reader," "mouse," "joy stick," "Koala and pen pad," "optical character readers (OCR)," and "touch sensitive screens" may also be used for data input (see Figure 2–8). Table 2–4 lists how these devices are used.

The keyboard, bar code reader, and cash register data entry devices have found the most use in business. For handicapped workers, special effects, and special situations, some of the other input devices are used.

Microcomputers can receive input from (and output to) other computers over telephone lines using modems (both input and output devices). Modems convert the signals that come over the telephone lines so the computer can understand them.

Output device:
A device connected to the microcomputer through which data and instructions are communicated to the user of other devices.

Output Devices

The primary **output devices** are the monitor and printer.

FIGURE 2–7
Microcomputer with Voice
Recognition

FIGURE 2–8   Input Devices: (a) Mouse, (b) Koala Pad, (c) Bar Code Reader, and (d) Touchscreen

(a)

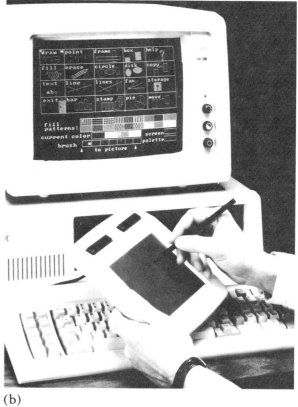

(b)

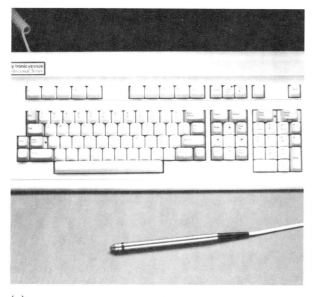

(c)

(d)

TABLE 2–4
Input Devices

Device	How used
Bar Code Reader	Device that reads cost and inventory bar codes.
Mouse	Controls screen cursor (pointer) by moving mouse across a flat surface.
Joy stick	Device used to control video games by moving a small stick or bar.
Koala pen pad	A surface, pad, is written on and the cursor moves in a similar manner on the monitor.
OCR	Optical character readers for printed characters and handwriting.
Touch sensitive screens	Selection from a screen list is made by pressing a finger against the screen.
Cash registers	Entry of data into the cash register is saved for future use.

Monitors The most common microcomputer output device is the monitor, the second most common is the printer. Purchasers of the IBM PC and look-alikes must select from color/graphic or monochrome monitors by installing a card to work with one of these output devices. The monochrome monitor produces a sharp character and is an outstanding selection for word processing. It will not produce graphics unless a special card is added.

The decision to use monochrome or color/graphics is dependent on the programs used. For example, the integrated spreadsheet program Lotus 1–2–3 requires a color graphics card to use its graphics functions. Lotus graphics will not operate on the IBM PC monochrome card.

The small screens on pocket and laptop computers are often LCD, liquid crystal displays, or electroluminescent (see Figure 2–9). These screens are flat and lend themselves to easy transport and storage.

There are two types of monitors. Monochrome monitors are green, amber, yellow, and black and white. Color monitors are composite (medium resolution) and RGB—red, green, and blue (high resolution).

There are currently four levels of resolution, or sharpness of image:

- Low: Monitors that can display 80 characters on a line.
- Medium: Capability to display 320 by 200 dots (**pixels**).
- High: Capability to display 640 by 200 pixels.
- Super-High: Capability to display up to 2048 by 2048 pixels.

The increase of screen resolution means a better image quality.

Pixels:
The dots on the microcomputer's screen used to create numbers, graphics, and other characters (letters, numbers, and symbols).

Printers The most common method of getting hard copy from a microcomputer is through a printer. The common types of printers are:

- dot matrix
- letter quality
- laser
- ink jet
- thermal
- plotters

The selection of a printer depends on printer type and your needs, as shown in Tables 2–5 and 2–6.

FIGURE 2–9
LCD on NEC

The dot matrix printer (see Figure 2–10) uses small pins to produce dots on paper to form letters and other characters. The quality of the letters is a function of the number of dots used per letter. The newer and more expensive models produce the highest quality output. Some dot matrix printers produce characters at the rate of 50 to 600 characters per second.

TABLE 2–5   Types of Printers

Type of Printer	Method of Letter Creation	Quality Dr af t	N. L. Q. *	L e t t e r	Graphics Variable Size Letters	Approximate Characters per Second	Price Range
Dot Matrix	Uses dots to create image	x	x		x	80 to 600	$100 to $2,000
Letter Quality	Typewriter style			x		12 to 55	$300 to $3,000
Laser**	Many dots per char.	x	x	x	x	8 pages per minute***	over $3,000
Ink Jet**	Uses ink jet	x	x	x	x	80 plus	$300 to $1,500
Thermal	Uses heat sensitive paper or ribbons	x	x		x	no limits	$50 up
Plotter	Uses pens				x	****	$350 to $10,995

*N.L.Q.—near letter quality.

** The laser and ink jet printers use a large number of dots per character. The more dots used, the nearer the output is to a character produced by a single impact.

*** Eight pages per minute is approximately 572 characters per second.

**** Plotters use pens to create a character. Their speed may be as slow as two characters per second, depending on the type of character and its size.

TABLE 2–6
Use of Printers

Application	Printer needs
Word Processing—Letters	Letter quality output.
Spreadsheets	Large number of characters per line and speed.
Data Bases	Large number of characters per line and speed.
Graphics	Dot addressable control and plotters.
Special effects	Proportional printing (such as in this book).

Dot matrix printers can produce small letters, compressed or condensed mode, to increase the number of characters output per line on standard paper. Businesses using data bases and spreadsheets often use the increased characters per line such printers provide. Special sideways printing programs are available when a greater number of characters per line is needed.

Special characters are available on many dot matrix printers including Greek and other foreign languages, scientific symbols, and (dot addressable) graphic characters. Some printers have the capability of allowing the user to define their own characters.

Letter quality printers use thimbles, balls, and daisy wheels (see Figures 2–11). The letter formed looks exactly like that produced by a typewriter. These printers are generally slower than dot matrix printers. Speeds vary from 12 to 55 characters per second.

The laser printer (see Figure 2–12) uses technology similar to some copying machines. The slower, low-cost models have maximum output of eight pages per minute. The quality of output is competitive with traditional letter quality printers. There are no limitations to the images that can be produced by a laser printer.

FIGURE 2–10
Dot Matrix Printer

FIGURE 2–11   Daisy Wheel Printer and Daisy Wheel

The ink jet printer (see Figure 2–13) produces letters by spraying a jet of ink through small pin-holes. It is not limited to letters and can produce many special effects. The speed is in the same range as dot matrix printers.

Thermal printers use a heating element to make a letter or character on either heat-sensitive paper or on regular paper with a heat-sensitive ribbon. The units vary from low-price units designed for home and traveling micro-computers to high quality, high speed, and high priced units.

FIGURE 2–12
Hewlett-Packard LaserJet Printer

FIGURE 2–13 Hewlett-Packard ThinkJet Printer and Print Head

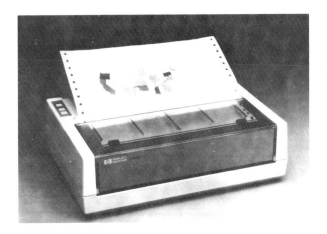 

Plotters use pens to produce their images (see Figure 2–14). Some hold the paper and move the pens, while others hold the printing head fixed and move the paper. Some use drums while others print on a flat surface. Generally, a plotter is much slower than other output devices. It is primarily used for graphics, CAD, CADD, and special effects.

There are four methods of feeding paper into a printer:

1. Single sheet friction feed
2. Automatic sheet feed

FIGURE 2–14
Hewlett-Packard Plotter

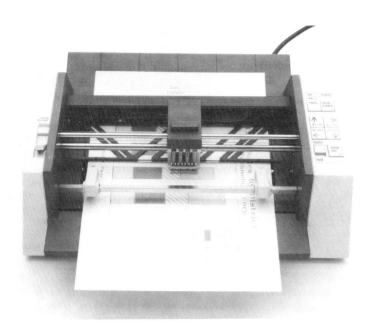

3. Pin feed
4. Tractor feed

Any and all types of paper may be fed in using friction feed (see Figure 2–15). Using pin or tractor feed, the paper must have a tractor along the outside edge to guide it.

On-Line Storage Devices

On-line storage means memory that is available to your microcomputer through communication cables. It is not part of the internal RAM or ROM. **On-line storage devices** are considered to be external to the microcomputer, even though they are commonly built into the same case as the microcomputer.

The lowest cost on-line storage device commonly used is a cassette tape recorder. The most popular device is a five and one-quarter inch floppy disk drive. Other devices used on microcomputers include hard disks (which are replacing the floppy disk drive in many business offices), eight-inch disk drives, quarter-inch (streaming) tapes, and three and one-half inch disk drives.

The Apple IIe, Apple look-alikes, IBM PC, IBM lookalikes, and most other microcomputers use cards, called disk controller cards, for controlling on-line storage devices. Each type of data storage device requires its own card.

The type of on-line storage device is a function of the availability, size, and application of the microcomputer. Table 2–7 lists the varieties of on-line storage media and devices, and where you may expect the device to be used. Figure 2–16 shows a briefcase computer that uses a built-in mini-cassette. Figure 2–17 shows some external on-line devices for a laptop microcomputer.

Five and One-Quarter Inch Disk Drives The most common data and program storage device is the five and one-quarter inch floppy disk drive. A floppy disk drive is an electromechanical device that rotates a disk and feeds

On/Off-line:
The operation of computer equipment at the same time as other equipment under the control of the microprocessor (on-line). Independent operation is called off-line.

On-line storage devices:
Devices available to the microcomputer through communication cables.

FIGURE 2–15 Mechanisms for Feeding Paper: (a) Sheet Feeder and (b) Tractor Feed

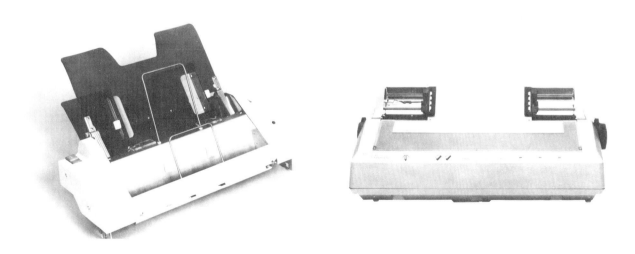

TABLE 2–7 On-Line Storage Media and Devices

Microcomputer Size	Cassette Tape *	Bubble memory inch	3½ inch	5¼ inch	8 inch	Fixed/Removable Hard Disks
Pocket Microcomputers	X					
Laptop Microcomputers	X	X	X	X		
Transportables			X	X	X	X
Desktop	**		X	X	X	X***
						****

* Both regular and mini-cassette tape recorders are used.

** Starter units, which are desktops when expanded, often use cassette storage in their minimum configuration. Some use the CMOS low power system for storage.

*** Other media and devices that are available but not widely used are the Bernoulli box, laser disks, ¼-inch streaming tape, RAM cartridges.

**** Cassette-type tapes are also used for backup of hard disks.

signals into and from the disk as directed by the controller circuits. The controller circuits are managed by a microcomputer through its operating system.

Three and One-Half Inch Disk Drives The Apple Macintosh introduced the three and one-half inch disk drive to the American market. Since its introduction, the three and one-half inch disk drive has found favor with laptop, portable, and desktop manufacturers due to:

- Economy
- Light weight (all-plastic construction)
- Storage capacity of more than 700K
- Compact size of disk drive
- Compact size of disk
- Hard shell of disk (protection of stored data)

Many MS/PC DOS microcomputers now use the three and one-half inch disk drive. When IBM used the three and one-half inch disk smaller drive on its Personal System/2 series, three and one-half inch disk drive became a second standard.

A three and one-half inch disk cannot fit into a five and one-quarter inch disk drive, and vice versa. Many leading software manufacturers are producing software in both sizes of media.

On-line storage media: Material used to store microcomputer files.

Eight-Inch Disk Drives The Radio Shack Models II, 12, and 6000 microcomputers, among others, use eight-inch disk drives (see Figure 2–18). The trend in the use of **on-line storage media** is towards small devices. The dominance of the five and one-quarter inch disk drive over the eight-inch drive seems to be primarily due to size and technology.

Hard Disk Drives The hard disk (Figure 2–19) provides mass storage of data in an efficient manner, providing greater operating speed, convenience, and economy. A 10 megabyte hard disk can store the equivalent of thirty-nine floppy disks and save you hundreds of hours of time in not having to switch disks in search of one special disk, or forgetting on which disk a particular file was stored. Many programs require the availability of a hard disk.

FIGURE 2–16
Epson with Built-in Microcassette

Hard disk drives can be internal or external with removable cartridges of 5 to 30 megabyte capacity that are often used for back-up storage. They allow the microcomputer mass storage capabilities from 1 to 800 megabytes.

Hard disks may be found in three and one-half, five and one-quarter, and eight inch sizes, with the five and one-quarter inch drive leading the way. The 5 to 10 megabyte standard size has given way to the 20, 30, and the 40

FIGURE 2–17
On-Line Devices for the
NEC–8201

FIGURE 2–18

Radio Shack Model 12 Eight-inch Disk Drive

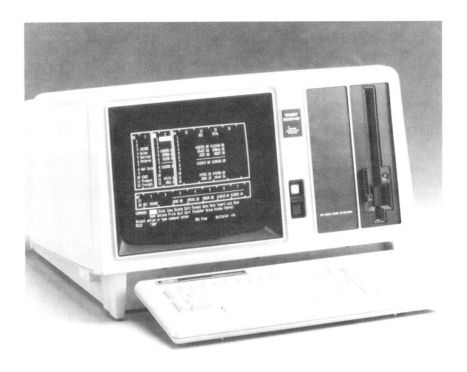

megabyte capacity. Manufacturers put 40 megabytes into a five and one-quarter inch, half height hard disk drive. There are internal hard disks with 103 megabytes and external with up to 800 megabytes.

Half height:
A disk drive that fits into half the height of the original IBM PC disk drives.

Not only have the capacities changed, but access speed has also quickened as the megabytes have increased. Early technology used the stepper motor, or incremental method of searching for data. Access time varies from 85 to 70ms (milliseconds).

Present technology uses a "voice coil" method of access that has reduced search time to 50 to 18ms for a 20 megabyte hard disk drive versus 65ms for the stepper motor. Access time depends on the technology and disk capacity (Table 2–8).

Hard disks may also be found in 10 and 20 megabyte capacities mounted on pc-boards (Figure 2–20) that fit into a slot on the motherboard. They come in varying thicknesses. One requires only one slot, one requires two slots. One that requires one and a half slots also provides space for use of a half-card function such as a half-card modem.

On-Line Storage Media

Many different types of media are used to record computer files.

Track:
A magnetic circle on a disk for storing data.

Sector:
A division of a track on a disk.

The disk is a plastic circle with a coating of magnetic material that rotates within the outer sleeve. You must be careful not to touch the magnetic surface. The oil from your fingers will damage the surface. Figure 2–21 is a sketch of a disk with its parts identified. Figure 2–22 shows the **track** and **sector** divisions of a disk.

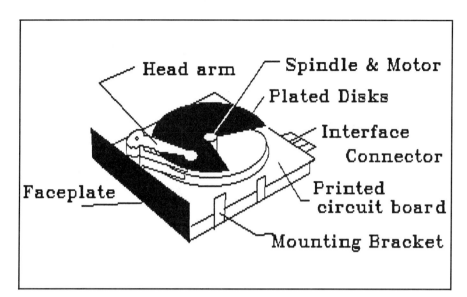

FIGURE 2–19
Hard Disk Components

On the upper right side is a square cutout. This is the write-protect notch. On eight-inch disks it must be covered for reading and writing, while on the five and one-quarter inch disk it must be uncovered for reading and writing. The eight-inch disk is uncovered for read only and the five and one-quarter is covered. The index hole on disks is used by some microcomputers to locate the data on the media. The rotation hole is in the middle of the disk and is used by the disk drive to rotate the media.

The three and one-half inch disk is similar internally to the larger disks, and has a hard plastic shell that opens automatically when inserted into the disk drive. It does not require a paper case or sleeve, but must be treated with care.

Handling rules for disks include:

1. Do not allow the disk to come near magnetic fields such as those generated by television sets and electric motors.
2. Do not remove the disk from the microcomputer when it is operating. (A red light indicates when a disk drive is moving.)
3. Do not force fit the disk into the drive.

Disk Storage Capacity Megabytes (MB)	Access Speed Milliseconds (ms)	
	Stepper Motor	Voice Coil
10	85–70	
20	85–70	50–35
30	85–60	40–25
40	65–28	25–40
60		30–20
75		40–22
100 +		30–15

TABLE 2–8
Disk Access Time

FIGURE 2–20
PC-Board Hard Disk

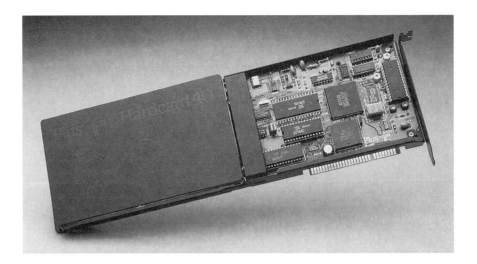

4.   Do not write on the disk with a hard device. It is best to write on the label before placing it on the disk.
5.   Do not touch the magnetic part of the disk.
6.   Do not expose the disk to the direct heat of the sun by storing it on the dashboard of your car or in a similar manner.
7.   Do not expose the disk to extreme cold.
8.   Do keep the disk in its protective envelope except when in use.
9.   Do handle the disk by its edges.

FIGURE 2–21
Disk

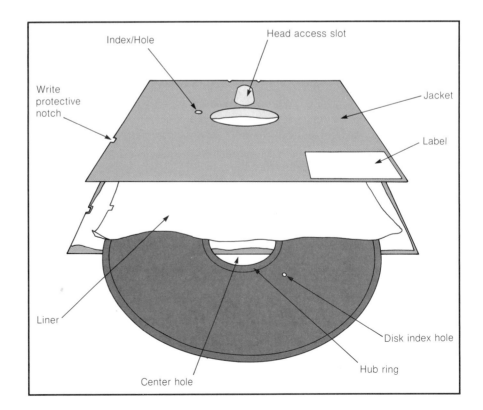

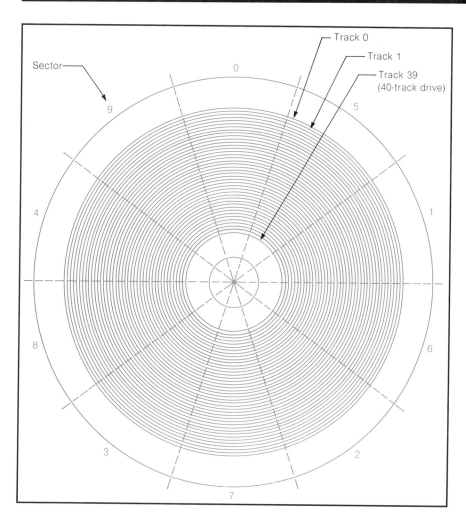

FIGURE 2–22
The Tracks and Sectors of a Disk

When placing a disk in a disk drive, the disk is held by the edge with the write-protect notch to the left and the label facing up. It is gently placed in the disk drive and the door is closed.

When a microcomputer is started, it will look for the operating system in a particular disk drive, called the default drive. When the disk drives lie side by side, the default drive on American-manufactured microcomputers is located on the left. When drives sit on top of each other, you must learn the disk drive designations, since they vary among manufacturers.

The size of a disk is not the only factor that determines the amount of data that may be stored. Disks may be single-sided/single-density (SSSD), single-sided/double-density (SSDD), double-sided/double-density (DSDD), and quad density (QD). Single-sided means that only one side of the disk is used to store information. The density rating indicates the closeness in which data is stored and determines the capacity of the storage media. For disks with storage densities greater than double density, the number of tracks is used as a measure of the potential capacity of the disk. Disks store from 50,000 to over a billion characters (see Table 2–9).

The type of disks to purchase should match your system specifications. If you are using a microcomputer such as the IBM AT with quad density 1.2 megabyte disks, this type of disk must be used.

Even when you handle disks carefully, they will fail. A copy of all program and data disks should be made and stored in a separate location for insurance.

USER WINDOW

HANDLING DISKS

The professor started her lecture on the care of disks. She read a set of instructions: "Remove the master disk from its envelope and insert in drive A."

She located a "master disk" and removed it from the booklet where it was stored. She then carefully pried off the "envelope" and removed the plastic disk. It did not fit into the disk drive. She smiled, laughed, and asked a student what was wrong.

REVIEW OF SELECTED SYSTEMS

There is a wide selection of microcomputers available in each size class: pockets, laptop transportables, and desktops. The numbers and capabilities of microcomputers in all size classes are great. We have selected typical microcomputers in each class as examples (see Tables 2–8 to 2–16).

Microcomputers change constantly. The IBM PS/2 (Personal System/2) series of microcomputers released in April 1987 has approximately

- 1,000 times more internal (RAM) memory
- 1,000 times more external (on-line) memory
- 4 times the data-carrying capacity
- 6 times the number of communication protocols
- 5 times the speed
- 2.5 times the disk retrieval speed
- 4,000 times the colors

TABLE 2–9 Commonly Used On-Line Storage Media and Devices—Approximate Capacities

	3½ inch	5¼ inch	8 inch	Fixed/Removable Hard Disks
Single-sided/Single-density		50K to 90K	92K	
Single-sided/Double-density	400	160K to 200K		
Double-sided/Double-density	400K to 800K	300K to 400K	500K	
Quad density	1.4Megabytes	750K to 3Megabyte	1.2Megabyte	5Megabyte to 1Gigabyte*

A Gigabyte is 1,000,000,000 bytes.

■ 4.8 times the screen resolution
■ 50 percent reduction in price
■ 50 percent reduction in size

than the original IBM PC released in 1981. Table 2–17 compares PS/2 microcomputers.

MICROCOMPUTER COMPATABILITY

When a business requires more than a single microcomputer it is important that they be able to function as a system. **Operational compatibility**—the capability of microcomputers to work together as a system—is one important aspect that must be considered in a professional environment where more than a single microcomputer is used. Physical compatibility involves the capability to exchange physical parts, such as the pc-boards used to add capabilities.

The single microcomputer office does not need to be concerned with compatibility except when expansion is anticipated or data is being transferred from an outside source. When the business professional must work with others who are using microcomputers, the need for compatibility begins. When a second or third microcomputer is added, the problem of compatibility becomes critical. The number of offices with multiple microcomputers is increasing rapidly.

Operational compatibility: The capability of microcomputers to work together as a system.

TABLE 2–10   Pocket (Hand-held) Microcomputers

Manufacturer	*Casio Computer Corp.*	*Sharp Electronics Corp.*	*Sharp Electronics Corp.*	*Tandy Corp.*
The CPU Box				
Model	FX–700P	PC–1250A	EL–550011	PC–4
Size (in.)	6.5×2.75×.375	5.3125×2.75×.375	6.6875×2.8375×.375	6.5×2.75×.375
Weight (oz.)	9	4	5.28	4
ROM	13K	24K	40K	16K
Software	BASIC	BASIC	BASIC	BASIC
RAM	2K	3.5K	4K	0.5K
Power	Battery	Battery	Battery	Battery
Expansion				
Cassette Interface	X	X	X	X
Printer		X	X	X
RAM				Expandable to 1K
Input devices				
Keyboard	X	X	X	X
Output Devices				
Display				
LCD Lines	1	1	1	1
Characters	12	24	16	12
On-line Storage	Cassette	Cassette	Cassette	Cassette
Notes			Has scientific calculator functions.	

The price of pocket computers varies from approximately $40 to $200 depending on configuration. Some units may be purchase with 10K of memory. Expansion memory is available for some models. BASIC is the dominant language of pocket computers. Users should know how to program and debug in BASIC.

TABLE 2–11   Laptop Microcomputers without Internal Disk Drives

Manufacturer	Epson America Inc.	NEC Home Electronics Inc.	Tandy Corp.
The CPU Box			
Model	HX–20	PC–8201A	Model 200
Size (in.)	11.67×8.5×1.75	11.875×8.5×2	2.1875×11.75×8.5
Weight (lb.)	4	3.75	4.5
Microprocessor	2 6301	80C85	80C85
ROM	32K	32K	72K
Software	BASIC Word Processing	BASIC Word Processing	BASIC Word Processing Communication
RAM	16K	16K	24K
Power	Battery	Battery/AC	Battery/AC
Expansion			
Cassette Interface	X	X	X
RAM	To 32K	To 64K	To 72K
External RAM		X	
Input Devices	Keyboard Bar Code	Keyboard Bar Code	Keyboard Bar Code
Output Devices			
Display			
LCD Lines	4	8	16
Characters	20	40	40
Printer			
Built-in	X		
External	X (Serial)	X (Parallel)	X (Parallel)
Serial Comm.	X	X	X
Modem			X
On-line Storage			
Microcassette	X		
Cassette	X	X	X
Floppy disk		X extra	X extra

Prices have been as low as $300 for some units. Maximum prices are usually under $1,000.

The problem of compatibility exists between different brands and even within the same brand of microcomputers produced at different times. The capabilities of microcomputers have grown. A five-year-old microcomputer may be expected to have some features that are not compatible with newer models of the same brand. For example, the IBM PC cannot read or write on the IBM AT 1.2 Megabyte disks.

The problem of operational compatibility is one problem that has not been completely solved. Microcomputers produced by different manufacturers, or different models produced by the same manufacturer, are often not compatible.

Operational compatibility has several aspects:

1. Being able to use the same organization for recording data on a disk.
2. Being able to write data on the same disk.
3. Being able to read common data files from disk.
4. Being able to use common data files.
5. Being able to use common programs created in BASIC or similar languages.
6. Being able to use common machine language programs.

TABLE 2–12   Laptop Microcomputers with Internal Disk Drives

Manufacturer	Data General	International Business Machines	NEC Home Electronics Inc.	Toshiba
Operating System	MS–DOS	PC–DOS	MS–DOS	MS–DOS
The CPU Box				
Model	Model 2	Convertible	MultiSpeed	T3100
Size (in.)	2.75×11.6×13.6	2.7×12.8×14.7	13.6×12.4×3.1	2×11.5×12
Weight (lb.)	13.7	12.5	11.2	14.6
Microprocessor	Intel 80C88	Intel 80C88	NEC V30	Intel 80286
Speed	4.77MHz	4.77MHz	4.77 & 9.54 MHz 9.54 MHz	8 MHz
RAM	256K	256K	640K	640K
ROM			Notepad/Speller Communication Outline/Filer	
Power	Battery AC	Battery AC	Battery AC	AC
Expansion				
RAM	To 640K	To 512K	To 640K	To 2.6MB
Input devices	All use the keyboard and may have a large variety of other input devices added.			
Output Devices				
Display				
LCD Characters	80	80	80	80
Lines	25	25	25	25
Printer				
Interface	X	X	X	X
Serial Comm.	X	X	X	X
Modem		1200 Baud		
On-line Storage				
Disk	one 3½ in.	two 3½ in.	two 3½ in.	one 3½ in.
Hard Disk	optional 10MB			10MB

Prices start at approximately $700 and may go as high as $5,000 depending on configuration. All systems have built-in disks drives (one or two), full-size screens, and use the MS/PC–DOS operating system; some include internal hard disk drives.

The first four aspects are the most important in many situations. An organization must have a common set of data, a common memory. Without a common memory, an organization is only a series of parts, often working at cross-purposes. The capability to use the same program on more than a single microcomputer is often not as important as the exchange of data files.

Data files may be transferred using communication methods such as those discussed in chapter 8, but this method of transfer is usually not as fast as direct disk reading and writing.

In many cases you may purchase, at extra cost, programs and special hardware that make it possible to overcome the limitations of your microcomputer and read disks from a foreign microcomputer. The cost of disk-reading systems varies from $30 to $300. When an organization has been using microcomputers for a number of years, such extra cost add-ons are useful when making the newly purchased microcomputer part of the existing system. Although these add-ons will solve some of the compatibility problems, it is best to avoid them in the first place.

TABLE 2–13 Transportable Microcomputers (Units with Separate Keyboards)

Manufacturer	AMQ	COMPAQ Computer Corp.	Panasonic Inc.	Sharp Electronics Corp.
Operating System	MS–DOS	MS–DOS	MS–DOS	MS–DOS
The CPU Box				
Model	AMQ 286e Model 1E	COMPAQ Portable III	Senior Partner	PC 7000
Size (in.)	$17.5 \times 8.5 \times 14.5$		$18.5 \times 13.1875 \times 8.25$	$8.5 \times 16 \times 6$
Weight (lb.)	Not Available	18	28.75	18.5
Microprocessor	Intel 80286	Intel 80286	Intel 8088	Intel 8086
Speed	10MHz	12MHz	4.77MHz	4.77MHz
RAM	128K	64K	128K	384k
Power	AC	AC	AC	
Expansion				
RAM	To 16MB	To 16MB	To 640K	To 704K
Input Devices	All use the keyboard and may have a large variety of other input devices added.			
Output Devices				
Display	Will accept optional display boards.		Will accept optional display boards.	
Monitor	9–inch Green	Gas-Plasma	9–inch Green	Backlit LCD
Printer				
Parallel	X	X	X Built-in	X
Serial	X	X	X	X
Serial Comm.	X	X	X	X
On-line Storage				
Disks	one or two $5\frac{1}{4}$ in. 1.2MB	one $5\frac{1}{4}$ in. 1.2MB	one $5\frac{1}{4}$ in.	two $5\frac{1}{4}$ in.
Hard Disk	extra	extra	extra	

Prices start at approximately $1,500 and may go as high as $3,000 depending on configuration. All systems have built-in disks drives (one or two), full-size screens, and use the MS/PC–DOS operating system; some include internal hard disk drives.

TABLE 2–14 Desktop Microcomputers

Manufacturer	Apple Computer Corp.	Atlantic Research Corp	International Business Machines	Leading Edge	Tandy Corp.
Operating System	Apple–DOS PRO–DOS, CP/M*	PC–DOS	MS–DOS	MS–DOS	MS–DOS
The CPU Box					
Model	Apple IIe	XT	IBM PC/XT	Model D PC	1000 EX
Footprint	$1.25 \times 1.5 \times .375$	$1.67 \times 1.25 \times .5$	$1.67 \times 1.25 \times .5$	$1.67 \times 1.25 \times .5$	Not Available
Disk drives	External	Internal	Internal	Internal	One
Microprocessor	Motorola 6502	Intel 8088	Intel 8088	Intel 8088	Intel 8088
RAM	128K	**Dealer Control	256K	256K	256K
Power	AC	AC	AC	AC	AC
Expansion					
RAM		To 640K	To 640	To 640	To 640
Serial Comm.	X	X	X	X	X
Parallel Printers	X	X	X	X	X
Input Devices	All use the keyboard and may have a large variety of other input devices added.				
Output Devices					
Display	Will accept a variety of optional display boards.				
Monitor	All monitors are external. Many options are available.				

TABLE 2–14 continued

Manufacturer	Apple Computer Corp.	Atlantic Research Corp	International Business Machines	Leading Edge	Tandy Corp.
Printer					
Parallel	X	X	X	X	X
Serial	X	X	X	X	X
Serial Comm.	X	X	X	X	X
On-line Storage					
Disks	one to four 5¼ in. 140K each	one or two 5¼ in. 360K each	one or two 5¼ in. 360K each	one or two 5¼ in. 360K each	one internal 5¼ in. 360K
Hard Disk	extra	May add hard disks up to 30MB with no special changes. Larger hard disks require special configuration.			

*CP/M add-on extra for Apple IIe.

** Each system is custom configured by the dealer for the customer.

Prices of IBM PC/XT (Intel 8088) and MS–DOS computers vary between $700 and $3,500 depending on brand and configuration.

TABLE 2–15

80286 Desktop Microcomputers

Manufacturer	Cordata	International Business Machines	TeleVideo
Operating Systems	PC/MS–DOS, 286DOS (when available), UNIX, and other operating systems.		
The CPU Box			
Model	CS–4200	AT	Tele–286
Footprint	18.25 × 16.00		
Disk Drives	1.2MB	1.2MB	1.2MB
Hard Disk	add-on	add-on	add-on
Microprocessor	Intel 80286	Intel 80286	Intel 80286
RAM	640K	640K	512K
Speed	8MHz	8MHz	6/8MHz
Power	AC	AC	AC
Expansion			
RAM	May add expansion memory beyond 640K.		
Serial Comm.	X	X	X
Parallel Printers	X	X	X
Input Devices	All use the keyboard and may have a large variety of other input devices added.		
Output Devices			
Display	Will accept a variety of optional display boards.		
Monitor	All monitors are external. Many options are available.		
Printer			
Parallel	X	X	X
Serial	X	X	X
Serial Comm.	X	X	X
On-line Storage			
Floppy Disks	1.2MB and 360K drives available.		
Hard Disk	Hard disks available with capacities of 300MB and more.		

The systems listed use 80286 chips operating at 6, 8, 10, and 12MHz. While prices for the basic unit and operating system start at $1,000, the cost of a complete system may be over $6,000.

TABLE 2–16
80386 Desktop Microcomputers

Manufacturer	Advanced Logic Research	COMPAQ	Kaypro
Operating Systems	MS–DOS, 286DOS/386DOS (when available) UNIX, and other operating systems.		
The CPU Box			
Model	Basic 386	Deskpro 386 Model 40	386 Model A
Footprint	24×19.5	16.5×19.8	21.25×17
Disk Drives	1.2MB	1.2MB	1.2MB
Hard Disk	Add-on	40MB	Add-on
Microprocessor	Intel 80386	Intel 80386	Intel 80386
RAM*	512K	1MB	512K
Power	AC	AC	AC
Expansion			
RAM	All are expandable to 4Gigabytes.		
Serial Comm.	X	X	X
Parallel Printers	X	X	X
Input Devices	All use the keyboard and may have a large variety of other input devices added.		
Output Devices			
Display	Will accept a variety of optional display boards.		
Monitor	All monitors are external. Many options are available.		
Printer			
Parallel	X	X	X
Serial	X	X	X
Serial Comm.	X	X	X
On-line Storage			
Floppy Disks	1.2MB and 360K drives available.		
Hard Disk	Hard disks available with capacities of 300MB and more.		

*Expandable to 1MB on the motherboard.

The systems listed use 80386 chips operating at 16 and 20MHz. While prices for the basic unit and operating system start at $4,000, the cost of a complete system may be over $20,000.

TABLE 2–17   IBM Personal System/2

Model	30	50	60	80
Operating Systems	PC–DOS 3.3	PC–DOS 3.3 OS/2	PC–DOS 3.3 OS/2	PC–DOS 3.3 OS/2, and UNIX
The CPU Box				
CPU	8086	80286	80286	80386
Speed	8MHz	10MHz	10MHz	16 or 20MHz
Size	4×6×15.6 on desk	23.5×6.5×19 on floor	23.5×6.5×19 on floor	23.5×6.5×19 on floor
Disk Drives (3½ in.)	720K (2 std.)	1.44MB	1.44MB	1.44MB
Hard Disk	Add-on	20MB	44MB	44MB
Options	20MB		115MB	115MB
Power	AC	AC	AC	AC
Serial Comm.	X	X	X	X
Parallel Printers	X	X	X	X
RAM Standard	640K	1MB	1MB	1 or 2MB
Maximum	Not available	7MB	15MB	16MB

TABLE 2–17   continued

Model	30	50	60	80
Input devices	All use the keyboard and may have a large variety of other input devices added.			
Output devices				
Display				
Monochrome	640×480 2 colors	640×480 64 shades	640×480 64 shades	640×480 64 shades
Color	320×200	640×480	640×480	540×480
	256 colors	16 colors	16 colors	16 colors
Printer				
Parallel	X	X	X	X
Serial	X	X	X	X
Serial Comm.	X	X	X	X

SUMMARY

You have learned the importance of hardware. It is the foundation upon which the microcomputer system is built. The parts of the microcomputer have been identified, as well as the ways in which they work together to form a system. Some of the systems currently available in the marketplace have been reviewed. The importance of compatibility when using different microcomputers has been reviewed.

The key points of this chapter are:

1. Hardware is the foundation upon which the microcomputer system is built.
2. The parts of a microcomputer include:
   a. In the CPU box
      ■ Microprocessor
      ■ ROM and RAM
      ■ Cards—PC-boards (Expansion)
   b. Input devices
   c. Output devices
   d. On-line storage devices (media).
3. The CPU box usually contains a microprocessor mounted on a printed circuit board, ROM and RAM, other printed circuit boards, and dip switches.
4. The keyboard is the most used microcomputer input device. Others include voice recognition devices, pads, a mouse, bar code readers, and joy sticks.
5. The primary output devices are the monitor and printer.
6. External storage devices are on-line, available to the microcomputer through communication cables.
7. There is a wide selection of microcomputers available in each size class: pockets, laptops, transportables, and desktops.
8. When an organization requires more than a single microcomputer, it is important that they be able to work together.

KEY TERMS

Compatibility
Configuration
DIP switch
Input devices
Microprocessor
Motherboard
On-line storage devices
On-line storage media

On/Off-line
Operational compatibility
Output devices
PC-boards
Physical compatibility
RAM
ROM

REVIEW QUESTIONS

1. Why is it important to know about microcomputer hardware?

2. What is compatibility? What does configuration have to do with compatibility?

3. What is the relationship of hardware and software?

4. What are the hardware parts of a microcomputer system?

5. What is the architecture of a microcomputer? Compare the design architecture of the Apple IIe and IBM PC.

6. What is a microprocessor?

7. What are RAM and ROM? Why are they important to the user?

8. How is the amount of memory in a microcomputer measured?

9. What are PC-boards and how can a user take advantage of them?

10. What is an input device? What is the most commonly used input device?

11. What is an output device? What are the most common output devices found on microcomputers?

12. What is resolution? What are the four levels of screen resolution?

13. Identify the types of printers available.

14. What is on-line storage? What is an on-line storage device?

15. What are the reasons for purchasing a hard disk?

16. What are the advantages of having a hard disk?

17. What are the typical sizes of hard disks? How do these capabilities compare with floppy disks?

18. What is the most common data and program storage device on a microcomputer?

19. What is on-line storage media?

20. Identify the parts of a microcomputer five and one-quarter inch disk.

21. What is the square notch on the right side of a disk and how is it used?

22. Review the rules for the correct handling of disks.

23. What are the six levels of operational compatibility?

DISCUSSION AND
APPLICATION QUESTIONS

1. From your local newspaper find some advertisements for microcomputers. Identify the microcomputers being sold and prepare a short discussion of the nature of these microcomputers.

2. Obtain a copy of a microcomputer magazine from your library, local computer store, or bookstore. Select any article relating to microcomputer hardware and prepare to discuss the information contained in the article.

3. Examine several copies of the *Wall Street Journal* or national news magazines. Identify some articles about microcomputer hardware and prepare a short discussion.

4. Identify the radio and television advertisements for microcomputer hardware currently being run. What type of hardware or store is being advertised?

5. Identify the type of hardware sold through:
    a. Local retail stores
    b. Discount and department stores
    c. Mail-order outlets
    d. Office supply outlets.

6. Look up the hardware outlets listed in the yellow pages of your telephone book. What equipment might you expect to be able to purchase locally?

SELECTED REFERENCES

Dologite, D. G. *Using Small Business Computers,* 2d ed. Prentice-Hall, 1988.

Freedman, Alan. *The Computer Glossary.* Prentice-Hall, 1983.

Lewis, Gerard. *Macintosh: The Appliance of the Future with Disk.* Banbury Books, 1984.

Shelly, Gary B., and Thomas J. Cashman. *Computer Fundamentals with Application Software.* Boyd & Fraser Publishing Company, 1986.

Sippi, C., and R. Sippi. *Computer Dictionary.* Howard W. Sams & Co., 1982.

Veit, Stanley S. *Using Micro-Computers in Business—A Guide for the Perplexed.* 2d ed. Hayden Book Company, 1983.

Zimmerman, Steven M., Leo M. Conrad, and Larry Goldstein. *Osborne User's Guide.* Brady Publishing Company, 1983.

3

GOALS

Upon completion of this chapter you will be able to:

Understand the importance of the operating system to the user.

Define the tasks of an operating system.

Identify and examine the features of the more popular operating systems.

OUTLINE

OPERATING SYSTEMS

An operating system is the program that controls the printer, monitor, one or two disk drives, and a hard disk drive, if connected, and central processing unit so they all work together. The user must be able to control all the microcomputer parts to obtain useful results.

An operating system consists of:

1. Functions: program-routines built into the operating system and always available.
2. Utilities: programs available on the disk with the operating system.

Many **functions** and utilities involve saving, recalling (**loading**), moving, changing, copying, and keeping track of **files.** Files usually contain data in the form of text and numbers or instructions in the form of programs.

Routines may be either functions or utilities depending on the operating system. Examples of routines are:

1. Preparing a disk to receive data or programs.
2. Copying a disk.
3. Saving a data or program file.
4. Bringing a data or program file into RAM.
5. Removing data or program files from the directory.

Microcomputers may be classified into "family" groups according to the operating system that is used. There are seven popular operating systems, or microcomputer **families:**

WHY YOU MUST KNOW ABOUT OPERATING SYSTEMS

You use the operating system to control the microcomputer when solving problems. Some of the output the user of a microcomputer might produce are letters, financial reports, evaluations, market surveys, invoices, and checks. Business users are not interested in how the program and data files used to create the business documents are saved, but they must know what to do and what not to do to ensure that errors are not made that may damage these files. Usually, application programs **interface** with the operating system, but sometimes the user must do so directly.

1. Apple-DOS, Apple Disk Operating System used on Apple computers.
2. Apple-Macintosh DOS, Apple Disk Operating System used on the Apple Macintosh.
3. CP/M, Control Program/Microcomputer—operating system for both eight- and sixteen-bit microcomputers.
4. MS/PC–DOS, Microsoft Disk Operating System/Personal Computer Disk Operating System used on the IBM PC, XT, AT, and compatibles.
5. OS/2, Operating System 2 for multi-tasking multi-user operation on the IBM Personal System/2 microcomputers and compatibles.
6. TRS–DOS, Tandy Radio Shack–Disk Operating System used in various forms on many Radio Shack microcomputers.
7. UNIX. The multi-user operating system developed by Bell Laboratories. Versions of UNIX include Venix and Xenix.

Functions (operating system):
Routines built into the operating system. These routines provide the user with the capability to perform often needed tasks. Functions are loaded into RAM with the operating system and remain there.

Load:
To transfer a file from an on-line storage media into the RAM of a computer so it may be used.

File:
A collection of related material. May be data or programs or both.

Routine:
A part of a program that performs specific tasks.

Families:
Groups of microcomputers that use the same or similar microprocessor and the same or similar operating system. These groups have similar capabilities.

Interface:
A common boundary between independent systems; in the field of microcomputers the connection between two parts of the system; the programs and hardware that make it possible for two parts of the microcomputer system or two computers to work together

You must know about the operating system because:

1. Knowledge is required to accomplish some tasks.
2. Knowledge solves problems when they occur.
3. Knowledge saves time.

Knowledge Required

You must know how to make **backup** copies of programs and data files. Having backup copies of programs and data eliminates the potentially devastating effects of storage media failures.

Backup:
A copy of a disk or file.

The creation and maintenance of a data set cost dollars for hardware, software, time, and effort. These dollars may be wasted if the data are lost due to the lack of backup copies and poor operating practices. Once a user becomes experienced in using a data set, it is difficult to do without it even for a short period of time.

Solves Problems

Problems occur even with the best-designed system and programs. When these problems occur, knowledge may turn a disaster into a simple inconvenience.

It is not uncommon for operating systems to be upgraded. With MS/PC–DOS version 2.0 came the capability to increase the amount of storage on a disk from 320K to 360K. With MS–DOS version 3.0 came the ability to store 1.2MB on disk and to read and write the 360K disk on the 1.2MB disk drive. Version 2.1 enabled the PC Jr. to read and write to a cassette drive. While version 3.2 brought with it the capability to read and write three and one-half inch disks. When systems older than 2.0 are used to read the high capacity disk, a lot of junk appears on the screen, but no damage is done to the disk. If the older system is used to change or write something on the new disk, program and data files could be damaged. Knowing that an error has occurred and what not to do may prevent the loss of valuable programs and data.

Saves Time

There are a number of ways to perform a task. Knowledge of the operating system makes it easier to select the best method.

In CP/M and MS/PC–DOS a text file may be examined by using a word processor, or by typing the word TYPE followed by the file specification and <CR> when in the disk operating system. The second method is much faster if the objective is to simply find out what is stored in a particular file.

<CR>:
Press the return or enter key.

TASKS OF OPERATING SYSTEMS

The operating system controls and coordinates the parts of a microcomputer system so they work together as a system. Operating system tasks are performed using built-in functions and add-on utilities. The operating system functions, utilities, and hardware define the limits of a microcomputer system's capabilities. For example, you cannot obtain printed output unless you have an operating system with the capability and the hardware to do the job.

Built-in functions are loaded into RAM when the system is loaded and are always available. Utilities are programs recorded on a disk. The user must tell the computer to load utilities into RAM when they are needed. That disk must be available when they are used.

A set of **conventions** (operating rules) makes it easier to use functions and utilities. There are conventions for communication between all the parts of the microcomputer system.

Internal Functions

The functions internal to the operating system provide capabilities that the user will need often. Routines commonly included as functions are:

1. System Operating Functions
   a. Booting the system (loading system from disk to RAM).
   b. Storage and retrieval of files on disk.
   c. Examining the directory of files.
2. Controlling Communication Functions
   a. Controlling screens, printers, and communication ports.
   b. Controlling the date and time.
3. Housekeeping Functions
   a. Transferring files between disks.
   b. Transferring systems between disks.
   c. Keeping track of what is on a disk.
   d. Erasing files from disks.
   e. Renaming files.
4. Additional Functions
   a. Windowing.
   b. Multi-tasking.
   c. Multi-using.

System Operating Functions—Booting the System The first thing an operating system must do is to get the system started. There are two methods of starting your microcomputer. One is with the machine turned off, called a cold boot. The second is with the machine turned on, called a warm boot.

There is a small program recorded in the ROM of your microcomputer that starts the process of reading the operating system code from disk or hard disk. This is called loading the operating system or boot strapping.

The boot strap routine is usually small, just large enough to read into RAM a set of instructions used to load the remaining operating system code from disk or hard disk into RAM. The Apple and MS/PC–DOS microcomputers start with a cold boot, while CP/M and TRS–DOS microcomputers are first turned on and then the disk is inserted before starting the booting process.

Most microcomputer operating systems will look for a program or data file on the disk drive that is the currently **logged drive.** When a system is started, the **default drive** that becomes the active drive is the lower numbered or lettered drive. Table 3–1 lists the default drive by operating system.

System	Default Drive (Originally Logged Drive)
Apple DOS	Slot # 6 * Drive # 1
Apple Macintosh	Internal drive
CP/M	A
MS/PC–DOS	A
TRS–DOS	System must be in drive 0. Does not use logged drive procedures.

*The Apple may have the disk controller card in different slots. The operating system will look at the first slot with a disk controller card as the default drive.

TABLE 3–1
Default/Logged Drives

The cold boot steps are:

1. Place a disk with an operating system in the default drive.
2. Turn the microcomputer on.

When the machine starts, the disk is read and the operating system is loaded. This is called a cold boot. Many CP/M and TRS–DOS users are warned not to use this cold booting method.

A warm boot may be used by most microcomputers. It starts with the microcomputer running, a disk with an operating system in the default drive, and a reset instruction. Table 3–2 lists the reset instructions for selected systems.

After giving the reset command, the boot strap program will take over in the same manner as a cold boot.

The operating system may be loaded directly from some hard disks. Usually, the microcomputer first looks for a disk in the default drive, and if one is not found, it then changes the default drive to the hard drive and continues with the process of loading the system into RAM. Some hard disk drive systems do not boot from the hard disk drive, but require that you load the operating system from the default drive or a pre-boot program (which transfers control to the hard disk drive.)

Some TRS–DOS and MS/PC–DOS versions require that you enter the date and time at the beginning of an operating session. In some cases you will be able to press <CR> and not actually enter the date. If a version requires that you enter certain information, it will not let you continue until you do.

Storage and Retrieval of Files on Disks After the system is booted, the task of organizing, indexing, and locating data and program files on data storage devices is one of the most important operating system functions. Table 3–3 is a review of the procedure for storage and Table 3–4 for retrieval of data and programs on cassette tape (to illustrate what must be done) and disk (to

System	Reset Procedures
Apple DOS	Press control, open apple, and reset keys together.
Apple Macintosh DOS	Reset key on side.
CP/M	Press reset key (location variable).
MS/PC–DOS	Press control, alt., and del. keys together.
TRS–DOS	Press reset key on side or top of keyboard.

TABLE 3–2
Reset Methods

TABLE 3-3

Steps Required When Recording Files

Cassette Tape	Disk
The recording of microcomputer programs or data on a cassette tape requires the user to perform the following housekeeping chores:	The disk operating system performs the task of keeping track of the programs and data stored on the disk:
1. Prepare a cassette tape by cleaning it with a bulk cassette eraser or start with a new tape. 2. Prepare the program or data to be saved. 3. Load a new cassette tape into the recorder. (Tapes may be erased and reused.) 4. Set the counter and locate where on the tape the beginning of the program or data file will be located. 5. Keep a careful record of where the recording starts. 6. Connect the recorder to the microcomputer. 7. Place the recorder in play/record mode. 8. Tell the microcomputer operating system to record the file. 9. Keep a careful record of where the recording ends.	1. Prepare a disk for program and data by placing a disk with the operating system on it in drive A and a new disk in drive B. The instruction to FORMAT the disk in drive B is entered. 2. Prepare the program or data to be saved. 3. Tell the operating system to save the program or data.

illustrate what the operating system does). The disk system is assumed to have two disk drives, the first one labeled A and the second B.

Your knowledge of how to save a file on a cassette tape recorder should help you understand what a microcomputer must do when saving a file on disk. The task that must be done is the same when saving a file on both a cassette tape recorder and a disk drive. (The cassette tape recorder is assumed to have a counter.)

When the microcomputer records the material, it starts by placing a beginning of file code marker, and then records the information followed by an end of file code marker, often called EOF. You must carefully record where on your tape you have saved material, in order to prevent the overwriting of valuable information.

FORMAT:

Instruction used to tell the microcomputer to prepare a disk for use. Magnetic marks are made on the media to identify tracks and sectors where data is to be stored.

The disk **FORMAT** instruction prepares a directory for the disk. The disk operating system records the name and location of each file on the disk in the directory.

Once the material is stored on tape or disk, you may shut off your microcomputer. The program or data may be reloaded into the RAM of your microcomputer as shown in Table 3-4.

The microcomputer operating system searches the tape until the beginning of file marker is found. It then reads the information stored on the tape into RAM until the EOF marker is encountered. The program or data can now be used. The process may be repeated as many times as you wish in a manner similar to replaying one of your music tapes.

The microcomputer disk operating system checks the disk's directory to find the file. The file is then loaded. The control that the operating system has over the recording and retrieval process is minimal with external cassette tapes, a little greater with internal minicassette tape recorders, and complete with disks and hard disk systems. One reason why cassette and other types of tape

TABLE 3–4

Steps Required When Recalling Files

Cassette Tape	Disk
1. Start the microcomputer with a warm or cold boot.	1. Start the microcomputer with a warm or cold boot.
2. Rewind the tape.	2. Put disk in drive B.
3. Connect the tape recorder to the microcomputer.	3. Tell the disk operating system to load the file.
4. Place it in the run mode.	
5. Tell the microcomputer operating system what to load. (Programs and data files are stored on tape.)	

storage have not been as popular as disk and hard disk storage is that data must be stored and accessed on tape sequentially. When a file is needed on a tape the computer must often start at the beginning of a tape and search for the file's beginning. On a disk the computer finds a directory track and then goes directly to where the file is stored.

There are a number of different methods for organizing files on a disk or hard disk. The most popular method for disks has been a series of individual files. For hard disks a **hierarchical file** structure (see Figure 3–1) is popular.

Examining the Directory Disk operating systems perform the function of keeping a list of the programs, data, and other files stored on a media. Directory is a common name for this file. Examining a directory is simple (see Figure 3–2). In CP/M, MS/PC–DOS, and TRS–DOS you simply type DIR<CR> to get the directory of the disk in the logged drive.

To get the directory of any other drive, the instruction is usually DIR n:<CR> in CP/M and MS/PC–DOS, where n stands for the letter of the drive (A, B, C, etc.) or the name of the subdirectory. In TRS–DOS the instruction for non-default disk directory is DIR:i<CR>, where i is the drive number 0, 1, 2, or 3.

Under Apple DOS 3.3 the directory instruction is CATALOG<CR> for the default drive, and CATALOG,D2<CR> for the second drive. Using PRO–DOS you will be given a menu of system utilities from which to select.

Most operating systems allow you to give instructions to your operating system using either upper- or lowercase letters. There are some exceptions. Some CP/M instructions and utilities cannot find a file saved using lowercase. UNIX uses lowercase letters for systems instructions. Apple DOS 3.3 requires the use of uppercase only.

For hard disks with large volumes of files, a tree directory structure has been developed. UNIX was the first operating system to use this type of directory. This type of directory is used under MS/PC–DOS 2.0, UNIX, and Apple's PRO–DOS among others. The number of branches is limited in some operating systems. The branches are called subdirectories. The set of subdirectories from the main directory to the one of interest is called a path.

If you are using a MS/PC DOS system with a hard disk divided into subdirectories, then you must either log into a subdirectory or use a path instruction to obtain the directory listing in a subdirectory. To log into a subdirectory type: CD\subname<CR>. CD is the change directory instruction. To return

Hierarchical Files:
A file structure consisting of a top down organization. Files are organized in what is often referred to as a tree structure. Some operating systems allow sophisticated security to be established for hierarchical files.

FIGURE 3–1
Hierarchical Files

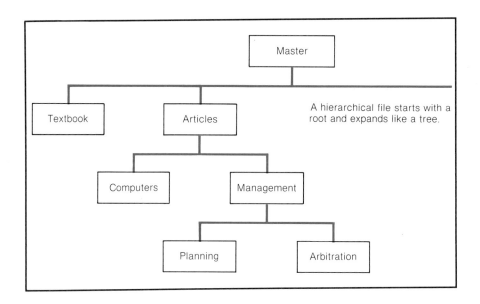

FIGURE 3–2
Examining the Directory of a Disk
Using MS/PC–DOS

to the root directory type: CD\<CR>. Once the system is logged into a subdirectory, the directory may be examined as noted above.

The path instruction is used to examine the directory of one subdirectory when the system is logged into another subdirectory. The path instruction is similar to the change directory instruction. For example, if you are logged into a subdirectory DOS on disk drive C, the instruction: DIR C:\PERT<CR> may be used to examine the directory of the subdirectory PERT without changing the logged subdirectory.

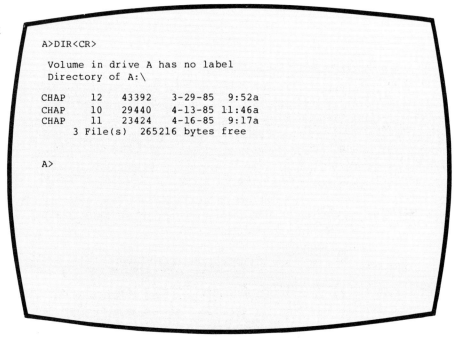

```
A>DIR<CR>

 Volume in drive A has no label
 Directory of A:\

CHAP    12    43392    3-29-85   9:52a
CHAP    10    29440    4-13-85  11:46a
CHAP    11    23424    4-16-85   9:17a
      3 File(s)  265216 bytes free


A>
```

The instruction may be given in uppercase or lowercase. The microcomputer tells you what files are on the disk, the size of each file, the date and time the file was started, and the amount of bytes still free to use on the disk.

Controlling Communications Functions The microcomputer communicates with printers, monitors, plotters, and communication devices through ports. Some of the more common ports found on microcomputers are:

1. **Centronics connection**, parallel printer port.
2. RS–232C serial communication and printer port.
3. Disk drive port.
4. Keyboard port.
5. Monochrome monitor (one color) port.
6. RGB (Red-Green-Blue, color) monitor port.
7. RS–422 serial port.
8. IEEE–488 parallel port for laboratory equipment.

Centronics connection: The name of the standard parallel connector. Centronics was the first printer company to make this connection popular.

One job of the operating system is to control the communication between the CPU and the ports (see Figure 3–3). Before this control can be executed, the hardware and software must be configured to operate with the operating system being used. As a user you need not concern yourself with the communication process. For example, when you type on the keyboard, the operating system is controlling the communication from the keyboard to the other parts of the system. Your concern is simply to type the characters correctly on the keyboard.

In MS/PC–DOS and some versions of TRS–DOS the time and date may be entered at the beginning of a session and used by all programs that require such information. Some microcomputer systems have printed circuit boards with clocks and batteries that provide this information automatically.

Housekeeping Functions No matter how careful you are in setting up a microcomputer system, it will require adjustments over time. A new application will occur that requires a different or improved collection of programs.

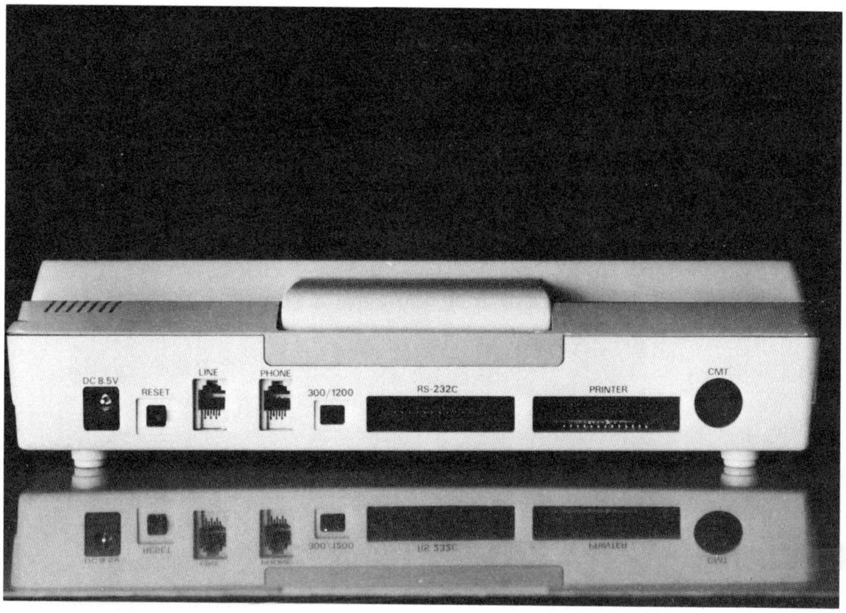

FIGURE 3–3
Outlet Ports on Microcomputer

MS/PC–DOS housekeeping functions such as COPY, and the utilities such as DISKCOPY, make it easier to move files to reorganize for the new needs.

It is also often convenient to erase files that are no longer wanted and to rename files to fit a new pattern. The MS/PC–DOS routine that performs this task is ERASE. During moving, erasing, and renaming, the operating system will keep track of what files are available and where on the disk they are stored.

Additional Operating System Functions Additional features some operating systems offer include windowing (see Figure 3–4), multi-tasking, and multi-using. Windowing allows you to split the screen into two or more "windows." You may view different combinations of files, parts of files, and different activities. The capability to look at two word processing documents and to transfer text between them may speed the creation of new documents.

Multi-tasking is the capability of a microcomputer to do more than one task at a time. A user can, for example, maintain communications with another computer while creating a document. Information from the second computer may be transferred into the document periodically.

FIGURE 3–4 Operating System Windows with Sidekick

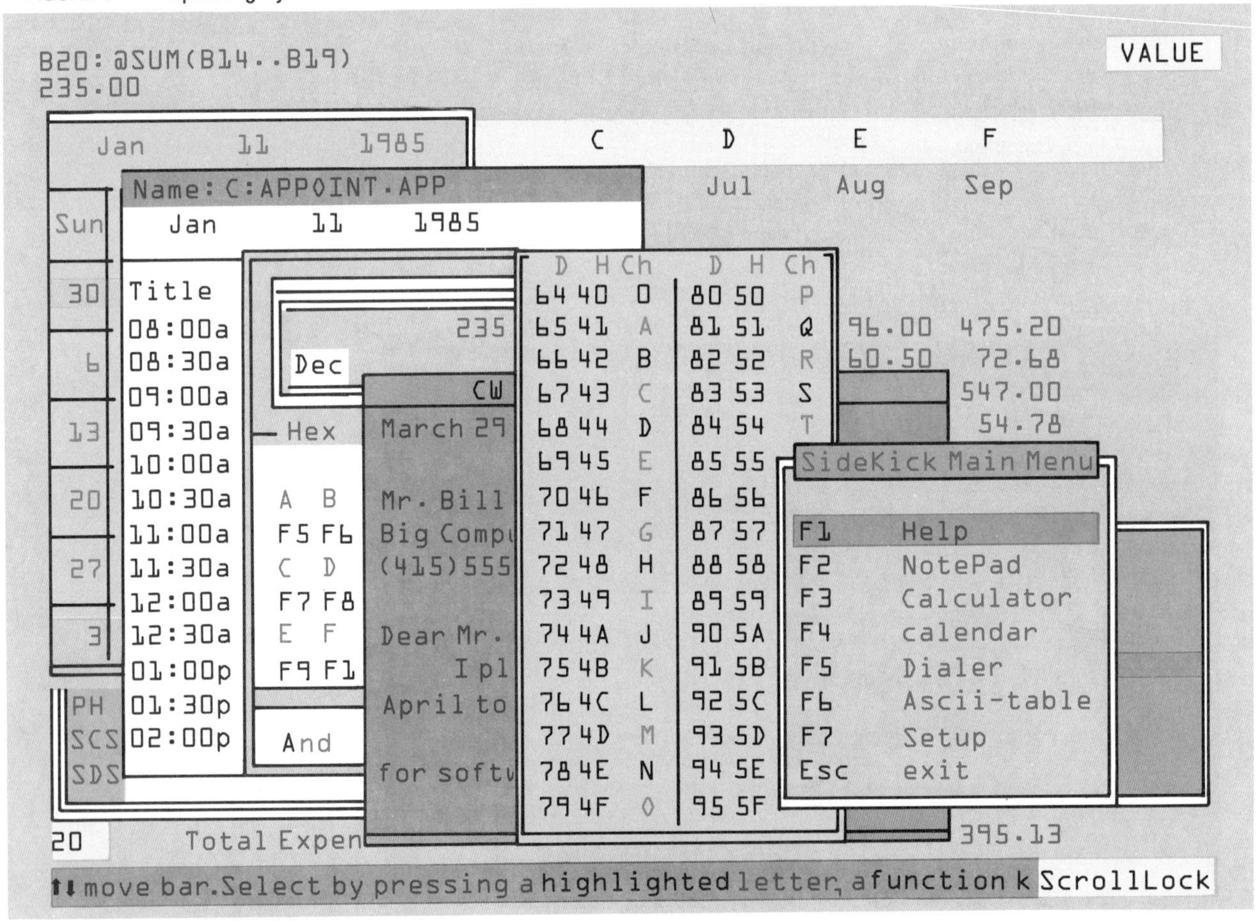

Multi-using gives the microcomputer **timesharing** capabilities for more than one **terminal** to share the same microprocessor. Individuals using these terminals share the microcomputer's microprocessor, data and program files, and peripherals.

Microcomputers may be connected in a LAN, local area network, to share files and peripherals. Networks are important to the business office where a number of individuals must use the same files or the number of peripherals such as printers is limited.

External Utilities

Utilities are external programs that add to the capabilities of an operating system; they are stored on the disk, not in RAM. Utilities include:

1. Housekeeping Utilities
   a. Preparing disks for use (FORMAT).
   b. Making backup copies of programs or data.
2. Additional Utilities
   a. Copying screens, text, and graphics.
   b. Sorting lists.
   c. Determining what printer port is used.
   d. Determining the configuration of the communication performed.

Housekeeping Utilities—*FORMAT* One utility that must be used each time a new data disk is created is FORMAT. This utility comes in a variety of names in different operating systems. Formatting is the process by which magnetic markers are placed on a disk to identify where data are to be stored. These locations are divided into tracks and sectors. One track is identified as the directory track, where the list and location of all files are maintained. The amount of data that can be stored on a disk is a function of the manner in which it is formatted (organized).

Timesharing:
More than one terminal may be connected to and operated at one time on the same microcomputer.

Terminal:
A computer work station, input/output device. It may consist of a keyboard and a monitor or be a microcomputer.

Utilities:
Programs that support the operation of the operating system by adding capabilities.

USER WINDOW

GETTING STARTED

The professor set up his new microcomputer on his desk. He checked the instruction book carefully and then selected the word processing program from the collection of programs he had purchased with his computer. He placed a data disk in the second disk drive.

After typing a short letter, he instructed the microcomputer to save it on the disk in his second disk drive. The program terminated with an error.

Following the instructions in the manual, he repeated the process over and over again, with the same results.

In walked a student who owned a microcomputer. After a short discussion the student asked him, "Did you FORMAT the data disk?"

As soon as the question was asked, the professor knew his problem was that he had not formatted the disk. Everyone makes errors when first learning to use a computer. A little knowledge about the operating conventions makes it easier to use the microcomputer.

There are file copy routines, copy routines, and hard disk backup routines available in most operating systems. The file copy routine copies individual files to a formatted disk. The disk copy routine copies an entire disk to a second disk. The hard disk backup routine copies the files from a hard disk to one or more floppy disks. In MS/PC–DOS the individual file copy routine is a built-in function; the disk copy routine, diskcopy, and the hard disk backup routines are utilities.

Copy protected (programs):
Programs sold with a limit placed on the number of copies a user may produce.

When a program is purchased or created, the first task should be to make a copy in case the original is damaged. Some programs are sold **copy protected** with limits on the number of copies that may be made to prevent illegal copying. The producers of these programs often provide a backup service to owners who register their purchases with the sellers.

After a program or data disk has been copied, we recommend that one copy be stored at a different location.

USER WINDOW

PLAY IT SAFE

Bill was almost finished with his term report. There was a rainstorm developing outside, but he did not notice until he heard thunder. Bill quickly saved the file and made a backup.

Soon there was a complete loss of power. The file in the machine was lost. After the storm the backup copy was used to complete the report.

It is best to shut down when a storm approaches. If you cannot stop, make extra backups and keep the second copy out of the microcomputer.

Making a Backup Disks and hard disks fail. Backup copies of disks are needed to prevent loss of data and program files. The process of making backup copies varies from system to system. Most failures seem to occur when you do not have a backup. When an individual first purchases a microcomputer, the instructions are to make a backup of the operating system disk store the master, and use the backup as the working disk. The documentation for this task is often poor, misleading, or missing. The user often has no microcomputer knowledge. Sometimes experience and knowledge gained on one system works to the user's disadvantage due to the manner in which the task is performed. In Table 3–5 is a listing of the names of the various functions and utilities used in different operating systems to make disk backups.

The backup routine can be started after the system has been loaded and the date and time questions answered as required. You should get in the habit of always placing the master in a specific drive and the new disk in the other. We recommend that you copy from 1 to 2 on the Apple (internal to external drive using the Apple IIc), 0 to 1 in TRS–DOS, and A to B on CP/M and MS/PC–DOS microcomputers.

Specific routines may be part of the operating system or they may be independent programs. The location varies between systems and versions of sys-

Apple-DOS	Apple-PRO–DOS	CP/M	MS/PC–DOS	TRS–DOS
COPYA	part of utilities menu	COPY* COPYDISK**	DISKCOPY	BACKUP

*Osborne 1 using CP/M.

**Epson QX–10 using CP/M.

TABLE 3–5
Names of Backup Function or Utility Routines

tems. Most backup routines are separate utilities. It is usually necessary to have the system disk in the microcomputer when the utility is called. To illustrate the different methods used in various operating systems to perform various routines, the backup routine has been detailed for the Apple DOS, MS/PC–DOS, and TRS–DOS.

Making a Backup on the Apple The Apple microcomputer operating under DOS 3.3 starts the backup process when RUN COPYA<CR> is typed. You must use uppercase only in the Apple. The first screen in the backup process is shown in Figure 3–5.

The Apple is designed with eight slots. Each slot is numbered. Slot 6 is the default (expected) location of the disk controller card. Each disk controller card can handle two drives, 1 and 2. You must know how the Apple you are using is set up. To complete the backup process you must follow the instructions on the screen.

Making a Backup Using MS/PC–DOS The DISKCOPY A: B:<CR> instruction in MS/PC–DOS results in the instruction shown in Figure 3–6.

Following these instructions carefully results in a copy of the disk in drive A being produced on the disk in drive B.

Making a Backup Using TRS–DOS When using TRS–DOS in the Radio Shack Model III, typing the word BACKUP<CR> starts the backup process. Figure 3–7 illustrates the starting screen.

The source drive may be identified as 0. The next question requires you to identify the destination drive, which may be 0 or 1. In this operating system each disk must be assigned a password. You must know the password of the source disk to complete the backup process.

Additional Utilities Almost any program may be added as a utility in a given operating system. A utility added to MS/PC–DOS is SORT. This utility sorts lists rapidly. It may be used to alphabetize the directory of files on a disk.

Normally the IBM PC uses a parallel printer. If a serial printer is used, the MODE utility is available to tell the microcomputer about the change in printers. This same utility is also used to tell the microcomputer what communication settings to use to communicate with this serial printer.

```
APPLE  DISK  DUPLICATION  PROGRAM

ORIGINAL SLOT:     DEFAULT = 6
```

FIGURE 3–5
Apple Backup

FIGURE 3–6
MS/PC–DOS Backup

```
Insert source diskette in drive A:
Insert target diskette in drive B:
Strike any key when ready
```

Communication Conventions

There are four instances in which conventions are used to communicate:

1. From microcomputer to user.
2. From user to microcomputer.
3. Between microcomputers.
4. From microcomputers to peripherals.

Communication requires conventions for the two partners to understand each other. As a professional user you must learn what is expected by the microcomputer when certain messages appear on the screen.

From Microcomputer to User Among the communication conventions from the microcomputer to the user are:

1. < CR > or an arrow that starts down and then turns left: Means press the carriage return or enter key.
2. Usually ∧n means to press the control or Ctrl key while simultaneously pressing the other key (n). C is the break instruction in some operating systems.
3. Esc means to press the escape key or to send the code number 27 to a device.
4. Filename refers to the name of a data or program file. Filespec refers to the disk drive where the file is located, a colon, the path (if any), the filename, a decimal point, and an extender. A path is needed on hard disks that are divided into subdirectories. See Figure 3–8.
5. .BAK as the extender on a filename means the file is a backup file.
6. .COM as the extender on a filename means the file is a command file. It is usually run by typing its name and pressing < CR >.
7. .BAS as the extender on a filename means the file is a BASIC program file.

From User to Micorcomputer Included in the communication conventions from the business professional to the microcomputer are:

1. The filename must fit the limitations of the operating system. Some accept blanks, most do not. Some do not limit characters such as , (a comma), others do.

FIGURE 3–7
TRS–DOS Backup

```
TRSDOS Model III Backup Utility Ver 1.3

SOURCE Drive Number?
```

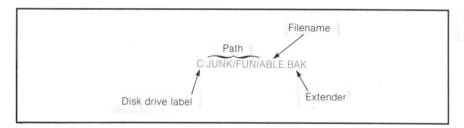

FIGURE 3–8
Sample Filespec

2. Most systems start on the default or logged disk drive. Drives are identified as A, B, C, ... or 0, 1, 2, ... or Slot 6–drive 1, Slot 6–drive 2. Each operating system has a convention.

3. When entering values into the microcomputer, most programs do not allow the use of commas in numbers. The number 1,000 must be entered 1000<CR>.

4. When using word processors, a carriage return is needed at the end of a paragraph. If you enter one on each line, the program usually will not work as expected.

5. There is a special code at the end of each file, called an end of file marker (EOF). In a word processing file it is usually necessary to press the enter key to make the program expand beyond the end of file. The down arrow will not work to expand a word processing file.

Between Microcomputers There are a number of communication conventions used by microcomputers to communicate with each other. The American Standard Code for Information Interchange, **ASCII,** is often part of the convention. In ASCII, numbers are used to represent a set of fixed characters. For example, capital Z is represented by the number 90, while the lowercase z is represented by 122. As far as the microcomputer is concerned, it records the numbers 90 and 122 as **binary numbers,** not uppercase and lowercase.

Microcomputers save program and data files in special binary code (machine language) and in ASCII. Most **binary files** are specific to a microprocessor and an operating system. ASCII files may be transferred between microcomputers.

From Microcomputer to Peripherals The communication of data from microcomputer to printer, printer plotters, and most other peripherals uses the same ASCII code that is used for communication between microcomputers. This is why a printer may be operated by many different microcomputers.

MICROCOMPUTER FAMILIES

The combination of microprocessor and operating system forms the basis for microcomputer families. Seven popular operating systems are:

1. Apple DOS and PRO–DOS
2. Apple Macintosh DOS
3. CP/M
4. MS/PC–DOS

ASCII:
American Standard Code for Information Interchange. ASCII is a seven-bit binary code. Numbers from 00 to 127 can be produced with a seven-bit binary number. The decimal number 90 is 1011010. Each number in ASCII stands for a character or control instruction.

Binary number:
A number consisting of 0 and 1. Each 0 or 1 is a bit. The decimal numbers 0 to 126 require 7 bits. To add the decimal numbers 127 to 255 requires the 8th bit.

Binary file:
Programs stored in machine language form. A binary file may be directly executed by the microcomputer.

5. OS/2
6. TRS–DOS
7. UNIX.

Operating systems are created for a specific microprocessor. They are a series of programs usually written in the basic **instruction set** of the microprocessor.

Each family is built on a different microprocessor, hardware system, and operating system. The general rule is that families are compatible. Families can:

1. Use the same machine language programs.
2. Use the same high-level language programs.
3. Use the same data files.
   The MS/PC–DOS family can read, write, and format the same disks.

In general, the only method of transfer between families is by use of ASCII files. The data files that may be saved in ASCII and our estimates of the percentage that can be saved in this manner are shown in Table 3–6.

Table 3–7 identifies six popular microcomputer families and the microprocessor upon which they are built.

The methods of transferring files between families include:

1. Communication over cables and telephone lines.
2. Use of special programs to read different disk formats.
3. The purchase of special printed circuit boards, pc-boards, that give a microcomputer in one family the capabilities of some other family.

The addition of special pc-boards is the only current method of using machine language programs from one family in another family. High-level programs, such as BASIC programs, may sometimes be transferred by converting to ASCII and then corrected to work in the second family.

There are many versions of each operating system. An operating system is like a language; it is alive and constantly growing and improving. As the capabilities of hardware improve, operating system programs are usually rewritten to take advantage of these enhancements. If an operating system stops improving, it will soon fall by the wayside since newer and better systems will take its place. New operating systems generally maintain the capability to do

Instruction set:
Instructions built into the computer. The instruction set is contained in the microprocessor.

TABLE 3–6
Use of all ASCII Files

Type of File	Percentage of Programs That Produce ASCII files
Word processing files	90%
Electronic spreadsheets	90%
Data base	70%
Graphics (data files)	60%
Picture files	10%
Communication	100%
Special application programs	80%

what the older systems do, i.e., they are downward compatible. The older system generally cannot have the newer capabilities added, as the systems are not upward compatible.

Apple DOS and PRO–DOS

The Apple family started with the Apple I and has progressed to the Apple II, II +, IIe, and IIc. All use the 6502 microprocessor family, including the Apple IIc, which is a portable and uses the 65C02 chip. The Apple operating system has developed through a number of versions. The most current versions are Apple DOS 3.3 and PRO–DOS, that operate on the Apple II +, IIe, and IIc. This long history has resulted in a large collection of programs available for Apple microcomputers.

Apple PRO–DOS is easier for the beginner to use because it is **menu** driven and the user does not have to remember how to perform specific functions. The PRO–DOS design and its hierarchical file structure are ideal for hard disk drives.

Many of the Apple disk operating instructions use unique words. For example, CATALOG<CR> or CAT<CR> calls up the directory of an Apple disk. DIR<CR> is used by most other systems for the same or similar instruction.

Menu:
A list of microcomputer actions displayed on the screen from which the user selects the one wanted.

Apple Macintosh DOS

The Apple Macintosh uses the Motorola 68000 microprocessor and has its own operating system. The Motorola 68000 is a 32–bit microprocessor with 16–bit I/O **buses.** The operating system of the Macintosh is visual. It is built around the use of a mouse that moves the cursor for menu selection. The system set a new standard in graphics capabilities that is being copied by special program developers for other systems.

The power of the Macintosh operating system is also one of its limitations. The operating system forces all program developers to use the visual approach rather than allowing the developer to create options for the user.

Bus:
Pathway or channel for data and instructions between hardware devices.

TABLE 3–7   Microprocessor and Operating Systems

Microprocessor		Apple/DOS	Macintosh	CP/M	MS/PC–DOS	ADOS* 286DOS*	386DOS*	TRS–DOS**	UNIX***
Zilog	Z80			X				X	
Motorola	6502	X							
Motorola	68000		X						X
Intel	8086				X	X	X		X
Intel	8088				X	X	X		X
Intel	80186				X****	X****	X****	X****	
Intel	80286					X	X		X
Intel	80386						X		X

*Operating systems under development.

**Tandy Radio Shack uses TRS–DOS title for the operating system built on a number of different microprocessors.

***UNIX is written in the C programming language. It will run on most systems with C available.

****Only a limited number of applications.

The Macintosh uses three and one-half inch disk drives. Without the addition of special hardware and software, disks from other microcomputers cannot be read. Programs and data files are best transferred using communication procedures or as part of a network.

CP/M—Control Program/Microcomputer

CP/M is the defacto standard operating system for eight-bit microcomputers based on the 8080, 8085, and Z80 microprocessors. There are versions of CP/M for sixteen-bit microcomputers such as CP/M–86, Concurrent CP/M, and MPM–86.

The eight-bit version of CP/M was designed with a few built-in functions and many separate utilities. This allows for a greater amount of RAM for application programs and data because the operating system needs only a small amount of RAM. You must learn the name of each utility and call it up directly from the disk's menu. The separate utilities include:

- ASM: Used to create a machine language file from assembly language code.
- DDT: Used to **debug** an assembly language program.
- ED: Used to edit a file.
- LOAD: Converts **Hex** files to COM files.
- MOVECPM: Used to relocate the system to make room for special programs.
- PIP: Peripheral Interchange Program used to transfer a file from one disk to a second.
- STAT: Used to check the status (how much memory is used for each file, the types of files, and how much memory is available for additional use) of disks and system.
- SYSGEN: System Generator used to generate a CP/M operating system on a new disk.

The utilities most users must learn about, such as STAT, PIP, and SYSGEN, are needed in many different applications.

Some of the advantages of CP/M for the experienced user are:

1. It is found on many microcomputers.
2. It is easy to switch from one CP/M machine to another.
3. Overlays using menus are available for the new user.
4. There are many special application programs available to work under CP/M.

Microsoft Disk Operating System (MS/PC–DOS)

Microsoft, an independent software company, developed PC–DOS, the operating system of the IBM PC, under contract with IBM. Microsoft also produces and markets MS–DOS, an operating system similar to PC–DOS, for independent manufacturers.

Some of the advantages of MS/PC–DOS are:

1. Standard disk format makes data file transfer easy.
2. Large number of programs available.

Debug:
To remove errors from a program.

Hex:
Hexadecimal. A Hex file is a file stored using numbers based on 16 digits.

3. Growing number of users means a continual growth of program availability.

4. It is easy to switch from one MS/PC–DOS machine to another.

5. Overlays using menus are available for the new user.

Independent manufacturers produce machines that are either close to the IBM PC for compatibility or have better speed, resolution, and other features. In putting a business system together involving several microcomputers, you must balance the compatibility factor with the increase in capabilities of these independently produced microcomputers.

The dominance of IBM in the microcomputer market has resulted in the MS/PC–DOS operating system becoming the defacto standard for 16–bit systems. The original version was PC–DOS 1.0, designed for the IBM PC with single-sided 160K disk drives. Each additional version of MS/PC–DOS was developed to add capabilities. The most important reason for PC–DOS 1.1 was to handle 320K double-sided disk drives. PC–DOS 2.0 was developed to handle 360K double-sided disk drives and hard disks. PC–DOS 2.1 was developed to handle the extra peripherals of the IBM PC Jr. PC–DOS 3.0 and 3.1 were developed to handle the additional capabilities of the IBM PC/AT such as multi-using, multi-tasking, and high-capacity disk drives.

OS/2

Operating system 2 (OS/2) is a graphics operating system. MS/PC–DOS are character-based systems. OS/2 will operate microcomputers using Intel's 80286 and 80386 microprocessors. It will not operate on computers using Intel's 8088 and 8086 microprocessors. Users of IBM PC, IBM PC look-alikes, and Personal System 2 Model 30 must continue to use MS/PC–DOS.

The graphics user interface of OS/2 creates a user environment that eliminates the need for the user to know or understand many aspects of an operating system. OS/2 requires more memory than MS/PC–DOS partially because it will include most external utilities.

The important features of OS/2 include

- Dual mode operation
- Consistent user interface
- Improved graphics
- Advanced data management
- Elimination of the 640K memory limitation.

Dual Mode OS/2 has two operating modes:

- DOS
- OS/2

The DOS mode emulates the operation of MS/PC–DOS. Many programs created for the MS/PC–DOS will only operate in this mode.

The OS/2 mode is multi-tasking and multi-user. Most new programs are being written to operate in the OS/2 mode, while older versions of programs are being revised to operate in the OS/2 mode.

Consistent Interface When computer users move between computer systems or between programs on the same system, they often must learn many new and different commands. OS/2 forces developers to use a consistent interface, so users of OS/2 only need to learn a single interface.

Improved Graphics OS/2 requires VGA, video graphics array. VGA produces a resolution of 640 by 480. Since the height of most screens is three-quarters of its width, the use of 640 by 480 results in a square pixel. The creation of graphics, such as round circles, are easy using square pixels.

The resolution of OS/2 results in screen displays that are pleasing to the eye and easy to read. Special character displays, such as those needed for electronic publishing, may be created.

Advanced Data Management OS/2 makes the transfer of data between applications easy. Data may be moved between word processing, spreadsheet, data bases, and graphics programs without the need for custom programs.

Uses Over 640K Intel's 80286 microprocessor may use up to 16 million bytes of memory and Intel's 80386 uses up to 4 gigabytes of memory. MS/PC–DOS can only use 640K. OS/2 is needed to take advantage of the larger memory.

Tandy Radio Shack (TRS–DOS)

Tandy/Radio Shack markets an array of microcomputers using a variety of microprocessors. With the exception of its TRS–80 Model 1000, 1200, and 2000 using MS–DOS, and its Model 6000 using Xenix (Microsoft adaptation of UNIX), all its microcomputers use the name TRS–DOS for the operating system.

The microcomputer models upon which "TRS–DOS" is used include:

Microprocessor	Model
Z80	4 (Also uses CP/M)
Z80/68000	12
Z80/68000	6000 (Also uses XENIX)
6809	Color Computer
80C85	100
80C85	200

Disk storage capacity of Tandy's computers starts at 50,000 and goes to over 1 million bytes. The capability varies by operating system release and model of microcomputer. It is often difficult to move data and programs between different models.

UNIX

Bell Laboratories developed UNIX in 1970 in assembly language and then redeveloped it in the C language. UNIX will work on most microcomputers that have the C language available. When a new microcomputer is developed, UNIX can be added easily when the C language becomes available.

In 1973, UNIX was distributed to many universities, nonprofit organizations, and government entities for use by larger computers. Many programming utilities and features were developed for UNIX by these groups. These utilities and features include:

1. Hierarchical file system for the control of files.
2. Multi-tasking.

3. Windowing.
4. Multi-using.
5. Enhanced communication capabilities.
6. Good programming environment.

UNIX is expected to continue to be a leader in innovative ideas and concepts. It led the way in the development of many features now found in other operating systems.

SUMMARY

Knowledge of the operating system is important to the microcomputer users. Knowing what an operating system does helps solves problems and increases the results obtained from using a computer. Among the important aspects of operating systems are:

1. An operating system is a program that controls the parts of the microcomputer so they all work together.
2. The professional uses the operating system to control the microcomputer when solving problems.
3. Internal functions that are often needed by users are built into the operating system.
4. External utilities are available that allow an operating system to perform tasks that are needed often, but not as often as internal functions.
5. External utilities are programs.
6. Communication conventions are needed for communications:
    a. From microcomputer to user.
    b. From user to microcomputer.
    c. Between microcomputers.
    d. From microcomputers to peripherals.
7. The combination of microprocessor and operating systems forms the basis for microcomputer families.

KEY TERMS

Backup	Functions
Default drive	Logged drive
Families	Operating System (OS and DOS)
File	Routine
FORMAT	Utilities

REVIEW QUESTIONS

1. What is the prime function of an operating system and what does it consist of?

2. What is the difference between functions, routines, and utilities?

3. What is a file? What is stored in a file?

4. Identify and explain five routines commonly available in operating systems.

5. Name the seven popular operating system families. What are the characteristics of a microcomputer family?

6. Why must the user know about operating systems?

7. What routines are commonly included as operating system functions?

8. What are the two methods of starting a microcomputer?

9. How does knowledge of what an individual does when saving a file on a cassette recorder help you understand what a microcomputer does when recording files on disks?

10. What is a hierarchical file? Why is the organization of this type of file compared to a tree?

11. What is the instruction to examine the directory of the disk in the default or logged disk drive?

12. What communications are controlled by the operating system?

13. What is done to a disk when it is formatted by the operating system?

14. Why should backup copies of disks be made?

15. What is the backup utility called on the Apple, CP/M, MS/PC–DOS, and TRS–DOS systems?

16. Name the four instances in which conventions are required in microcomputer communications.

17. Identify some of the communication conventions you must know as a user when communicating with a microcomputer and its operating system.

18. What is a code? What is ASCII? What is the difference between lowercase letters and uppercase letters in ASCII?

19. In what ways might you generally expect compatibility within a family?

20. What are the three methods of transferring files between microcomputer families?

21. What are some of the advantages of MS/PC–DOS?

22. When did universities get involved with UNIX, and what was their contribution?

23. Identify some of the special features developed for UNIX.

24. What is the main difference between MS/PC–DOS and OS/2?

25. On which PS/2 model will OS/2 not work?

26. What are the features of OS/2?

27. What are the dual modes of OS/2? Explain the differences.

28. What is VGA? What is its resolution?

1. Get a microcomputer magazine with an article on disk operating systems out of the library or from your local bookstore. Prepare a short discussion of the material in the article.

2. Survey organizations (business, academic offices, government) and identify the type of microcomputer and the operating system in use. Why do you think the hardware and operating system was selected?

3. Interview a faculty member or other microcomputer user who is an advocate of a particular operating system and summarize his/her views.

4. From a recent issue of a microcomputer magazine, identify current developments in operating systems and their meanings for the user.

5. From material in the chapter and your library, review the operating systems currently in use and their features. Prepare a forecast of future developments in operating systems.

1. This set of assignments is to get you started.
    a. Make a backup (DISKCOPY) of the disk.
    b. Examine the directory of the disk and, if possible, type a copy of the directory.
    c. Identify the routines performed by three of the utilities or programs listed in the directory.

2. Use the FORMAT command to prepare a disk for use.

3. Use your operating system to copy a disk file from one disk to another.

4. Use the TYPE instruction in MS/PC–DOS and CP/M to examine the contents of individual files. Which files are ASCII, which are not?

5. The following is a list of MS/PC–DOS utilities. Use them or their substitutes in the operating system available:
    a. SORT
    b. CHKDSK
    c. MODE
    d. TREE

Explain the tasks performed by each of these routines.

Caggiano, Joseph. *The Easy Guide to Your Macintosh.* Sybex Books, 1984.
Chertok, Barbara Lee. *IBM PC Owner's Manual.* Prentice-Hall, 1983.
Copeland, Cody T., and Jonathan Bacon. *Understanding and Using MS–DOS/PC DOS.* West Publishing Company, 1987.

DeVoney, Chris. *MS–DOS User's Guide.* Que Corporation, 1983.

DeVoney, Chris. *PC DOS User's Guide.* Que Corporation, 1983.

King, Richard Allen. *The IBM PC DOS Handbook.* Sybex Books, 1984.

McGilton, Henry, and Rachel Morgan. *Introducing the UNIX System.* A Byte Book, McGraw-Hill Book Company, 1983.

Miller, David. *Apple ProDOS Data Files.* Prentice-Hall Books, 1984.

Murtha, Stephen, and Mitchell Waite. *CP/M Primer.* Howard W. Sams & Co., Inc., 1980.

Operating Manuals for Apple, CP/M (Osborne 1 and Epson QX–10), MS–DOS and PC–DOS, TRS–DOS, and UNIX V.

Ruff, Laura B., and Mary K. Weitzer. *Understanding and Using MS–DOS/PC DOS.* West Publishing Company, 1986.

Sippi, Charles, and Roger Sippi. *Computer Dictionary.* Howard W. Sams & Co., Inc., 1982.

Thomas, Rebecca, Ph.D., and Jean Yates. *A User Guide to the UNIX System.* Osborne/McGraw-Hill, 1982.

Zimmerman, Steven M., Leo M. Conrad, and Larry J. Goldstein. *Osborne User's Guide.* Robert J. Brady Co., 1983.

4

WORD PROCESSING

MICROS IN ACTION

Doug Houston Real Estate is a two-person real estate office consisting of one broker and one agent. The agency's business is primarily concerned with the sale of commercial investment property, including hotels, motels, apartments, and large tracts of land for development.

When evaluating the feasibility of starting a new business, they identified their microcomputer needs as

1. Word processing for
   a. Contacting potential sellers.
   b. Organizing the property list.
   c. Developing "packages" describing the financial picture (market and income analysis), physical location, and values of similar properties.
   d. Aiding in handling the closing details.
2. Spreadsheets for
   a. Developing "packages" describing the financial picture (market and income analysis), physical location, and values of similar properties.
   b. Operating and managing investment properties.
3. Data base for
   a. Organizing and managing investment groups for the purchase and operation of investment properties.
   b. Operating and managing investment properties.

They expected that most of the associate's time would be spent communicating with buyers and sellers. This communication places a heavy demand on word processing and requires a letter quality printer.

Word processing:
The creation, storage and retrieval, and printing of text files.

Text file:
A computer file that contains words and characters. Such files are commonly created during word processing.

Text:
Characters found on paper, on the screen, or stored in a microcomputer text file. Text may be a letter or a manuscript length book.

The microcomputer may be used as a word processor. **Word processing** programs can create/edit, save, recall, and print word processing **text files**. The user can start a document, save it, and then return to complete it at some future time.

Word processing is the creation of quality documents for professional or other purposes. Electronic word processing is the creation of documents on a microcomputer, using a word processing program. Basic word processing program features include

1. Creating the **text** file.
2. Editing the text file.
3. Saving and recalling the text file.
4. Printing the text file.

Additional features found in some word processors include

1. Special printing effects.
   a. Boldfacing.
   b. Additional fonts such as italics.
   c. Proportional spacing
2. Document assembly from files with pre-written text.

3. Print spoolers.
4. Windows.

Commonly found add-on utility programs include

1. Spelling checkers.
2. Merge print for mass mailing.
3. Table of contents generators.
4. Index generators.
5. Footnote programs.
6. Style checkers.

WORD PROCESSING HARDWARE

Word processing requires a microcomputer, a word processing program, and a printer. The minimum hardware requirements include

1. Enough RAM to support the word processing program.
2. An input device such as a keyboard.
3. A monitor upon which to edit.
4. A printer that can produce output of the desired quality.
5. A storage device such as disk drives or memory, which retains text when the microcomputer is turned off.

RAM Needs

The amount of RAM needed for a particular word processing program depends on how the program is written and upon the operating system of the microcomputer. You will find some word processors operating under CP/M in 64K, which require 128K in MS–DOS due to additional features.

Input Device—Keyboard

All microcomputers have some type of input device. The one most often used for word processing is the keyboard (see Figure 4–1). Other devices such as optical character readers and voice recognition devices are available.

Monitor

The two types of monitors are: monochrome monitors green, amber, yellow, or black and white; color monitors composite or RGB (red, green, and blue).
Some monitors produce higher quality characters than others. Some monitors designed for graphics will not produce as sharp a letter as a monitor designed for text. Color monitors often produce a poorer quality letter than black-white, amber, and green screen monitors. Generally, you get what you pay for in monitors. High-resolution color monitors are available at additional cost.
For word processing, the standard monitor produces 80 characters across, and either 24 or 25 lines down. A full page of text is 66 lines in length. Some

FIGURE 4–1
Keyboards: (a) Dvorak Layout,
(b) QWERTY Layout

microcomputer monitors are capable of handling 66 lines, allowing the user to see the entire page at once.

Most word processors work with all combinations of color or monochrome monitors, but in a different manner. Many word processors display underlining and boldface type correctly on one or the other configuration, some display the output correctly on both. If you want to take advantage of all the features of a word processor, you must make sure you have the correct configuration.

Printers

A word processing microcomputer must be able to control a printer. This is done through ports. Printers are available for both parallel and serial ports.

All types of printers may be used for word processing. The most commonly used printers include letter quality printers and dot matrix printers (see Figure 4–2). The letter quality printer produces a document in the same manner as a typewriter, and is limited only by the daisy wheel, ball, or thimble **fonts** available. Printers that produce characters from dots or in a similar manner come with many features that make it possible to produce special effects (see Figure 4–3):

Font:
A style of letter or character such as Italic, Courier, or Prestige.

1. Enhanced (large) print.
2. Compressed or condensed print.
3. Special fonts (italic, scientific, Greek).
4. Underlining.
5. Bold and near letter quality letters.
6. Subscript and superscript.
7. Graphics.

To obtain all the features available in a printer, it must be matched (configured) with the word processor so that the proper codes are sent between the microcomputer and printer. Some word processors have special menu-driven routines that make configuration easy.

Storage Devices

Word processing requires a method of saving text. Any of the devices discussed in chapter 2 may be used. The most common configuration is a two disk drive system or one disk drive and a hard disk.

Dot Matrix   Letter Quality

FIGURE 4–2
Dot Matrix versus
Letter Quality Letters

FIGURE 4–3
Dot Matrix Output—
Special Effects

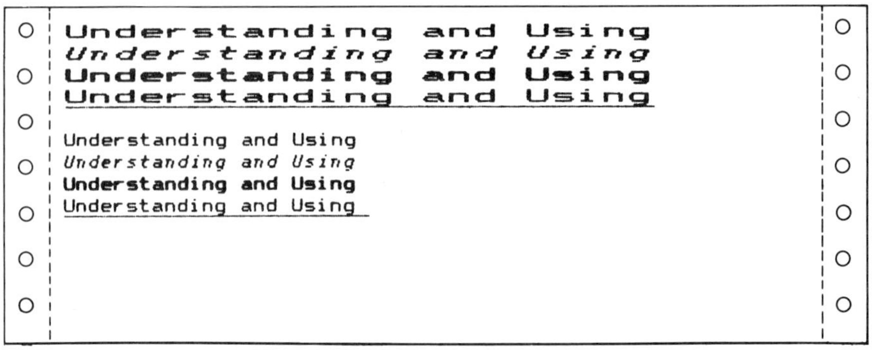

WHY YOU SHOULD KNOW ABOUT WORD PROCESSING

Word processors are valuable tools for the user. Professionals who do their own typing and those who use secretaries can profit from word processing programs. Those who use the word processor themselves receive direct benefits.

The amount of time needed to produce an individual letter becomes important as the number of letters created becomes large. Some users spend over half their time producing letters. Microcomputer word processing reduces the amount of time between creation and production of a printed document.

A completed document with an error, an excessive amount of correction fluid, or any other mark of poor quality makes a negative impression on a contact. Word processing helps produce quality documents by allowing screen editing for easy correction of errors and by creating hard copies quickly without introducing new errors that might need correction fluid.

USER WINDOW

TERM PAPERS

Have you ever done this?

After working on a term paper for two weeks, the final typed copy is read and two misspelled words are found. The decision is made to "live with it" because the time and effort required to make the corrections are just not worth it.

Many users have some typing training but are not expert typists. Professionals with marginal typing skills may take over the entire typing and letter creation process and produce quality documents exactly the way they are wanted.

Microcomputer word processing programs commonly cost between $39 and $700. Most microcomputers are equipped to handle word processing with no additional costs for hardware other than a printer. A printer capable of producing the type of output wanted is often the only additional expense other than the word processing program.

For the professional who has typing assistance, the word processor makes things easier, faster, and improves the document quality. The use of microcomputer word processing changes the skills needed by the secretary typist from speed and accuracy on the keyboard to knowledge in the use of the microcomputer and its programs. The secretary may increase his or her output in the same manner as the professional who directly uses the microcomputer and its word processor.

A document needs to be proofread once, and then only the changes need be proofed as they are made. Errors may be introduced during editing, but this is rare. No new errors are introduced with the printing of the revised document. The time to prepare the first copy of a document may not be significantly reduced with word processing, but if a second or third draft is needed, the word processor can turn them out with ease.

The advantage of microcomputer word processing over a typewriter depends on:

1. The microcomputer system.
2. The specific typewriter.
3. The skill of the user of alternate equipment.

The advantage to the user of the IBM PC type microcomputer with a word processing program over an electric typewriter include:

1. The availability of screen editing.
    a. The ability to overwrite, insert, and delete.
    b. The ability to reformat and control the margins without retyping.
    c. The ability to make global changes and search for strings.
    d. The ability to make block moves of text.
    e. The ability to send the printer special instructions.
2. The ability to save and recall for later edit.
3. The ability to produce a hard copy with a few key strokes.
4. The ability to use the add-on utility programs.

When similar letters are being prepared, the word processor makes the job easier:

1. The original letter is copied under a new filename.
2. The word processor is used to edit the new letter for the next addressee.
3. With a few keystrokes, the word processor is instructed to print the letter on the printer.

On a typewriter each letter would have to be completely retyped.

WORD PROCESSING FEATURES

The features of word processing programs make text creation easy. Word processing program features may be classified into four groups:

1. General features.

2. Text creating and editing features.
3. Saving and recalling the text file features.
4. Printing the text file features.

General Features

There are some general features found in most word processing programs. They include:
1. Menu driven versus function keys.
2. Conventions.
3. Type of file backup.
4. Types of printer control.
5. Disk or RAM based.

Function keys:
Keys found on the left side of the IBM PC keyboard, or the top of some lookalikes, that send custom instructions to the microcomputer. In some programs the user may define the instructions sent by the function keys.

Block:
A collection of characters with beginning and ending markers that must be entered by the user.

Menu versus Function Keys Most word processors on MS/PC–DOS microcomputers use the **function keys** to send special instructions from the user to the microcomputer. On the IBM PC the function keys are located on the left side of the keyboard. In CP/M, the control key in combination with keyboard numbers on the top or side of the microcomputer is often used as a function key. In WordStar, the "begin underline" instruction may be sent by pressing Ctrl P and then Ctrl S. On the IBM PC in WordStar the underline instruction is sent by pressing function key F5. A function key may be used to move to the beginning of a text file, mark the ends of a **block,** mark the beginning and ending of underlining and boldfacing, and to perform other special tasks saving keystrokes.

Generally, function keys are used in combination with the on-screen menu. A menu is a selection of different actions that may be taken. For example, in PCWrite, you will see the menu shown in Figure 4–4 on the screen.

FIGURE 4–4
Word Processing Menu

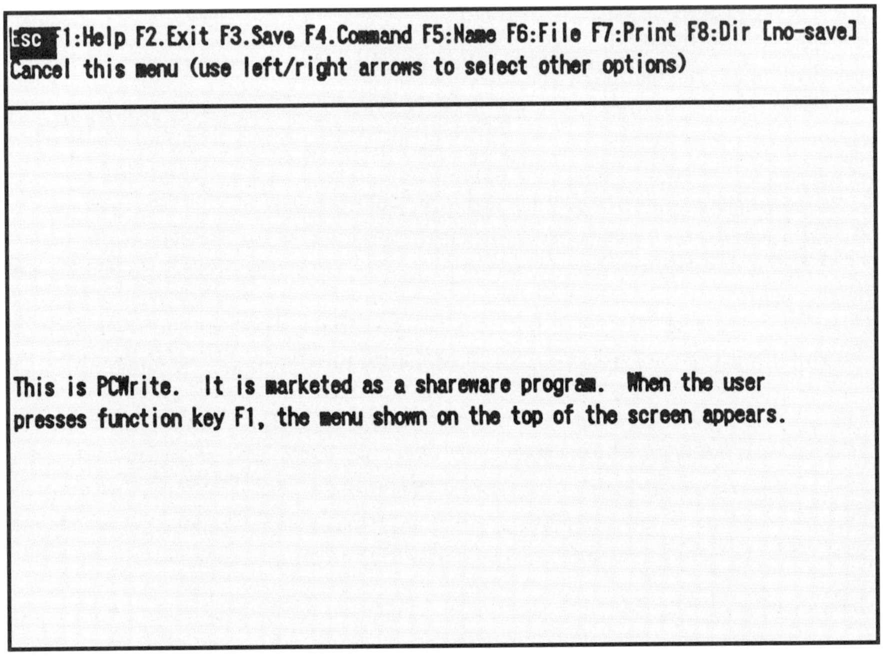

```
Esc F1:Help F2.Exit F3.Save F4.Command F5:Name F6:File F7:Print F8:Dir [no-save]
Cancel this menu (use left/right arrows to select other options)




















This is PCWrite.  It is marketed as a shareware program.  When the user
presses function key F1, the menu shown on the top of the screen appears.
```

This menu allows you to choose whether you want to begin to edit your document, to define the formats used to produce the page, to print the current file, to read a text file from disk or save or remove, to clear the text from the memory of your computer, or to exit the system.

In PCWrite, function keys F1 and F10 have several uses. Pressing F1 at any time will result in a "HELP" appearing on the screen. Help menus and aids are available in many programs. They are screen explanations that may be called up by the user when needed to aid in learning or remembering how some task is performed. Careful reading of screen instructions and use of the help menus often make using programs easier.

Conventions Word processing programs, as a group, have a number of conventions that are usually followed. Three common ones are:

1.   <CR> should not be used at the end of each line.
2.   The control key " ∧ " is used in combination with other keys to perform special functions.
3.   The Esc key is used for special printer instructions.

Do Not Press <CR> Each Line You should not press the carriage return at the end of each line due to word wrap. **Word wrap** occurs in most word processing programs automatically when the text reaches the end of a line. The last word is moved to the next line when there is no more room on that line, according to the margins you have specified. You may override the automatic word wrap by entering a <CR> at the end of a line.

Word wrap:
The moving of the last word in a line to the next line when there is no room between margins.

USER WINDOW

DO NOT PRESS <CR>

The first time a letter was typed, the user pressed the carriage return at the end of each line. The letter was then re-written with new material inserted. The program would not line things up correctly.

After reading the manual, the user removed the carriage returns. The program was allowed to take over and control the form of the letter. The results were much better.

The Control Key Microcomputer keyboards have a limited number of keys. Each key sends a number to the computer. These numbers instruct the microcomputer to perform specific functions. Some special functions require numbers that can be produced only with a combination of the control key and some other key being pressed at the same time. For example, the number 26 is produced by pressing ∧Z. It is used to signify the end of file in some systems. Most programs insulate the user from such details by entering such end of file markers automatically.

The Esc Key The Esc key creates the number 27. Often, combinations of numbers such as 27,21 are sent to printers to give them special instructions.

MICROS IN ACTION

Backup Procedures

Doug Houston Real Estate considered three optional backup procedures:
1. Use of disks and the limitation of each subdirectory on their hard disk to the size of a floppy disk.
2. Purchase and use of tape backup.
3. Purchase and use of removable hard disk cartridge.

For economical and volume reasons, they decided on making copies of subdirectories onto floppy disks daily. The copy is taken to the home of one of the brokers each day in case of potential problems.

The 27,21 combination, when sent to a Radio Shack Daisy Wheel II printer, tells it to line feed as needed by an IBM PC type microcomputer. The 27,21 codes must be sent to the printer each time it is turned on. These codes may be sent by a special program and by many word processing programs. These numbers are referred to as codes.

Type of File Backup Some word processors add the extender .BAK to the old copy of the text file for backup purposes, while the current working text file is saved under the original name.

We recommend that you use the disk utilities to make a copy of your disk periodically. A copy on two physically separate disks is better than two copies on the same disk.

Types of Printer Control Word processors may be classified into two types. The first type is on screen formatting and is often referred to as:

"What you see is what you get."

Word processors of this type allow you to create text on the monitor that is then copied "exactly" to the printer. There are no word processors that do this job completely, although some come very close. Word processing programs of this type include:

- PCWrite
- Microsoft Word
- WordStar

The match between what you see on the monitor and what is produced on a printer is not perfect, because the capabilities are not matched. Printers can handle superscripts and subscripts, compressed and expanded print. At present, monitors cannot handle all these capabilities.

Originally, word processors could boldface or underline on the printer but not on the monitor. Many of the newer word processors can perform these tasks on the screen. Some word processors are near to the goal of producing on the screen what is printed on the printer. As the number of pixels (dots) available on the monitor increases, the goal comes closer. The monitor and printer capabilities must be matched.

The second type of word processor is off screen formatting called:

"Embedded printer commands."

Word processors of this type include:

- Electric Pencil
- Volkswriter

These programs make it easy for you to type text into the word processor in an efficient manner. Printer instructions are embedded into the text. For example, a special character such as a dot, semicolon, or "$>$" is placed in the first position on a line. Following the special character is an instruction, such as "LS $=$ 2". This means to switch to double spacing when the text is printed.

As in many real-life situations, most word processors do not necessarily fit into one or the other classification but both on and off screen formatting.

Disk or RAM Based

Word processing programs may be designed to be:

1. Program and text all in RAM.
2. Program in RAM, text recalled from disk as needed.
3. Parts of program stored on disk recalled as needed, text in RAM.
4. Parts of program stored on disk recalled as needed, text recalled from disk as needed.

Generally, the greater the parts of the program and text in RAM, the greater the speed of the program. The capacity of RAM based programs is limited by the amount of RAM, while the capacity of disk based programs/text is limited by the amount of on-line storage. The difference in performance of word processing program design has been reduced as speed, RAM capacity, and on-line storage capacity of microcomputers have increased.

Text Creating and Editing Features

The text creating and editing features are what make the word processor valuable to the user. These features include:

1. The capability to overwrite, insert, and delete.
2. The capability to reformat and control the margins without retyping.
3. The capability to make global changes and search for strings.
4. The capability to make block moves of text.
5. Rulers.
6. Headers and footers.
7. Page numbering and page breaks.
8. Soft hyphen.

Text editors are programs that allow you to enter text (create) easily. Thereafter, characters, words, or complete paragraphs may be inserted or deleted anywhere in the text file. You can make changes with ease, and you can see the changes as they are made on the monitor.

Text editor:
Software that makes creating, changing, storing, and retrieving of text in a file possible.

The microcomputer monitor is an ideal place to accomplish the editing task. Most word processors allow for full-screen editing. This means you may move the **cursor** to any location on the monitor and make whatever changes, additions, or corrections needed. You may **scroll** through a document (text file), looking at it over and over again.

One advantage of electronic editing is that, once you have entered the text, you do not need to type the material a second or third time. You enter the text once, and save it as a text file on a computer storage media.

The Capability to Overwrite, Insert, and Delete A word processor may be in the overwrite or insert modes. Some word processors control the shape or size of the cursor, to let you know which mode they are in, while others will display the words INSERT ON.

Overwrite means the word you are entering replaces the text that was formerly at the location of the cursor. **Insert** means that when a word is typed into existing text, the text following it is moved to the right to make room.

Figure 4–5 shows a word processing screen in overwrite mode, with the cursor located at the beginning of the word "displayed." The words "OVER-WRITE ON" in the upper right part of the screen often do not appear. The absence of any words means the overwrite mode is on.

Starting with Figure 4–5 the words "We are now overwriting" are typed. Figure 4–6 indicates the results.

Many IBM PC word processors use the "Ins" key, found in the lower part of the numeric keypad, to switch between insert and overwrite mode. It is next to the "Del" key, which is used to **delete** unwanted letters by many word processors. In some word processors, pressing the Del key will delete the character to the left of the cursor, rather than the one at the place where the cursor is located. The use of special keys such as Ins and Del are program specific.

Cursor:

A symbol on the monitor that indicates where text will be typed. The cursor is often a line (____) or a box. It may be steady or blinking.

Scroll:

Text is moved up or down to display text that cannot be shown on the monitor at one time.

Overwrite:

When a character is typed, it replaces the character formerly at the location of the cursor.

Insert:

When a word is typed into existing text, the text that follows it moves over to make room.

Delete:

An instruction to remove a character, block, or file. When characters are removed, the text closes up.

FIGURE 4–5
Diskette Misspelled

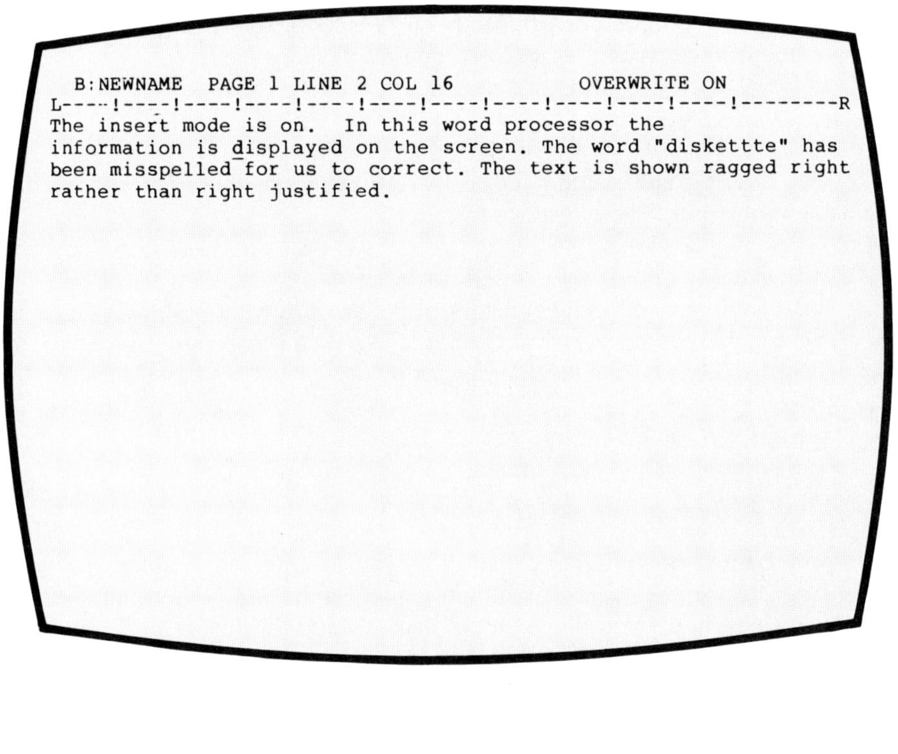

```
     B:NEWNAME   PAGE 1 LINE 2 COL 16          OVERWRITE ON
     L----"!----!----!----!----!----!----!----!----!----!--------R
     The insert mode is on.  In this word processor the
     information is displayed on the screen. The word "diskettte" has
     been misspelled for us to correct. The text is shown ragged right
     rather than right justified.
```

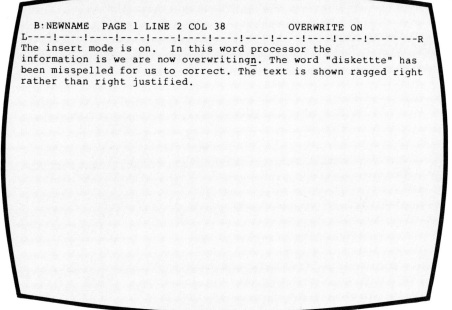

FIGURE 4–6
Overwriting in Word Processing

```
   B:NEWNAME   PAGE 1 LINE 2 COL 38              OVERWRITE ON
L----!----!----!----!----!----!----!----!----!----!----!--------R
The insert mode is on.  In this word processor the
information is we are now overwritingn. The word "diskettte" has
been misspelled for us to correct. The text is shown ragged right
rather than right justified.
```

Changing from the overwrite mode to the insert mode results in Figure 4–7.

If the words "WE ARE NOW INSERTING" are typed, the screen will change to Figure 4–8.

The plus + sign in line two of Figure 4–8 indicates that the line flows off the screen because of the newly inserted material. The text is not lost;

FIGURE 4–7
The Insert Mode is Turned On

```
   B:NEWNAME   PAGE 1 LINE 2 COL 38              INSERT ON
L----!----!----!----!----!----!----!----!----!----!----!--------R
The insert mode is on.  In this word processor the
information is we are now overwritingn. The word "diskettte" has
been misspelled for us to correct. The text is shown ragged right
rather than right justified.
```

FIGURE 4–8
The Act of Inserting

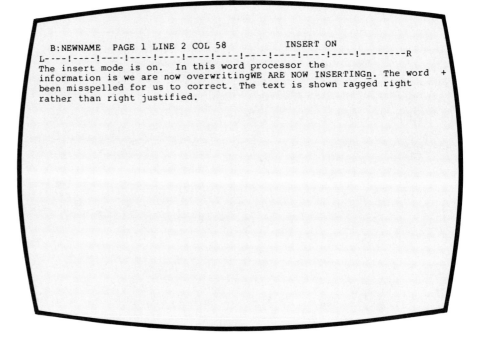

```
    B:NEWNAME   PAGE 1 LINE 2 COL 58            INSERT ON
L----!----!----!----!----!----!----!----!----!----!----!--------R
The insert mode is on.  In this word processor the
information is we are now overwritingWE ARE NOW INSERTINGn. The word  +
been misspelled for us to correct. The text is shown ragged right
rather than right justified.
```

reformatting puts the text back on the screen between existing margins. Some word processors do this while others will push all the material down as shown in Figure 4–9.

Figure 4–10 shows a word processing screen with some text, with the cursor located in the upper-left position and the insert mode on.

FIGURE 4–9
The Results of Inserting

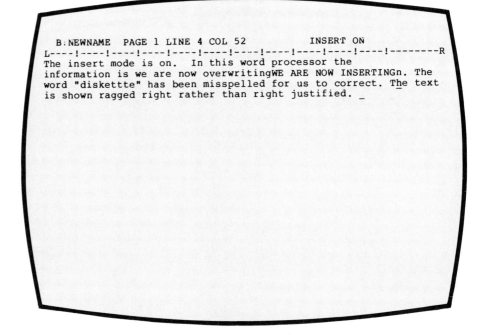

```
    B:NEWNAME   PAGE 1 LINE 4 COL 52            INSERT ON
L----!----!----!----!----!----!----!----!----!----!----!--------R
The insert mode is on.  In this word processor the
information is we are now overwritingWE ARE NOW INSERTINGn. The
word "diskettte" has been misspelled for us to correct. The text
is shown ragged right rather than right justified. _
```

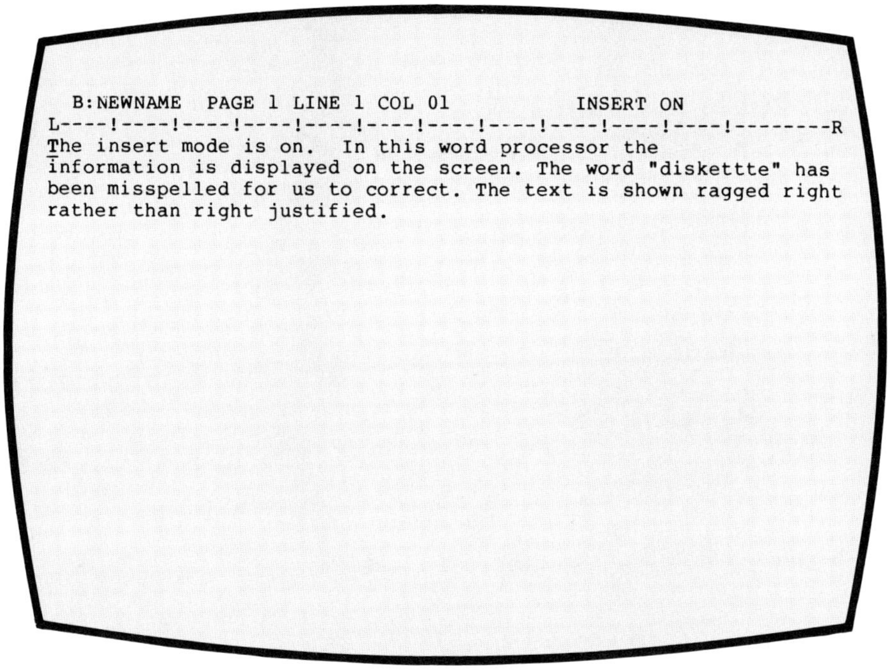

```
    B:NEWNAME   PAGE 1 LINE 1 COL 01            INSERT ON
L----!----!----!----!----!----!----!----!----!----!----!-------R
The insert mode is on.  In this word processor the
information is displayed on the screen. The word "diskettte" has
been misspelled for us to correct. The text is shown ragged right
rather than right justified.
```

FIGURE 4–10
Starting Over Again
without Changes

One way to correct the misspelling in Figure 4–10 is with the use of the Del key. Figure 4–11 shows the cursor located under one of the letters "t" that must be removed.

After the delete instruction is given the screen changes to that shown in Figure 4–12.

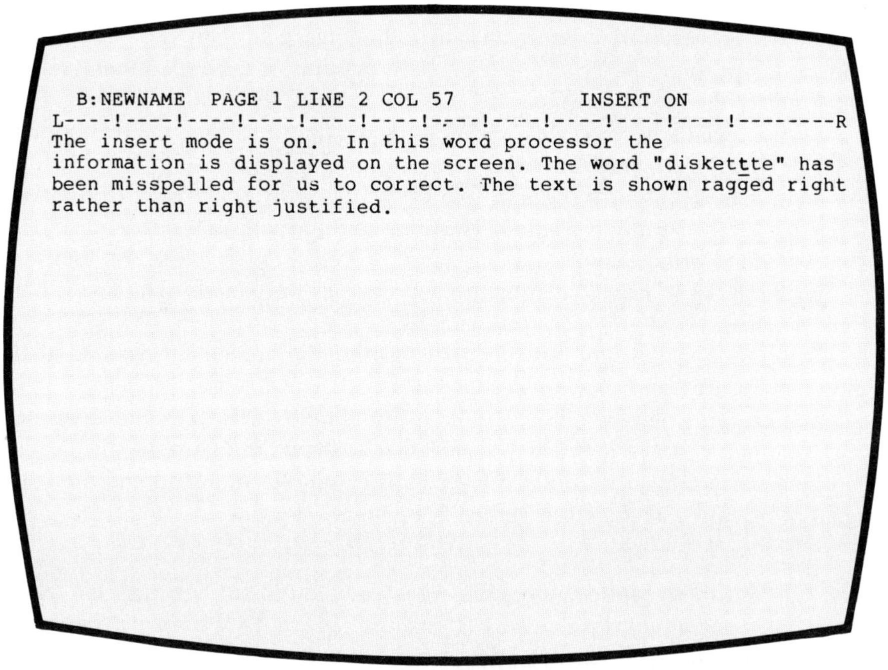

```
    B:NEWNAME   PAGE 1 LINE 2 COL 57            INSERT ON
L----!----!----!----!----!----!----!----!----!----!----!-------R
The insert mode is on.  In this word processor the
information is displayed on the screen. The word "diskettte" has
been misspelled for us to correct. The text is shown ragged right
rather than right justified.
```

FIGURE 4–11
Correcting Spelling

FIGURE 4–12
Delete Key Corrects Spelling

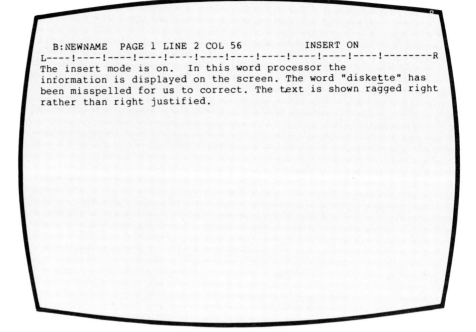

```
   B:NEWNAME   PAGE 1 LINE 2 COL 56          INSERT ON
L----!----!----!----!----!----!----!----!----!----!----!--------R
The insert mode is on.  In this word processor the
information is displayed on the screen. The word "diskette" has
been misspelled for us to correct. The text is shown ragged right
rather than right justified.
```

Word processors operating in microcomputers without special keys, such as Del and Ins, use the control key with combinations of other keys to perform the same tasks. The availability of special keys makes the use of word processing programs a little easier.

The Capability to Reformat and Control the Margins without Retyping
The word processor is capable of controlling margins with the press of a button. It can then line up the text on both margins, if desired. When text is lined up evenly on the right margin, it is called right justification.

In the "what you see is what you get" type word processor, the text on the monitor occasionally must be reformatted. Most word processing programs do this automatically. One, WordStar, requires you to instruct the microcomputer when such reformatting is wanted. This type of reformatting is not required in the embedded printer command type word processor, such as Electric Pencil.

Figure 4–13 shows the text before any changes were made. The text is not right justified.

After the justify-right instruction is given, the screen changes to that shown in Figure 4–14.

The margins may be adjusted with a few simple keystrokes and then the microcomputer can be instructed to reformat as shown in Figure 4–15.

Line spacing may be adjusted with another simple command and the text again reformatted as shown in Figure 4–16.

The Capability to Make Global Changes and Search for Strings One term commonly used in word processing is "strings." A **string** is simply a character or group of characters. All word processors have the capability to search for a string and/or to replace one string with another.

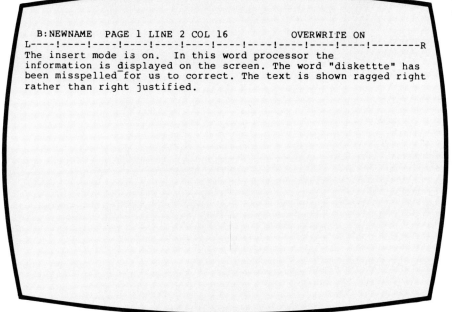

```
    B:NEWNAME   PAGE 1 LINE 2 COL 16           OVERWRITE ON
L----!----!----!----!----!----!----!----!----!----!----!--------R
The insert mode is on.  In this word processor the
information is displayed on the screen. The word "diskettte" has
been misspelled for us to correct. The text is shown ragged right
rather than right justified.
```

FIGURE 4–13
Starting Over with
Diskette Misspelled

String searches and replacements are made in different ways. For example, some word processors, when told to find the string "the", will include the string "The" (that is, they will find all words spelled t–h–e regardless of whether the "t" is uppercase or lowercase). Others will ask you if uppercase and lowercase should be ignored before performing the search. Some word processors are capable of an exact match only.

String:
A character or characters. Strings may be one or more characters in length.

```
    B:NEWNAME   PAGE 1 LINE 2  COL 01           OVERWRITE ON
L----!----!----!----!----!----!----!----!----!----!----!--------R
The insert mode is on.  In this word processor the information is
displayed on the screen. The word "diskettte" has been misspelled
for us to correct. The text is shown ragged right rather than
right justified.
```

FIGURE 4–14
Right Justified
(The Text Is Now in Error)

FIGURE 4–15
Margin Adjustment

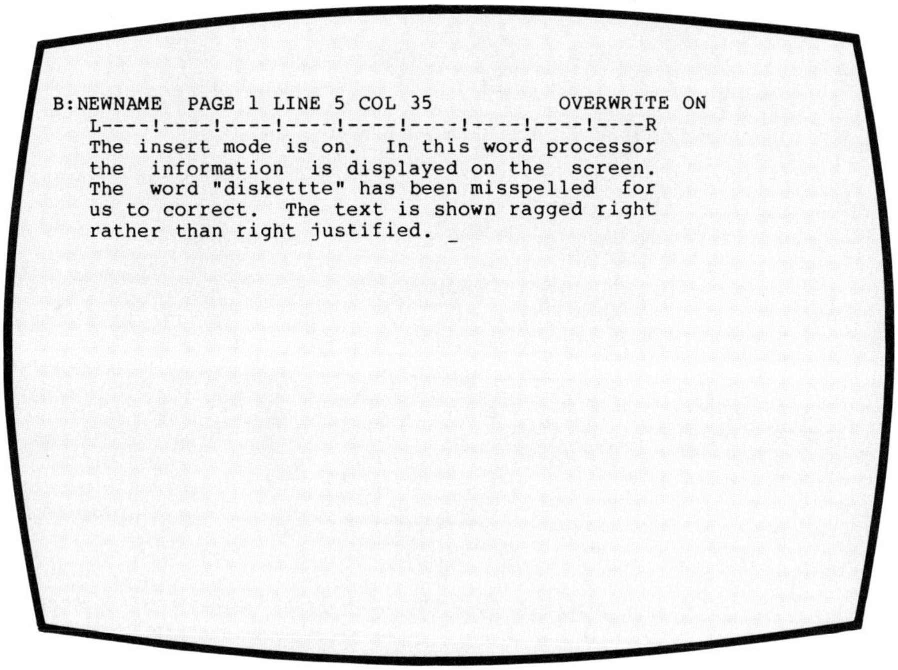

```
B:NEWNAME   PAGE 1 LINE 5 COL 35           OVERWRITE ON
  L----!----!----!----!----!----!----!----!----!---R
  The insert mode is on.  In this word processor
  the  information  is displayed on the  screen.
  The  word "diskettte" has been misspelled  for
  us to correct.  The text is shown ragged right
  rather than right justified. _
```

Copy:
To duplicate an image of a block at a new location.

Move:
To relocate a block.

The Capability to Make Block Moves of Text A block is a section of text identified with beginning and ending markers that must be entered by the user. The marker at the beginning may be the same as at the end, or different. Once identified, the block may be copied, moved, or erased. **Copy** means another image of the block is created at a new location. **Move** means the original copy is erased, and the block appears at another location. **Erase** means the

FIGURE 4–16
Double Spacing

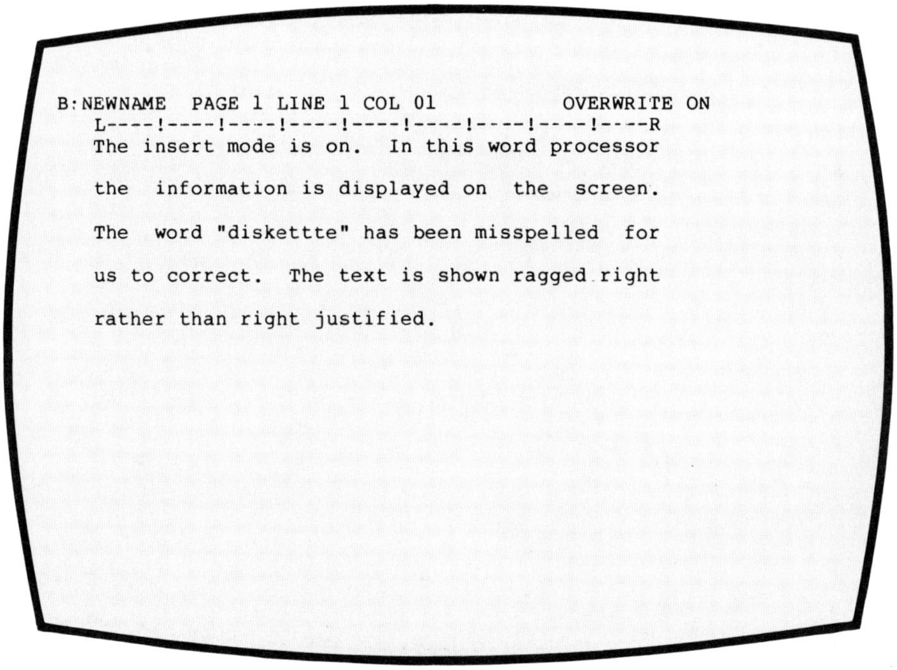

```
B:NEWNAME   PAGE 1 LINE 1 COL 01           OVERWRITE ON
  L----!----!----!----!----!----!----!----!----!---R
  The insert mode is on.  In this word processor

  the  information is displayed on  the  screen.

  The  word "diskettte" has been misspelled  for

  us to correct.  The text is shown ragged right

  rather than right justified.
```

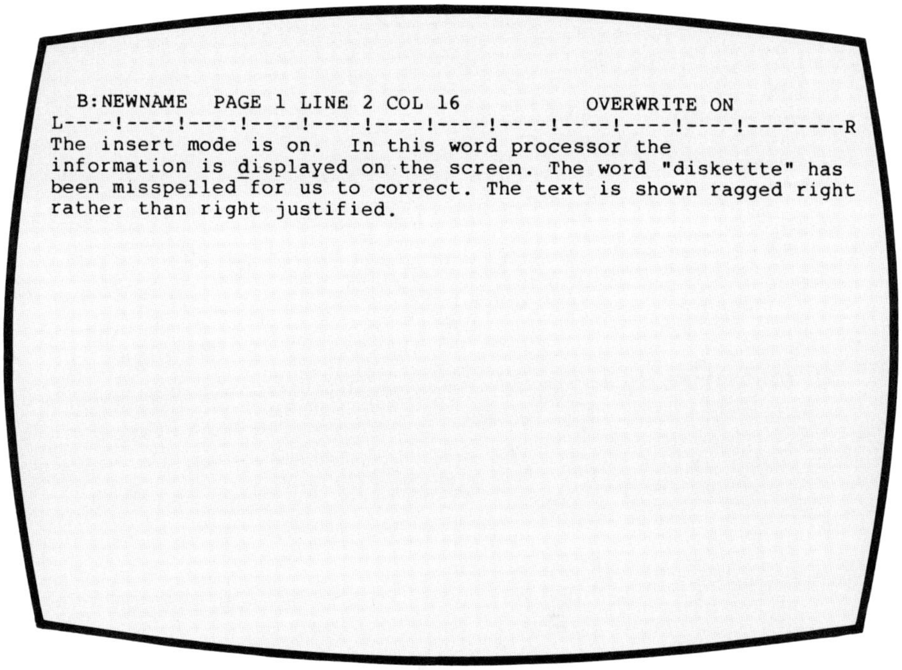

FIGURE 4–17
Starting Again

```
   B:NEWNAME   PAGE 1 LINE 2 COL 16           OVERWRITE ON
L----!----!----!----!----!----!----!----!----!----!----!--------R
The insert mode is on.  In this word processor the
information is displayed on the screen. The word "diskettte" has
been misspelled for us to correct. The text is shown ragged right
rather than right justified.
```

block is removed from the file. A number of word processors can insert a block of text saved under a filename on a disk, or find a block of text in the middle of one file and move it to another.

Figure 4–17 shows the screen before beginning the block operation.

A block is marked by identifying its beginning and end as shown in Figure 4–18.

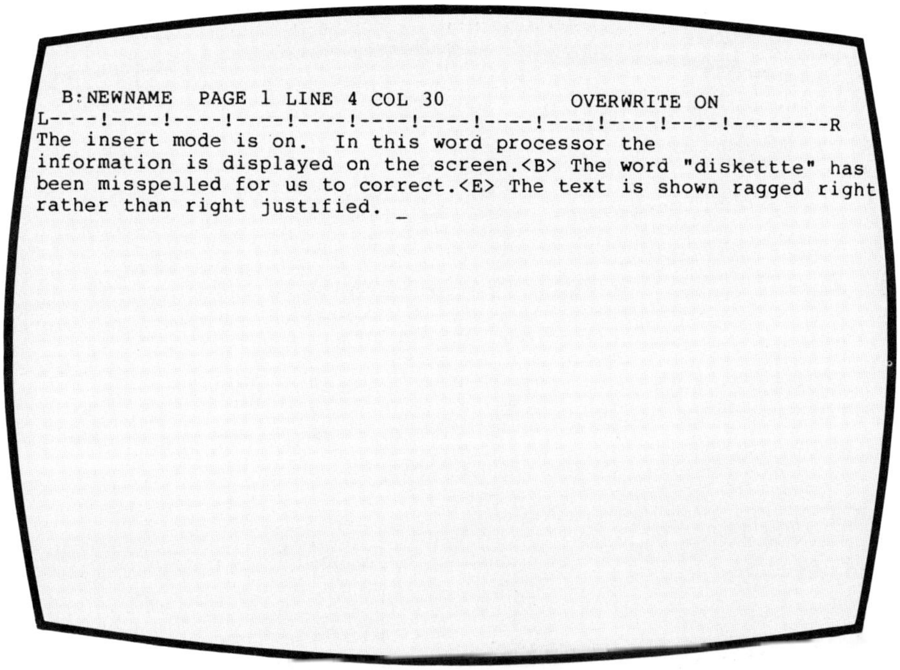

Erase:
To remove a block.

FIGURE 4–18
Marking the Block

```
   B:NEWNAME   PAGE 1 LINE 4 COL 30           OVERWRITE ON
L----!----!----!----!----!----!----!----!----!----!----!--------R
The insert mode is on.  In this word processor the
information is displayed on the screen.<B> The word "diskettte" has
been misspelled for us to correct.<E> The text is shown ragged right
rather than right justified. _
```

FIGURE 4–19
Copying a Block

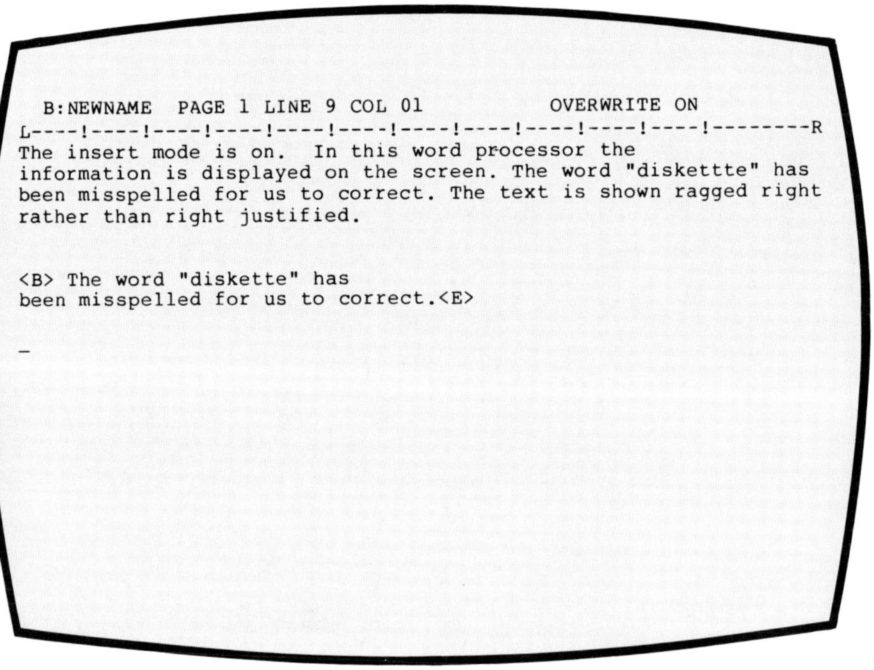

```
     B:NEWNAME   PAGE 1 LINE 9 COL 01              OVERWRITE ON
L----!----!----!----!----!----!----!----!----!----!----!--------R
The insert mode is on.  In this word processor the
information is displayed on the screen. The word "diskettte" has
been misspelled for us to correct. The text is shown ragged right
rather than right justified.


<B> The word "diskette" has
been misspelled for us to correct.<E>


_
```

After moving the cursor beyond the end of the text and giving the copy instruction, Figure 4–19 results. If the move instruction is given, Figure 4–20 results. If the erase instruction is given, Figure 4–21 results.

Some word processors will leave the text formatted as shown while others will fill in and reformat. Most move the block markers to the new location along with the block. Sometimes you will need to "unmark" text before proceeding.

FIGURE 4–20
Moving a Block

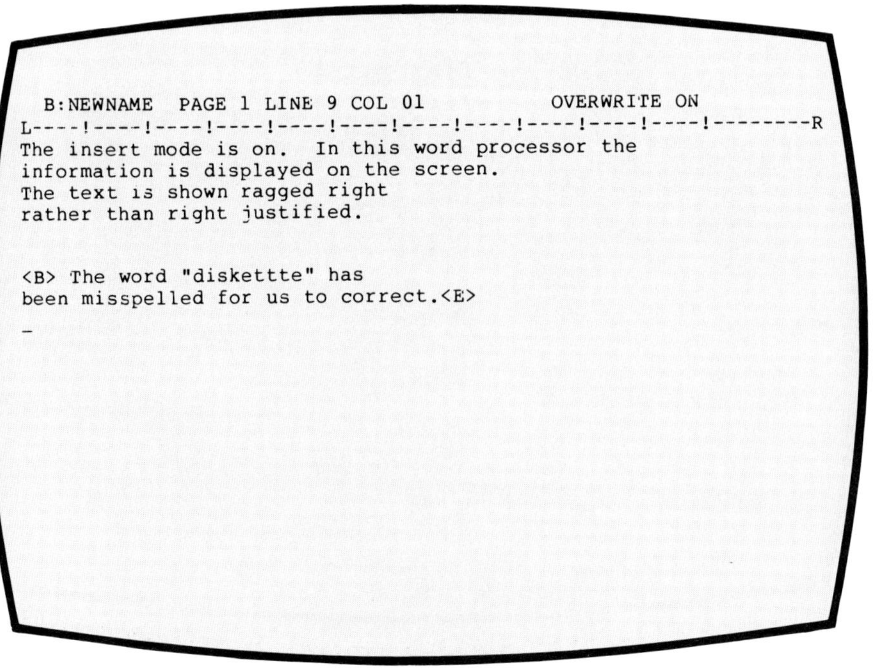

```
     B:NEWNAME   PAGE 1 LINE 9 COL 01              OVERWRITE ON
L----!----!----!----!----!----!----!----!----!----!----!--------R
The insert mode is on.  In this word processor the
information is displayed on the screen.
The text is shown ragged right
rather than right justified.


<B> The word "diskettte" has
been misspelled for us to correct.<E>

_
```

MICROS IN ACTION

Learning to Move Blocks

The word processor was used for three months before the capability to move blocks was needed by one of the agents. The need arose in a large proposal in which several alternate designs for a building were being considered. There were a number of common aspects of each design that would have had to be retyped without the block moving capability. Approximately three hours of typing was saved on this one project.

Rulers Each word processor displays its screen differently. Along the top or bottom of the screen you will generally find a ruler that helps the user locate the cursor and tab locations. Word processing users should check the screen layout.

Headers and Footers The addition of page headers and footers can be important when you are assigned the task of producing a document in a specific format. In the past, most publishers and universities had specific methods for handling headers and footers. The trend is for them to be more flexible. However, you may still find yourself faced with the problem of a specific location and format requirement for footnotes and page titles.

Page Numbering and Page Breaks The default mode of many word processors is to print the page number, while others will not do so unless instructed. Some locate the page number on the top of the page while others put it on the bottom.

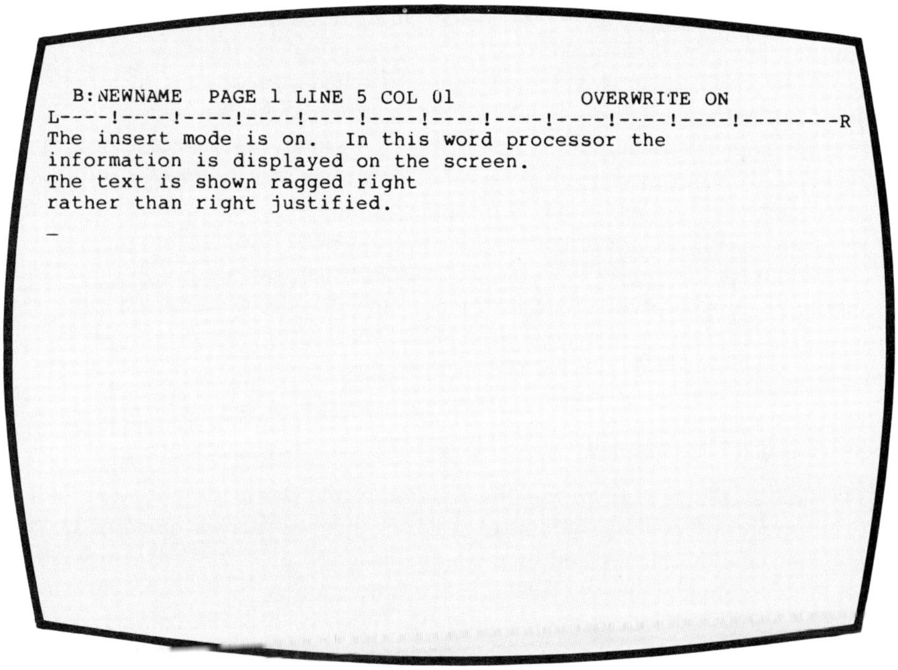

FIGURE 4–21
Erasing a Block

```
   B:NEWNAME   PAGE 1 LINE 5 COL 01             OVERWRITE ON
L----!----!----!----!----!----!----!----!----!----!----!--------R
The insert mode is on.  In this word processor the
information is displayed on the screen.
The text is shown ragged right
rather than right justified.
 _
```

A word processor that automatically locates the page number in the manner wanted may be the best selection. If your needs are for letters and other such documents, you should select a word processor that defaults to no page number.

Generally, only word processors that format on the screen will be able to display page breaks during the editing process. If page breaks and other on-screen formatting are important, the selection of an on-screen word processor is best.

Soft Hyphens and Hard Spaces The placement of proper hyphenation has not generally been solved. Some word processors will aid you in the placement of (hard) hyphens during the editing process. Others allow you to place a (soft) hyphen in a word or words to be used, if that word appears at the end of the line.

You may sometimes wish to control the location of two or more words so they are on the same line. The placement of a hard space between the words in some word processors forces the program to handle the string as a single word during format. The two words will always appear on the same line. A soft space allows the word processor to separate the words on two lines if required by the format process.

Saving and Recalling Text File Features

Text must be saved on disk and then recalled for future editing. All word processing programs save text files. Some save the text as ASCII files, some as near ASCII files, and some in special code. A near ASCII file is a file that uses the ASCII codes, has some additional control codes, and may be edited to an ASCII file without excessive effort.

Word processors that may produce ASCII files include Electric Pencil, Volkswriter, and WordStar (in its non-document mode). WordStar document files are near ASCII because they include hidden characters that are not consistent with the ASCII standard.

A standard, such as ASCII, is required when you transfer files between word processing programs. The standard is also used for transferring information between microcomputers, spreadsheet programs, and database programs. The ASCII file printed on disk by other programs may be moved into many word processing programs for additional editing and report preparation. Many word processing programs come with utilities to ease file transfer.

When transferring files between programs that use ASCII files, problems should be minimal. Embedded instructions may have to be removed either before or after transfer. For creating ASCII files in programs using near ASCII files, you may need to purchase special programs.

Printing Text File Features

The final step in a word processing program is the production of a hard copy. Printer controllers are programs or routines that are part of the word processor; they take the file created by the text editor and produce hard copy using a printer. Usually the print routine is called from a menu, by function keys, using a combination of several keys, or directly from the disk operating system by calling a printer program.

You may find a printed draft is unnecessary. We recommend that you edit on the monitor, and then use a printed draft for additional error corrections. Examination of the screen helps find some errors, while examination of a printed document helps find others.

ADDITIONAL FEATURES OF WORD PROCESSORS

Word processors have special features of value in particular situations. Some word processors come as complete or almost complete packages, while others that are limited may have their capabilities expanded by the addition of special utilities. Some of the additional features you may expect in many word processors are:

1. Special printing effects.
   a. Boldfacing.
   b. Additional fonts such as italics.
   c. **Proportional spacing**.
2. Document assembly from files with pre-written text.
3. Print spoolers.
4. Windows.

Proportional spacing: Allows for difference in letter size to make the document look like typeset material.

Special Printing Effects

Many printers are capable of producing special effects, such as large print, compressed print, lines, graphics, boldface, subscripts, superscripts, proportional spacing, and enhanced print. Table 4–1 lists some of the capabilities of the Epson FX–80 printer and the codes used to start and stop these capabilities.

Printer codes may be sent using decimal numbers, hexadecimal numbers, symbols, or by a combination of keyboard keys. The word processor being used determines the method in which the user enters the codes. In all cases only binary numbers are sent to the printer.

A common method of entering control codes in MS/PC–DOS word processors is to use the Alt key combined with the numeric key pad. To send the binary number 15 to an Epson printer and make it change to compressed mode, the procedure is:

- Hold the Alt key down
- Type 15 on the numeric keypad
- Lift up on the Alt key

Either nothing or a character similar to * will appear on the screen. This character will not be printed. When the binary number 15 is received by the printer, it will switch to compressed mode.

If you want to change to a subscript and need a number of codes such as

<Esc> 83 1

the procedure is

- Hold the Alt key down
- Type 27 on the numeric keypad to send the <Esc> instruction
- Lift up on the Alt key
- Hold the Alt key down

TABLE 4–1
Epson FX–80 Codes

Font or Printer		Epson FX–80		
Action	Esc	Decimal	Hex	Symbol
Backspace		8	08	BS
Compressed				
Start		15	OF	SI
	< Esc >	15	OF	SI
Stop		18	12	DC2
Double Strike				
Start	< Esc >	71	47	G
Stop	< Esc >	72	48	H
Enlarged				
Start		14	OE	SO
	< Esc >	14	OE	SO
	< Esc >	87	57	W
Stop		20	14	DC4
	< Esc >	14	OE	SO
Emphasized				
Start	< Esc >	69	45	E
Stop	< Esc >	70	46	F
Proportional Spacing				
Start	< Esc >	112	70	P
Super and subscript				
Start	< Esc >	83	53	S
Stop	< Esc >	84	54	T

For Subscript send the three instructions:
< Esc > 83 1

For Superscript send the three instructions:
< Esc > 83 0

Underline				
Start	< Esc >	45	2D	—
Stop	< Esc >	45	2D	—

- Type 83 on the numeric keypad
- Lift up on the Alt key
- Hold the Alt key down
- Type 1 on the numeric keypad
- Lift up on the Alt key

Three characters similar to ↑SΩ will appear on the screen when you have completed the instructions.

Document Assembly

When the same words are used over and over again, as in a legal office, document assembly capabilities of word processors make the task easier and more efficient.

There are five ways to assemble a document:

1. Insert or merge text on the screen.
2. Create a file from other text files that are called during the printing process.

3. Append at the end of files other text files to be called during printing.
4. Use a menu driven program to assemble a document.
5. Use the capability in DOS to add one file to another.

Many applications including advertising, law, academic proposals, medical reports, contracts, and more require a word processor with this capability.

Print Spoolers

Programs are available that set aside part of RAM or create a special file on the disk to be used to hold text that is on its way to the printer. The text is fed into the reserved area faster than it would be into a printer. As soon as all the text is in the reserved area, the microcomputer is free to perform other tasks.

Print spoolers are often referred to as print buffers when they are external to the microcomputer. Printers may be purchased with built-in RAM to act as print spoolers. The print spooler is an example of multitasking; the microcomputer can do two things at the same time.

Print spooler:
A program that sets aside part of RAM or the disk to receive text being sent to the printer.

Windows

A feature that is most useful when performing word processing is splitting the screen into "windows" (see Figure 4–22). Each word processor with windows uses them a little differently. In general, each window may display a part of the same document or entirely different documents. Text may be transferred between windows. Windows are most useful when creating a custom document from a series of other documents.

FIGURE 4–22   Word Processing Windows

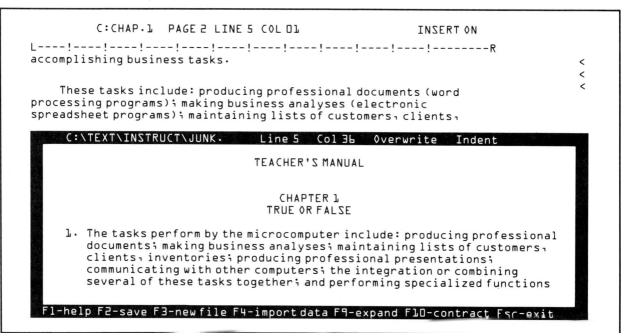

MICROS IN ACTION

Spelling Checker

The brokers and agents found that a spelling program reduced the amount of time required for proofreading. The spelling program helped improve the quality of documents and was more than worth its purchase price.

COMMONLY FOUND ADD–ON UTILITIES

You may often buy add-on programs to perform routines that are not available in a particular word processor. Some commonly found add-on programs are:

1. Spelling checkers.
2. Merge print for mass mailing.
3. Table of contents generators.
4. Index generators.
5. Footnote programs.
6. Style checkers.

Spelling Programs

Spelling programs help produce documents without errors. These programs use several different methods for checking spelling. One method is a table look-up type, where words are compared to a pre-recorded dictionary. Generally, spelling programs will work on any ASCII file, including programs saved as near ASCII files.

USER WINDOW

SPELLING CHECKERS

The writer prepared to use his spelling program for the first time. After the corrections were made and the letter mailed, he took one more look at the results. The word "computer" was spelled "commuter"!

A week later while reading the magazine to which the letter was mailed, the writer spotted the same spelling error. Spelling programs help but do not eliminate the need for careful proofreading of your documents.

Spelling programs will not identify words that are not in their dictionary. The word may not be in the dictionary because:

1. It is a proper name.

2. The word is not included in the dictionary.
3. The word is misspelled.

Some spelling programs will help you find the correct spelling for a word by displaying similar words on the screen. Some programs point out the problem and let you solve it. If you spell the word "computer" as "commuter", this error will not be identified. Commuter is a word. The spelling program can find misspelled words, not misused words.

Merge Print for Mass Mailing

An example of a merge printing program for mass mailing is MailMerge, an add-on to the word processing program WordStar. It allows the preparation of mail list data files that may be used to produce multiple letters addressed to different individuals. MailMerge aids in the preparation of envelopes, document assembly, and the continuous printing of multiple files. Mailing list programs allow the use of names and addresses for business applications. Some mailing programs personalize mass mailings.

Table of Contents, Index Generators, Footnote Programs

Completing a large manuscript involves many details. The creation of a table of contents, the searching and identification of terms for an index, and the proper location of footnotes are just a few of these details. There are a number of programs that facilitate these tasks. Each works a little differently and have different levels of user involvement. Most programs are designed to operate with a specific word processing program or with word processors that produce ASCII files.

Style Checkers

Style (grammar) programs will check a document for common typographical errors, writing style, and sentence level. Common errors, such as writing the word "can not" as two words rather than one, will be found by grammar programs, but not by spelling programs. Words such as "very" will be identified by grammar programs as being unnecessary. Wordy phrases such as "in the case of" will be found by a grammar program. Double words such as "the the" will be found. This error is common in word processing.

These style programs make great teaching aids. They will point out questions and problems without becoming annoying. Most of the current versions cannot correct errors, but just alert the writer to possible stylistic errors.

COMPARING WORD PROCESSORS

The features of word processing programs are compared in Table 4–2. These comparisons relate to the stated versions only and are based on available data before pubpublication.

TABLE 4–2
Comparison of Word Processing Features

Features	DisplayWrite 4	PC Write 2.7	Volkswriter III	WordPerfect 4.2	WordStar 4.0
Configuration					
RAM required	341K	128K	256K	256K	256K
Disk drives	1	1	1	1	1
Hard drive	supported	supported	supported	supported	supported
General					
Function key		x	x	x	x
Menu driven	x		x	x	x
Windows		no	no	yes	yes
Document Assembly	yes	yes	yes	yes	yes
Spell checker	yes	yes	yes	yes	yes
Help screens	yes	yes	yes	yes	yes
Math					
Line draw	yes			yes	yes
On screen bold	yes		yes	yes	yes
underline	yes		yes	yes	yes
Undo				yes	yes
Macros	yes			yes	yes
GOTO page	yes	yes	yes	yes	yes
Use DOS functions				yes	yes
Headers/footers	yes	yes	yes	yes	yes
Indexes/Outliner				yes	yes
Save/Recall					
Backup		yes	user control	user control	yes
File Type					
ASCII	yes	yes	yes	yes	yes
DIF				yes	
WordStar			yes		yes
Printing					
Proportional	yes	yes	yes	yes	yes
Spooler	yes	yes		yes	yes

Printer controls work only if the printer has the capabilities called for by the program.

The price of word processing programs starts as low as $40 and may be as high as $1,000. Some programs are sold as shareware. The user may obtain a copy, try it out, and then become a registered owner if the program proves useful.

SUMMARY

Word processing is one of the more important programs to computer users. Word processing capabilities make it easy to produce quality reports and letters. The important concepts include:

1. The microcomputer may be used as a word processor.
2. Word processing saves time, increases document quality, reduces the typing skill level needed, reduces the amount of coordination needed between individuals, and does not require a large investment.
3. Word processing requires a microcomputer, a word processing program, a printer that can produce text of the quality needed by the application, and usually two disk drives.
4. Electronic word processing programs have general, text creating/editing, saving and recalling, and printing features.

5.   The general features of a word processor include the trade off between menu-driven program and function keys, the conventions used, the type of file backup procedures, and the type of printer control designed into the system.

6.   Text editing involves overwriting, inserting, and deleting, formatting and margin control, and the movement of strings and blocks.

7.   Text must be saved on a disk and then recalled for future editing.

8.   No program can do everything you need. Each has some feature that is of special value in a particular situation.

9.   You may often buy add-on programs to perform routines that are not available in a particular word processor.

KEY TERMS

Block	Move
Copy	Overwrite
Cursor	String
Delete	Text editor
Erase	Word processing
Function key	Word wrap
Insert	

REVIEW QUESTIONS

1. What is word processing?

2. What is text? What is a text file?

3. What are the basic features of a word processing program?

4. Identify some of the commonly found add-on utility word processing programs.

5. Identify the minimum hardware needs for word processing.

6. What are some of the special printer effects useful in word processing?

7. How does the word processing program help produce quality documents?

8. How does word processing help the professional with marginal typing skills?

9. What are the advantages of electronic word processing over using a standard typewriter?

10. Identify some of the general features of word processing programs a user should be concerned with.

11. Identify three common word processing conventions.

12. What are two general types of word processing programs?

13. What is a text editor? What is the importance of such a program?

14. What is full-screen editing?

15. Identify the exact meaning of overwrite, insert, and delete.

16. What is right justification?

17. What is a string?

18. What is a block? What does it mean to copy, move, and erase a block?

19. Why is a standard ASCII file needed in word processing?

20. What is a print spooler?

21. What do style programs do?

DISCUSSION AND APPLICATION QUESTIONS

1. Find a magazine advertisement for a word processor. How much does one cost? What kind of features is being advertised?

2. Survey an office that uses electronic word processing. What kind of word processor is being used? Why was this one selected for this office? Was it a good choice?

3. Use the yellow pages of your telephone book to identify where word processing programs and equipment may be purchased.

4. Identify alternate equipment and techniques to word processing. Where are they available locally?

5. After being introduced to the use of word processing in your laboratory, use magazine and other sources to study electronic typewriters. How do the two compare?

6. If the school's mainframe computer has a word processing program, find out about it. How does it compare to the one available on your microcomputer?

7. Examine the school's bulletin board for advertisements for typing and word processing services. What do they cost? What is being offered?

8. Examine your local newspaper and the telephone yellow pages for word processing services. What is available?

LABORATORY ASSIGNMENTS

All assignments start with the same letter. The DOS copy utility should be used to make copies of the original letter for the additional assignments.

Assignments:
1. Enter the following letter and save it on your disk.

```
                    John Quartize
                     President
              American Indian Foundation
                 123 Far West Lane
               Way Out, Arizona 55555

                   212-555-55555

               January 3, 1999
```

Mr. William Snodgrass
Office of Senator Avert
Capitol Building
Washington, DC 55551

Dear Sir:

The research on the farming conditions on the XZP Indian Reservation has been
completed and forwarded to your office under separate cover. We feel the results justify additional investigation, and a grant to develop new crops for
the particular soil conditions found on the reservation.

We would like an appointment to meet with you in May during our trip to
Washington.

Sincerely,

John Quartize, President

2. Starting with the letter in assignment 1, create a memo telling members of
the tribal council that a letter has been written to the office of Senator Avert.
Save the memo on your disk.

The organization of this memo should be:

Date: _____
Subject: _____
From: _____
To: _____
Subject: ....

3. Starting with the letter in assignment 1, restyle the letter with paragraphs
that are indented and the "sincerely" and name placed in the middle of the
page, rather than the left side. Save the memo on your disk.

4. Create the following letter:

```
                    John Quartize
                     President
              American Indian Foundation
                 123 Far West Lane
               Way Out, Arizona 55555

                   212-555-55555

               January 3, 1999
```

Mr. William Snodgrass
Office of Senator Avert
Capitol Building
Washington, DC 55551

```
Dear Sir:

We are inviting all candidates for the office of senator to join us on our ra-
dio station for a debate on local issues. We have made arrangements with all
local newspapers to cover the event and help us in getting out support.

Your participation would be appreciated. We will schedule the event to meet
your requirements.


Sincerely,


John Quartize, President
```

5. Prepare a newspaper release based on the previous assignment. Assume a date has been set by the senator.

6. Prepare a memo to your tribe on the debate from assignment 4.

7. Redo assignment numbers 4–6 using margins of left 10, right 50. Assume the material will be included in a newsletter.

8. Change all words "the" to "help" in assignment number 4.

9. Use the block move capability of your word processor and make ten copies of paragraph two in assignment 4.

10. Add three user-controlled page breaks to assignment 9.

11. If your word processor does not automatically put in page numbers, add them to the letter in assignment 4. If your word processor does put in numbers, delete them.

12. Follow the text instructions to load PRAC.002 and PRAC.001 into a single file. Create a standard ASCII file using the COPY CON:XX DOS instruction and add this file to your working document.

13. Make a copy of assignment 1. Import into the middle of this assignment a copy of the letter from assignment 4.

14. Type a short description of how to import a file in your word processor. Create a README file from this description.

15. Mark the second paragraph of the letter prepared in assignment 4 as a block. Save the block as a separate file.

16. Make hard copies of the editing assignment. Create a new document to experiment with the capabilities of your printer.

17. Prepare a memo detailing the capability of your word processor-printer to:

- Bold
- Underline
- Use compressed print
- Use expanded print
- Use special characters
- Use superscripts and subscripts

18. Prepare a meeting announcement for a local club. Use the power of your printer.

19. Prepare a program for a classroom presentation. Use the power of your printer.

20. Prepare a set of handouts to be made into overhead slides for a classroom presentation. Use the power of your printer.

21. Prepare a report showing a formula. Use superscripts and subscripts.

SELECTED REFERENCES

Lund, Patsy H., and Barbara A. Hayden. *Understanding and Using WordPerfect.* West Publishing Company, 1987.
Lund, Patsy H., and Barbara A. Hayden. *Understanding and Using WordStar 4.0.* West Publishing Company, 1988.
Maiorana, Victor P. *Understanding and Using PCWrite.* West Publishing Company, 1988.
Ross, Steven C. *Understanding and Using WordStar.* West Publishing Company, 1986.
Weitzer, Mary K., and Laura B. Ruff. *Understanding and Using MultiMate.* West Publishing Company, 1986.
Weitzer, Mary K., and Laura B. Ruff. *Understanding and Using pfs:WRITE.* West Publishing Company, 1986.
Zimmerman, Steven M., Leo M. Conrad, and Larry Goldstein. *Osborne User's Guide.* Brady Publishing Company, 1983.

5

GOALS

Upon completion of this chapter you will be able to:

List some special hardware needs of electronic spreadsheets.

Review the importance of electronic spreadsheets.

Outline general characteristics of electronic spreadsheets.

List electronic spreadsheet applications.

Identify the more popular electronic spreadsheets.

List some electronic spreadsheet features.

OUTLINE

ELECTRONIC SPREADSHEETS

A1: 'Hotel Analysis Model   READY

	A	B	C	D	E	F
1	Hotel Analysis Model					
2		Category	2			
3		Region	E			
4			'80 Act	'81 Act	'82 Pro	'83 Pro
5						
6	Avg night rental		$61.38	$65.06	$68.31	$78.56
7	Occupancy rate		79.21%	75.23%	74.29%	73.35%
8	Revenues		$9,927,488	$9,890,117	$10,381,964	$11,789,462
9						
10	Expenses					
11		Salaries	$2,242,332	$2,233,891	$2,324,500	$2,651,510
12		Maintenance	$3,474,621	$3,461,541	$3,633,687	$4,126,312
13		Supplies	$1,342,196	$1,337,144	$1,403,642	$1,593,935
14		Utilities	$519,704	$517,748	$543,496	$617,178
15		Other	$1,699,586	$1,693,188	$674,828	$2,298,945
16	Profit (Loss)		$649,049	$646,606	$1,801,812	$501,582
17						
18		1982	1983	1984	1985	
19	Inflation	5%	15%	9%	10%	
20						

CALC

MICROS IN ACTION

Scott Paper Company, including international operations, is the world's leading manufacturer and marketer of sanitary tissue-paper products. In the United States, a broad range of products for the home and away-from-home are sold through the Packaged Products Division. Internationally, Scott operations are located in twenty countries and primarily manufacture and market sanitary paper products similar to those produced in the United States.

Scott's S. D. Warren Division produces coated and uncoated printing, publishing, and specialty papers, principally for United States markets. The National Resources Division is responsible for Scott's 3.3 million acres of woodlands in the United States, Canada, and Brazil, and directs the company's land management and pulp and forest products marketing and mineral activities. Scott also manufactures nonwoven materials in their Nonwoven Division.

The Scott family includes approximately 20,600 employees in consolidated operations and more than 19,700 in affiliated companies.

The initial application of electronic spreadsheets started in the accounting department. An advertisement for an electronic spreadsheet indicated that a microcomputer program that solved problems using the same structure as the manual method was available. An electronic spreadsheet program and a microcomputer were purchased to try it out.

The use of electronic spreadsheets grew throughout the company. Spreadsheets and spreadsheet graphics are now used for applications in
- Financial analysis
- Monthly accounting statements
- Budget control
- Production planning
- Engineering analysis
- Quality control
- Tracking inventory
- Tracking labor and organizational performance

Electronic spreadsheets have proved to be an economical method of doing the job that must be done.

Many different brands of electronic spreadsheets are used at Scott Paper, including VisiCalc, SuperCalc, Multiplan, and Lotus 1–2–3.

Spreadsheet:
A method for organizing, calculating, and presenting financial, statistical, and other business data for decision-making.

Labels:
Words identifying columns, rows, or overall titles.

Numbers:
Mathematical values.

Electronic spreadsheet programs solve problems using **labels, numbers,** and **formulas.** They divide the computer screen into a series of **columns** and **rows** (cells). Many electronic spreadsheets use capital letters, A, B, C, etc., to identify columns that appear across the top of the screen. A row extends across the screen and is usually labeled by number down the left side of the screen. **Cells** are identified by their column-row or row-column position, such as G4, meaning column G and row 4.

The **spreadsheet** is a tool for planners, budgeters, mathematicians, engineers, accountants, and others. It has been used to solve numeric problems since the invention of pencil and paper. A spreadsheet is a method for organizing, calculating, and presenting financial, statistical, and other numeric data that are used as the basis for decision-making.

Examples of applications for spreadsheets include budget control and forecasting, accounting ledgers and working papers, production planning, investment, cash flow, and annual operating data. Most business, financial, mathematical, and statistical problems that may be solved with pencil and paper are spreadsheet type problems.

As a student you will find electronic spreadsheet programs among the most valuable programs available for the microcomputer. The electronic spreadsheet has become a best seller mainly because it allows the user to solve business, financial, and other numeric problems on the microcomputer without the help of professional programmers. It performs calculations at high speed without errors, formats and prints reports automatically, and makes it easy to create a variety of graphs.

There are a number of spreadsheet programs available for microcomputers. The first spreadsheet program, VisiCalc, was followed by SuperCalc, Multiplan, and Lotus 1–2–3 among others.

BASIC HARDWARE NEEDS

Electronic spreadsheets require standard microcomputer hardware but may need extra RAM. The microcomputer hardware needs for electronic spreadsheets include

1. RAM
2. Input Device—Keyboards
3. Monitor
4. Printer
5. On-Line Storage

RAM

Electronic spreadsheet programs are limited to the

- Number of columns and rows (cells).
- Number of cells with characters.
- Amount of data entered into the spreadsheet.
- Number of features (such as graphics).

There are no simple rules for determining the number of columns-rows and cells with characters for a specific program on a specific computer with a given amount of RAM. Each spreadsheet program requires a minimum amount of RAM to begin operation. Most student assignments may be solved with the minimum RAM. Organizational problems may require additional RAM.

MS/PC–DOS spreadsheet programs use up to 640K of RAM. Some spreadsheet programs are able to use add-on extended memory storage (EMS) on special C-boards of two megabytes and more. The Apple Macintosh, Amiga, and others have over a million bytes of RAM that may be used by spreadsheet programs.

Formula:
A rule defining the relationship (outcome) between numbers used in the spreadsheet. Electronic spreadsheet formulas often use cell references as variables.

Column:
Vertical division of screen and spreadsheet.

Row:
Horizontal division of screen and spreadsheet.

Cell:
The column (vertical division) and row (horizontal division) intersection on screen and spreadsheet.

Electronic spreadsheets:
Programs used for calculation (formula oriented) and presentation under the control of the user.

Input Devices—Keyboards

Data may be entered into electronic spreadsheet programs using any of the many devices available on microcomputers. The keyboard is the most common.

Monitor

Monitors with 80 columns and 24 or 25 lines are sufficient for most spreadsheet needs. C-boards that display 132 columns by 25 or 44 rows on monochrome and color monitors are available to view a larger portion of a spreadsheet. Combinations of C-boards and custom monitors can display even more rows and columns.

When using custom monitor displays, special drivers or custom adjustments may have to be made to many spreadsheet programs. Some electronic spreadsheets may not work with some combinations of hardware. Newer versions of spreadsheet programs may or may not be compatible with the custom displays.

Printers

The number of spreadsheet columns produced on a printer is a function of its size and capability to produce compressed print. Table 5–1 identifies the number of nine-character spreadsheet columns different sized printers may produce. The maximum capacity of printers is lower than the smallest spreadsheet program. To obtain a complete copy of a spreadsheet with more columns or rows than a printer can produce, it is necessary to print it in parts and "cut and paste" the parts together.

Programs are available for selected dot matrix printers that allow you to print down the page (sideways), rather than across the page. This capability may help produce a complete report without cutting and pasting in some situations.

On-Line Storage

Spreadsheets require a minimum of a single disk drive to a maximum of a disk drive and a hard disk. The sum of all program and data file storage determines

TABLE 5–1

Printer Size versus Spreadsheet Columns

Printer Size	Number Characters	Number of Nine-Character Spreadsheet Columns
Normal Carriage		
Regular Size Print	80	8
Compressed Print	132	14
Wide Carriage		
Regular Size Print	132	14
Compressed Print	220	24*

*Some printers can print as many as 255 characters, resulting in 28 columns of 9 characters each.

Wide-carriage printers are usually more expensive than smaller-carriage printers of the same type.

on-line storage requirements. The size of a single spreadsheet may exceed the capacity of a floppy disk. Some programs have the capability to save a single spreadsheet on more than a single floppy disk.

WHY YOU SHOULD KNOW ABOUT ELECTRONIC SPREADSHEETS

Electronic spreadsheets save time, increase calculation accuracy, and make it possible to perform powerful evaluations. Electronic spreadsheets are often based on manual spreadsheets (see Figure 5–1, An Accounting Ledger).

Spreadsheet programs may be used in many different areas. Some business applications are listed in Table 5–2.

FIGURE 5–1   An Accounting Ledger

		1	2	3	4	5	6
			Home Office	Pascagoula	Gautier	ALCO	Chickasaw
1	Revenues		0	139796	16503	0	57920
2	Operating Expenses						
3	Advertising		11357				
4	Automotive		1371				
5	Bank Charges		144	188			104
6	Contributions		100				
7	Depriciation			16559	5095	2396	14315
8	Dues & Subscriptions		279				
9	Entertainment		1832				
10	Insurance		815	653			
11	Intrest		978				
12	Janitorial		70				
13	Maintenance & Repairs		360	1005	820	215	2379
14	Miscellaneous		1184	10			
15	Office		11404	562	127		301
16	Postage		108				
17	Professional Fees		8665				
18	Rent		1630	3750	2720	867	1540
19	Salaries- Officers		64923				
20	Salaries- Other		14240	15673	4436		9798

Interim Statement of Operation
For the Six Months Ended Febuary 28, 1985

TABLE 5–2

Applications of Electronic Spreadsheets

Professional Area	Applications
Accounting	General ledgers, trial balances, checkbook balancing, data collection reports, amortization schedules, depreciation schedules.
Banking	Ratio analysis, cash budget, capital budgeting–net present value, internal rate of return, profitability index, optimization analysis, loan analysis.
Finance and Economics	Ratio analysis, cash budget, capital budgeting–net present value, internal rate of return, profitability index, optimization analysis, amortization schedules, depreciation schedules.
Marketing (Transportation and Logistics)	Analysis of marketing surveys, marketing projections, inventory control analysis, location evaluation, marketing mix analysis, distribution analysis.
Personnel Administration	Personnel needs analysis, personnel use analysis, insurance needs, job analysis and evaluation.
Quantitative Management	Optimization applications, inventory analysis and control, production control, Performance Evaluation and Review (PERT).
Retail Merchandising	Pricing, inventory control, marketing mix, turnover analysis.
Statistics	Analysis of variance, regression analysis, calculations of averages and standard deviations.
Training	Training records, tests records, performance analysis.

Electronic spreadsheets have been modeled after manual ones. They both have labels, numbers, and formulas. Figure 5–2 shows a spreadsheet for adding up a column of numbers that represents incomes from different sources. Cell A1 contains the word "Income."

The spreadsheet in Figure 5–2 has labels "Income", "-----", and "= = = = =". It has a single formula: "SUM(A2:A4)." This formula form is found on many different spreadsheet programs. It means to add up the values in cells A2, A3, and A4, and then place the result in cell A6. In some spreadsheet programs "@SUM(A2:A4)" or "@SUM(A2 . . . A4)" may be the formula format required.

In an electronic spreadsheet you enter the labels, the formulas, and the numbers; then, the program takes over. When a value is changed, the system automatically performs the calculations needed.

FIGURE 5–2

A Simple Spreadsheet

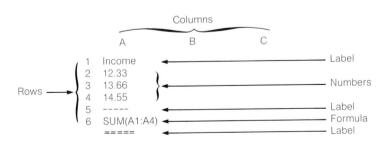

Electronic spreadsheets solve numeric problems. They

1. Save calculation time and increase accuracy.
2. Make "what if" calculations possible.
3. Produce a final report.
4. Produce graphs.
5. Save and recall spreadsheets for reuse.
6. Do not require a big investment.

Save Calculation Time and Increase Accuracy

Calculations take time. Add a column of numbers; the spreadsheet does it faster.

Add the values in a column a second time. Often, the results are not the same as the first. Even with the use of a calculator with a print-out tape, there are problems in getting the numbers correct.

USER WINDOW

MANAGING SALES

Sales managers may save time and effort by using spreadsheets to calculate sales, commissions, costs, and profit.

"What If" Calculations

The capability of the electronic spreadsheet to perform automatic recalculation means you may make many changes and see the results of those changes immediately throughout the entire spreadsheet. This type of an analysis is often referred to as performing a "**what if**" change or a "sensitivity analysis." Questions such as "what if the sales were 50 percent of the estimate," or "what if sales were 200 percent of the estimate," may be answered quickly. The sensitivity of the results to particular estimates may be determined.

What if?:
The investigation of economic and business consequences by changing the assumptions on which decisions are to be made, and the conditions under which the decisions are made.

Produce Graphs

Bar and other charts may be created by many spreadsheet programs. The charts are displayed on the screen or printer. Each time a value is changed on the spreadsheet, the chart is also changed. Figure 5–3 is a spreadsheet bar chart.

The steps required in many spreadsheets to create a graph are:

1. Enter the formulas, numbers, and labels.
2. Call up the graph routine.
3. Identify the cells to be graphed.
4. Select the screen display routine.

Many different functions including SIN(X) may be graphed using spreadsheets. Being able to see what a function looks like helps you understand the concepts being studied. Figure 5–4 is a graph of SIN(X)/X varying the value of X from –22 through + 22 in steps of 2.

The quality and accuracy of spreadsheet graphs are beyond the manual ability of most individuals. Graphs help the understanding of both the creator and the individuals for whom the graphs are being prepared.

Produce a Final Report

When working with manual calculations, the last step is to have the results organized and typed or otherwise prepared for use by other managers. The microcomputer produces a nicely typed copy, without errors and ready for managerial analysis and use. Electronic spreadsheets, like all other microcomputer programs, may produce bad results due to incorrect data and formulas. "GIGO" means garbage in, garbage out.

Save and Recall Spreadsheets

Professionals must perform calculations over and over again. Governments perform calculations many times when performing tax analysis and collections. Other organizations must produce a dues collection report each and every time period. Each week or each month the same spreadsheet must be produced. The electronic spreadsheet may be saved on disk or hard disk and then recalled. After dates have been changed, new values entered, and fresh reports generated, the spreadsheet can be saved again for reuse during the next period. The labels and formulas, once entered, do not have to be entered a second time. The more an electronic spreadsheet is used, the greater the benefits derived from it.

Do Not Require a Big Investment

The cost of an electronic spreadsheet varies from $50 to $1,000. Unless you have a need for unusually large spreadsheets, there are no special microcomputer hardware purchases required.

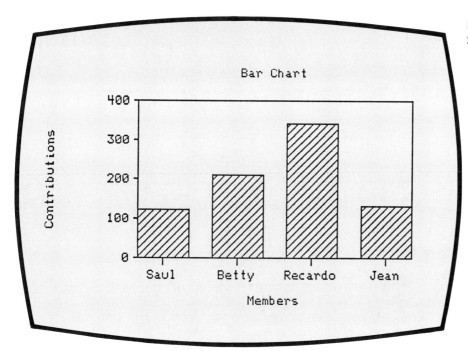

FIGURE 5–3
Spreadsheet Bar Chart

GENERAL CHARACTERISTICS

A spreadsheet cell is commonly nine characters wide and one line high. You may control the width of individual columns on many spreadsheets. The maximum number of columns and rows is determined by the specific program used. The original version of VisiCalc had 64 columns and 254 rows, most current programs have greater capacities.

A cursor, which may be a line or reverse video (the background of the cell is light and the letters dark), is used to indicate which cell is active or current. Labels, numbers, or formulas may be entered only into the active cell.

The methods used to move around spreadsheets vary depending on the program. In Lotus 1–2–3 (version V.1a and V.2), SuperCalc4, and others, the options include:

1. Press function key F5 to call a go-to option. You enter the cell you wish the cursor to move to, such as B7, and the program moves the cursor as instructed.
2. Use of PgUp, PgDn, Home, and End keys on the numeric keypad. Home returns the cursor to cell A1. The End key and the down arrow key pressed sequentially move the cursor to the last entry in the spreadsheet.
3. Tab to move the cursor to the right. From column A the cursor is moved to column I, from column I to column Q. Shift Tab moves the cursor to the left in a similar manner.
4. Pressing the Scroll Lock key results in the cursor remaining in a fixed position and the spreadsheet moving around it. Pressing Scroll Lock a second time returns the cursor to the original method of moving.

MICROS IN ACTION

A Common Application

A Scott Paper Company accountant set up an electronic spreadsheet form using labels and mathematical formulas. A clerk without mathematical training was given the form to fill in with the correct information.

After the form was completed, the accountant checked the input and found only one number had to be changed. The amount of professional time and cost was reduced by allowing most of the calculations to be performed by the clerk.

SAMPLE ELECTRONIC SPREADSHEET

Figure 5–5 illustrates the layout of a spreadsheet with cell C2 identified by asterisks and the characters "C2".

Keyboard input may be used to enter a label in position C2 of the electronic spreadsheet. After the cursor is located in the correct cell, you need to tell the program that you are going to enter a label. Some programs require the quote (" or '); other programs assume labels are being entered unless you tell it otherwise by entering a mathematical operator, such as a plus sign.

The following steps enter a label:

1. Use arrows to locate the cursor at the desired cell.
2. Type the instruction telling the computer that a label is being entered.

FIGURE 5–4
XY Chart

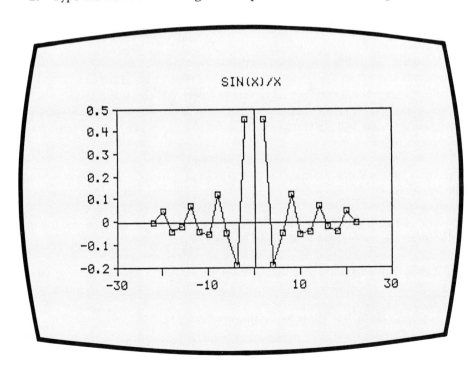

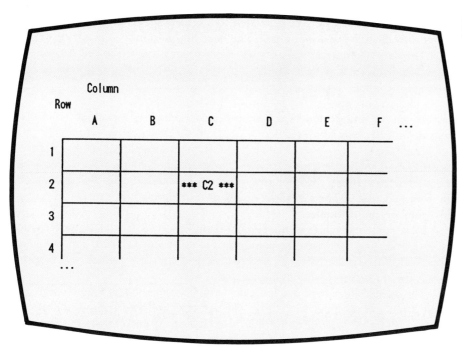

FIGURE 5–5
The Layout of a Spreadsheet

3. Type the label and press enter.

Figure 5–6 is a spreadsheet with the title "Commission Report" and cursor in cell A1.

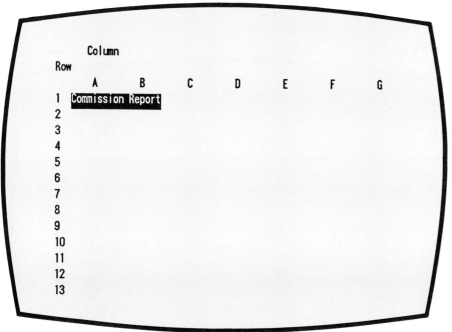

FIGURE 5–6
Entering a Label

The spreadsheet used assumes labels overflow to next cell when they are too large to fit into a column. Some spreadsheets truncate the display to the number of characters available in a cell. The characters not shown are still in the computer's memory.

The title and date may be separated so a spreadsheet is usable for different months by changing the input data. The next step is to move the cursor to cell D1. The date "January 1999" is typed. The cursor is moved to cell A4, where the salesperson's name, "Pia Martin," is typed and the cursor is moved to cell A6, and the label "Type Sales" is typed (see Figure 5–7).

The numbers are located on the right side of the cell, while the labels are located on the left. Numbers usually default to being right justified, while labels default to being left justified.

Justified:
Lined up. Left justified means lined up evenly on the left, while right justified means lined up on the right.

The "Rate" and "Sales" labels for the column headings in row 6 have been limited to fewer than the nine characters allowed to make them look good. The row labels, "Computers," "Software," and "Furniture" are added in rows 7, 8, and 9. The spreadsheet as shown in Figure 5–8 is ready for entering numbers and formulas.

Next enter the values of the percent commission (8, 9, and 10 percent) in cells C7, C8, and C9. Place the amounts of sales in cells D7, D8, and D9. The commission dollar amount may be calculated in cells E7, E8, and E9. Figure 5–9 is the spreadsheet with all numbers entered.

The spreadsheet formula for calculating commission is Commission = Sales * percent commission * 0.01. The asterisks are used for multiplication. The reason for multiplication by 0.01 is to change the percent commission to a decimal.

For sales of computers, C7*D7*0.01 must be entered in cell E7. Cell C7 contains the percent commission, and cell D7 contains the amount of sales. The percent commission was entered as a whole number in location C7.

To enter a formula, the steps are:

1. Tell the computer a formula is being entered with a mathematical operator if needed.
2. Type the formula and press <CR>.

FIGURE 5–7
Enter Dates and Names

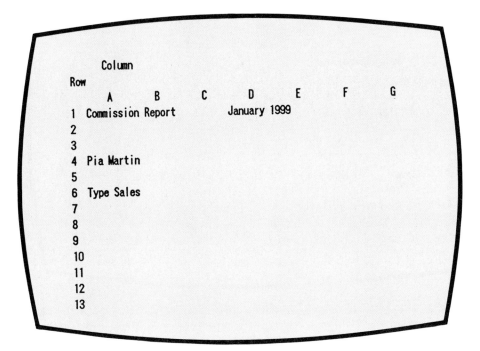

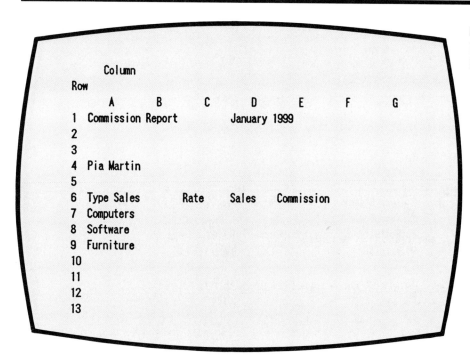

FIGURE 5–8
Ready for the
Numbers and Formula

Figure 5–10 is the spreadsheet including all commission formulas. Cell E7 shows the number 1840, not the formula. The formulas are invisible; only the result of the calculation is displayed. The formula for software, C8*D8*.01 (cell E8), and the formula for furniture, C9*D9*.01 (cell E9), are also in Figure 5–10.

The format of the output is not consistent in Figure 5–10. There are spreadsheet commands for controlling display formats.

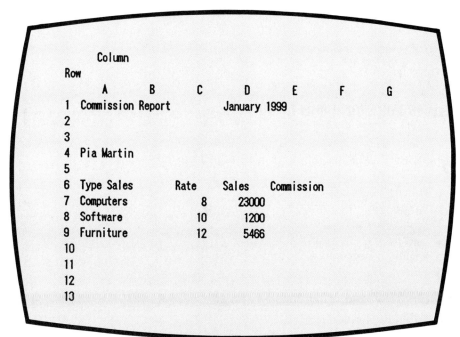

FIGURE 5–9
Entering the Numbers

FIGURE 5–10
Formula Results

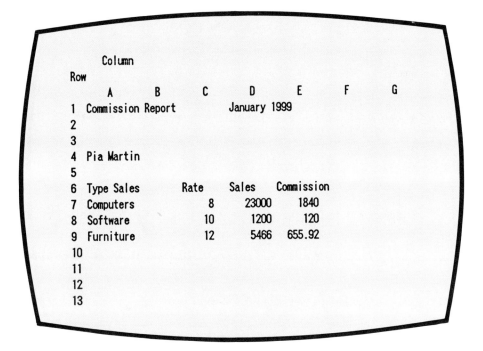

A line consisting of nine minus signs as a label in cell E10, and a second line consisting of nine equal signs as a label in E12, is used to indicate the column is summed. Most electronic spreadsheet programs require a quote when using a mathematical operator as a label.

One more formula in cell E11 (Figure 5–11) completes the spreadsheet. Two alternate forms are possible: +E7+E8+E9 or @SUM(E7...E9). The second form is similar for different spreadsheets. The @SUM(cell start ... cell end) form means to add the values in all cells from the starting cell to the ending cell inclusive. For adding large columns of numbers, the @SUM method is more convenient.

ELECTRONIC SPREADSHEET FEATURES

Electronic spreadsheet programs have some general, configuration, interfacing, and add-on features. The features of electronic spreadsheets may be classified as

1. Function keys and extenders
2. Range
3. Display format
4. Calculation
   - Built-in Functions
5. Editing
   - Recalling cells
   - Inserting/deleting columns and rows
   - Cell Replication
   - Search and format features

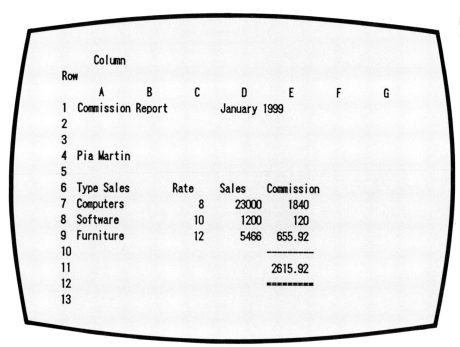

FIGURE 5–11
One More Formula Is Added

6. Graphing
7. Storing and recalling
8. Printing
9. Windows
10. Interfacing
11. Integrated spreadsheet programs
12. Add-on features.

Function Keys and Extenders

Function keys are used differently in each spreadsheet program. Table 5–3 details how they are used in Lotus 1–2–3 and SuperCalc4.

The three-character extender on the filename is used by many spreadsheet programs to identify the type of file stored on the disk. Table 5–4 identifies the use of extenders in spreadsheet programs.

Range

The **range** of cells is referred to for format control, creating **protected cells**, and printing, among other purposes. Figure 5–12 is a spreadsheet sheet with the range (B6 through E9) of cells defined. Table 5–5 is the range commands of Lotus 1–2–3.

Display Format

Figure 5–13 illustrates numbers (values) presented in currency, date, fixed, general, percent, scientific, +/−, and comma (,) formats. In some spreadsheets the +/− format is not available, and * is used for a bar type chart on the spreadsheet.

Range (spreadsheet):
The identification of the cells in a spreadsheet by the specification of the cell in the upper-left position and the cell in the lower-right position. The range A5 . . . C7 identifies the cells A5, A6, A7, B5, B6, B7, C5, C6, and C7.

Protected cells:
Cells that have been protected from change by the spreadsheet designer. It is good practice to "protect" the cells with labels when a standard form is created.

TABLE 5–3
Function Keys

	Lotus 1–2–3 and SuperCalc4
Function Keys	*Application*
F1:Help	Display Help screens—press [Esc] to return to ready mode
F2:Edit	Switch to/from Edit Mode for current entry
F3:Name	(Point Mode only) Display menu of range names
F4:Abs	(Point Mode only) Make/Unmake cell address "absolute"
F5:Goto	Move cell pointer to a particular cell
F6:Window	(Split-screen only) Move cell pointer to other window
F7:	
Lotus:Query	Repeat most recent Data Query operation
SuperCalc:Calc	Recalculate worksheet
F8:	
Lotus:Table	Repeat most recent Data Table operation
SuperCalc:Resume	Continue operation
F9:	
Lotus:Calc	Ready Mode: Recalculate worksheet Value and Edit Modes: Convert formula to its current value
SuperCalc:Plot	Print active graph according to most recent graphing specification
F10:Graph	Draw active graph according to most recent graphing specification

Calculation

A number is a value that you place in a cell to use in your calculations, such as the cost of an item, the volume sold, etc. A mathematical formula is a defined relationship that you place in a cell to calculate the desired results. The formula will appear in a section of the screen at the top or bottom, but not in the body of the spreadsheet. In the body of the spreadsheet you will see the results of the formula. A number is a mathematical formula equal to a constant, the number.

All mathematical operations—addition ($+$), subtraction ($-$), multiplication ($*$), division ($/$), and raising to a power ($\hat{\ }$)—may be performed by

TABLE 5–4
Spreadsheet File Extenders

Extenders	*Application*
.CAL	SuperCalc spreadsheet file
.COM	Program file
.DAT	Program data file
.DOC	Text file with documentation *
.EXE	Program file
.HLP	Help file
.MSG	Message file
.OVL	Program overlay file
.PIC	Graph (picture) file
.PRN	Print (text) file
.PRO	Program file
.WKS	Lotus V.1 spreadsheet file
.WK1	Lotus V.2 spreadsheet file
.XQT	SuperCalc macro-execute file

Programs that have documentation on the disk.

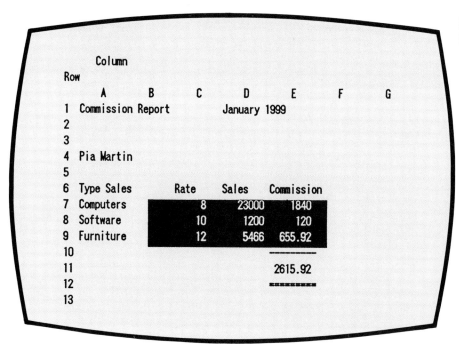

FIGURE 5–12
Range Defined

electronic spreadsheet programs. In addition, most programs provide special mathematical capabilities, such as adding all values in a column or row, most trigonometric functions, and others.

Electronic spreadsheet programs may or may not use all the mathematical **precedence** rules. Precedence is the order in which **mathematical operators** are executed. It requires all operators ($+$, $-$, $/$, $*$, $\char`^$) inside parentheses to be performed first, followed by power calculations, multiplication and division, and finally by addition and subtraction. Operations at a common level of precedence are performed from left to right.

The formula: $A = 5 + 2 * 4$, yields the result 28 when executed from left to right. It yields the result 13 when the order of precedence is considered. The $2 * 4$ operation should be executed first and then the value 5 added to that result.

Precedence (math): The order in which mathematical operations are executed. The standard order is parentheses, power, multiplication and division, and addition and subtraction.

Mathematical operator: Symbol that indicates a mathematical process such as $+$ (addition), $-$ (subtraction), $*$ (multiplication), $/$ (division), and $\char`^$ (raising to a power).

Commands	Application
Format	Number/Formula display
Label-Prefix	Alignment of labels
Erase	Erase cell entries
Name	Maintain set of names for ranges
Justify	Adjust width of label "paragraph"
Protect	Disallow changes to cells (if Protection Enabled)
Unprotect	Allow changes to cells
Input	Restrict pointer to unprotected cells

TABLE 5–5
Range Commands of Lotus 1–2–3

FIGURE 5–13
Format Options

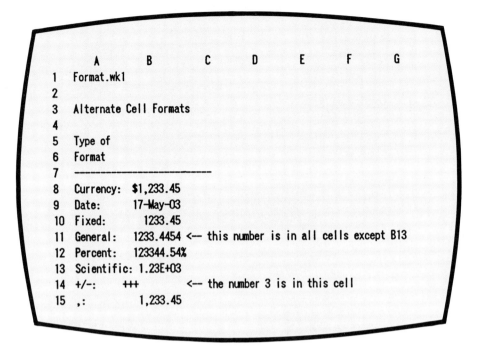

```
           A         B        C        D        E        F        G
 1  Format.wk1
 2
 3  Alternate Cell Formats
 4
 5  Type of
 6  Format
 7  ─────────────────────────────
 8  Currency: $1,233.45
 9  Date:      17-May-03
10  Fixed:       1233.45
11  General:     1233.4454 <-- this number is in all cells except B13
12  Percent:  123344.54%
13  Scientific: 1.23E+03
14  +/-:       +++            <-- the number 3 is in this cell
15  ,:           1,233.45
```

Care must be taken when using precedence. For example, the square of a negative number may or may not be a positive number (Table 5–6). When calculating $-1 \char`^ 2$, some spreadsheet programs square the one and then consider the negative sign. Other spreadsheet programs square $-1$. All spreadsheet programs obtain $+1$ when calculating $(-1)\char`^ 2$. We recommend that you use parentheses to control the order of calculations.

Functions A variety of special functions are built into spreadsheet programs. Some spreadsheet financial functions are shown in Table 5–7.

The PMT(prn,int,term) function (Figure 5–14) finds the equal payment required to pay off a loan for the value **prn**, at a periodic interest rate of **int** (in decimal format), in **term** payments. The variables may be either numbers or numbers found in cells. To use a function found in a specific spreadsheet program, you must know how the data is entered into the function.

Logical and Special Functions Spreadsheets may contain logical and special functions such as conditional "If" statements, among others. Table 5–8 is a list of the logical and special functions found in Lotus 1–2–3.

TABLE 5–6
Calculating

Spreadsheet	Results
ExpressCalc	-1
Lotus	-1
Multiplan	$+1$
SuperCalc	$+1$
VisiCalc	$+1$

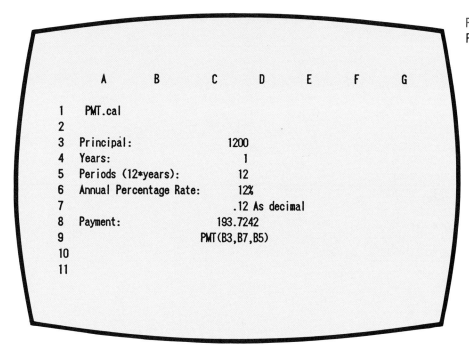

FIGURE 5–14
Financial Functions

The logical function allows you to direct the actions of the spreadsheet program with the values entered. For example, the @IF(cond,x,y) function calculates the formula entered into the conditional position, and, if the number is non-zero, executes the instruction in the x position. If the number is zero, the instruction in the y position is executed.

Some spreadsheets include logical operations in their precedence rules. The arithmetic and logical operators of a spreadsheet program and their precedence are shown in Table 5–9.

Circular Calculations Some spreadsheets calculate by rows while others calculate by columns. Some allow the user to determine the order of calculation. Most of the time, the different order of calculation results in only a slightly different round-off. In some situations involving a circular set of calculations, such as that shown in Figure 5–15, the different order of calculation may yield totally different results. The general rules are do not use circular references, and always check your results to be sure the spreadsheet formulas are performing the way you want.

TABLE 5–7
Spreadsheet Financial Functions

Financial Functions	Application
IRR(guess,range)	Internal rate of return
NPV(x,range)	Net present value
FV(pmt,int,term)	Future value
PV(pmt,int,term)	Present value
PMT(prn,int,term)	Payment

Lotus 1-2-3 requires an @ preceding all functions.

TABLE 5–8
Lotus 1–2–3 Logical and Special
@ Functions

Logical Functions	Application
@FALSE	0 (FALSE)
@TRUE	1 (TRUE)
@IF(cond,x,y)	x if cond is TRUE (non-zero)
	y if cond is FALSE (zero)
@ISNA(x)	1 (TRUE) if x = NA
@ISERR(x)	1 (TRUE) if x = ERR

When determining the truth value of a formula, Lotus 1–2–3 considers any non-zero value to be TRUE. Only 0 itself is FALSE.

Special Functions	Application
@NA	NA (not available)
@ERR	ERR (error)
@CHOOSE(x,v0,v1, . . .,vN)	Select value
@HLOOKUP(x,range,offset)	Table lookup index row
@VLOOKUP(x,range,offset)	Table lookup index column

Editing

A saved electronic spreadsheet may be recalled and reused. The date and sales numbers may be replaced. If other changes occur, such as the commission rates, they may also be replaced. "What if" calculations may be made by changing individual values and examining the results.

The spreadsheet may be used by more than one individual by replacing the name and the values with those associated with the second individual. You do not recalculate. You enter the new data and the electronic spreadsheet produces the results. The output is typed for you so neither you nor your secretary has to type reports.

TABLE 5–9
Arithmetic and Logical Operators

Operators	Application	Precedence #
^	Exponentiation	7
+	Positive	6
−	Negative	6
*	Multiplication	5
/	Division	4
+	Addition	4
−	Subtraction	4
=	Equals	3
<	Less than	3
< =	Less than or equal	3
>	Greater than	3
> =	Greater than or equal	3
< >	Not equal	3
#NOT#	Logical not	2
#AND#	Logical and	1
#OR#	Logical or	1

Operators with larger precedence numbers are performed first, unless overridden by parentheses. Operators with equal precedence are performed left to right.

FIGURE 5–15
Circular Calculations

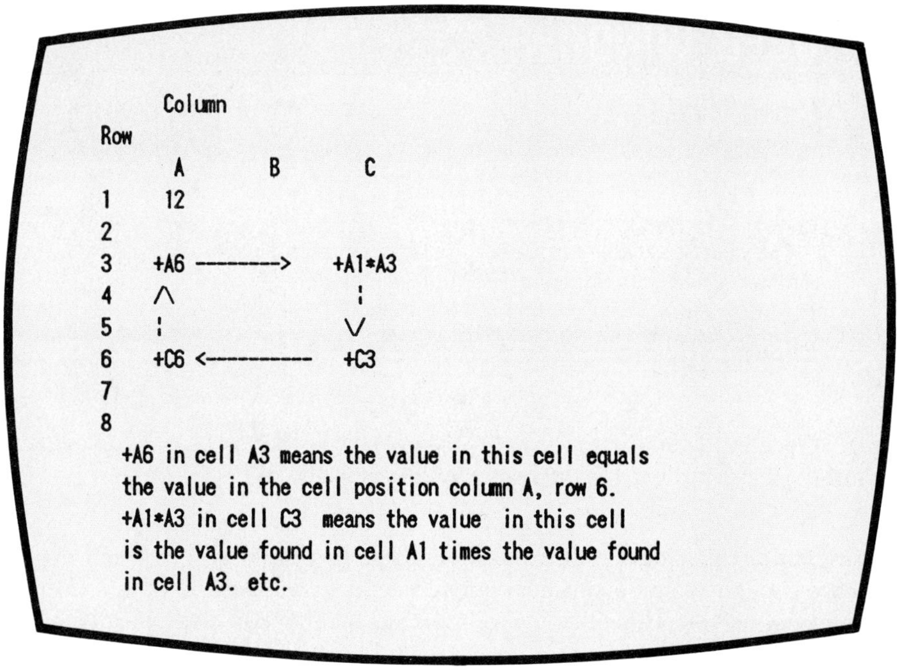

```
           Column
     Row
           A        B        C
     1     12
     2
     3     +A6 --------->    +A1*A3
     4      /\                 :
     5      :                  V
     6     +C6 <-----------   +C3
     7
     8
           +A6 in cell A3 means the value in this cell equals
           the value in the cell position column A, row 6.
           +A1*A3 in cell C3  means the value  in this cell
           is the value found in cell A1 times the value found
           in cell A3. etc.
```

+A6 in cell A3 means the value in this cell equals the value in the cell position column A, row 6.

+A1*A3 in cell C3 means the value in this cell is the value found in cell A1 times the value found in cell A3, etc.

USER WINDOW

CORRECTIONS ARE EASY

The manager reviewed the formula used and its results in a spreadsheet. A series of numbers did not seem to be correct.

After a short period of time, one formula was found to have an error. The editing capability was used to correct the error and the evaluation was re-done in seconds.

Editing functions include the capability of:

1. Editing a cell.
2. Inserting/deleting columns or rows.
3. Cell replication.

Editing a Cell Common methods of entering the edit mode are

1. Place the cursor in the cell to be edited.
2. Press a function key (F2 in Lotus and SuperCalc4) or press /E (all versions of SuperCalc).

USER WINDOW

HOMEWORK

The student set up his accounting homework on a spreadsheet. After one hour he looked up. It was the first time he had ever been able to get a trial balance to balance on the first try.

The student was able to eliminate his errors and complete most of his assignments in less time and with less effort than required manually.

Once in the edit mode the cursor keys such as home, arrows, delete, and insert are used to change the text or numbers in the cell.

Inserting/Deleting Columns and Rows If you make an error and do not leave enough room on a manual spreadsheet, you will have to copy it over. In an electronic spreadsheet, you may insert a column or row when needed with a few simple menu-driven instructions. All formulas will be adjusted to the new location of the values upon which they are based.

In like manner, a column or row may be deleted. If you delete a cell that has a base number or formula in it, you may get an error. The commands used to delete columns or rows are similar between spreadsheets.

Cell Replication When replicating or copying a formula, you must be careful how cells are addressed. A formula may refer to a cell using either an "absolute" or "relative" reference.

An **absolute reference** refers to a fixed cell. For example, if the interest rate is located in cell B12, all formulas in the spreadsheet should be using B12, no matter where these formulas are or are moved.

A **relative reference** is one that refers to a cell a fixed distance (in terms of columns and rows) from the cell where the formula is located. For example, if the formula in cell C22 uses the information in cell A21, this means to use a cell two columns left and one row up. A cell reference may have one parameter fixed and the other relative. In Lotus 1–2–3 and SuperCalc4, a relative cell is assumed unless a dollar sign is placed in the formula (Table 5–10). In some spreadsheets, the nature of a cell is defined during the move or copy operation.

Absolute reference (spreadsheet): The indication of where specific data are found in a fixed column/row location. When cells are moved or copied, absolute references do not change.

Relative reference (spreadsheet): The indication of where specific data are found in terms of a fixed number of columns and rows from the cell where the data are needed. When cells are moved or copied, the relative references are changed to maintain their relative position.

TABLE 5–10

Types of Cells in Formulas Lotus 1–2–3 and SuperCalc4

Type of Cell	Cell Indication
Relative cell	B5
Absolute column, relative row	$B5
Relative row, absolute column	B$5
Absolute cell	$B$5

Graphing

Spreadsheet programs may be used to produce graphs using internal routines or by data transfer to custom charting programs. The types of charts produced include

1. Area, Line, and XY: Charts that show trends or changes over time. May be single, multiple, additive, negative, and positive.
2. Bar: Charts that use bars to compare selected items. Bar charts may be horizontal and vertical.
3. Hi-lo: Charts that can graph the high, low, opening, and closing price of a stock over time.
4. Stacked-bar: Bar charts that illustrate parts of a whole.

Figures 5–3 and 5–4 illustrate bar and XY charts. Figures 5–16, 5–17, 5–18, and 5–19 were produced using Lotus and SuperCalc to illustrate area, hi-lo, line, and stacked-bar charts.

The line and XY charts are similar. Some programs do not differentiate one from the other. In general, line charts require the data to be evenly spaced along the X axis and allow the use of text labels. XY charts use numeric data for both the X and Y scales and will perform automatic scaling.

To create a graph in a spreadsheet, the steps are

1. Identify the range of the X variable.
2. Identify the range of each Y variable.
3. Add headings and other identifying data.
4. Specify colors if available.
5. Save and print the results.

Storing and Recalling

Spreadsheet programs allow you to save all the information in a spreadsheet, or just the labels and formulas. When a spreadsheet is being used as a form, the labels and formulas only are saved. All data must be saved in a completed form.

Once saved, the spreadsheet file may be recalled for use at any time. By editing or overtyping, new data is entered and the analysis is updated for the next period. A spreadsheet saved for future use is often referred to as a **template**.

Saving a spreadsheet file is simple and often menu driven. Table 5–11 is a listing of the commands in the file save menu (/F) of Lotus 1–2–3.

Printing

The spreadsheet printing instruction starts with identifying the material to be printed. Usually the number of columns/rows to be printed do not match the standard page format of the printer. There are programs that allow you to print spreadsheets sideways if a better fit can be obtained by this change.

Template:
A model saved on disk to be recalled into a spreadsheet or other program as a pattern for future applications. Templates for many user applications may be purchased on disk or copied out of books.

FIGURE 5–16
Area Chart

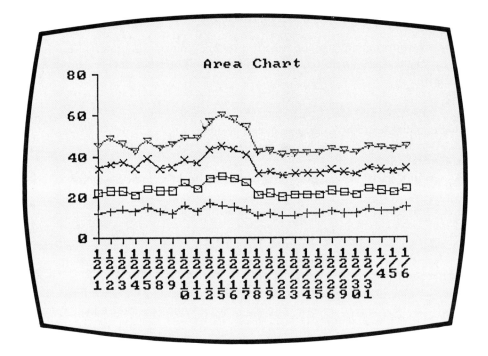

The printer instructions are menu driven (Tables 5–12 and 5–13) in most spreadsheets and are specific to a particular spreadsheet program. Many spreadsheet programs allow printing to a file as well as a printer. The file printed is an ASCII file that may be transferred to a word processor or used with a sideways printing program.

FIGURE 5–17
Line Chart

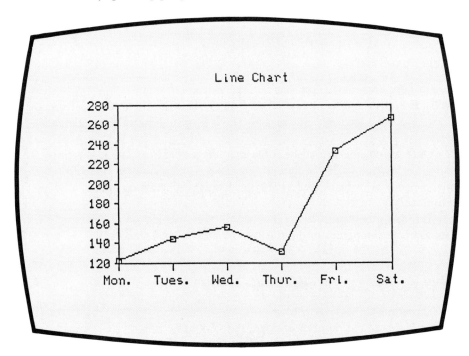

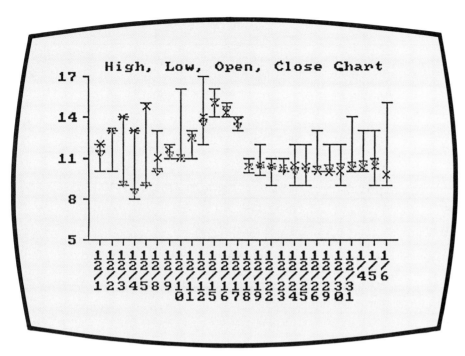

FIGURE 5–18
Hi-Lo Chart

The printer setup codes are sent in a variety of ways. For example, compressed mode on an Epson printer requires the code number 15 be sent. The Lotus setup string is \015. The SuperCalc3 setup string is ∧O (Control and Fifteenth letter of the alphabet sends a 15 to the printer). SuperCalc4 uses either ∧O or \015.

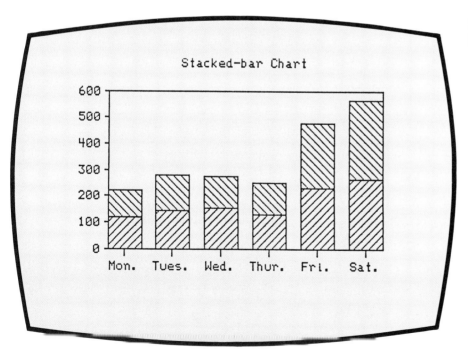

FIGURE 5–19
Stacked-bar Chart

TABLE 5–11
/File Menu of Lotus 1–2–3

Instruction	Function
Save	Stores entire worksheet in worksheet file.
Retrieve	Restores data from worksheet file.
Combine	Incorporates (part of) worksheet file into Current worksheet:
	Methods: Copy, Add, Subtract use Entire-file or Named-Range only.
Xtract	Stores range of entries in worksheet file: save Formulas or current values only.
Erase	Erases one or more 1–2–3 data files.
List	Lists names of 1–2–3 data files, reports disk space.
Import	Incorporates print file into worksheet: treats lines as Text or as Numbers and quoted text.
Directory	Changes current directory assignment.

Windows

A spreadsheet may be divided into windows as shown in Figure 5–20. You may display the labels with either column or rows showing in one window, as data is entered into the part of the spreadsheet in the second window. Almost all spreadsheets have this capability.

Macros

Macros:
Custom routines that substitute a few keystrokes for many. They may be created by the user and saved on disk as routines that are recalled with a few keystrokes when needed.

Macros are keystrokes that may be saved and used over and over again. Macro files may be recalled in total with a few simple keystrokes. Lotus macro files are part of the spreadsheet. SuperCalc4 macro files may be internal and/or external.

In some spreadsheets you can create your own menus using macro files for custom templates. The custom templates are similar to custom programs in a programming language.

The /X command is used in Lotus to create menus. Table 5–14 is a listing of the options in this menu.

TABLE 5–12
Printer Menu for Lotus 1–2–3

Function	Application
Printer vs. File	Direct output to printer or print file.
Range	Range to be printed.
Line	Advance printer one line.
Page	Advance printer to top of next page.
Options	Page formatting:
Headers, Footers	Set page header/footer line.
Margins	Left, right, top, bottom.
Borders	Graft extra columns/rows to print range.
Setup	Set printer-control characters.
Page-Length	Set number of lines.
Other	As-displayed vs. cell-formulas:
	Printing of formula texts.
	Unformatted vs. formatted.
	Suppress headers, footers, page breaks.
Clear	Cancel print settings.
Align	Reset line-number counter to 1.
Go	Print the selected range.

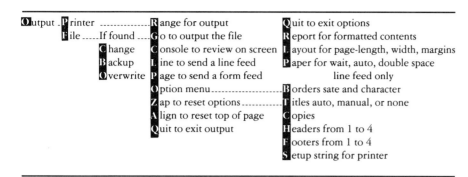

TABLE 5–13
Printer and File Menu for
SuperCalc4

Transferring Data and Output

Spreadsheet results and data may be transferred or exported to and imported from:

1. Other spreadsheet programs.
2. Word processing programs.
3. Data base programs.
4. Graphics programs.
5. Special purpose programs.

When you first develop applications with an electronic spreadsheet, the need to transfer data between programs may not seem important. After a

TABLE 5–14
/X Menu in Lotus 1–2–3

Instruction	Application	Notes
/XClocation ˜	Call	Continue reading keystrokes at location (cell address, range, or range name). When a /XR command is encountered, return to the point just beyond the /XC location ˜ command.
/XR	Return	(Must follow /XC command.) Return to reading keystrokes just after the corresponding /XC location ˜ command.
/XGlocation ˜	Go To	Continue reading keystrokes at location (cell address, range, or range name). No "return" is possible.
/XIformula ˜	If-Then	If the formula is TRUE (i.e., has a non-zero value), continue reading keystrokes in the same cell. If the formula is FALSE (i.e., zero), continue.
/XMlocation ˜	Process a Menu	Allow user to make a menu choice and branch on the choice. Lotus 1–2–3 constructs the menu from the menu range whose upper-left corner is at location (cell address, range, or range name).
/XLstring˜location˜	Label Entry	
/XNstring˜location˜	Number Entry	Display the specified string as a prompt in the control panel, accept an entry from the keyboard, and store the result as a left justified label (/XL) or as a number (/XN) at location.
/XQ	Quit	Enter macro execution and return to Ready mode.

The character ˜ is used to indicate a ⟨CR⟩.

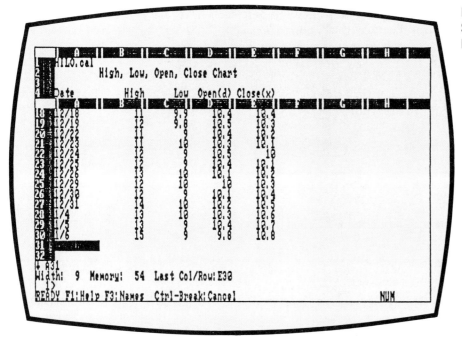

FIGURE 5–20
Spreadsheet Screen
Divided into Windows

number of years you will find yourself with a collection of programs and data in many different formats. You will also find the need to transfer electronic spreadsheet programs into word processing or data base programs. For example, you have to prepare a report based on the output of calculations performed in an electronic spreadsheet. The output of the spreadsheet may be saved as an ASCII (DOS) file and then transferred into a word processor text file to save you typing.

If an electronic spreadsheet program can read ASCII files, and most do, it is generally easy to transfer data into it.

Most electronic spreadsheet programs can print files to a disk. This capability usually produces an ASCII file that may be transferred to a word processing program for report preparation.

In addition to ASCII files there are a number of other "standard" formats used in spreadsheet work. Data interchange format file, DIF, first developed for the electronic spreadsheet VisiCalc, is used by a number of programs as an aid in interfacing. DIF files are ASCII files in a specific format. Many spreadsheet programs allow you to save your spreadsheet in DIF format.

SuperCalc4 can read and write Lotus 1–2–3 V.1a and V.2 files. It can import and export files to and from earlier versions of SuperCalc.

Integrated Spreadsheet Programs

Another approach to moving data among spreadsheet applications is the integrated program. Integrated programs often use a spreadsheet program as a foundation. Integrated programs built on a spreadsheet foundation often include:

1. Word processing
2. Spreadsheets
3. Data base
4. Graphics
5. Communication

Integrated program growth has occurred partially because of the increase in the amount of RAM available and the reduction in its cost.

Lotus 1–2–3 was one of the first programs to combine spreadsheet, graphics, and data base capabilities. Symphony, a product of the same company, has added word processing and communication to the package.

The original version of SuperCalc was a spreadsheet program only. SuperCalc3 has added some outstanding graphics.

VARYING CAPABILITIES OF ELECTRONIC SPREADSHEET PROGRAMS

The basic operations of spreadsheet programs are similar, yet each program has unique capabilities. All spreadsheet programs use labels, numbers, and formulas displayed in columns and rows on the microcomputer's monitor. The main menus of six selected spreadsheets are shown in Figure 5–21.

FIGURE 5–21
Spreadsheet Menus

Lotus 1-2-3

MENU

Worksheet Range Copy Move File Print Graph Data Quit
Global, Insert, Delete, Column-Width, Erase, Titles, Windows, Status

Multiplan

COMMAND: **Alpha** Blank Copy Delete Edit Format Goto Help Insert Lock Move
Name Options Print Quit Sort Transfer Value Window Xternal
Select option or type command letter

ExpressCalc

| 67K | Arrange | Blank | Configure | Delete | Edit | Format | Global | Insert |
| | Load | Print | Quit | Replicate | Save | Title | Xternal | Zap |

SuperCalc3

Enter A,B,C,D,E,F,G,I,L,M,O,P,Q,R,S,T,U,W,X,Z,/?

SuperCalc4
Arrange Blank Copy Delete Edit Format Global Insert Load Move Name
Output Protect Quit Save Title Unprotect View Window Zap /more

VisiCalc (The Original Spreadsheet)

Command: BCDEFGIMPRSTVW-

All the spreadsheet programs listed in Figure 5–21, except Multiplan, call up menus by pressing the "/" key. The Multiplan menu is always on the screen.

Spreadsheet programs tend to be either menu or function key driven. The beginner or occasional user often finds the more complete menus convenient, while the experienced user frequently prefers to use function keys.

User aids in the form of command cards (cards listing the meaning of the letters in the menu), keyboard overlays (command cards that fit over the keyboard), and key labels (stick-on labels that may be attached to specific keys to define their functions) are available for most spreadsheets.

Spreadsheet programs often have add-on capabilities to perform graphics and data base tasks such as rearranging either columns or rows according to the labels in a row or column. These add-on features often become the determining factor when deciding on what spreadsheet program to select (Table 5–15).

TABLE 5–15
Comparison of Electronic
Spreadsheets

Hardware	Apple Works	Express Calc	Lotus 1–2–3 V.2	SuperCalc4*	Multi-plan
Microcomputer	Apple II	—IBM/compatibles—PC/XT/AT			
RAM					
Minimum RAM	64K	256K	256K	256K	128K
Maximum RAM used	128K	—	over 2MB	over 2MB	1000K
General					
Number of Colums	200	64	256	255	255
Number of Rows	250	256	8192	9999	4095
Windows per screen	2	2	2	2	8
Calculations					
Average	yes	yes	yes	yes	yes
Logarithmic	no	yes	yes	yes	yes
Percentage	yes	yes	yes	yes	yes
Trigonometric	no	yes	yes	yes	yes
Programming statements	if-then, else	if-then, else	if-then, true/ false, and/or	conditional expression	if-then, else
Editing					
Insert/delete columns/rows	yes	yes	yes	yes	yes
Duplicate columns/rows	yes	yes	yes	yes	yes
Duplicate screen to another area	yes	yes	yes	yes	yes
Global search	yes	no	yes	yes	no
Right, left, and center justify	yes	yes	yes	R & L	yes
Other Features					
Protect/unprotect indiv. cells, rows	yes	yes	yes	yes	yes
Underline/flashing or inverse video	yes	no	yes	yes	yes
Vary width of more than one cell	yes	yes	yes	yes	yes
Can $ be displayed	yes	yes	yes	yes	yes
Use commas with numbers	yes	yes	yes	yes	yes
Copy protected	no	no	yes	no	yes
Interfacing					
File Type DIF	x		x	x	
ASCII		x	x	x	
WordStar				x	

TABLE 5–15
Continued

Hardware	Apple Works	Express Calc	Lotus 1–2–3 V.2	SuperCalc4*	Multi-plan
dBase II			x	x	
Lotus			x	x	
SYLK					x
VisiCalc	x				
Add-On Features					
Word processing	yes	no	no	no	no
Graphics	As extra	Bar charts	yes	yes	no
Data base	yes	no	yes	yes	no
Communication	no	no	no	no	no

** SuperCalc is available for the Apple, CP/M, and MS/PC DOS systems.

Memory utilization of over 640K requires expanded memory system.

SUMMARY

It is important to learn to use electronic spreadsheet programs because they perform many standard mathematical operations and data manipulations commonly used in business and other applications. Generally, electronic spreadsheets divide a screen into columns and rows. In each column-row, cell labels, numbers, or formulas may be entered. Any problem that can be solved with pencil and paper can be solved by electric spreadsheet programs.

Spreadsheets do not usually require special hardware. Some large spreadsheets may require extended memory cards.

The key points learned in this chapter are:

1. The spreadsheet is a tool used to solve numeric problems since the invention of pencil and paper.
2. Electronic spreadsheets save time, increase calculation accuracy, make it possible to perform powerful evaluations, produce final reports, create valuable graphics, and store spreadsheets for future recall and reuse, without requiring a large investment.
3. Electronic spreadsheets require a microcomputer, large amounts of RAM, data entry devices, a monitor, a printer, and usually two disk drives or a single drive and a hard disk drive.
4. Electronic spreadsheet programs divide the screen into column-row cells.
5. Electronic spreadsheet programs have some general, configuration, interfacing, and add-on features.
6. Electronic spreadsheet programs solve problems using labels, numbers, and formulas.
7. Electronic spreadsheets allow you to divide the screen into windows, protect cells, underline, control the size of cells, and control the numerical format.
8. The basic operation of spreadsheet programs is similar, yet each has unique capabilities.
9. Spreadsheet data may be transferred to other programs.

KEY TERMS

Cell	Precedence
Column	Protected cell
Electronic spreadsheet	Range
Formulas	Reference absolute
Labels	Reference relative
Macros	Row
Mathematical operator	Spreadsheet
Numbers	Template

REVIEW QUESTIONS

1. What is a spreadsheet?

2. What information is entered in a spreadsheet?

3. What is an electronic spreadsheet?

4. Define the following electronic spreadsheet terms:
   a. label
   b. numbers
   c. formula
   d. column
   e. row
   f. cells

5. Identify five spreadsheet applications.

6. What does a spreadsheet do for you as a student?

7. Which commercial spreadsheet was the first one available for microcomputers?

8. Why do some spreadsheet applications require large amounts of RAM?

9. What is the most common input device used when creating electronic spreadsheets?

10. Identify the need for monitor displays by spreadsheet users.

11. What are the special printer needs of spreadsheet users?

12. What are the special on-line storage needs of spreadsheet users?

13. Give an example of a common manual type of spreadsheet.

14. Detail the six things that electronic spreadsheets do that make them important to many users.

15. Set up a simple spreadsheet illustrating all of its important parts.

16. How does the spreadsheet program help you perform a ''what if'' analysis?

17. Identify some of the common types of graphs produced by spreadsheet programs.

18. Detail the five steps needed to create a graph in a spreadsheet program.

19. Name three applications of spreadsheets in:
    a. Accounting.
    b. Banking.
    c. Education and Training.
    d. Finance and Economics.
    e. Marketing (Transportation and logistics).
    f. Personnel administration.
    g. Quantitative management.
    h. Retail merchandising.
    i. Statistics.

20. What is a cursor? How is it displayed in a spreadsheet program?

21. How do you communicate to an electronic spreadsheet program that you are entering a label?

22. When the words "Inexpensive, but it floats" are typed into a single nine-character cell, what happens if the spreadsheet truncates? If the spreadsheet overflows?

23. Give an example of a spreadsheet formula.

24. When you enter a formula into an electronic spreadsheet, what appears on the screen?

25. Give an example of a spreadsheet function.

26. How are function keys used in spreadsheet programs?

27. Give five examples of the extenders used in spreadsheet files and explain what they mean.

28. What is a range? How is it used in a spreadsheet program?

29. Give three examples of the formats used to display values on spreadsheet programs.

30. What is mathematical precedence?

31. What is a mathematical operator?

32. When you enter $-1 \wedge 2$ in a spreadsheet, do you always get the same result?

33. Give an example of a logical function found in spreadsheet programs.

34. Why must you be careful to avoid circular calculations?

35. Identify some editing features found in spreadsheet programs.

36. What are some reasons for inserting or deleting columns and rows?

37. What is the difference between absolute and relative references and when is it important?

38. What is a macro? How are they used in spreadsheet programs?

39. What is a spreadsheet window? Why would you want to use one?

40. Why would you want to transfer a spreadsheet file to another program?

41. How are ASCII files useful in electronic spreadsheet work?

42. What are DIF files?

43. What programs are found in an integrated spreadsheet program?

44. What are some of the additional features found in many spreadsheet programs?

DISCUSSION AND APPLICATION QUESTIONS

1.   Identify several courses you have taken, and several you plan to take, in which electronic spreadsheets could help you complete the assignments.

2.   Select a problem that can take advantage of spreadsheet graphics from a math, statistics, finance, or similar course. Identify how spreadsheet graphics help in the solution of the problem.

3.   Examine advertisements for electronic spreadsheet programs in a microcomputer magazine. What features are now being promoted?

4.   From the advertisements reviewed in question 2, determine the amount of RAM that may be used by electronic spreadsheet programs.

5.   Use the yellow pages of your telephone book to identify several businesses that have uses for electronic spreadsheet programs. How do you think the programs might be used?

6.   Use the yellow pages to find where you can purchase electronic spreadsheet programs in your area.

LABORATORY ASSIGNMENTS

1. Load an electronic spreadsheet into a microcomputer. Enter a label, enter two values, enter an equation based on the values entered, and then check the results.

2. Develop a spreadsheet to calculate gasoline mileage. The output should be:

	A	B	C	D	E
1	GAS.wk1				
2					
3		Tank #	Miles	Gallons	Miles/Gallon
4		1	300	11.8	25.42372
5		2	334	12.4	26.93548
6		3	333	12.3	27.07317
7		4	288	11.9	24.20168
8		5	345	10.3	33.49514
9		6	355	12.1	29.33884
10		7	301	12.1	24.87603

Column A is a counter for the tank number. Column B is the number of miles driven on the tank. Column C is the amount of gasoline purchased to fill up the tank. Column D is the calculation of miles divided by the gallons used.

3. Develop a spreadsheet to calculate the batting average of the members of a baseball team. The output should be:

	A	B	C	D	E	F	G
1	BAT.wks						
2							
3							
4							
5	Player	Number of	Number of				
6		times at bat	Singles	Doubles	Triples	Homers	Total Hits
7	Jim Jones	34	4	1	2	3	0.294117
8	Stan Smith	45	5	3	3	1	0.266666
9	Carol Kim	33	4	2	2	2	0.303030
10	Andy Rodrege	23	2	3	0	0	0.217391
11	Samual Smith	12	1	1	0	1	0.25
12	Andress Able	44	4	1	1	0	0.136363

Column A is the player's name. Column B is the number of times the player was at bat. Columns C through F are the types and number of hits of each type the player had. Column G is the calculation of the sum of all types of hits divided by the number of times at bat.

4. The election for the president of the senior class is conducted by sections. There are five sections and three candidates. The spreadsheets are as follows:

	A	B	C	D	E	F	G	H
1	ELECT.wks							
2								
3	Section	Names						
4		Jones, John		Fransisco, July		Rodrigus, Manuel		
5	1	102		132		122		
6	2	122		255		345		
7	3	200		234		322		
8	4	123		122		344		
9	5	333		234		546		Total
10		-------		-------		-------		Votes
11	Total	880		977		1679	3536	
12		-------		-------		-------		
13	Percent	24.88687%		27.63009%		47.48303%		
14		-------		-------		-------		

In row 11 the sum of all the votes for a candidate is calculated. In H11 the total of the votes cast is calculated. Row 13 is the percentage of votes each individual earned.

5. Change the values in assignment 2 for amount of gas used and the mileage driven to match an automobile with which you are familiar.

6. Use the baseball batting average spreadsheet in assignment 3 and replace the names of the players shown with the names of players on a team that interests you. Enter data to match the performances of the players entered. Use the editing capability to make the changes and add players to complete your team.

7. Redo the election spreadsheet in assignment 4 to match the way it is done in your school. Add or delete sections, and substitute names of the candidates in the current or last election.

8. Clear your spreadsheet. Enter the number 1 in cell A1. Enter the formula +A1 +1 in cell A2. Use the copy command to replicate down the page for 12 periods.

9. Clear your spreadsheet. Enter the number 1 in cell A1. Enter the formula +A1 +1 in cell B1. Use the copy command to replicate across the page for 12 periods.

10. Place the number 2 in cell A1 and the number 3 in cell B7. Place the formula: +B7 +$A$1 in cell C7 and copy it into the next ten columns. Place the formula: +B7 +$A$1 in cell B8 and copy it into the next ten rows.

(The objective of this assignment is to learn to use absolute and relative addressing. If your spreadsheet does not use the dollar sign for absolute addressing, substitute the method used.)

11. Place a label in cell A1. Copy it both down and across the page.

12. Set up a grade sheet for a class. Calculate the average of each grading criteria, each student's average, and the class average.

13. Create a spreadsheet to calculate the average and standard deviation of a set of data. The formulas used are:

- Average = SUM(range)/COUNT(range)
- Variance = SUM (average − each data point) $\wedge$ 2/(Count(range)−1)
- Standard deviation = Square root (Variance)

Where SUM is a spreadsheet function for adding the values in a range of the spreadsheet and COUNT is a spreadsheet function for finding the number of data points in the same range. If there is an AVERAGE function it should also be used and the results compared.

If your spreadsheet has a variance or standard deviation function try it and compare results. If they are different use Count(range) rather than Count (range−1) in the variance formula and try again.

Use the following data for a trial run:

12 23 12 13 23 24 24 15 17 15 13 13 14 15 13 14 15

14. Create a report on the finances of a student club or other activity. Use the manual finance report as a model.

15. Create a report on the finances for a class trip. Use the manual finance report as a model.

16. Create an invoice using the model below:

```
         A          B          C          D          E          F          G
 1  INVOICE.wks
 2                                        I N V O I C E
 3   ---------------------------------------------------------------------------
 4  From:                            To:
 5  Professional Sales and Services  A&Z Management, Inc.
 6  3375 Somewhere Lane              4151 Bay Front Road
 7  Santa Clara, CA 55555            Atlanta, Alabama 35555
 8  (555) 555-5555                   Atten: S.M. Zimmerman
 9   ---------------------------------------------------------------------------
10  QUANTITY DESCRIPTION                       PRICE    AMOUNT
11   ---------------------------------------------------------------------------
12
13
14
15
16
17
18   ---------------------------------------------------------------------------
19                                           TOTAL
20                                                  =========
```

The amount should be calculated by multiplying the quantity times the price. The total is the sum of all the individual amounts.

17. Create a spreadsheet for accounting working papers. Use the model shown below:

```
     A     B      C      D          E      F      G      H      I      J      K      L      M      N
 1  ACCT.wks
 2  X&Z Incorporated     June 1999                              Adjusted        Earnings
 3                                      Trial Bal.  Adjustments  Trial Bal.  Statement  Balance Sheet
 4  Type  Chart of Accounts            Dr.   Cr.    Dr.   Cr.    Dr.   Cr.    Dr.    Cr.   Dr.    Cr.
 5  ----  -------------------          ----------------------------------------------------------------
 6  A     Cash                         6500                      6500               6500
 7  A     Accounts receivable          16000                     16000              16000
 8  A       Allowance for bad debts          200          670           870                        870
 9  A     Prepaid rent                 800                 400    400                400
10  A     Equipment                    17300                     17300              17300
11  A       Accumulated depreciation         3200        2330          5530                       5530
12  L     Accounts payable                   6500                      6500                       6500
13  L     Accrued salaries payable                 3500          3500                       3500
14  L     Capital                            9000                      9000                       9000
15  L     Retained Earn.                     5000                      5000                      14800
16  I     Sales commissions                  68000                     68000        68000
17  E     Salaries expense             34500        1330          35830  35830
18  E     Administrative expense       4800         1200          6000   6000
19  E     Rent expense                 10050        1800          11850  11850
20  E     Bad debts expense            1950         170           2120   2120
21  E     Depreciation expense                      2400          2400   2400
22                                     -----  -----  ----   ----   -----  -----  -----  -----
23                                     91900  91900  6900   6900   98400  98400  58200  68000
24                                     =====  =====  ====   ====   =====  =====
25        Net Earnings                                                  9800
                                                                 -----  -----  -----  -----
                                                                 68000  68000  40200  36700
                                                                 =====  =====  =====  =====
```

Column A identifies the type of asset, column B is the chart of accounts, and columns E and F are the Trial Balance. The number in the trial balance columns E and F and the numbers in the adjustments (G and H) are input data. In the adjusted trial balance all debit balances are calculated by adding columns E and G, subtracting columns F and H. The credit balances are calculated by adding columns F and H, subtracting columns E and G.

The earnings statement is created by copying all the debit and credit balances for income and expense accounts from the adjusted trial balance. The difference between the sum of the credits and the sum of the debits is the net earnings.

The balance sheet is created by copying all asset and liability accounts from the adjusted trial balance and adding the net earnings into the retained earnings.

18. Create a spreadsheet to model a check book. A checkbook register contains the following information:

Date	Check Number	Check issued to or deposits received from	Amount Deposited	Cleared	Amount of Check	Balance
—	—	Original balance				$2,300.00
8/13	233	Rent			$167.88	
8/14	234	Utilities			133.44	
8/14	235	Telephone			51.22	
8/14	—	Salary check	$1,200.77			
8/15	—	Sold radio	33.45			
8/15	236	Cash			165.44	
8/16	237	Food store			87.88	

The bank records show:

Previous Balance	We have added:		We have subtracted:			Current Balance
Statement	Number	Deposits	Number	Checks	Serv.Charg	
$2,300.00	3	$1,400.77	5	676.86	1.44	3022.47

Checking Account Transactions

Date	Amount	Description
8/15	1,200.77	DEPOSIT
8/16	33.45	DEPOSIT
8/16	100.00	DEPOSIT

Checks

Date	Amount
8/17	167.88
8/17	133.44
8/18	165.44
8/18	87.88
8/18	122.22

At the beginning of the period your balance and the bank's balance were the same. There were no outstanding transactions of any type.

On your spreadsheet start with your balance, add the not-cleared checks, subtract the unrecorded checks, subtract the not-cleared deposits, add the unrecorded deposits, make adjustments for errors in recording and service charges, and produce a final balance to be compared with the bank's.

19. Re-call the assignments selected above.

20. Create an ASCII file identical to the following in your word processor.

"This table is for the student to transfer"

"Table 1–2 A Table"

"From/To:"	1	2	3	4	5	6
"Able"	12	22	2	12	21	34
"Baker"	15	15	16	5	6	8
"Charley"	13	13	13	16	7	9
"Dog"	23	23	24	54	21	22

Read the file into your spreadsheet using its import capability. Use both the text and number option. Note the differences in the results.

21. Print the contents of a template. Use the setup codes to control your printer. Print an ASCII file.

22. Re-call the assignments selected above and print the template on the printer.

23. Re-call the assignments selected above, print an ASCII file, transfer the file to your word processor, and include it in a report. Use the power of your word processor and printer to enhance the format of the spreadsheet.

24. Look up the setup codes for your printer. If available, use your spreadsheet printer routine to produce a report in compressed mode.

1. (Education.) A class consists of twelve people. Their names and student numbers are:

Number	Student	Student Number
1.	Mary Lenissa	12234
2.	Ivan Petrushian	22445
3.	Stanley Michel	12554
4.	Neal Roberts	43223
5.	Bruce Davis	11447
6.	Kim Aguilar	43556
7.	Kim McCreary	45669
8.	Sven Torgeson	19854
9.	Wayne Bonnana	18888
10.	Anna Spatulski	16431
11.	Jean Angstreich	25647
12.	Chang Ho Quon	54678

Set up a class roll and grade sheet that can be used by the instructor. Identify headings for each column including spaces for roll checking, grades for quizzes, final exams, and course grades.

There are five grading criteria in the class. The first two are reports with a weight of 5% each. The second and third are quizzes with a weight of 10% each. The last is the final exam with a weight of 70%. The class meets twice a week for five weeks.

Identify the formulas used to calculate the student's average for the term, the class average, and class standard deviation. Lay the grade sheet out on a piece of paper in preparation for making an electronic spreadsheet. Identify the location of these formulas.

2. (General.) Develop a budget in the form of a spreadsheet for a dual-career couple in which the wife works as an accountant for $22,000 per year, and the husband attends graduate school full time at a nearby university. The monthly costs for various budget items are:

Number	Item	Monthly Budget
1.	Rent	$344
2.	Food	280
3.	Babysitting	100
4.	Utilities	200
5.	Books	30
6.	Tuition	200
7.	Clothing	200
8.	Travel/auto	200
9.	Savings or entertainment	
10.	Miscellaneous	
11.	Gifts/donations	

Using spreadsheet format, lay out the above budget for the year on a month-by-month basis. Assume that church donations will total $50 a month except during December, when a $300 donation is planned. Include a special birthday present costing $200 for the couple's daughter in June. Lay out the above as a spreadsheet, locating all labels and formulas. Identify the formulas needed. The objective is to determine the cash available per month.

3. (General.) The couple in problem 2 has a 10–year–old girl who is a member of a youth group. The group is planning a 3-day, 300-mile trip to the state capital. The costs include:

Number	Item	Cost
1.	Rent on bus	$600
2.	Meals per day per person	18
3.	Camping fees for the group	50
4.	Museum entrance fees per person	8
5.	Insurance	75
6.	Camping supplies	50

Lay out a spreadsheet to determine the total cost for the group, and to identify the cost per individual if there are twenty-two children and four adults making the trip. Identify all labels, numbers, and formulas.

4. (General business.) A checkbook check register contains the following information:

Date	Check Number	Check issued to or deposits received from	Amount Deposited	Amount of Check	Balance
—	—	Original balance			$2000.00
8/13	202	Rent		$150.00	
8/15	203	Utilities		125.36	
8/16	204	Phone		39.87	
8/17	—	Salary check	$1500.26		
8/18	—	Gift	12.15		
8/18	205	Cash		175.00	
8/18	206	Food store		97.83	

The bank records show:

Balance Last Statement	We have added: Number	Deposits	We have subtracted: Number	Checks	Serv Chg	Balance
$2000.00	1	$1500.26	8	587.01	1.22	2912.03

Checking Account Transactions

Date	Amount	Description
8/19	1500.26	DEPOSIT

Checks

Date	Amount
8/15	100.22
8/19	39.87
8/19	5.21
8/19	12.55
8/20	6.33
8/24	175.00
8/25	97.83
8/25	150.00

At the beginning of the period, your balance and the bank's balance were the same. There were no outstanding transactions of any type.

Set up a spreadsheet to start with your balance, add the not-cleared checks, subtract the unrecorded checks, subtract the not-cleared deposits, add the unrecorded deposits, make adjustments for errors in recording and service charges, and produce a final balance to be compared to the bank's.

5. (Accounting.) Set up and organize a spreadsheet for the ledger of Western Gas with the following chart of accounts:

Balance Sheet	Debit	Credit
Cash account	5,000	
Accounts payable		7,000
Accounts receivable	1,200	
Building	100,000	
Equipment	59,800	
Reserve for depreciation		30,000
Land	75,000	
Notes payable		55,000
Capital		150,000
Retained earnings		9,000
Supplies	10,000	

Place the accounts in order of current assets, fixed assets, current liabilities, and long-term liabilities, followed by stockholder's equity.

Locate where all labels and formulas will be and identify these formulas in terms of spreadsheet location.

6. (Marketing.) You have a job working for the local computer store to determine the number of spreadsheet users on your campus. A questionnaire has been designed. Most questions are designed to be answered with a "Yes," "No," or "I do not know." Some questions require the respondent to identify the type of computer or program being used. The questions to be answered by the survey include:

1. Do you know what a spreadsheet is?
2. Are you currently using an electronic spreadsheet?
3. Do you have a microcomputer available?
4. What kind of microcomputer do you use?
5. Do you have an electronic spreadsheet program available?
6. What electronic spreadsheet program do you have?
7. How long have you had the program?
8. How much did you pay for the program?
9. If you do not have a spreadsheet program, are you planning to purchase one?
10. How often do you use your program?
11. Do you plan to purchase a microcomputer? When?

Organize the questions onto a spreadsheet. Identify all questions, the numbers you generate, the formulas needed and their location. The objective is to give the store management some idea of how large a market exists for electronic spreadsheets and microcomputers on campus.

7. (Statistics.) The formulas for the average and standard deviation of a sample are:

- Average = (Sum X(i))/N
- Standard Deviation = Square Root ((Sum (Average–X(i)))/(N–1))

Set up a spreadsheet for a sample size of 10 to:

1. Find sum X(i).

2. Identify where N is.
3. Find sum (average–X(i)).
4. Find the average.
5. Find the standard deviation.

Analyze the following sample data set:

Number	Data
1	12.32
2	12.99
3	13.55
4	16.55
5	11.23
6	12.24
7	13.66
8	12.45
9	12.54
10	12.00

Identify the labels, the numbers, the formulas, and the location of each item.

8. (Accounting/Finance.) Lay out a spreadsheet for the preparation of an amortization schedule for the first twelve months of an equal monthly-payment mortgage. The mortgage is for $40,000 with a thirty-year payout at 12.5% annual percentage rate. Identify the location of all labels, all numbers entered, and all formulas. Specify the formulas needed.

9. (Other courses.) From any course being taken this term or last, propose a spreadsheet application for the instructor's approval. After approval, lay out a spreadsheet for the selected application.

SELECTED REFERENCES

Allegretti, Enzo V. *Understanding and Using Symphony.* West Publishing Company, 1987.

Clark, Roger E. *Executive SuperCalc3.* Addison Wesley, 1984.

Maiorana and Strunk. *Understanding and Using ExpressCalc.* West Publishing Company, 1987.

Ross, Steven. *Understanding and Using Lotus 1–2–3.* West Publishing Company, 1986.

Ross, Steven. *Understanding and Using Lotus 1–2–3 Release 2.* West Publishing Company, 1987.

Ross, Steven, and Judy Reinders. *Understanding and Using SuperCalc3.* West Publishing Company, 1987.

Ross, Steven, and Judy Reinders. *Understanding and Using SuperCalc4.* West Publishing Company, 1987.

Watterson, Karen L. *Understanding and Using FRAMEWORK.* West Publishing Company, 1986.

Weber System Inc. *Lotus 1–2–3 User's Handbook.* Ballantine Books, 1984.

Witkens, Ruth. *Managing Your Business with Multiplan.* Microsoft Press, 1984.

Zimmerman, Steven M., Leo M. Conrad, and Stanley M. Zimmerman. *Electronic Spreadsheets and Your IBM PC.* Hayden Book Company, 1984.

6

GOALS

When you complete this chapter you will be able to:

Understand why data base programs are important to the user.

Define the tasks of a data base program.

Understand the steps needed to set up and operate a data base system.

Identify some commercial data base programs.

OUTLINE

Data base

MICROS IN ACTION

An agent for the Schneider-Fleming Insurance agency identified his microcomputer needs as:

1. Customer data base file.
2. Word processing-letters, proposals, and contracts.
3. Custom program or spreadsheet client analysis.
4. Communication capability with the central office.

The data base need was the most critical because agency research has shown that appointments per phone call and sales per appointment could be increased if the calls could be coordinated with events in the clients' lives. Among the more important events were:

1. Birth of a child.
2. Graduation of a family member from high school or college.
3. Obtaining a new job.
4. Purchase (sale) of a house.
5. Family member's death.
6. Serious illness of a family member.
7. Marriage (divorce) of a family member.
8. A child's first car.

A data base also made sales easier by providing the knowledge necessary to maintain contact with a client. If contact is not made for one year, the probability of client loss to another agency is increased.

Knowledge:
The assignment of meaning to information by a human being.

Facts:
Something having real, demonstrable existence.

Information:
Data that has been processed and recalled from a data base in an organized manner.

A data base is a collection of data used for one or more purposes. An electronic data base program is one that is designed to operate on a computer. A data base program takes care of organizing data for storage on disk and usually includes a screen editor that allows data entry and update, and a report generator that produces custom business reports. **Knowledge** starts as **facts** about some situation, it becomes data when it is entered into a data base. The output of a data base turns data into **information.** When it is read and used by a human being, knowledge is gained.

USER WINDOW

PUTTING DATA BASES TO WORK

A young lady was hired as a new car salesperson. She faced the problem of contacting as many friends and acquaintances as possible in order to start building a client group. She started with a list of her high school graduation class and the members of her church.

She used her mother's microcomputer to type a letter. She typed a mailing list of all the names she had collected into the microcomputer for her mail-list data base.

She then proceeded to send all her friends a computer-produced letter. This is a simple and effective use of a data base.

Microcomputer users create and maintain data bases for their own personal and business needs by acquiring one of the many data base programs currently available.

These programs vary from **file maintenance** and **report generators** with limited capabilities, to programs that are, in effect, very high-level, special purpose microcomputer languages in themselves. The **non-procedural language** data base programs can perform almost any data base task, as well as many other tasks.

The data base system installed in your microcomputer has a number of functions. First, it is a data storage entry device. The method of organizing the file into which the data is stored must be defined in a setup routine. This is the step that requires the most research and effort. A little extra care and effort in setup greatly adds to the value of a data base in the future as a business problem-solving tool. Once the file is set up and organized, facts must be collected and recorded in the data base as data.

The capabilities of data base systems vary from simple file maintenance to computer languages. Data base programs allow you to search for a particular record with specified characters.

File maintenance:
The entering and updating of data in a data base.

Report generation:
The creation of a formatted report to output information from the data base.

Non-procedural language:
A programming language that does not require programming techniques to be used. It allows the user to send instructions to the computer in English-like statements.

DATA BASE HARDWARE NEEDS

The development and application of microcomputer data bases are dependent upon the capabilities and capacities of the available hardware. The hardware needed for a microcomputer data base includes:

1. RAM
2. Input devices
3. Monitor
4. Printers
5. On-line storage

RAM

Most data base programs, both file maintenance and very high-level language programs, have no special RAM requirements. A number of programs which were transferred and re-written from larger computers do have large RAM needs.

Input Devices

Data base input methods include:

1. Keyboard
2. Point of sale (cash register)
3. Light pens
4. Optical character readers
5. Communication programs using other data bases

The most often-used method of data entry and data base update is the keyboard. Data base programs can be designed to take advantage of many

MICROS IN ACTION

Sizing a Data Base

The Schneider-Fleming insurance agency created a master file of all the agency's clients. The maximum number of clients was estimated to be five thousand. The number of characters stored per client was estimated to be one thousand. Multiplying the two numbers together resulted in an estimated five megabytes needed for storage.

other methods. Point of sales data entry, light pens, and optical character readers are often used for inventory control.

Microcomputer data bases are often used in conjunction with central computer data bases. Communication and transfer of files between the central computer and the microcomputer are common; they will be covered in more detail in the communication chapter.

Monitor

The monitor is used as a primary output device for data base programs. Almost any monochrome or color screen will satisfy the data base user's needs. If the data is to be used for color or high-resolution graphics, a monitor with the required capability is needed.

Printers

Data bases often produce lists and tables. Users of data bases and spreadsheets often have the same need for wide carriage printers. The discussion of printers in chapter 5 applies to data bases as well as to spreadsheets.

On-Line Storage

Data bases need on-line storage devices that can handle large amounts of information. As the amount of on-line storage availability has increased and its costs decreased, the number of programs and applications of data bases on microcomputers has increased as well. Early data bases on microcomputers were simple due to the limited hardware capacity and software capability. Only when low cost (under $1,000), hard disk devices (over 5 million bytes) and increased RAM (beyond 64K) became available did the number of programs and applications expand.

You may not need a hard disk because the size of your data base may fit on a floppy disk system. However, you will find that some data base programs were developed because of the expansion of this market. Table 6–1 lists the capacity of storage on floppy disks in microcomputer terms.

In data base programs using ASCII files, the number of bytes is equal to the total number of characters in the data base including control codes and spaces. Most data base programs use ASCII files. Data base programs using compressed code are able to store more data in the same space than an ASCII

Microcomputer Operating System	Floppy Disks
Apple DOS	140K to 720K–1.4MB
CP/M	90K up to 760K
MS–DOS/PC–DOS	160K to 380K, 760K, and 1.2MB
TRS–DOS (Models I, III, 4)	80K to 180K

TABLE 6–1
Media for Storing Data

file. The storage requirements of files created by a data base program can be determined only from studying its specifications.

Many data base applications are initially set up using floppy disks, then moved to a hard disk as the system grows. Hard disks can store from 5 megabytes to over 500 megabytes of data. The greater the capacity, the greater the absolute cost, but the lower the cost per byte. Laser disks are under development and are expected to have capacities near 500 megabytes.

WHY YOU SHOULD KNOW ABOUT DATA BASE PROGRAMS

Information is a resource. Data base helps individuals manipulate information. Businesses require many different data bases, for example:

- Accounts payable
- Accounts receivable
- Customer lists
- Vendor lists
- Employee records
- Inventory
- Product information
- Sales records
- Suppliers
- Year to date accounting performance data

The availability of accurate, up-to-date information can help management earn or save dollars. Management decisions must often be made immediately, and the availability of information from the data base can mean additional profit. Errors in judgment may occur when working without key facts. The cost of creating and maintaining a data base must be balanced with the value of the data to the business.

The question "What is the potential size of the microcomputer college market, if the current price of equipment were reduced by 50%?" cannot be answered by a data base because it is a prediction. The question "What are the current and past sales of microcomputer equipment in different types of colleges in different locations around the country?" can be answered by a data base. Having the answers to the second question can aid a manager in making a better decision about how to service the college microcomputer market.

The principal limitations to the creation of data bases are the needs and imagination of the professional. Data base design begins with an in depth understanding of your needs.

MICROS IN ACTION

A Data Base Helps Sales

One agent for Schneider-Fleming insurance set up his own data base. His clients' names and life information needed to provide insurance services were entered into the data base.

The extra work slowed down the number of sales calls at first but resulted in a good long-term relationship and repeat business from the client base, once it was established.

Some of the data needed were identified as:
1. Name
2. How called (how the individual wants to be addressed)
3. Address
4. Phone number
5. Date of last contact
6. Number in family
7. Names and dates of birth of each family member
8. Approximate date of next life event
9. Home ownership
10. Automobile ownership
11. Unusual or serious illness of a family member.

THE LANGUAGE OF DATA BASE

Some basic terms must be understood when learning about data bases. To understand a data base some basic concepts are needed. These concepts include:

1. File management concepts
   a. Files
   b. Records
   c. Fields
2. Data base concepts
   a. Facts
   b. Data
   c. Information
   d. Knowledge
   e. Decision making

File Management Concepts—File, Record, and Field

Record:
A collection of facts about an entity.

Entity:
Something that has separate and distinct existence.

A data base file is a collection of similar records. An example of a file is a file cabinet containing all the data pertaining to a group of housing units owned by a real estate investor. A data base file is stored on your disk in the same manner as text or program files.

A **record** is a collection of facts about an **entity.** The rent record form in a file folder in a housing unit file cabinet may contain historical rental facts about a particular housing unit. This form is a record. A collection of forms constitutes a file.

A **field** stores data about an **attribute** of the entity. If there is a location to enter the telephone number of the current occupant of a housing unit on the rent record form, this "location" could be considered a field. The telephone number is an attribute. Figure 6–1 illustrates a file, record, and field.

A data base of personnel records may consist of a series of files. In each file may be different job skills. The record or entity would be an individual. The fields in the record would contain the individual's name, sex, pay rate, number of dependents, address, telephone number, etc. The more information in the data base, the more potential applications of the data base. The more information, however, the greater the cost of setup and maintenance.

In many data bases, fields and records contain a fixed number of characters or numbers. If the data in a field does not take up the entire field, the remaining space is wasted. Every wasted character cuts the amount of data that may be stored in a given file, on a given type of computer storage media. When you assign characters to fields, you must be careful to balance the loss of information of small fields with the waste of space caused by too large a field. An example of wasted space is a last name field of ten characters with the name JONES in it. JONES uses five characters, the extra space for the five additional characters is wasted.

Field:
A unit of data about an attribute of an entity.

Attribute:
A particular characteristic of interest about an entity.

FIGURE 6–1   A (a) File, (b) Record, (c) Field

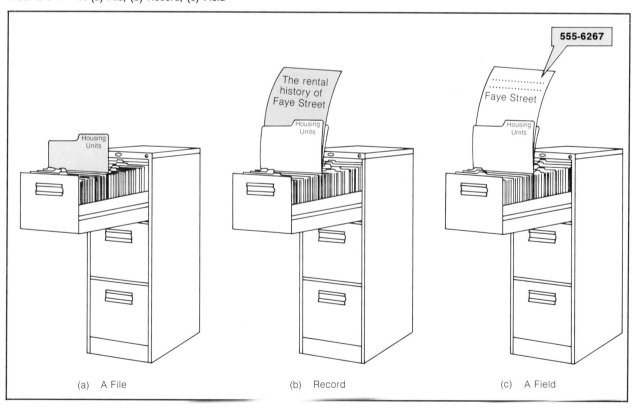

(a)   A File   (b)   Record   (c)   A Field

Data Base Concepts—Facts, Data, Information, Knowledge, and Decision-Making

Definitions of data base terms vary between writers and over time. The meaning of the words facts, data, information, knowledge, and decision-making gives structure to the field of data base management.

The objective of a data base system is to collect facts, store selected facts as data, recall, and present the data as information to a knowledgeable worker. The individual may then turn the information into knowledge for decision-making. The system starts with the collection of facts and ends with a decision.

Facts are available everywhere, about everything. The colors of your car and house are facts. Your age and the grade you earned in your last English course are facts. Facts may be considered raw data. Facts do not become data unless they are selected and stored or organized in some manner. Data bases are used to store and organize data for future use.

The data in a data base becomes information when the data is received by a human being in a form that has meaning.

Only a person can have knowledge. Knowledge is the assignment of meaning to information by an individual. You know something about a person or object when the information has meaning. When making a purchase decision, the prices of similar articles are knowledge.

When the value of information is great enough that it pays to create and maintain a data base, then and only then should one be created. The trade-off is the cost of the information versus its value. The low cost of microcomputer data base programs justifies many applications.

The decision to purchase a piece of real estate depends on information. If you are an investor making many such decisions, you may have a need for a personal data base. The value of information about the current real estate market and future trends is great to the investor.

If you are an individual purchasing your first house, then some information is needed. The value of the information is not as great as it is to the investor, but it still has value. Individual home buyers may depend on real estate agents and other professionals for knowledge, rather than set up a system to manage the data themselves.

DATA BASE PROGRAM FEATURES

Data base programs vary from file management-report generators to computer languages. A classification of data base programs helps in the selection of the proper program for your needs. Characteristics of candidate programs may be used to identify a program that matches a need.

The important characteristics of a data base program include:

1. Classification/type
2. Type of index organization
3. Compatibility
4. Other features
   a. File maintenance, report generators, and calculations
   b. Function keys and menus.

Classifications/Types

Data base programs may be simple file managers, complete languages in which many applications may be created, or something in between. The classification (general type) of data base management programs determines the type of problem the program can solve:

1. File management-report generator data bases
2. Relational data bases
3. Hierarchical data bases
4. Network data bases
5. Free format data bases
6. Multi-user data bases
7. Computer languages.

Most of the data base programs currently available for microcomputers are file management-report generators or relational types.

File Management-Report Generator Data Bases The needs of many business professionals are satisfied by **file management-report generator** data base programs. This type of program is not a true data base; it is often used to create and manage a single file for some single purpose with limited on-line storage capacity. A file management-report generator program controls a file that is organized into records and fields, and produces reports from the data. Figure 6–2 illustrates a file management file layout.

Relational Data Bases A relational data base is organized using files, records, and fields in a manner similar to file management systems. Relational data base systems have the additional capability to combine the data from a series of records that have a field with a matching relationship. Relational data bases do not have to be as carefully organized as file management systems, but the poorer the organization, the more slowly the system will operate. Figure 6–3 shows a relational data file layout.

The organization of relational and file management data bases looks the same. The difference is that relational data base programs have a "join" command that allows searching for all individuals with a given characteristic in a specified field, and to combine in a variety of ways the data pertaining to that characteristic. You may produce a list of all individuals in a file who live in the same zipcode area.

Hierarchical Data Bases A data base organized from the top down is called hierarchical. Such a data base does not have to be divided into fields. The hierarchical structure allows us to search the data base without being limited to

File management-report generators:
Programs designed to store, update, and retrieve business data. These programs are limited to managing simple files with narrow objectives.

```
File — scoutmasters in a district
    Record — a scoutmaster
    Fields — troop/name/street/city/
            zipcode/telephone
```

FIGURE 6–2
File Management File Layout

FIGURE 6–3
Relational Data File Layout

File — scoutmasters in a district
    Record — a scoutmaster
        Fields — troop/name/street/ . . .
You may join all records that pertain to a
given city.

searching each field. The record contents are not limited by the nature of the search procedures. The file organization determines the location of a record in the hierarchy, not the contents of a file. The organization is similar to the hierarchical organization of MS–DOS files. In the hierarchical system (see Figure 6–4) each record is related to the next higher level by its location.

Network Data Bases A network (see Figure 6–5) is similar to a hierarchical system, with the exception that it allows for multiple relationships among levels. Microcomputer programs for this type of data base are limited.

Free Format Data Bases Free format data bases (see Figure 6–6) combine different forms of data entry including text, lists, tables, charts, and graphs. Key words located in the stored data base are used to retrieve the material. Programs for microcomputers that handle this type of data base are not readily available.

Multi-User Data Bases The hardware and software technology for multi-user data bases is currently undergoing rapid change. A multi-user data base is one that allows more than a single user access at the same time. This means that two or more microcomputers are connected together and use the same on-line storage device. The problems of two users changing a record at the same time and of file security become more complex when there is more than a single user of a data base.

FIGURE 6–4
Hierarchical Data File Layout

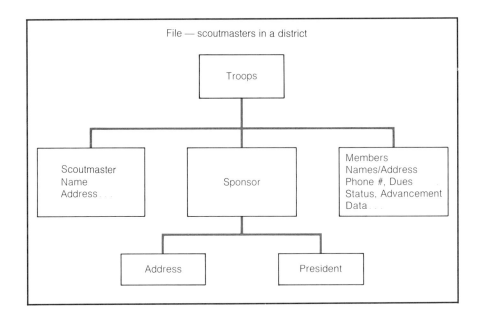

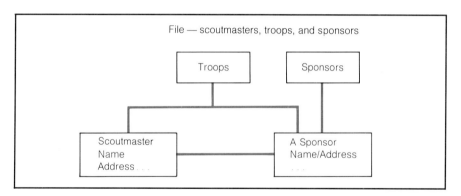

FIGURE 6–5
Network Data File Layout

Computer Languages There are few limits to the problems that may be solved by some data base programs. Complete accounting systems may be created entirely in a data base program. Computer language data base programs fit the definition of a high-level computer language: a set of near English codes used to give instructions to a computer. These data base programs often include specialized statements which make the creation and use of data bases easier than if a general purpose language were used in their creation.

Types of Index Organization

Indexing schemes reduce the amount of time needed to find data in a data base. Indexing is the manner in which a program orders the records in a file. It is often invisible to the user. The important aspect of record indexing is the amount of time needed to find the data wanted. A sequential search, starting at the beginning of a file, examining each record in turn, and seeking a particular record, quickly results in long delays for even small files, and is not an acceptable method for most data bases. The schemes commonly used for indexing are detailed in the appendix.

Compatibility

The capability to transfer files to and from data bases is a form of compatibility. A data base program is more useful if you are able to transfer files between it and other applications. There are several standards:

1. ASCII, American Standard Code for Information Interchange.

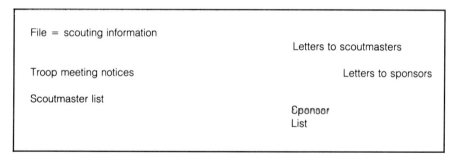

FIGURE 6–6
Data Base Free Format

2. DIF, Data Interchange Format (designed for VisiCalc).
3. SYLK, Symbolic Link (designed for MultiPlan).

Data base programs that can read and write ASCII files are able to interface with the maximum number of other data base, word processing, spreadsheet, and graphics files.

The DIF, data interchange file, is an ASCII file that is arranged in a special manner. It was developed for the spreadsheet VisiCalc to make the transfer of data between programs easier.

SYLK, Symbolic Link, is a specially formatted ASCII file created to make file transfer with MultiPlan easier.

Your ability to take advantage of new data base programs will be limited if your file cannot be transferred. Retyping a data base is expensive and subject to the introduction of costly errors.

Data base programs are often combined with other programs such as word processing, spreadsheets, communications, graphics, or others. These integrated programs, which include one or more functions, are often selected because the integrated program takes care of file transfer. All parts of the program use the same data file and operate using similar menus or functions.

Some data base programs, such as dBase II, dBase III, and dBase III Plus, include non-procedural programming languages in addition to standard data base features. A program of this nature may be used to create many different applications. You may have to balance your needs for fast results and flexibility. Programmers often find it easier to create complex applications with these very high-level non-procedural language tools. The more a program adds capabilities and approaches a very high-level language, the more difficult it is to learn and use.

Other Features

Microcomputer data base programs aid in data entry, report generation, and in custom calculation of information based on data in the data base. Report generators take the data from the file and produce hard copy using a microcomputer printer. The types of reports produced by data base programs vary from accounting to zoology.

USER WINDOW

STUDENT GRADES

Think about the amount of time it would take your university to produce your grade report by hand. Visualize the potential errors that could be produced in a manual system.

On-screen editors allow you to enter and update data in a data base. No data base remains fixed. Constant update is needed. Most programs allow you to make changes with ease, and to see the changes on the computer's monitor.

One advantage of electronically maintained data bases is that once you have entered the data, you need only update the changes and then press a key to produce a new report.

Data Base Program Function Keys and Menus PC File III uses the function keys on the IBM PC, found on the left side of the keyboard, in combination with screen selection menus. A menu is a list of different actions that may be taken. For example, in PC File III the screen looks like the one in Figure 6–7.

The PC File III menu allows you to enter the design file (edit) mode, to go to a second menu to define the formats used to produce the page, to print the current file, or to go to a second menu where you can read, save, or remove a text file from disk. You may also clear the text from the memory of your computer. This file management program places all the text in the RAM, and it may be cleared with ease.

STEPS REQUIRED IN DESIGNING AND OPERATING YOUR DATA BASE

Microcomputer data base creation requires careful planning. The functions of management are:

1. Planning (including goal setting)
2. Organizing
3. Directing
4. Controlling

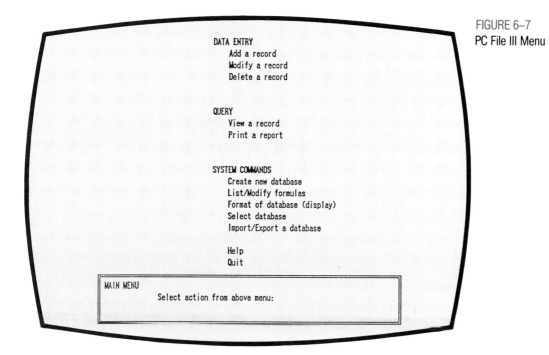

FIGURE 6–7
PC File III Menu

The data base program allows the professional user to:

1. Design the screen format used for data entry
2. Design the reports to be generated
3. Select the facts to be stored
4. Input facts
5. Update the data
6. Generate reports as needed
7. Sort the data
8. Query the data base for specific data.

The business plan and organization determine the data base reports, other outputs, and their frequency. The desired output of a data base determines how it must be designed and operated. Output includes reports and screen displays.

The steps in designing a data base are as follows:

1. Identification of output needs (reports and other output).
2. Identify the data required, sources, and the input format.
3. Design structure and size for data storage (identify file, records, and fields).
4. Identify what must be done with the input data to generate the reports and output required.
5. Identify data security needs.
6. Select and use data base program to:
   a. Create the data structure.
   b. Design the data input formats.
   c. Enter preliminary data.
   d. Design procedures for processing the data.
   e. Design outputs.
   f. Trial run.
   g. Evaluate performance.
   h. Redesign and repeat steps a–g until satisfied.
7. Operate and manage the data base.

There are constraints on all steps. Some of the facts you need may not be available. In the health business, information on personal health is restricted. Detailed financial facts are also often difficult to obtain.

User Output Needs

User needs will dictate the direction of a data base. Data bases are tools for the professional to accomplish specific objectives. The reports and other outputs are the physical manifestations of the objectives and government regulations. Examples of reports and outputs include a list of customers, employees, church members, property for sale, mailing lists, mailing labels, and automatic addressing of letters.

Figure 6–8 illustrates a report design with records referring to an individual and the following fields:

■ Last name

- First name
- How called (how the individual wants to be addressed)
- Phone
- Company
- Address
- City
- State
- Zip code
- Numerical code
- Alphabetical code

The form in Figure 6–8 was produced according to the specifications in Figure 6–9.

Some microcomputer data base programs are very high-level microcomputer languages, and they are capable of producing customized reports such as general ledgers, income and expense statements, inventory reports, telephone calls, graphic presentations, communication with other computers, and more.

The most common output from a data base is a report on a piece of paper. Reports are limited by the space available on screen and printer. There are programs that allow you to print sideways on a sheet of paper to overcome the limitations of paper size in a printer (see Figure 6–10).

Figure 6–11 is a 65–column report layout. Sixty-five columns is the default limitation on many word processors. The 65–column limitation was used to illustrate the types of problems that are encountered.

The titles and data are too long for some of the fields. There are no spaces left over to insert blanks between each field. The data will run together. Data base programs are not limited to storing the same information that is printed in a report. Using an output device that handles more than 65 columns or more than a single line for output, both data and title output may be expanded.

The four-digit numeric and alpha-numeric codes are assumed to be needed for the objective. Most data base programs differentiate between numeric data and alpha-numeric or character data. They may represent an income level, a credit rating, a health problem type, a preference in cars, computers, copiers, types of TV sets, or cameras. The data are shown in Figure 6–12.

The limitation of 65 columns reflects the users' decision to design a report that would fit on normal width paper. Most data base programs allow you to enter a greater number of characters in a given field than are printed.

Examine each field to see if the output would be useful for a business application. Since the space is limited the data printed will not be usable for

FIGURE 6–8

The Required Report as Implemented in dBase III Plus

Last	Firs t	Call	Phone	Company	Address	City	Zip S T	S Num	Alp
Prieto	Juan	Smit ty	205-555-1 212	Able Compute r Company	11 First Street	Mobile	1234 5	A L	1255	99A A
Snodgr ass	Mary	Leni.	123-555-1 111	AZ Managem ent Service s In	4151 Bay Avenue	Atlant a	4444 5	N J	5555	AlB B
Conrad	Leo	Dr. Leo	123-555-1 116	Imagine ering Concept s Inc.	1234 Park Drive	Atlant a	4444 5	N J	5556	A2A A
Timbal ov	Step hani e	Dr. T	123-555-1 111	AZ Managem ent Service s In	4151 Bay Avenue	Atlant a	4444 5	N J	5555	B2B B
Rockab le	Bett y	Rock y	333-555-1 111	Lost Lane School	55 Byte Drive	Miami	1111 2	N Y	2222	A3C C
Duval	Robe rt	Bob	333-555-2 222	Western Wear Clothes Inc.	12 Label Lane	Miami	1111 2	N Y	2223	A3C C
Kahn	Joe	Joe	205-555-1 233	Able Compute r Company	11 First Avenue	Mobile	1234 5	A L	5555	AlA A
Cheng	Thuc	Thuc	333-666-1 111	Boston Compute r Company	11 First Avenue	Wester n	1111 5	A L	5555	A2B B
Anders on	Stev e	Mr. Ande rs	222-444-5 555	Eastern Microco mputer Co.	1 Compute r Lane	Boston	9999 5	C A	5555	B6X X
Zimmer man	Caro l	Caro l	123-555-1 lll	AZ Managem ent Service s In	4151 Bay Avenue	Atlant a	4444 5	N J	5555	B2B B

Printer output from different versions of dBase is similar.

many applications. As a user you must determine your output needs and the limitations of the equipment used and then make a careful trade-off between them if a conflict occurs, as in this case. Some fields are fixed, such as the telephone number and zip code. The code fields must also be shown in their entirety. Some data base systems allow you to add spaces and the extra characters in phone numbers and zip codes that make them more readable. The layout of a report requires a lot of careful counting and consideration of each output.

Data Required, Sources, Input Format, Design Structure, and Size

The data base output defines the needed input. The report in our example includes the last name, first name, how called (for personal letters), phone number, company name, address, city, state, zip code, and two codes for customer information. These facts must be found someplace. Sources include salesperson reports, other data bases, and copies of orders. Once located, the data must be entered into the data base. Figure 6–13 illustrates a typical input screen for these facts.

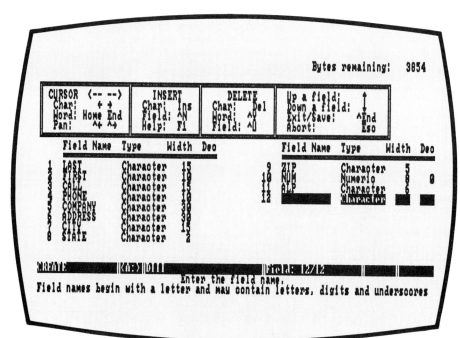

FIGURE 6–9
Defining Fields in dBASE III PLUS

The facts, once obtained, must be entered into the data base. Most entries will be through the keyboard onto a form designed and displayed on the screen. Some data may be entered directly from other data bases by **downloading** the data electronically. Data may also be **uploaded** to a data base from a microcomputer.

The data entry screen format must usually be defined by the data base user. Figure 6–14 shows how the screen format is defined in dBASE II and III. The same care used in laying out the output format pays dividends when defining the input format. The data entry task is made easier by a careful layout. Following the layout of the source documents, if there is a consistent one, is often useful.

Downloading:
The transfer of data from another computer into yours.

Uploading:
The transfer of data from your computer to another computer.

Operations

The operations needed in the simple example are sorting, querying, report generation, and some addition. Most data base programs provide all these capabilities with the exception of addition. You must examine your requirements, determine what you plan to do with the data, and then eliminate from consideration all data base programs which do not have the capabilities required.

Security

Management has a professional, social, moral, and legal obligation to control the quality and use of the data in their data base. A data base must be protected from both internal and external contamination and misuse. Equipment must be protected from damage and theft. A data base with contaminated data may lead

FIGURE 6–10
Sideways Printed Report

	Aug.	Sep.	Oct.	Nov.	Dec.
		(last 5 months projected)			
	405,075	567,516	554,109	575,362	617,345
	116,213	127,423	124,687	175,298	135,083
	42,052	46,284	48,219	50,045	57,225
	50,999	50,417	50,372	55,058	60,118
	614,339	791,640	777,387	855,763	869,771
	236,225	230,128	219,613	218,449	220,123
	8,449	9,207	8,763	8,789	8,884
	14,880	14,501	13,435	11,238	12,433
	36,738	30,777	41,122	43,972	42,873
	296,292	284,613	282,933	282,448	284,313
	17,817	18,552	19,001	19,224	17,335
	61,085	60,135	59,245	61,444	60,187
	1,046	1,030	1,555	1,322	1,088
	79,948	79,717	79,801	81,990	78,610

to decisions that hurt both the individuals whose data is in the data base and the company. The misuse of data by both employees and outsiders can damage all involved. The loss of equipment is the least crucial loss although it does cost the company dollars.

Data may be contaminated by the entry of bad data. This can happen in the normal course of business, and management must develop methods to detect and purge bad data.

Data contamination can also occur when an employee who is unhappy enters bad data to damage the company. If your system uses telephone communication input, an unauthorized outsider may break into your system and enter bad data. The bad data could result in millions of dollars of funds being transferred to an account out of the country, or your company could injure someone because of the bad data, and you could find yourself on the receiving end of a lawsuit.

FIGURE 6–11
Definition of Field Size For
65–Column Report

Last Name	First Name	How Called	Phone	Company	Address	City	St	Zip	Numeric Code	Alpha Code
5	5	4	9	8	7	6	2	3	3	3

There are ten spaces between fields for a total of 55 plus 10 or 65 spaces.

FIGURE 6–12   The 65–Column Report

```
O | Last    First How Phone       Company Address City    StZip  Num Alph | O
  | Name    Name Calle                                     Code Code Cod  |
O | Prieto Juan Smitt2055551212Able Coml1 FirstMobile AL12345125599AA      | O
  | SnodgraMary Leni 1235551111AZ Manag4151 BayAtlantaNJ444455555AlBB      |
O | Conrad Leo  Dr. L1235551116Imaginee1234 ParAtlantaNJ444455556A2AA      | O
  | TimbaloStephDr. T1235551111AZ Manag4151 BayAtlantaNJ444455555B2BB      |
O | RockablBettyRocky3335551111Lost Lan55 Byte Miami   NY111122222A3CC     | O
  | Duval  RoberBob  3335552222Western 12 LabelMiami   NY111122223A3CC     |
O | Kahn   Joe  Joe  2055551233Able Coml1 FirstMobile AL123455555AlAA      | O
  | Cheng  Thuc Thuc 3336661111Boston Cl1 FirstWesternAL111155555A2BB      |
O | AndersoSteveMr.An2224445555Eastern 1 ComputBoston CA999955555B6XX      | O
  | ZimmermCarolCarol1235551111AZ Manag4151 BayAtlantaNJ444455555B2BB      |
```

Some report generators truncate as shown. Others print the entire contents of a field, and wrap-around the output when it does not fit in the space available.

The destruction of data may be caused by individuals who are part of your organization or external to it, or by some electronic power or hardware failure. Good backup procedures help protect you against these problems. With good backup procedures it is not difficult to replace data that has been destroyed. It is often less costly to have all your data destroyed than to have it polluted or misused.

For individual users of microcomputers, data security may mean locking up the floppy disks when they are removed from the microcomputer, locking up the microcomputer if using a hard (fixed) disk system, adapting a software protection scheme, using passwords and account numbers, or a combination of these measures.

The security problem becomes more complex when there is a number of users of the same microcomputer with a fixed non-removable hard disk. If you have an automatic answering telephone device on your microcomputer or use the microcomputer as part of a network, you will have the same security problems as a large computer timesharing system.

Suggested security procedures include:

1. Long passwords to make exhaustive searches difficult.
2. Passwords containing random characters.
3. Limiting the number of trials to three or less.
4. Invisible passwords during operation.

```
RECORD # 00003
LAST:NAME  :Conrad        :
FIRST      :Leo      :
HOW:CALLED :Dr. Leo   :
PHONE      :123-555-1116:
COMPANY    :Imagineering Concepts Inc:
ADDRESS    :1234 Park Drive        :
CITY       :Atlanta:
STATE      :NJ:
ZIP        :44445:
NUM:CODE   :5556:
ALP:CODE   :A2AA:
```

FIGURE 6–13
Screen Input

FIGURE 6–14
dBase II and dBase III
File Organization Specification

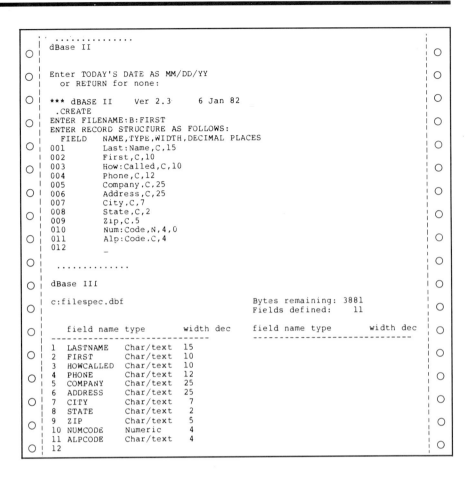

```
. . . . . . . . . . . . . .
dBase II


Enter TODAY'S DATE AS MM/DD/YY
  or RETURN for none:

*** dBASE II    Ver 2.3    6 Jan 82
  .CREATE
ENTER FILENAME:B:FIRST
ENTER RECORD STRUCTURE AS FOLLOWS:
  FIELD    NAME,TYPE,WIDTH,DECIMAL PLACES
001       Last:Name,C,15
002       First,C,10
003       How:Called,C,10
004       Phone,C,12
005       Company,C,25
006       Address,C,25
007       City,C,7
008       State,C,2
009       Zip,C,5
010       Num:Code,N,4,0
011       Alp:Code,C,4
012       _


. . . . . . . . . . . . .

dBase III

c:filespec.dbf              Bytes remaining: 3881
                            Fields defined:    11

   field name  type     width dec   field name type      width dec
---------------------------------   --------------------------------
 1  LASTNAME   Char/text  15
 2  FIRST      Char/text  10
 3  HOWCALLED  Char/text  10
 4  PHONE      Char/text  12
 5  COMPANY    Char/text  25
 6  ADDRESS    Char/text  25
 7  CITY       Char/text   7
 8  STATE      Char/text   2
 9  ZIP        Char/text   5
10  NUMCODE    Numeric     4
11  ALPCODE    Char/text   4
12
```

5. Careful administration of passwords.

6. Multi-level system: One password for read only; second password for read and write.

7. Change passwords often (monthly).

8. Create special operating procedures for when your security system is attacked.

9. Holding area for new data—data check before it is added to the data base.

10. Limiting remote access to read only or input to holding area only.

11. Dial back devices.

12. Logs of data use and access.

It is difficult to protect yourself completely from other computer users who wish to break into your system when it is on line with an auto-answer telephone device and in an unattended mode. Timesharing managers spend many hours developing schemes to protect their computers from outsiders. If you are concerned with data security, we recommend that you not use an auto-answer device.

Your company is responsible for what is in the data base and for the use of that data. Social attitudes toward information about individuals recorded in data bases are changing, along with the laws governing the use of such information. You must make sure you operate within current legal and moral constraints. It is important to enter accurate data into your data base, and to carefully control the data's distribution.

Selecting and Using Data Base Programs

The objective determines the size of the file, record, fields, and the type of record/field (fixed or variable). Most data base programs require that each record and field be a fixed size. Fixed size records and fields waste space. Programs often have fixed records and fields because it is easier for the programmer to create other capabilities with these limitations.

Variable size fields often mean larger data bases may be maintained in the given amount of on-line storage. The business need for large data bases must be balanced with the data base program's capability to manipulate the data.

The selection of a data base program is the matching of needs with program capabilities. The needs include output requirements, data required, sources, input format, structure and size for data storage, operations, data security, and the management procedures planned for the system's operation.

Operating and Managing the Data Base

To be useful to the user, a data base must produce results that are:

- Relevant
- Accurate
- Reliable
- Timely
- Available
- Secure
- Flexible
- Economical

The relevancy of the output of a data base often depends on how it is managed and operated as much as on the selection of the data base program. Only the user can determine if the facts contained in a data base are of value in a given situation.

The expression "garbage in garbage out" has been picked up for popular use in the computer field. "Garbage in garbage out" (or GIGO) refers to the necessity of carefully controlling and selecting the facts that go into a data base to make sure the information wanted is available when requested. The facts entered into a data base must be both accurate and measured in a consistent manner for the facts to be reliable for making decisions.

If a data base requires constant update, management must make sure the updates are made. Old data may often have no value or even a negative value in a given business decision-making situation.

One reason for the growth of microcomputer data bases is that they provide the professional with a method of getting the information needed to perform. The facts stored in the data base are readily available. There are "user friendly" data base programs designed to make it easy for the computer beginner to get started. But "user friendly" programs also tend to be "abuser friendly" programs, that is, unauthorized individuals can break in and get information out of such systems.

A data base program must be flexible. Business exists in an ever-changing environment. Objectives change as the environment changes. Data bases must change and adapt to the changing business objectives. This means a continual management commitment to operating and directing the data base.

Information has value. It costs money to create and manage a data base. If at any time the value of the information generated by a data base is less than the cost of operating the system, the continued existence of the data base must be questioned.

VARYING CAPABILITIES OF DATA BASE PROGRAMS

All data base programs make it possible to create, maintain, and use data bases, but there are many data base programs available. Table 6–2 compares some of the more popular data base programs.

TABLE 6–2

Comparison of Data Base Programs

Features	dBASE III Plus	Knowledgeman	PC File III	R-base 5000	Reflex
Configuration—					
RAM required	256K	320K	128K	128K	384K
Disk drives	2	2	2	1	2
Hard drive	supported	supported	supported		supported
General					
Function key	yes	yes	yes	yes	
Menu driven	yes	yes	yes	yes	yes
Family			yes		yes
Fixed fields	yes	yes		yes	
Fixed records	yes	yes		yes	
File management			yes	yes	
Relational	yes	yes			
Math	yes	yes	limited	limited	yes
Data Entry & Update					
Sort	yes	yes		yes	yes
Index	7	4	none		none
Search	yes	yes	yes	yes	yes
Save/Recall					
Auto backup	no	no	no	no	no
Merge files	yes	yes	yes	yes	yes
Change file	yes	yes	yes	yes	yes
definition	yes	yes	yes	yes	yes
Import/export					
ASCII	yes	yes	yes	yes	yes

The price of data base programs start as low as $40 and may be as high as $2,000. Some programs are sold as shareware. The user may obtain a copy, try it out, and then become a registered owner if the program proves useful.

The user needs data base programs for maintaining personal, professional, and other business records. Setting up data bases requires careful work and attention to details. There are many commercial data base programs that make the setup and operation of these programs easy for end users. Some of the important aspects of data bases are:

1. A data base is a collection of data used for a series of different purposes.
2. Data base programs solve problems.
3. The development and application of microcomputer data bases are dependent upon the capabilities and capacities of the available hardware.
4. There are some basic terms that must be understood when learning about data bases.
5. Data base programs vary from file management-report generators to computer languages.
6. Data bases are classified as file management, relational, hierarchical, network, free format, or multi-user.
7. Indexing schemes reduce the amount of time needed to find data in a data base.
8. The capability to exchange files between data bases is a form of compatibility.
9. Microcomputer data base programs aid in report generation and in custom calculations of information based on data in the data base.
10. Microcomputer data base creation requires careful planning.
11. Needs dictate the direction of a data base.
12. Errors will be made when entering data into a data base. There are easy methods for updating and correcting errors.

KEY TERMS

Attribute	File maintenance
Data	File management-report generator
Data base	Information
Data base management program	Knowledge
Facts	Non-procedural language
Fields	Record
File	Report generation

REVIEW QUESTIONS

1. Define the following key terms.
   a. Facts
   b. Data
   c. Information
   d. Knowledge

e. Data base

f. Data base management program

2. What is file maintenance and report generation?

3. Give some examples of input devices used to enter data into data bases.

4. Why did the number of microcomputer data base programs and applications start to increase?

5. Give some examples of data bases used in business.

6. What is a data base file, a record, a field, an attribute?

7. Name the classifications (general types) of data base programs.

8. What is a file management-report generator program?

9. What is unique about a relational data base program?

10. What is a hierarchical data base?

11. What is a network data base?

12. What is a free format data base?

13. What is unique about a multi-user data base?

14. What is indexing? What is a sequential search?

15. Identify some standard file transfer formats used for data base files.

16. What are the decision-making areas of management?

17. Identify the steps in designing a data base.

18. What is the relationship between reports and objectives?

19. How is data base output related to the input?

20. What is uploading/downloading?

21. What may result from contaminated data?

22. What is the trade-off between user friendly and abuser friendly designed programs?

DISCUSSION AND APPLICATION QUESTIONS

1. Identify some data bases where you would expect to find information about yourself listed.

2. Identify some data bases maintained by your university.

3. Identify some data bases maintained by your religious organization.

4. Identify some data bases maintained by your local government.

5. Visit a local business and identify some data bases it maintains.

1. Load your data base program into a microcomputer. Enter the structure:

Field	Size	Type	Decimal Points
Last Name	22	Character	—
First Name	22	Character	—
How called	15	Character	—
Identification Number	9	Character	—
Telephone Number	10	Character	—
Street Address	22	Character	—
City	15	Character	—
State	2	Character	—
Zip Code	5	Character	—
Amount	9	Number	2
Date Due	6	Special*	

*Use the procedure in your data base for handling dates. If there is not one, enter the date as a single number YYMMDD. Save, display, and print a copy of the structure.

2. Enter and save the data into the structure developed in assignment 1.

Last Name	First Name	How Called	Id. Number	Telephone Number	Street Address	City	State	Zip	Amount	Date Due
Boothe	Frank	FB	155260223	2055555555	123 West End Lane	Atlanta	AL	55555	$456.77	12/12/86
Armenable	Leanoria	Leo	111223333	1112223333	8564 Lost Lane	Mobile	NJ	11111	$122.33	01/13/88
Poser	Judy	Judy	222113333	9992221111	12 Bay Road	New Orleans	GA	22222	$ 12.33	02/12/89
Renser	Raymond	Ray	999229999	8882221111	65 Red Lane	New York	WI	44444	$987.22	02/02/88
Candely	Fred	Candy	222334444	5556667777	88 West Wood	Miami	FL	23442	$786.99	03/03/87

Print the data entered to demonstrate it was entered and saved.

3. Identify the help routine in your data base and make a screen copy of one of the help screens.

4. Develop a data base to store the amount of miles traveled and the amount of gasoline used per tank. The objective is to calculate the gasoline mileage of each tank.

Structure Field	Size	Type	Decimal Point
Miles	7	Numeric	2
Gallons	7	Numeric	2

Gasoline mileage report:

Tank #	Miles	Gallons	Miles per gallon
1	220	11.9	
2	234	11.0	
3	263	11.1	
4	248	12.2	
5	245	11.3	
6	256	11.4	
7	266	11.5	

The last column must be calculated by your data base.

5. Develop a data base to calculate the batting average of the members of a baseball team. The output should be:

Player	Number at bat	Number of Singles	Doubles	Triples	Homers	Total Hits
Jim Jones	34	4	1	2	3	0.294117
Stan Smith	45	5	3	3	1	0.266666
Carol Kim	33	4	2	2	2	0.303030
Andy Rodrege	23	2	3	0	0	0.217391
Samual Smith	12	1	1	0	1	0.25
Andress Able	44	4	1	1	0	0.136363

Add to the data base players' telephone numbers and address. Produce a report sorted by batting average from high to low. This is an expansion of a spreadsheet assignment.

6. Print an ASCII text file for one of the assignments you have completed. Transfer the file to your word processor and use it to create a report including a number of different fonts as are available in your printer.

7. Setup a data base for a company with the following fields:

Field	Size	Type	
Date	6	Number or Special	
Stock Name	22	Character	
Price	15	Numeric	3 beyond decimal point
Shares	5	Numeric	0 beyond decimal point

After creating the data base, enter the closing value of the stock's selling price for fifteen days. Produce a report that calculates the closing value of the stock.

8. Print an ASCII file from assignment 2 above. Prepare the data for transfer to some other program.

9. Develop a method to produce a mailing label from a data base containing names and address.

10. In assignment 1, a data base was created including:

- Last Name
- First Name
- How called
- Identification Number
- Telephone Number
- Street Address
- City
- State
- Zip Code
- Amount
- Date Due

Sort the records in the data base according to last name. Create an index for city, state, zip code, amount, and date due. Print reports in order of the data base records and each index.

11. Use the baseball team data base in assignment 3 as a foundation for a data base of your favorite team. Maintain the records in last-name order. Add indexes for the number of times at bat, batting average, and position. Print the data base according to last name, number of times at bat, batting average, and position.

12. Create (program) a grade sheet for a class. Include freshman, sophomore, junior, senior. Calculate the average of each grading criteria, each student's average, and the class average. Produce a report of the grades of all freshmen separated from all other members of the class. Produce a report for the class.

13. Create (program) a data base to maintain the finances of a club. Develop a report on the finances of a student club or other activity. Use the manual finance report as a model.

14. Data base number one contains the following:

Field	Size
Company Name	22
Street Address	22
City	15
State	2
Zip	5
Contact	22
Code Number	9

Data base number two contains:

Field	Size
Code Number	9
Date of transaction	6
Quantity	12 with 2 decimal points
Description	22
Price	12 with 2 decimal points

One objective is to create an invoice using the model below:

```
                          I N V O I C E
- - - - - - - - - - - - - - - - - - - - - - - - - - - - - - - - - - - - - -
From:                                 To:
Sales and Services, Inc.                 _____
3375 Bay Lane                            _____
Brooklyn, NY 55555                       _____
(555) 555-5555                        Atten: _____
- - - - - - - - - - - - - - - - - - - - - - - - - - - - - - - - - - - - - -
QUANTITY DESCRIPTION                                  PRICE     AMOUNT
- - - - - - - - - - - - - - - - - - - - - - - - - - - - - - - - - - - - - -




- - - - - - - - - - - - - - - - - - - - - - - - - - - - - - - - - - - - - -
                                                 TOTAL
                                                 = = = = = = = = = =
```

The amount should be calculated by multiplying the quantity times the price. The total is the sum of all the individual amounts.

15. The troop budget report contains the following fields:

- Date received from or paid to
- Dues income
- Registration income

- Magazine income
- Other income
- Registration cost
- Magazine cost
- Insignia cost
- Supplies cost
- Special fund cost
- Material cost
- Activities cost

In addition to the detailed field data, a report is required to have a sum of the incomes, a sum of costs, and a balance.

Prepare a structure. Use your best estimates for size of fields and type. Enter in the following data and prepare a report.

					Income				Expenses						
Date	Activity	Income	Expenses	Balance	Dues	Reg.	Mag.	Other	Reg.	Mag.	Insigna	Supplies	Special	Mat.	Act.
	Original Bal.			855.44											
12/1	Annual dues	122.34			122.34										
12/8	Headquarters		98.00						98.00						
12/15	Material		5.45											5.45	

16. Create a data base to model a checkbook. A checkbook register contains the following information:

Date	Check Number	Check issued to or deposits received from	Amount Deposited	Cleared	Amount of Check	Balance
—	—	Original balance				$2,300.00
8/13	233	Rent			$167.88	
8/14	234	Utilities			133.44	
8/14	235	Telephone			51.22	
8/14	—	Salary check	$1,200.77			
8/15	—	Sold radio	33.45			
8/15	236	Cash			165.44	
8/16	237	Food store			87.88	

The bank records show:

Previous Balance	We have added:		We have subtracted:			Current Balance
Statement	Number	Deposits	Number	Checks	Serv.Charg	
$2,300.00	3	$1,400.77	5	$676.86	$1.44	$3022.47

Checking Account Transactions

Date	Amount	Description
8/15	$1,200.77	DEPOSIT
8/16	33.45	DEPOSIT
8/16	100.00	DEPOSIT

Checks

Date	Amount
8/17	$167.88
8/17	133.44
8/18	165.44
8/18	87.88
8/18	122.22

At the beginning of the period your balance and the bank's balance were the same. There were no outstanding transactions of any type.

In your data base start with your balance, add the not-cleared checks, subtract the unrecorded checks, subtract the not-cleared deposits, add the unrecorded deposits, make adjustments for errors in recording and service charges, and produce a final balance to be compared to the bank's.

Compare the use of a data base and spreadsheet to solve this problem.

1. (General Business.) Set up a data base for inventory control with the following fields:

- Stock number
- Description
- Wholesale unit cost
- Quantity on hand
- Quantity on order
- Reorder point
- Sales this month
- Sales year to date

Enter the following data:

Stock Number	Description	Wholesale Unit Cost	Quantity on Hand	Quantity on Order	Reorder Point	Sales Month	Sales Year to Date
15525	RS–232 cable	9.55	8	12	12	5	36
15684	Parallel cable	8.22	15	0	12	9	44
14871	Null modems	20.11	2	0	1	0	8
12322	Cable ends	1.00	22	30	24	12	78
23232	Cable tool	5.22	5	6	5	3	22

Produce reports of entire inventory and stock numbers with orders outstanding.

2. (Clubs.) Use your data base to set up a club membership record keeping procedure. Each member must be listed, with telephone number, the academic division, dues status, and attendance record.

Some data base programs may be used to solve the same type of problem that may be solved using spreadsheet programs. If you have a program such as dBase II or III, you may solve all of the problems in Chapter 5. Below are some additional problems of this type.

3. (Education.) Create a data base for a class roll:

Number	Name	Student Number	Exam #1	Exam #2	Final Report
1.	Mary Prieto	11122			
2.	Leo Anderson	12345			
3,	Fred Prieto	54123			
4.	Bill Cheng	13487			
5.	Jean Beitel	78451			
6.	Carol Baker	02635			
7.	Fred Osborne	11223			

Add equations to find the sum, average, and standard deviation of each grading criterion, each student, and the total class effort.

4. (General Business.) A checkbook register contains the following information:

Date	Check No.	Checks issued to or deposits received	Amount Deposit	Amount Check	Balance
—	—	Original balance			1,225.22
9/1	210	Rent		150.00	
9/2	211	Utilities		101.00	
9/3	212	Telephone		31.22	
9/6	—	Salary check	1,500.26		
9/7	213	Cash		160.00	
9/11	214	Food store		102.33	

The bank record shows:

Balance last Statement	We have added: Number	Deposits	We have subtracted: Number	Checks	Service Charge	Balance
1,225.22	2	2,000.26	6	644.55	1.22	2579.71

Checking Account Transactions

Date	Amount	Description
9/6	1,500.26	Deposit
9/8	500.00	Deposit

Checks

Date	Amount
9/2	150.00
9/5	101.00
9/8	31.22
9/8	100.00
9/12	160.00
9/15	102.33

At the beginning of the period your balance and the bank's balance were the same. There were no outstanding transactions of any type.

Set up a data base program to start with your balance, add the not-cleared checks, subtract the unrecorded checks, subtract the not-cleared deposits, add the unrecorded deposits, make adjustments for errors in recording the service charges, and produce a final balance to be compared to the banks.

5. (Accounting.) Set up and organize a data base to enter a chart of accounts, a debit and credit field. Add the capability to sum both the debits and credits.

Chart of Accounts	Type	Liquidity	Debit	Credit
Cash account	A	L	9,200	
Accounts receivable	A	L	1,200	
Accounts payable	L	C		1,400
Retained earnings	E	T		2,000
Capital stock	E	T		4,000
Supplies	A	L	500	
Building	A	F	12,000	
Build-reserve for Depreciation	A	F		4,000

Chart of Accounts	Type	Liquidity	Debit	Credit	
Trucks	A	F	8,000		
Truck-reserve for Depreciation	A	F			3,000
Equipment	A	F	22,000		
Equip-reserve for Depreciation	A	F			6,000
Notes payable	L	C			8,000
Loans payable	L	T			24,500

Under type A is an asset, L is a liability, E is for stockholders equity.
Under liquidity L is for liquid, C is for current, T is for long-term, and F is for fixed.
Use the codes to help sort the data base into a good presentation order.

SELECTED REFERENCES

Ruff, Laura B., and Mary K. Weitzer. *Understanding and Using pfs: FILE/REPORT.* West Publishing Company, 1986.

Fife, Dennis W., W. Terry Hardgrave, and Donald R. Deutsch. *Database Concepts.* South-Western Publishing Co., 1986.

Harrison, William. *Computers and Information Processing.* West Publishing Company, 1985.

Hetzel, William, and David R. Adams. *Computer Information Systems Development.* South-Western Publishing Co., 1985.

Loomis, Mary E. S. *The Database Book.* Macmillan Publishing Company, 1987.

Ross, Steven C. *Understanding and Using dBASE III.* West Publishing Company, 1986.

Ross, Steven C. *Understanding and Using dBASE III Plus.* West Publishing Company, 1988.

Schnake, Marilyn A. *The World of Computers and Data Processing.* West Publishing Company, 1985.

Watterson, Karen L. *Understanding and Using R:BASE 5000.* West Publishing Company, 1987.

7

GOALS

Upon completion of this chapter you will be able to:

Identify the hardware needed for microcomputer graphics.

List the types of microcomputer graphics.

Review the differences between types of graphic programs.

Identify where graphics are needed.

Discuss the fundamental tasks of graphics.

List some popular graphics programs.

OUTLINE

Chapter Goals

Graphics Hardware Needs
Internal Memory (RAM and ROM)
Input Devices
Output Devices
On-Line Storage

Why You Should Know about Graphics Software
Using Graphics

Standard Charts
Spreadsheet and Data Base Graphics
Chart Programs
Analytical Graphics Programs

Image Creating and Editing
Draw, Freehand, and Paint Programs
Assembly–Clip-Art Programs
Screen Capture Programs
Font Control

Graphics and Text Output
Desktop Publishing
Slide, Animation, and Sound Shows
Engineering Applications

Comparing Graphics Program

Summary

Key Terms

Review Questions

Discussion and Application Questions

Laboratory Assignments

Selected References

GRAPHICS

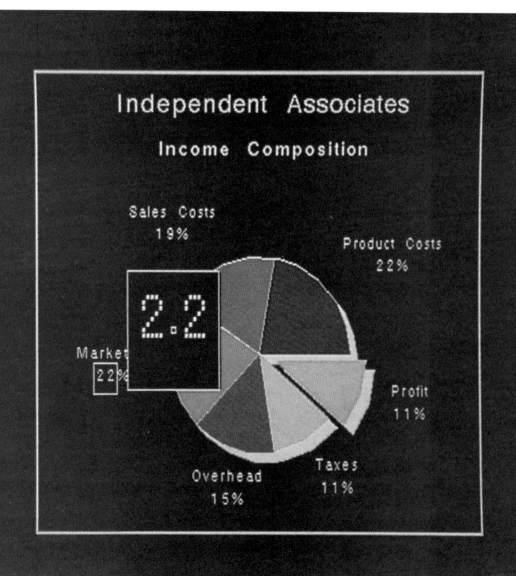

MICROS IN ACTION

Jean King and Associates, a public relations and advertising agency, is approximately seven years old and employs four individuals. It has maintained a rapid growth in sales and client base.

Among other activities the staff prepare presentations for meetings and publications in which graphics play an important part. They have identified their microcomputer needs as:

1. Graphics for client presentations.
2. Word processing for letters, presentations, and contracts.
3. Data base for client characteristics and advertising outlets.

The types of graphics needed include bar charts, pie charts, and some special presentation capabilities that combine microcomputer outputs with pictures. They use static slide shows, animation, and animation combined with sound.

The microcomputer is a tool for creating graphic displays on screen, paper, film, and other media. Graphics involves picture and picture-text creation and processing. The microcomputer and its graphic programs can help you create/edit, store/recall, display, and print graphic presentations more quickly and easily than any manual method.

Microcomputer graphic programs may be classified as:

- Standard Charts
- Image Creation and Edit
- Graphics and Text Output (Desktop Publishing)

Standard charts include the creation of line, bar, pie, XY, and scatter charts. Many standard charts are produced by spreadsheet programs. The variety and options available in stand-alone graphics programs require that examination. Figure 7–1 is pie chart produced by Lotus and Figure 7–2 is a three-dimensional pie chart not currently available in spreadsheet sheet programs.

Image creating and editing programs help the user create images, combine images, and edit images. Figure 7–3 is a house that is part of an image library (also referred to as **clip-art** or symbol libraries) of PC-Key-Draw.

Graphics and text output programs combine the products of word processing and graphics programs. Figure 7–4 is output that uses the capability of a word processor to select from the variety of fonts available to a printer and the capability of a graphics-merging program to insert graphics into the text.

Image creating and editing programs:
Programs that help the user create original images, assemble images from a variety of sources, and edit or enhance images.

Clip-art library:
A collection of images provided with image-creation drawings that may be recalled and used to create new illustrations.

GRAPHICS HARDWARE NEEDS

The graphics application determines the type and amount of:

- Internal memory (RAM and ROM)
- Input devices
- Output devices
- On-line storage

MICROS IN ACTION

Graphic Stories

Jean King and Associates uses the exploded pie chart because it allows them to highlight a selected factor when making a presentation for fund-raising campaigns and government analysis. They also use bar charts and line charts.

Internal Memory (RAM and ROM)

Screen graphic resolution determines the amount of RAM and ROM needed. Table 7–1 lists the number of bytes of RAM required for some selected screen resolutions.

Three bits per pixel are needed for eight shades of brightness. A 1024 by 1024 screen in eight shades or colors requires a total of 3,145,728 bits or 393,216 bytes. Table 7–2 illustrates the method for using three bits to create eight shades.

ROM may be designed to contain special graphics generators for screen output and special fonts for printer output. Some printers have ROM with five or more complete sets of fonts. Figure 7–5 illustrates laser printer fonts by their code number.

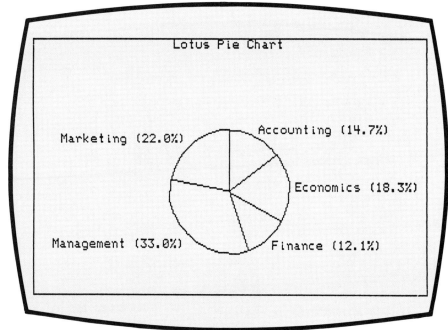

FIGURE 7–1
Lotus Pie Chart

FIGURE 7–2
Energraphics Three-Dimensional
Pie Chart

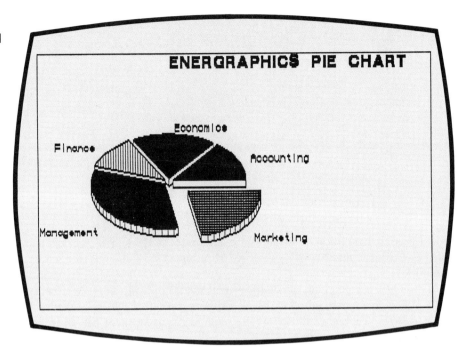

Input Devices

The keyboard, mouse, and scanner (digitizer) are common methods of data input for graphic programs. Mouse programs often will not work with the keyboard arrow keys. Some graphics programs use joy sticks and digitizing pads.

FIGURE 7–3
PC–Key-Draw House

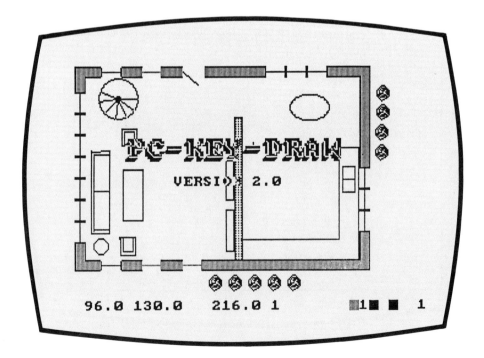

FIGURE 7–4
Graphics and Text Output

A scanner (optical character reader) has a lens with which it views a picture or image. Electronics converts the picture to digits (bits) to be produced as a pixel pattern on a screen. There are scanners that can recognize a letter and save the ASCII code associated with the letter.

Output Devices

Graphics requires good quality monitors for editing, and good quality printers for hard copies. The cost of this equipment is related to the resolution that it can produce.

Generally monochrome, EGA, or PGA monitors are needed. Monitor resolution depends on the monitor and the codes sent to it. Printed circuit boards, monitors, and programs may be purchased to:

- Display 80 columns by 66 rows
- Display 132 columns by 44 rows
- Display graphics and text
- Display special characters

Printers vary in price according to their speed of output. Dot matrix, laser, ink jet, plotter, or similar printers may be used to copy microcomputer screen

Screen Pixels	Bits (Pixels)	Bytes (8 bits per byte)
640 by 200	128,000	16,000
1024 by 1024	1,048,576	131,072
1024 by 1024 and 8 colors	3,145,728	393,216

TABLE 7–1
Resolution versus RAM

FIGURE 7–5
Fonts QMS Kiss Laser Printer

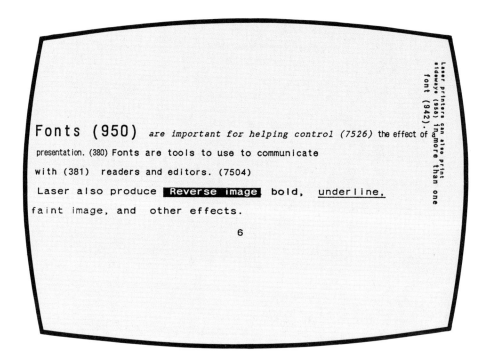

graphics. A printer that allows you to control the color and position of each individual dot or to direct pen strokes must be used. Figure 7–6 shows a color printer that allows the user to control individual dots.

Usually, the number of dots produced by a printer does not match the number of dots (pixels) on most microcomputer screens. The quality of hard copy is a function of the number of dots produced per square inch by a dot matrix or laser printer.

Plotters vary in price depending on speed, quality, and the size of the drawing produced. Figure 7–7 illustrates a plotter.

Plotter printers are programmed in a manner similar to the technique used to create graphics on a microcomputer screen. Plotters use ballpoint and felt-tip pens to produce their images. They are slow but may be controlled directly by the microcomputer through special programs.

Screen graphics do not look the same when copied by plotter printers or other devices, because the height-to-width ratio and media is different.

TABLE 7–2
Shades

Shade	Three-bit pattern
1	0 0 0
2	1 0 0
3	0 1 0
4	0 0 1
5	0 1 1
6	1 0 1
7	1 1 0
8	1 1 1

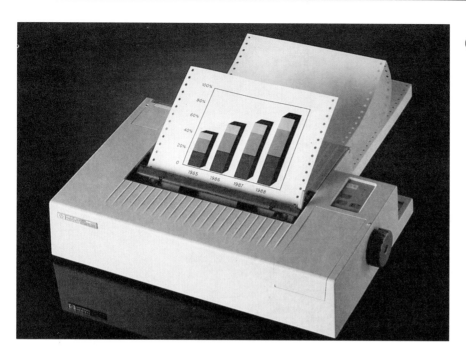

FIGURE 7–6
Color Printer

Utilities for sale as separate programs for the Apple, IBM PC, and other microcomputers can copy both monochrome and color screens. Color printers, plotters, and image cameras (Figure 7–8) make it almost as easy to produce color graphics as black and white pictures. An image camera directly captures the screen display before it is sent to the printer.

FIGURE 7–7
Plotter

FIGURE 7–8
Computer Image Recorder

On-Line Storage

Graphics programs may come on a series of as many as five or six disks. It is easier to use a hard disk where all the programs may be recorded. A floppy disk user of large graphics programs often finds it necessary to change disks.

A graphic image requiring over 360K cannot be stored on a single floppy disk. Hard disks are needed for many graphics applications.

WHY YOU SHOULD KNOW ABOUT GRAPHICS SOFTWARE

Academic and professional reports may be enhanced through the careful use of graphics. Reports enhanced with graphics earn better grades, sell more products, help obtain jobs, and usually result in greater benefits than the effort used to produce the graphics.

USER WINDOW

GRAPHICS IMPROVES REPORTS

Judy was taking a course in economics. Her homework assignment required her to study the use of funds in city government. She used a program to produce a pie and bar chart for her report showing a departmental breakdown of costs.

The results impressed both her fellow students and the instructor.

The variety of graphics programs includes:

- Standard Charts
    Spreadsheet and Data Base Graphics Programs
    Chart Programs
    Analytical Graphics Programs
- Image Creation, Assembly, and Enhancement
    Draw, Freehand, and Paint Programs
    Assembly–Clip-Art Libraries
    Screen Capture Programs
    Font Control
- Graphics and Text Output
    Electronic Publishing
        Page Layout Programs
        Merging Programs
    Slide, Animation, and Sound Show Programs.

USING GRAPHICS

A user can select from a large number of graphics displays and programs. Each program has different controls and capabilities. For example, controls available for the creation of a pie chart determine:

- Which piece (if any) is exploded.
- What color or shade is selected for each piece.
- The type of fonts used.
- Two- or three-dimensional format depending on:
    The objective of the display.
    The audience.
    The method of presentation and reproduction.

If the display's objective is to show that a department is spending less than other departments, the piece of the pie representing expenditures could be exploded and colored more boldly than the other pieces. In a similar manner, the department spending the most may be highlighted.

A graphics display may be used in a:

- Publication.
- Presentation using
    An overhead projector.
    Photographic slides.
    The computer screen.

Each type of presentation may be the product of a different process. Computer output methods include:

- The screen
- A variety of printers
- A plotter printer

Screen resolution (image sharpness) depends on the number of dots produced on the screen (pixels, or picture elements). The number of dots used to produce a character on a dot matrix and laser printer determines the resolution on the printed page.

MICROS IN ACTION

Professional Presentations

Jean King and Associates requires specialized, custom presentations for specific business objectives. They prepare slides using screen copy equipment for meetings and hard copy for stockholder reports and similar publications. They use graphics slides, films, and television tapes for audiovisual presentations.

The creation of pictures with dots is called digitizing. When a picture is created by dots, it is also called a bit map. Raster graphics refers to the use of bit-map graphics.

A plotter printer uses lines (vectors), rather than dots to create images. Lines and directions may be used to create images on the screen. Vector graphics is the creation of images on the screen using lines and directions rather than dots.

STANDARD CHARTS

Many programs (Table 7–3) are available to produce the standard charts and graphs. Standard chart-producing programs may be classified as:

- Spreadsheet and Data Base Graphics
- Chart Programs
- Analytical Graphic Programs

Examples of standard charts produced by selected programs are listed and illustrated in Figure 7–9. There are many programs available in addition to the ones used to produce the charts illustrated.

TABLE 7–3 Standard Charts and Graphs Packages

Charts	Boardroom Graphics	Business Graphics	Chart-Master	Energraphics	Lotus 1–2–3	pfs Graph	Printer Perfect	ProGraf	Stat Graphics	SuperCalc 4
Area				x			x	x	x	
Bar	x	x	x	x	x	x	x	x	x	x
Flow			x	x			x	x		
Functions			x	x	x		x	x	x	x
Gantt					x					x
Hi-Low			x	x	x		x	x	x	x
Line/XY	x	x	x	x	x	x	x	x	x	x
Organization	x		x	x				x		x
Pie	x	x	x	x	x	x	x	x	x	x
Scatter diagram	x	x	x	x	x		x	x	x	x
Stacked bar			x	x	x		x	x	x	x
Text	x			x				x		
Three-dimensional	x			x				x	x	

Gantt charts may be created on a Lotus or SuperCalc spreadsheet with a custom template.

Spreadsheet and Data Base Graphics

Graphics-producing spreadsheet and data base programs:

1. Create graphics from data stored for some other purpose.
2. Update the graph when a change is made in the source data.

The first spreadsheet to include graphics was Lotus 1–2–3. Graphics routines are now popular in spreadsheet programs and some data base programs.

Chart Programs

Charting programs are stand-alone programs that produce charts and graphs through the use of a keyboard (and other devices such as a mouse) for data entry. They can import data from other programs, and many can capture data from a screen display.

Charting programs produce a number and variety of charts and graphs that are an order of magnitude greater than spreadsheet programs.

Charting programs usually have limited data organization capabilities and do not perform any analysis. Data must be entered through the keyboard, captured from data files prepared by spreadsheet and data base programs, or captured from a screen display.

If data has already been entered into a data base or spreadsheet program, importing data into a graphic chart program saves time and reduces errors.

Analytical Graphics Programs

Analytical graphics programs are programs that use graphics in the performance of statistical analysis, project control, quality control, and other specialized procedures. The charts and graphs produced by these special-purpose programs include all the standard charts and graphs and a large variety of additional charts and graphs specifically required by the analysis performed. Most of these programs can import and export data in spreadsheet and some data base formats.

USER WINDOW

GRAPHICS HELPS UNDERSTANDING

Peter was employed as a mathematical research assistant. He worked on a finance problem for over a month without being able to determine why the mathematical methods being used would not work.

Out of desperation, he used a graphics program to see what the function looked like. The graph showed the function was almost a straight line.

An hour after seeing the graph of the function, he was able to solve the problem.

FIGURE 7–9   Standard Charts and Graphs

Area Charts: A line graph in which the area under the horizontal line represents a quantity.

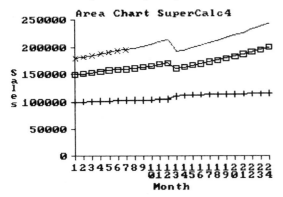

Bar Charts: Charts that compare parts to the whole using bars.
Vertical Bar:

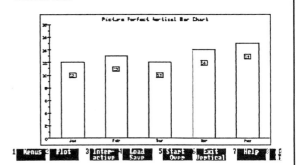

Flow Charts: Charts that trace the sequence of activities.

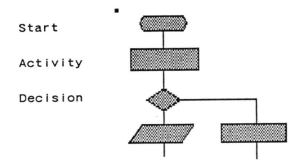

Functional: Graphs showing the behavior of a dependent variable to an independent variable.

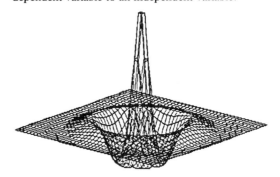

Hi-Low Chart: A line graph showing the high, low, open and closing values of a stock over time.

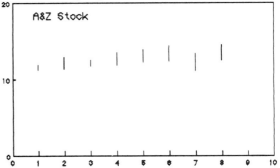

Gantt Chart: Chart showing the scheduling of activities and events.

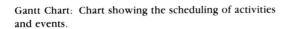
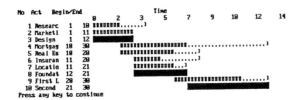

FIGURE 7–9   Continued

Line/XY Chart: Chart that shows the behavior between two variables. A line chart requires even divisions of the X scale while the XY performs scaling.

Lotus Line Chart

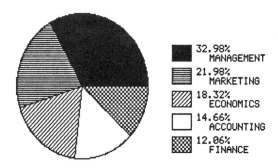

Organization Chart: A chart that demonstrates position or rank within an organization.

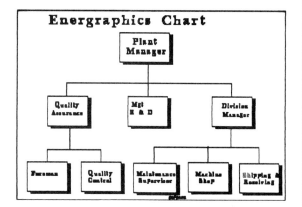

Pie Chart: A chart that compares parts to the whole using a circle.
pfs GRAPH pie chart:

PFS:GRAPH PIE CHART

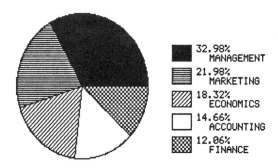

Scatter Diagram: A line chart with points plotted only, may be two or three dimensional.

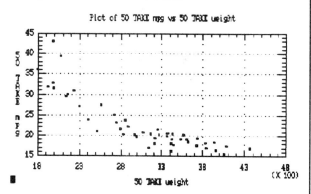

Text Chart: A display using words rather than images.

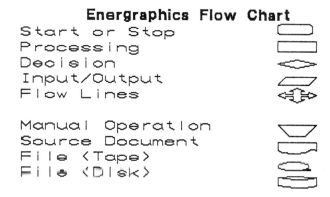

IMAGE CREATING AND EDITING

Image creating and editing programs include:

- Draw, Freehand, and Paint Programs
- Assembly–Clip-Art Libraries
- Screen Capture Programs
- Font Control Programs

Image-creating programs help the user create, assemble, and edit pictures using image libraries, colors, and cross-hatching. These programs can produce any image that the user can create in his or her imagination.

Draw, Freehand, and Paint Programs

Drawing, freehand, and paint programs help the user create, assemble, and enhance images. Using these programs the user manipulates:

- Arcs and circles
- Curves
- Lines and boxes
- Paint (color and cross-hatching)
- Points
- Text
- Symbol Sources:
    Earlier created symbols
    Other programs
    Clip-art libraries
    Bit images from digitizers

to produce an illustration in black and white or color. Figure 7–10 is a PC Paintbrush screen showing a drawing screen with an arc, circle, line, painted area, box, and text.

Symbols may be obtained by saving a completed or partially completed drawing for future use. These drawings, once created and saved on disk, become part of a symbol or clip-art library. Symbols may also be obtained by capturing the display of other programs and from scanners and digitizers.

Image creating and editing programs are designed to:

- Create/edit
- Store/recall
- Print graphic images.

Text output is enhanced by the capability to use different fonts and different size letters in a presentation, for example, large letters for titles and headers, normal size for text, italics and similar output for special effects. The separation between word processing and graphics becomes unclear when topics such as this are considered. Future word processors will be expected to handle text and graphics in the same file.

Creating and Editing Graphics creating and editing programs include the capability to:

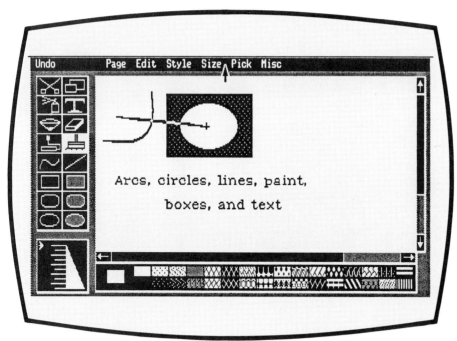

FIGURE 7–10
PC Paintbrush Screen

- Draw and paint
- Zoom
- Copy, enlarge, and shrink
- Rotate and inverse images
- Window.

The graphics editor performs a variety of tasks including:

- Area identification.
- Area move, copy, and delete.
- Area color.
- Enter text.
- Erase lines, characters, colors, and shapes.
- Create curves, shapes, and lines.

Most of these tasks may be performed by cursor movement and a menu or function key instruction. Differences between programs include:

- The ease of use.
- The number of utilities available for special shapes.
- The size of the drawing.
- The use of the keyboard, mouse, digitizer pad, and scanner.

Draw and Paint Many programs automatically produce circles, boxes, lines, and curves. The user simply specifies the location of the image, its type and size, and the program performs the rest of the task.

Figure 7–11 is the PC Paintbrush screen that shows the icons on the left. The empty circle icon is a light color indicating that it has been selected. The cursor was moved to the middle of the screen with a mouse and the center of the circle located. The cursor is now being used to control the diameter of the circle.

Icon:
A character display on the screen that usually represents a menu selection.

FIGURE 7–11
PC Paintbrush Circle Draw

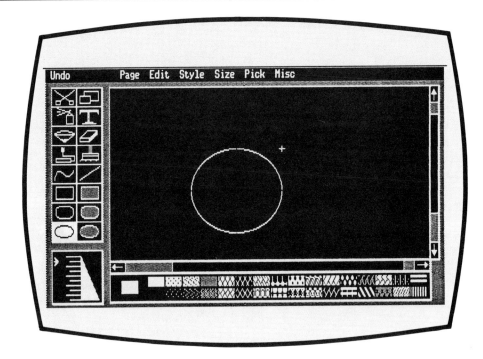

Figure 7–12 is PC–Key-Draw being used to create a box. The first corner is located with the cursor. Function key F2 is pressed and the box is created as the arrow keys are used to located the far corner.

Most programs have a cursor showing where the next character or symbol will be placed on the screen. Many have a column and row location indicator, a color indicator, and a direction of movement indicator.

FIGURE 7–12
PC–Key-Draw Box

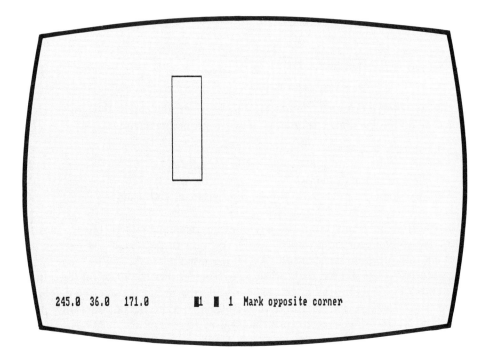

Columns are usually one pixel wide and run up and down as in a spreadsheet. The origin, the point from which counting starts, is often in the upper left corner of the screen or the middle of the screen. Figures 7–11 and 12 are 640 pixels across. Up and down movement is across rows. There are 280 rows in the illustration shown in Figures 7–11 and 12.

In programs that do not use a mouse, cursor movement is usually controlled by the arrow keys found on the numeric keypad. Pressing the right arrow key moves the cursor to the right, etc. Cursor speed can often be controlled by using a function key or a control key combined with some other key.

To paint the circle in Figure 7–11, the spray can icon is selected with the mouse, the cursor is moved to the inside of the circle, and a mouse key is pressed. To paint the box in Figure 7–12, function key F4 is pressed, l is selected for light shades, m for medium, or d for dark. Figure 7–13 shows the box filled in.

Zoom Most graphics programs have a zoom utility. The cursor is moved to a particular location on the screen and the instruction to zoom is given. The screen changes to a display showing only the local area in the neighborhood of the cursor. Figure 7–14 shows a normal image and Figure 7–15 shows the image after the zoom instruction is executed.

Changes may be made to the enlarged portion of an image. This capability gives the user additional control of the final product. Some programs allow users to control each and every pixel on the screen. They may be turned on or off, or their colors changed.

Copy, Enlarge, and Shrink Figure 7–16 is the original screen showing the name of the package boxed by four points. After the enclosed area has been captured, it can be reproduced as shown in Figure 7–17.

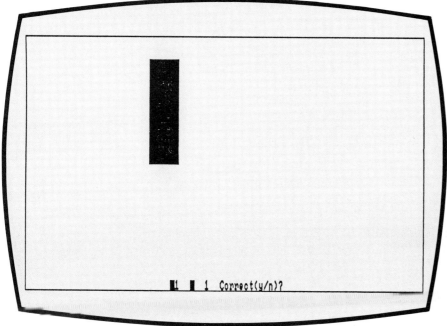

FIGURE 7–13
Painted Box

FIGURE 7–14
Before Zoom Executed

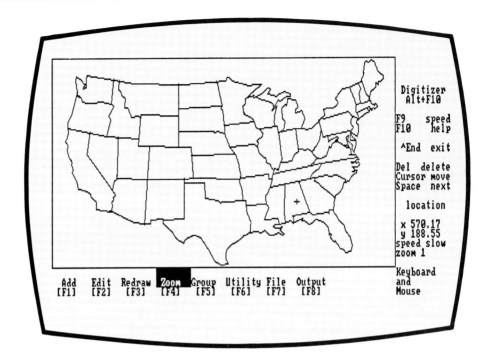

Rotation:
Moving an image around its
own axis.

Inverse:
A mirror image.

The relative size of part of a drawing may have to be changed. Figure 7–18 shows the second image in Figure 7–17 enlarged both vertically and horizontally.

Rotate and Inverse Images The process of rotating or inverting of images begins with identifying the area involved. A box is drawn around the area and

FIGURE 7–15
After Zoom Executed

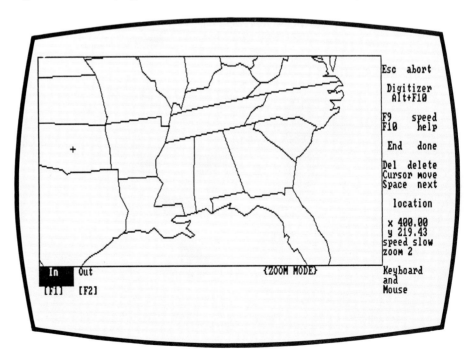

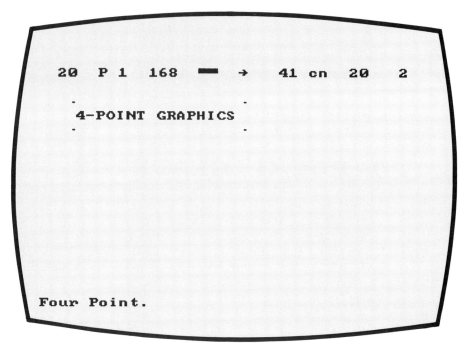

FIGURE 7–16
4–Point Graphics
Starting to Copy

the instruction is given to invert or rotate the image. Figures 7–19, 7–20, 7–21, and 7–22 illustrate an image that has been boxed, then rotated, then inverted.

In PC Paintbrush (Figure 7–20) the terms "flip horiz" and "flip vertic" stand for inverting an image, inverse for reversing the colors.

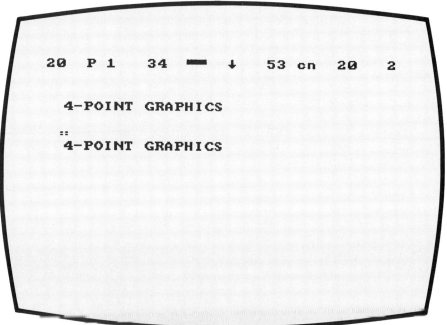

FIGURE 7–17
Image Copied

FIGURE 7-18
Enlarged Image

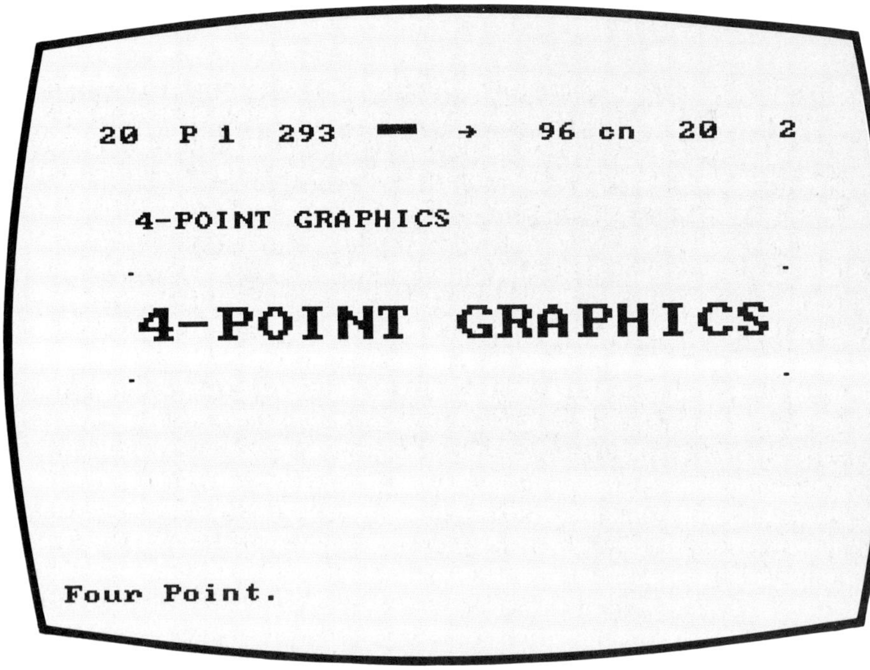

```
20 P 1 293 ▬ → 96 cn 20 2

4-POINT GRAPHICS

        .                                    .

4-POINT GRAPHICS

        .                                    .

Four Point.
```

Virtual screen:
A video memory created in the RAM of the computer. The physical screen examines a part of the memory at a time.

Windows The microcomputer screen is too small to create large-quality images. Programs can increase the size of the working space available by creating a virtual screen and using the physical screen as a window into the virtual screen. Figure 7–23 illustrates a window onto a larger virtual screen.

A part of an image may be created in part of the virtual screen. The cursor is moved to another part of the virtual screen and then the image is completed. When the results are printed, the entire image is shown.

Saving and Recalling Most graphics programs have their own data file storage method. A few programs can read files created by other programs. There are some transfer programs available to move files from one format to another.

One reason for differences between program graphics data files is the method of data representation. Some programs use raster (digital) information while others use vector information.

Digitized data are what you see on the screen. A line consisting of 50 pixels in a row is saved as 50 lighted pixels.

A vector is defined by:

1. The X and Y position of its starting point.
2. The distance, or length of the line.
3. The angle it goes from the starting point.

Images saved as digitized graphics may result in errors when the scale of a drawing is changed, expanded, or contracted. A vector is independent of scale. The scale of graphics saved as vectors can be changed with no loss of quality.

As indicated in Table 7–4, programs using digitized data allow you to enter data by moving the cursor to draw a line or a figure. Programs using vector

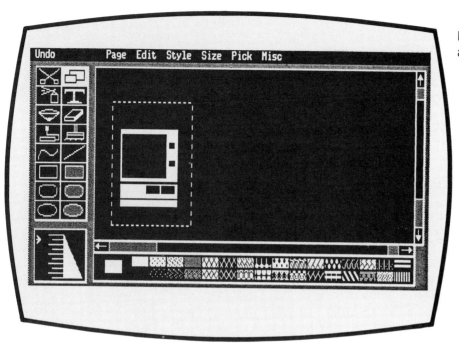

FIGURE 7–19
Boxed, Rotated,
and Inverted Image

graphics data require the identification of the beginning and end of a line. Vector graphics are independent of the number of pixels on a screen, and are often selected for technical drawing by engineers and architects.

Graphics save routines for raster and vector data are similar to those used in saving other types of data files. Some programs require you to log onto a

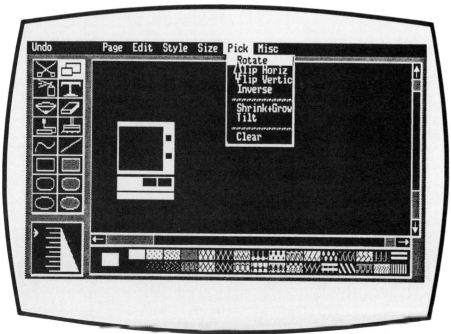

FIGURE 7–20
Ready to be Rotated

FIGURE 7–21
Rotate to Left

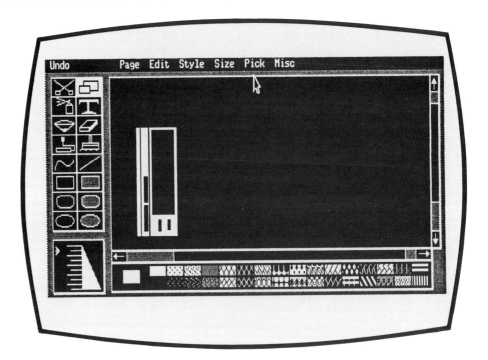

data disk or subdirectory when the system is started. Some accept the DOS path statement.

Printing Graphics The capability to print graphics is a function of both the printer-plotter hardware and the software. The software must send specific

FIGURE 7–22
Inverted

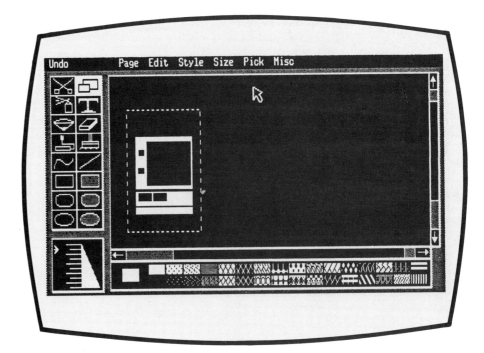

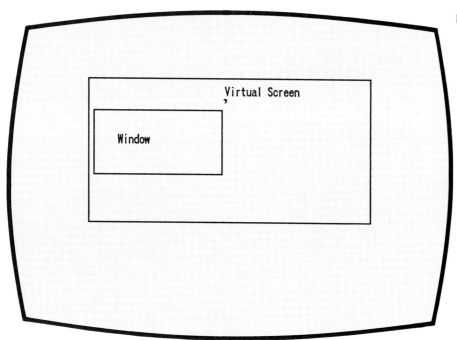

FIGURE 7–23
Physical Window to
Large Virtual Screen

codes to the printer or plotter to make it perform in a particular manner. Care must be taken to make sure a software package supports the specific printer or plotter.

Graphics programs come with a number of printer-plotter drivers that are installed when the program is first used or are selected when the print command is given. Each printer-plotter driver is designed to handle a set of codes. Some coding systems are used on a variety of different printers. The Epson codes are popular with many printer manufacturers, however, there is no standard for plotters. Thus, if a specific plotter is not listed, it probably cannot be used.

Laser printers may be designed to emulate a number of printers. When a laser is emulating a particular printer, the codes used for that printer will produce the same results on the laser as on the original printer. Emulations allow the user to have the features of a number of machines available in one machine. One emulation may be used for text, the other for graphics on the same page.

Emulate:
Hardware or software that permits one device to act like another.

Hard copy of graphics images is limited by hardware more than software and so requires a printer-plotter that uses dots, ink jet, or lines. Generally, a daisy wheel printer that produces a solid character cannot be used for graphics. An exception to this rule is a daisy wheel printer with special characters that may be combined to create images.

Digitized Data	*Vector Data*
Move the cursor to draw a line.	Identify the beginning and end of a line. Tell program to draw.

TABLE 7–4
Line Draw

Among the more popular hard copy graphics production methods (black and white and color) are:

- Screen photography
- Dot matrix and laser printers
- Ink jet printers
- Pens on plotter printers

Assembly–Clip-Art Libraries

Clip-art libraries are collections of images and symbols purchased or saved from earlier work. Many drawing programs are sold with a symbol library. It is easier to create a display using predesigned art from a symbol library than to create a display from scratch.

The bridge and plane in Figures 7–24 and 7–25 are part of the Diagraph symbol library. The Diagraph library is sold on several disks. A basic library comes with the program, and additional symbols may be purchased as needed.

Figure 7–26 is the drawing screen for the draw function of Enertronics "Energraphics" program. The map shown is part of the Enertronics symbol library.

Screen Capture Programs

A screen capture program captures and stores screen displays created by other programs. The screen is stored in RAM, along with other programs, and called when needed with a special set of key strokes. The screen display is frozen, captured, and saved on disk. The image is recalled from the disk file into a draw, freehand, or paint program. You may use the facilities of a draw, freehand, or paint program to edit the images as required.

FIGURE 7–24
Diagraph

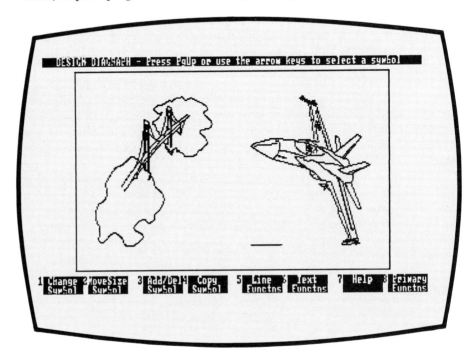

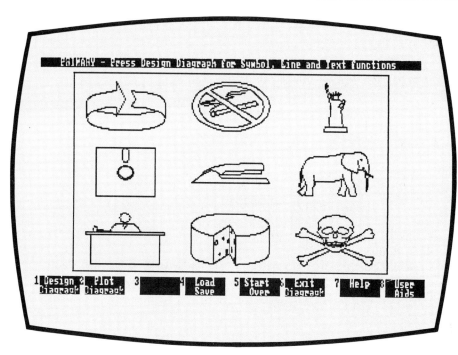

FIGURE 7–25
Diagraph Symbol Library

Data file transfer between graphics programs is more difficult than between text or characters programs. Graphics programs lack a standard file code such as ASCII, so screen capture programs are needed.

Figure 7–27 illustrates the screen when INSET is being used to capture a Lotus 1–2–3 graphics screen.

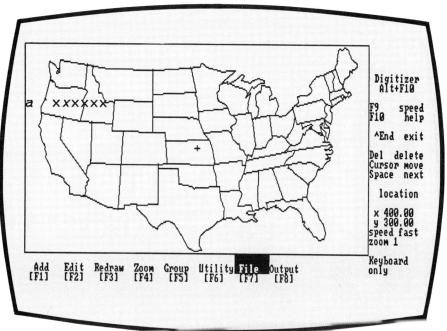

FIGURE 7–26
Energraphics

FIGURE 7–27
INSET Screen Capture

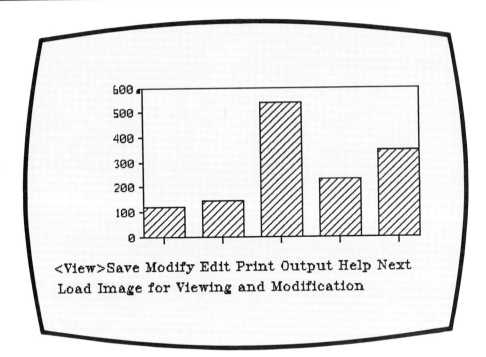

The map in Figure 7–28 was imported into PC Paintbrush from another program's symbol library. PC Paintbrush is a bit-image graphics program. The original map was created using vector graphics, saved using a screen capture program, and then imported into PC Paintbrush. Since the screen capture and PC Paintbrush use bit-image graphics, the map became a bit-image display. It is possible to transfer vector graphics to raster, but difficult to transfer raster to vector.

FIGURE 7–28
PC Paintbrush

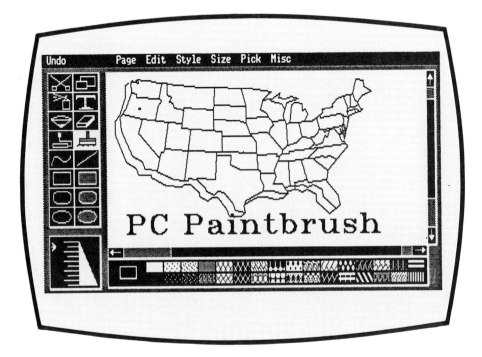

Once in PC Paintbrush, the bit image of the map may be changed and edited. States may be colored and text added. Figure 7–29 shows the state changed to a different one, with its capital marked and named.

Many different graphics displays may be created using a combination of clip art, screen capture, and editing. Figure 7–30 was created by:

1. Recalling three figures from the Computer Support Corporation Diagraph illustration library.
2. Combining them into a single screen using the Diagraph editor.
3. Capturing the screen with ZSoft Corporation's Frieze.
4. Performing some final editing with ZSoft Corporation's PC Paintbrush.

Font Control

A font is the size and shape of a letter. Printer fonts may be stored:

- In printer ROM
    Internal to the printer.
    On an add-on PC board.
- Downloaded from computer to printer RAM.
- On a physical device such as a daisy wheel.

- In computer ROM
    Internal to the computer.
    On an add-on PC board.
- By software in computer RAM.

Dot matrix, ink jet, and laser printers can often be instructed to switch between a variety of fonts. Special codes are sent to the printer to tell it to switch between fonts.

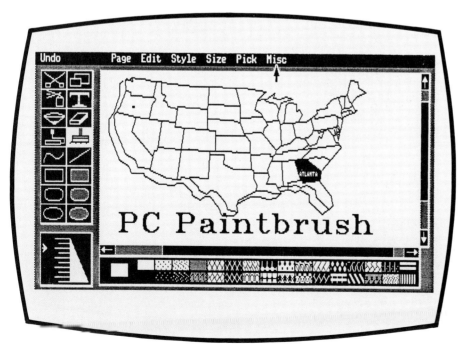

FIGURE 7–29
Map Edited

Epson printers usually start printing compressed print when the binary number 15 is received. Methods of instructing programs-computers to send a binary 15 to the printer include:

■ Pressing ^O (Press control key and the letter O)
■ Typing \015

The letter O is the fifteenth letter of the alphabet. When ^O is pressed the binary number 15 is sent to the printer.

The code \015 also sends a binary 15 to the printer. The printer must receive the number 15 to change into compressed mode. The software determines how the user must give the instruction to send the code.

The code <27>[382;0;1s is used in a QMS Kiss laser printer to change the font from what it is, to Epson compressed. This is the same font as produced by most Epson printers when the number 15 is received. Figure 7–31 illustrates Kiss printer fonts and codes.

Figure 7–32 is a screen display from a font creation program. The screen shows the design of the font for ASCII code number 050, a 2. The font being developed is rotated ninety degrees to print sideways. The user can control each dot produced by the printer to obtain the effect needed. Custom characters may be created using this technique.

Some custom font-printing programs are RAM-resident and work with the printer driver of word processors. Others are independent printing programs that must be used in place of the normal printer driver.

GRAPHICS AND TEXT OUTPUT

Computer graphics are often needed in written documents or as part of a computer-generated slide presentation. Desktop publishing (Dtop) is a collection

FIGURE 7–30
Using a Menu

of hardware and software for producing written documents. Computer-generated slide presentations may be still or animated.

Desktop Publishing

Desktop publishing is the creation of printed output that equals or closely approaches the results expected from typeset output. Desktop publishing programs integrate the output of word processors, graphics programs, and scanner inputs into a single document. There are two approaches to desktop publishing programs:

1. Merge programs using word processors.
2. Page layout programs (WYSIWYG).

Merging Programs Some merge programs are similar to the embedded-command word processing programs. A code is placed where a graphic image is desired and the graphics are added during the printing process. Some of these programs have screen preview capabilities. These programs approach the capacity of a page layout program.

Merge programs are usually RAM-resident. A series of symbols such as

[xxxx]

are used as a code to instruct the computer to imbed in the middle of a text display a graphics display saved in a disk file named xxxx. When a graphics monitor system is used, some merging programs can display a box such as Figure 7–33 to identify the future location of the graphics. Some programs display the graphics in location during the word processing sessions (Figure 7–34).

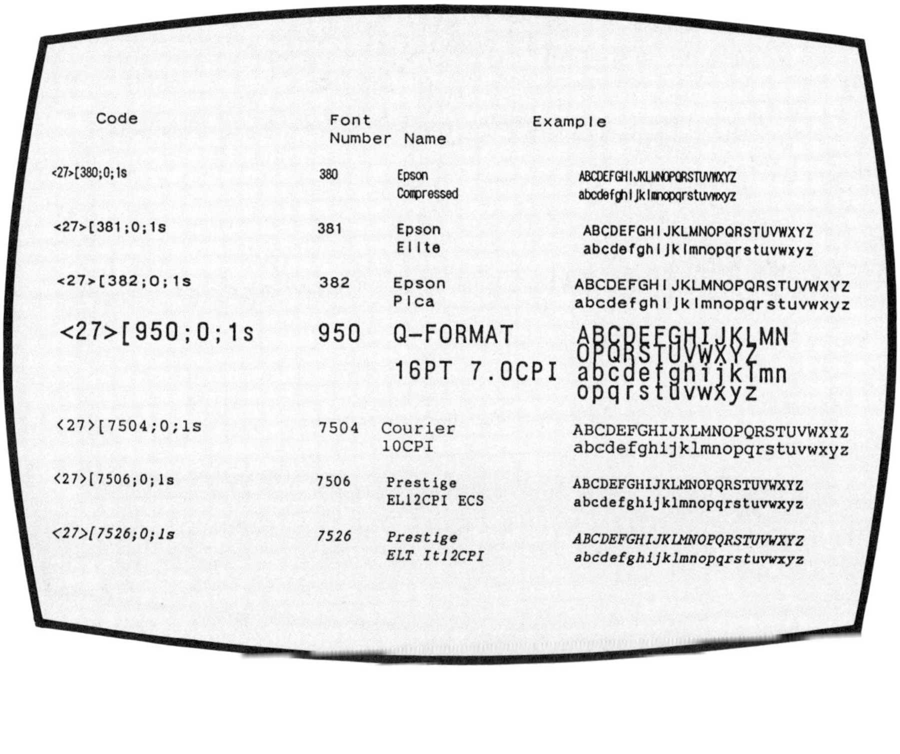

FIGURE 7–31
Kiss Printer Fonts

FIGURE 7–32
Font Design Using FONTASTIC

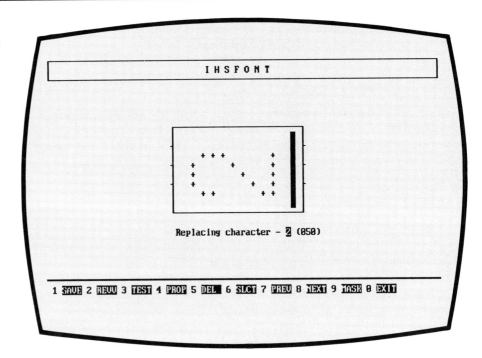

Page Layout Programs A page layout program is a graphics-text program that displays on a monitor what can be produced by a printer. The objective of these programs is true WYSIWYG (what you see is what you get). Fonts are correctly sized and graphics are displayed.

FIGURE 7–33
Locating an Image

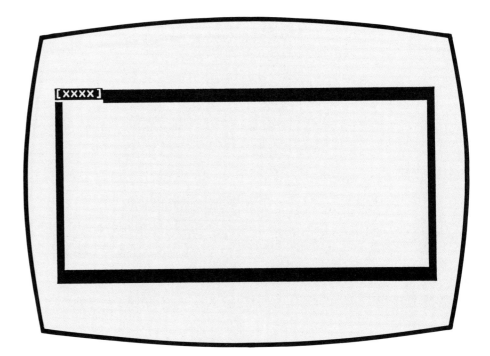

A page layout program (Figure 7–34) produces screen text and graphics on a printer. Screen, printer technology, and program capabilities have been in a constant state of change. Seldom has there been a balance between what printers can output and what monitors can display. We can now purchase, at extra cost, the capability of producing a match on both screen and printer. To obtain an exact page layout, we need both extra hardware and software.

There are many hardware-software page layout systems that approach the goal of an exact match for a special application at a reduced cost. These lower-cost systems may satisfy the need of many users.

Font:
A set of type characters similar to each other in size, weight, and design.

Special characters:
Foreign language letters like Greek and mathematical and scientific signs and symbols.

Graphics:
Photographs, charts, and clip art.

Slide, Animation, and Sound Shows

A slide show is the display of a series of static pictures on

- Film
- Transparency
- Computer screen

or some other media. There are devices available to enlarge and project an image produced by a computer screen (Figure 7–35).

An animated slide show displays moving pictures using film, computer screen, or some other media.

A sound show adds sound to slides or animation. The technology is available for the integration of sound with slides and animation. Extra-cost hardware and custom software are needed.

Slide shows may be a series of individual screen displays. Some programs such as Enertronics Energraphics (Figure 7–36) have up to ten slide merging options to control the transition from one slide to another:

0   Top to bottom
1   Left to right
2   Upper left to lower right
3   Center to edge horizontally
4   Edge to center vertically
5   Corners to center
6   Five vertical strips at the same time
7   Center to edges in a spiral
8   Edge to center in a spiral
9   Pseudorandom

A few programs such as 4Point have the capability to produce animation. Animation makes it seem as if an object is moving. A user may use an animation program to develop a presentation that starts with a pie chart. The part of the pie chart relevant to the audience could be made to move out from the rest.

Microcomputers can produce sound. Sound may be combined with either slide or animation presentations. The ultimate combination of sound and graphics is the motion picture that is available to the computer on CD ROM (compact-disk read-only memory). This technology is available at an extra cost.

Engineering Applications

Programs designed to allow engineers and designers to create images usually use vector graphics. These programs include:

> CAD —Computer-Aided Design
> CAM —Computer-Aided Manufacturing
> CADD—Computer-Aided Design and Drafting.

In operation, these programs are similar to other vector graphics programs. They are designed to help the professional user meet his/her specific graphics needs and have aids built in for that purpose.

Computer-aided design, CAD, describes the software and hardware available to help an individual with a design task. The microcomputer may produce a 3–D image of an object and then, with little effort, rotate the object so the designer can see it from a different point of view. With the addition of a CAD data base, an engineering evaluation of the design can be produced. Many software packages devoted to different design problems are available for microcomputers.

Computer-aided manufacturing, CAM, refers to controlling production equipment with your computer. A machine tool can be programmed to perform a variety of operations more quickly and accurately than its human counterpart.

CADD refers to computer-aided design and drafting. Not only can the microcomputer help the engineer see what the product looks like, but it can also be used to produce the many working drawings needed to transfer the idea into a product. Microcomputers can produce and update drawings with greater accuracy in less time than is possible by humans.

FIGURE 7–34
Page Layout With Merge
Program

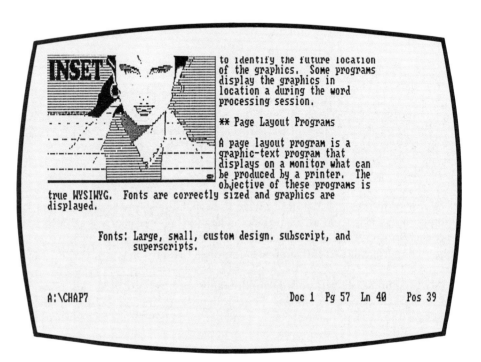

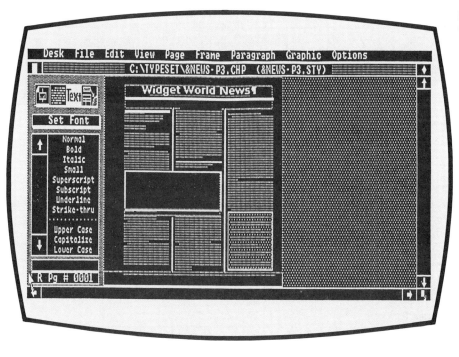

FIGURE 7–35
Ventura Screen

COMPARING GRAPHICS PROGRAMS

Graphics programs are designed to work with monochrome monitors and a graphics card
with a variety of pixel columns and rows, color CGA, EGA, and PGA. They are also
configured   for   use   with   black-and-white   and   color   printers

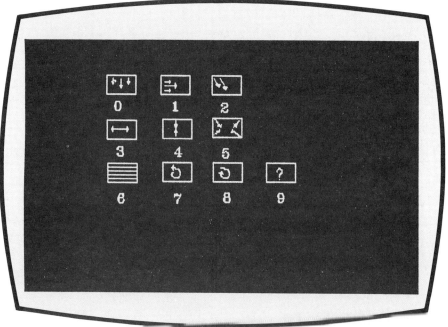

FIGURE 7–36
Screen Projector

TABLE 7-5   Hardware Needs of Graphics Packages

Hardware	4Point	DiaGraph	Energraphics	Fontastic	INSET	PC Paintbrush + Frieze	PC-Key-Draw	Print Master	Printer Perfect	Stat Graphics
RAM requirements	256K	512K	384K	under 128K	128K	192K + Frieze	256K	under 128K	448K	512K
Color CGA	x	x	x		x	x	x			
EGA		x	x		x					
Monochrome graphics card		x			x	x	x	x	x	x
Graphics printer	x	x	x	x	x	x	x	x	x	x
Color Print Plotter		x	x		x					

Some programs will perform a screen dump to a graphics and or color printer-plotter only with the addition of a special utility.

TABLE 7-6   Features of Graphics Software Packages

Features	4Point	DiaGraph	Energraphics	Fontastic	INSET	PC Paintbrush + Frieze	PC-Key-Draw	Print Master	Printer Perfect	Stat Graphics
Standard Charts			x						x	x
Draw, freehand, & paint	x	x	x		x	x	x	x		
Clip art	x	x	x			x	x	x		
Screen Capture					x	x				
Font Creation				x						
Merge Word Processing					x					
Slide show	x	x	x			x	x			
Animation	x									

and plotters. Table 7–5 details some of the hardware needs for some selected packages.

Graphics programs have a mixture of capabilities. Table 7–6 classifies a selection of programs according to general categories.

SUMMARY

Graphics solves many problems for microcomputer users. The quality and ease of producing microcomputer graphics mean that everyone can take advantage of the capabilities. There are three types of graphics programs:

■ Standard charts
   Spreadsheet and data base graphics
   Chart programs
   Analytical graphic programs
   Sample charts

- Image creation, assembly, and enhancement
    - Draw, freehand, and paint programs
    - Assemble clip art programs
    - Screen capture programs
    - Font control
- Graphics and text output
    - Desktop publishing
        - Page layout
        - Merging programs
    - Slide, animation, and sound shows

Spreadsheet and data base graphics are part of these programs. The spreadsheet and data base user can produce pie charts, bar charts, XY charts, and high-low-close charts, among others, with a simple press of a few keys.

Spreadsheet and data base data may be transferred to charting programs. These programs produce enhanced charts and graphs. Analytical graphics programs can produce specialized charts and graphs and may import data from other programs.

Image creation, assembly, and enhancement programs give the microcomputer user the capability to produce banners, greeting cards, and business illustrations with ease. Users with a minimum of art training can produce fine quality illustrations to help present their ideas and concepts.

The enhancement program may either produce graphics from scratch or use the products of other programs. It gives the user the capability to design the output to fit a specific need. These programs make it easy to create and edit graphics.

To produce graphics images, a dot matrix, laser, or ink jet or plotter printer is needed. These devices are available at reasonable cost.

The amount of RAM and ROM needed for graphics is greater than for some other microcomputer applications. The price of computer memory has fallen to a level that puts a large storage capacity within the reach of many users. As the number of users increases, the quality and amount of software will increase.

KEY TERMS

Animation
Bit map
Desktop publishing
Digitizing
Enlarging
Graphics
Icon
Pixel

Raster graphics
Slide show
Variable
Vector
Virtual screen
Window
Zoom

REVIEW QUESTIONS

1. What type of graphics is available on the microcomputer?

2. Why would you decide to use each type of microcomputer graphics program?

3. What special hardware is needed to perform microcomputer graphics?

4. Why do graphics require a large amount of RAM?

5. What is a pixel?

6. How are bit codes used to produce shades and colors?

7. Identify some of the fonts available for a dot matrix, ink jet, or laser printer?

8. What is a scanner? What two types of scanners are available?

9. How does a plotter differ from a printer?

10. What capability is provided by an image camera?

11. Why are hard disks often needed for graphic programs?

12. Why should you know about microcomputer graphics?

13. What three factors determine the creation of a graphics display?

14. What are some alternate methods or mechanisms for displaying graphics?

15. What is the difference between bit-mapped and vector graphics?

16. Give some examples of standard charts and graphs.

17. Give some examples of what image creation, assembly, and enhancement programs do.

18. Identify each of the following and its application:
    a. Area chart
    b. Bar chart
    c. Flow chart
    d. Function chart
    e. Gantt chart
    f. Hi-Low chart
    g. Line/XY chart
    h. Organization chart
    i. Pie chart
    j. Scatter diagram
    k. Text chart

19. Identify some varieties of bar charts.

20. Identify some varieties of pie charts.

21. What is the difference between a line and XY chart?

22. How are spreadsheet and data base graphics programs different from charting programs?

23. Why are both spreadsheet or data base programs and charting programs used together?

24. Identify the need for analytical graphic programs.

25. What are some of the tools used in draw, freehand, and paint programs?

26. How is a vector defined?

27. How does the creation of a digitized line differ from that of a vector line?

28. What is an important advantage of using vector over bit image drawing programs?

29. What are CAD, CAM, and CADD?

30. How are circles and boxes created in a graphics drawing program?

31. How is an image filled in with a different color or shading pattern?

32. What is the zoom capability? How and why is it used?

33. What are the copy, enlarge, and shrink capabilities and why are they of value?

34. What are the rotate and inverse capabilities and why are they of value?

35. What is a virtual screen in a drawing program? What is a window?

36. What is a clip-art library?

37. How may a clip-art library help you create images?

38. Review some examples of clip art.

39. Why is a screen capture program valuable?

40. Why must a screen capture be stored in RAM along with other application programs?

41. What can be done with a captured screen after it has been saved?

42. Where are fonts stored?

43. How do you change from one printer font to another?

44. How is a font created?

45. What is desktop publishing?

46. What are two approaches to desktop publishing?

47. What is the difference between animation and a normal slide show?

48. How can a graphics slide program be used?

DISCUSSION AND APPLICATION QUESTIONS

1. Using magazines and newspapers, find an article on microcomputer graphics and report on its observations.

2. Find an article on the use of television cameras and computer graphics. What do you think future developments in this area will be?

3. Find an article on the use of computer-generated backgrounds for movies and television in either computer magazines or industrial publications. What potential use do these capabilities have in business?

4. Detail the value of microcomputer-generated graphics in presentations in other courses and in reports for other courses.

1. Use the data given below to create one of each of the types of charts available in your spreadsheet or chart program.

Data set A		Data set B		Data set C	
Andy	12	July	22	12	122
Judy	22	August	24	13	133
Carol	21	September	33	14	123
Andress	17	October	34	15	155

Produce a chart with headings on both screen and printer.

2. The class budget for a party is:

Drinks	$34.00
Hot food	23.00
Cold food	12.00
Treats	10.00

Make a pie and bar chart of the budget.

3. (Accounting.) Use the data from the balance sheet and income and expense statements shown below to create a pie and bar chart comparing:

    a. Sources of income
    b. Alternate expenses
    c. Assets
    d. Liabilities

Income Statement for the three-month period ending December 31, 19xx:

REVENUE			
Rent Unit 1		$ 35710	
Rent Unit 2		26590	
Total Revenue			$62300
EXPENSES			
Wages Expense	$ 750		
Rent Expense	2500		
Advertising Expense	2430		
Travel Expense	920		
Supplies Expense	1700		
Insurance Expense	700		
Depreciation Expense	2400		
Total Expenses			11400
NET INCOME			$50900

Balance sheet as of December 31, 19xx:

ASSETS		
Cash		$ 56300
Supplies		2900
Prepaid Wages		2100
Equipment	93500	
. . . Dep.	34900	58600
Accounts Rec.		1800
		121700

LIABILITIES
  Accts. Payable   3900
  Loans   550
  Wages Payable   750
STOCKHOLDERS EQUITY
  Retained Earnings   86500
  Capital   30000
        121700

4. (Algebra.) Use a spreadsheet or chart program to chart the following functions:

  a. $f(x) = SIN(x)/x$ for $-22 <= x <= 22$ in steps of 22.
  b. $f(x) = x^2 + 3*x + 2$ for $-10 <= x <= 10$

5. (Economics.) Given that the quantity demanded and the amount supplied are functions of price:

$$Demand = -Price * 22 + 300 \quad 1.00 <= price <= 25.00$$
$$Supply = Price * 12 + 22 \quad 1.00 <= price <= 25.00$$

graph the supply and demand curves as a function of price.
    Using algebra to find the price as a function of quantity, the results are:

$$Price (demand) = -(Quantity - 300)/22$$
$$Price (supply) = (Quantity + 22)/12.$$

Graph the supply and demand curves for quantities from 0 to 280 in steps of 10 units.

6. (Management.) The economic order quantity formula is:

$$f(Q) = 122 * 1200 / Q + (Q/2) * 12.33$$

for values of Q greater than zero. Graph the formula from Q equals 20 until 500 in steps of 20.

7. Look through your local newspaper. Find some data that fits the form of the data in problem 2. Make a pie and bar chart with headings from the data.

8. Using a drawing program and clip-art library, create a joke similar to one found in this chapter or your daily newspaper.

9. Start with one of the clip-art symbols in your clip-art library and enhance it for a business logo.

SELECTED REFERENCES

Conklin, Dick. PC Graphics: Charts, Graphs, Games and Art on the IBM PC. John Wiley and Sons, 1983.
Cuellar, Gabriel. Graphics Made Easy for the IBM PC/XT. Prentice-Hall, 1984.
Ford, Nelson. Business Graphics for the IBM PC. SYBEX, 1984.
Fowler, John. The IBM PC/XT Graphics Book. Prentice-Hall, 1984.
Harold, Fred G. Introduction to Computers With BASIC. West Publishing Company, 1984.
Hearn, Donald, and M. Pauline Baker. Computer Graphics for the IBM Personal Computer. Prentice-Hall, 1983.
Volkstorf, J. Edward. Graphics Programming on the IBM Personal

8

GOALS

When you complete this chapter you will be able to:

Understand why microcomputer communication is important.

Understand some theory, the steps needed to set up, and how to operate a communication session.

Understand the role of some of the special microcomputer communication hardware.

Name and identify the tasks performed by communication within a microcomputer system and between microcomputers.

OUTLINE

Chapter Goals

Communication Hardware

Modems
Cables and Null-Modems
Mechanical and Electronic Switching Devices

Why You Must Learn about Microcomputer Communication

Need for Speed
Need for Computer Data
Low Cost
Controlling the Parts of a Microcomputer System
Controlling External Devices and External Data Collection Devices

Communication Theory, Background, and Programs

Microcomputer Communication—Two Smart Devices
Serial and Parallel Connections
Asynchronous or Synchronous
Communication Using ASCII
Communication Parameters
Setting Up Communication Parameters
Communication Programs

Communication with Peripherals

Off-Line Data Entry Devices

Communication between Microcomputer Systems

Read-Write-Format Programs
Other Special Communication Procedures

Comparing Communication Programs

Summary

Key Terms

Review Questions

Discussion and Application Questions

Laboratory Assignments

Selected References

MICROCOMPUTER COMMUNICATION

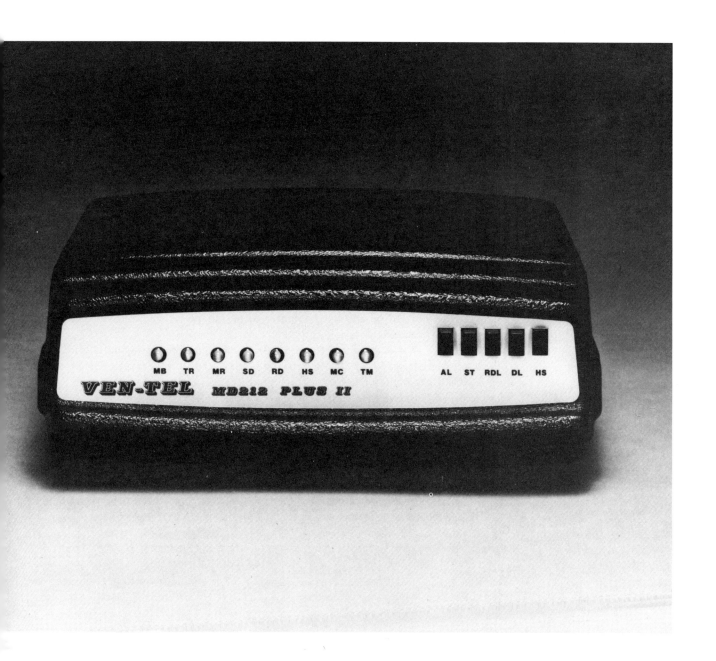

MICROS IN ACTION

Gleem Paint Center in Mobile, Alabama, is a retail store approximately 50 feet by 200 feet in size with an inventory of over $100,000 in paint and painting supplies.

An analysis identified their microcomputer needs as a data base for
- Inventory control
- Accounts payable
- Accounts receivable.

A spreadsheet or a specific application was also needed for the general ledger.

A data base for inventory control was identified as the most necessary. Each month a physical inventory had to be taken for cost control. Each item in the store had to be counted, the records updated, and then a value calculated.

The required microcomputer equipment included:
- A desk top microcomputer
- A printer
- A laptop microcomputer
- A bar code reader.

The Epson HX–20 and IBM PC were selected so data could be communicated between them.

Communication is the transfer of data and/or (microcomputer) instructions from one computer to another or to peripherals. Microcomputer communication within a system is similar to communication between different microcomputer systems. This chapter deals with data and instructions between the parts of a microcomputer system and between individual microcomputers.

Microcomputer communication is necessary when data exists on one computer that is needed on another computer or peripheral or when instructions must be sent from one device to another.

The hardware needed for communication between microcomputers and their parts or between microcomputers and other microcomputers includes the cables used to connect the parts of a system, special communications cables, modems, and telephone lines.

This chapter will help you understand and use the communication capabilities of the microcomputer.

COMMUNICATION HARDWARE

The microcomputer requires a communication port for input and output to a second device. Computers communicate with the world through ports:

Input Ports	Output Ports	Input/Output Ports
Keyboard	Monitor	RS–232C
Bar code reader	Printer (Parallel)	(Communication)
Joy sticks	IEEE 488 (lab equipment)	(Printer)
Voice recognition	Voice synthesis	(Plotter)
Koala pads		(Device control)
		Disk drives
		Hard drives

Some ports are for input or output, others for both. The RS–232C port is commonly used for communication, and can be used both for input and output. The microcomputer must have an RS–232C port for most communications discussed in this chapter. Figure 8–1 shows the ports at the rear of a microcomputer.

The ports of a microcomputer may be designed to send and/or receive data. Often, even those ports that you most likely would assume are one way only are actually both sending and receiving. For example, the parallel port is typically a conduit to the printer. This port usually receives input on the status of the printer. Notice how the microcomputer waits for the printer to perform its task, no matter how slow it is. The microcomputer is receiving information from the printer at the rate of flow of data the printer can handle.

Each port on a microcomputer requires a special connector. The RS–232C and Centronics parallel connectors are quasi-standard. The use of differently styled plugs with different numbers of active lines for varied purposes is often used by the manufacturer to make it difficult to make errors when connecting equipment. This practice usually means that special cables are needed for each application.

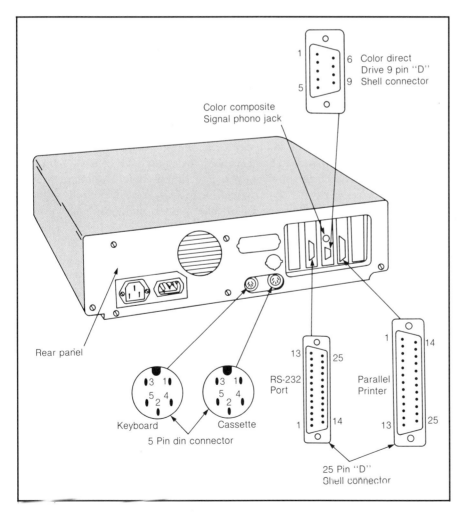

FIGURE 8–1
Ports of a Computer

FIGURE 8–2
Direct Connect Modem

Modem:
A device to connect the microcomputer to the telephone. It changes binary codes to sound for telephone transmission, and then back again.

Baud rate:
Usually refers to the transmission rate. 1200 baud is 120 characters per second.

Special communication hardware devices are available for using the telephone, connecting to a central computer, and connecting two microcomputers together. Some of these devices fit into the expansion slots, while others are external.

Modems

The built-in or add-on RS–232C serial port connects the microcomputer to a **modem**. A modem is a device that changes the binary code generated by the microcomputer to a sound so it may be sent over telephone lines to a second modem that changes the sounds back to binary code. The word modem comes from the tasks it performs, to MOdulate and DEModulate. Some microcomputers have internal modems.

Answering microcomputer-modems send their code on one frequency, while the originating microcomputer uses another. This is why one microcomputer must be the originator and the other the answerer.

A modem may be a direct connect modem or it can use an acoustical coupler. A direct connect modem is connected directly into the telephone line (see Figure 8–2). It works well in a home where telephones may be easily disconnected. An acoustical coupler is a device that cradles the telephone receiver (see Figure 8–3). It may be used anywhere: your office, a telephone booth, or your home.

Most acoustical couplers are limited to 300 baud, while direct connect modems can often handle 300, 1200, 2400, 4800, 9600, and 19,200 baud. Modems with the capability of using faster **baud** are more expensive and are currently under development. Direct connect modems are less likely to cause errors than are acoustical couplers.

In laptop microcomputers, it is common to find internal modems. These microcomputers are designed to be carried to remote locations for the communication of information back to a desktop microcomputer or central computer.

Modems may be simple devices for connecting the microcomputer to telephone lines, or smart devices that dial automatically, control the log-on information, and answer the telephone when called. Smart modems must be direct connect.

One advantage of smart modems is that you may use the microcomputer to call other microcomputers automatically in the middle of the night when long distance telephone costs are at their lowest. The microcomputer may be instructed to send a series of prepared files for processing the next day, and then break the connection. The smart modem also allows the microcomputer to answer incoming calls and receive and store messages, as well as send automatic messages.

Special programs are needed for both the automatic send and receive functions. This feature opens the microcomputer to all the security problems of the national data base operator. Users of auto-answer modems may have unwelcome users break into their systems and damage files or obtain confidential information.

Cables and Null-Modems

Another way to use the communication capabilities of laptop computers is to collect information in their fulltime or low power memories for transmission to

FIGURE 8–3
Acoustical Modem

MICROS IN ACTION

Data Transfer

Gleem Paint Center had the option of using a modem or null-modem to connect the HX–20 with the IBM PC. Since both were at the same location, a null-modem was selected. After a little experimentation, the printer cable of the HX–20 was found to work as if it were a null-modem to connect the two microcomputers together.

desktop computers through the use of direct wired connections (Figure 8–4) and a null-modem. A **null-modem** is a way of wiring microcomputers together, making them think a modem is being used to connect them when there is none. Baud rates of up to 9600 are commonly used for null-modem file transfer with the proper software.

Null-modem:
Device that makes the computer behave as if it is connected to a telephone to allow communication between computers.

Mechanical and Electronic Switching Devices

More than a single printer may be connected to a microcomputer with the aid of switches. The first time many microcomputer users think of controlling a printer as a communication task is when a second printer is needed. This need may arise when a letter-quality printer is needed for correspondence, and a dot matrix printer is needed for business graphics.

If one printer is parallel and the other serial, it is possible to connect one to each port and instruct the microcomputer which port to use for each task. MS/PC–DOS microcomputers equipped with more than one serial port may control one device per port. When both printers use the same communication port, both may be connected at the same time with a switch. Connecting and disconnecting a cable will soon damage the connection on either cable or microcomputer or both if a switch box is not used (see Figure 8–5).

FIGURE 8–4
Serial Cables

An RS–232C connector cable is soldered with the pins connected as indicated:

Pin	1	to	Pin	1
	2	to		3
	3	to		2
	4	to		5
	5	to		4
	6	to		6
	7	to		7
	8	to		20
	20	to		8

Pins 8 and 20 are shorted

A female connector was placed at the end of each cable. This cable was used as null-modem (a substitute for a modem) with many combinations of microcomputers. It does not work for all combinations.

FIGURE 8–5
Switch

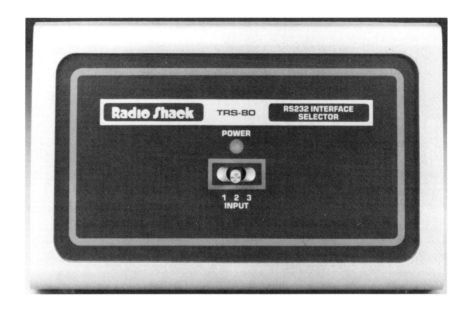

There are switches available for both parallel and serial controlled devices. Most switches are mechanical, while others use electronic switching. The need for electric power generally indicates the presence of electronic switching.

Serial devices use 25 pin connectors, but may use as few as 3 active pins. Since the actual pins used for specific purposes are not standard, you must be careful when purchasing switches to make sure they work for the purpose intended, with the cables available.

Most devices are interchangeable among brands, but there are exceptions. Cables and switches may be used to connect different brands of peripheral devices and microcomputers, but you need to learn about your system and how it works.

In addition to connecting two printers to one microcomputer, it is possible to connect several microcomputers to a single printer. It is also possible to connect one or more microcomputers together to form a simple network for the exchange of files and programs. Usually the data sent must be converted to ASCII code before being sent from one microcomputer to another.

WHY YOU MUST LEARN
ABOUT MICROCOMPUTER COMMUNICATION

Knowledge of communication procedures helps the user get the most from each part of a microcomputer system. Users need electronic data and instruction communication when:

1. There is a need for high-speed data and instruction transfer.
2. The data at both ends of the transfer are needed ready for computer use.
3. The cost of electronic transfer is less than alternate means.
4. One part of the microcomputer system must control a second part.
5. An external device must be controlled.
6. Data are being collected by an external device.

Need for Speed

Data and/or instructions may be sent over regular telephone lines from one microcomputer to another. Auto-answer modems provide microcomputers with the capability of answering the telephone without human assistance. Microcomputers may be left on standby waiting for messages that may be sent at any time by other microcomputers. Business transactions depend on timely communication. A late letter or contract can mean a lost sale.

Need for Computer Data

Entering data into a computer is time consuming and subject to errors. If data are already in a form usable to a computer, it is wasteful to transfer it to hard copy and re-enter it into a computer.

Data and/or instructions in one microcomputer may be required in a second microcomputer at a different location. If the computers use the same disk format, the data and instructions may be sent on disk. If the formats do not match, the data and instructions may have to be sent using either telephone or direct wire transfer.

Low Cost

The cost of a telephone call from one microcomputer to another may be the most economical method of transferring data and instructions. Data and instructions sent this way are usually in the form needed for printing or use by the second microcomputer.

Controlling the Parts of a Microcomputer System

Data and instruction transfers from a microcomputer to its printer, disk drives, monitor, and hard disk are the same as or similar to the data and instruction transfers between two microcomputers. For example, to be able to use all the capabilities of a printer, the user must know what instructions are needed to make the printer perform a task, and how to get the microcomputer to send these instructions.

Many printers can boldface, underline, subscript, superscript, produce extra large type, produce small type, change fonts, and do many other things. Some programs make it easy to perform these tasks while others make it difficult or impossible. The user must know:

1. The need.
2. What the device can do.
3. What the program can do.

The accomplishment of a result depends on the capability of the device and program. If the device can, but the program cannot, accomplish a desired result, the user must find new programs or ways to change the available program to get the job done. If the device cannot do the job, it must be replaced with a device that can.

Controlling External Devices and External Data Collection Devices

Analog devices:
Devices used to monitor real-world conditions such as temperature, sound, and movement. These devices use continuous voltage rather than the binary coding system of the microcomputer.

Microcomputers can communicate with **analog devices** that measure continuous changes in voltage. A special interface such as the IEEE 488 is required to allow a computer that is a binary device to understand an analog device. Laboratory equipment, machine monitors, and other data collection devices are often designed to operate as analog devices.

With external devices, the microcomputer can control the temperature in a room, the lights in a house, the flow of liquid in an experiment, and many other things in both an office and industrial plant. In many cases the microcomputer must first be able to determine facts about the process being controlled, in order to make feedback adjustments needed to control the process.

COMMUNICATION THEORY, BACKGROUND, AND PROGRAMS

The user must understand some of the theory and know some of the terms and programs to obtain the most benefit from the communication capabilities available. The user needs the microcomputer to perform a specific task or set of tasks. If a system cannot be purchased ready to perform a needed task, one must be assembled from products supplied by a number of different vendors. To match different vendors' products, the communication procedures often require configuration. The user who does the configuration must know some theory and terms and must be knowledgeable about the programs available. Some things the user must study are:

1. The nature of communication between two smart devices.
2. Serial and parallel connections.
3. Communications parameters (asynchronous or synchronous).
4. Communication parameters (ASCII).
5. Other communication parameters.
6. Communication programs.

Microcomputer Communication—Two Smart Devices

Communication between microcomputers and from microcomputers to peripherals (Figure 8–6) is the transfer of meaningful data and instructions in the form of bits. Bits may be part of a standard coding system, such as ASCII, or a custom code of a particular system.

When the devices at both ends of the communication link are smart, often, one device will try to outsmart the other and cause communication failure. It is best to let one communication partner standardize on the communication parameters (speed and other settings), then adjust the second partner to fit the needs of the first.

Serial and Parallel Connections

The most common method of connecting two microcomputers together, or a microcomputer and a peripheral, is by serial or parallel cables. The standard serial communication port is the RS–232C. A serial RS–232C port uses a

MICROS IN ACTION

Data Storage

Gleem Paint Center selected the Epson HX–20 because bar code readers were available. Inventory data is collected by the HX–20 bar code reader and stored in its CMOS memory for printing or communication at some later time. (The purchase of a commercial null-modem from your dealer is recommended. Hardware requirements change over time.)

standard connector with 25 pins, not all of which are active. In serial communication, data is transmitted one bit at a time through a single wire to a specific pin.

Serial RS–232C communication is used for both peripherals and between microcomputers. It may be used to connect additional devices to a telephone to allow a microcomputer to communicate over telephone lines.

Parallel (Centronics) connections are commonly used for printers and other peripherals. Figure 8–7 illustrates different types of connectors. Parallel connections transmit all the bits used along a set of wires at the same time. Many devices may be connected in either serial or parallel. Most microcomputers use both types of connections. There are additional connections and ports to communicate with the keyboard, bar code readers, and other devices.

FIGURE 8–6
Setting Up Communications

Communication can occur only between two communicating partners. A Radio Shack Model 100 with a custom program and an IBM PC with a custom program are connected using their standard modem cables and a null-modem adapter.

Both microcomputers are turned on and communication is established using:

For the IBM PC	For the Radio Shack Model 100
1200 baud	1200 baud
Eight-bit character (default)	Eight-bit character
No parity (default)	No parity
	1 Stop bit
	XON/XOFF disable
	Echo Yes
	Reflect line feed No
	On send do not add line feed
	Print own output Yes
	To screen add line feeds

The Radio Shack program allows the microcomputer to originate or answer using a null-modem. Either end of the communicating pair may be used to control any of the configuration parameters. The decision was to use the default setting for the IBM PC and then use the custom program in the Radio Shack Model 100 to match the communication settings. If any one of the settings is different, communication will not occur.

FIGURE 8–7

(a) Male and Female RS–232C Plug, and (b) Male and Female Centronics Parallel Plug

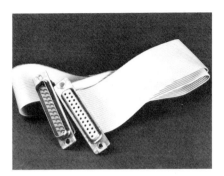 

Asynchronous or Synchronous

There are two types of computer communication:

1. Asynchronous
2. Synchronous

Asynchronous is commonly used on microcomputers. Only during data transmission is timing critical in **asynchronous communication. Synchronous communication** requires continuous timing.

In asynchronous communication, the microcomputers control the timing only when a character is sent. Communication may start at any time and end at any time. During the period when a character is being sent, the timing is important.

Synchronous communication requires that the timing of the transmission from the beginning of to the end of a communication session be synchronized, coordinated. Synchronous communication is used predominantly with central computers.

Communication Using ASCII

ASCII is the standard used by most of the microcomputer industry. ASCII uses seven-bits, the decimal numbers from 00 to 127, to define specific characters and control codes (see Table 8–1).

The codes from 00 to 31 are mostly control codes. Some microcomputers and printers use different control codes. There is a degree of inconsistency in how the codes from 00 to 31 are used by different printers and microcomputers. Line feed (10) and carriage return (13) are quasi-standard. However, some microcomputers only use carriage return (13). When communicating from one microcomputer to another, it is common to get double line feeds or none because of this inconsistency. Programs can often solve these problems.

Esc code (27) is widely used to send special instructions, but again it is not universal. Common end-of-file markers in CP/M and MS/PC–DOS are usually 26, while in TRS–DOS zero is used.

Using a seven-bit character with one **stop bit,** the first bit is a **start bit** telling the receiving computer that asynchronous communication is about to start. The next seven bits are the ASCII code. The next bit is usually the **parity bit,** and the last bit is the stop bit.

Asynchronous communication: Communication that requires timing only when a bit is being transmitted.

Synchronous communication: Communication that requires continuous timing.

Stop bit: The bit that tells the second microcomputer the character is complete.

Start bit: The bit that tells the second microcomputer a character is being sent.

Parity bit: Error checking bit.

Binary No.	Decimal No.	Character	Binary No.	Decimal No.	Character
0000000	000	control	1000000	064	@
0000001	001	control	1000001	065	A
0000010	002	control	1000010	066	B
0000011	003	control	1000011	067	C
0000100	004	control	1000100	068	D
0000101	005	control	1000101	069	E
0000110	006	control	1000110	070	F
0000111	007	Bell	1000111	071	G
0001000	008	backspc	1001000	072	H
0001001	009	tab	1001001	073	I
0001010	010	Line fd	1001010	074	J
0001011	011	control	1001011	075	K
0001100	012	form fd	1001100	076	L
0001101	013	carr ret	1001101	077	M
0001110	014	control	1001110	078	N
0001111	015	control	1001111	079	O
0010000	016	control	1010000	080	P
0010001	017	control	1010001	081	Q
0010010	018	control	1010010	082	R
0010011	019	control	1010011	083	S
0010100	020	control	1010100	084	T
0010101	021	control	1010101	085	U
0010110	022	control	1010110	086	V
0010111	023	control	1010111	087	W
0011000	024	control	1011000	088	X
0011001	025	control	1011001	089	Y
0011010	026	control	1011010	090	Z
0011011	027	Esc	1011011	091	[
0011100	028	control	1011100	092	\
0011101	029	control	1011101	093	]
0011110	030	control	1011110	094	^
0011111	031	control	1011111	095	=
0100000	032	blank	1100000	096	`
0100001	033	!	1100001	097	a
0100010	034	"	1100010	098	b
0100011	035	#	1100011	099	c
0100100	036	$	1100100	100	d
0100101	037	%	1100101	101	e
0100110	038	&	1100110	102	f
0100111	039	'	1100111	103	g
0101000	040	(	1101000	104	h
0101001	041	)	1101001	105	i
0101010	042	*	1101010	106	j
0101011	043	+	1101011	107	k
0101100	044	,	1101100	108	l
0101101	045	—	1101101	109	m
0101110	046	.	1101110	110	n
0101111	047	/	1101111	111	o
0110000	048	0	1110000	112	p
0110001	049	1	1110001	113	q
0110010	050	2	1110010	114	r
0110011	051	3	1110011	115	s
0110100	052	4	1110100	116	t
0110101	053	5	1110101	117	u
0110110	054	6	1110110	118	v
0110111	055	7	1110111	119	w

TABLE 8–1

American Standard Codes for Information Interchange—ASCII

Table 8–1 continued

TABLE 8–1
continued

Binary No.	Decimal No.	Character	Binary No.	Decimal No.	Character
0111000	056	8	1111000	120	x
0111001	057	9	1111001	121	y
0111010	058	:	1111010	122	z
0111011	059	;	1111011	123	{
0111100	060	<	1111100	124	:
0111101	061	=	1111101	125	}
0111110	062	>	1111110	126	~
0111111	063	?	1111111	127	special

The microcomputer often sends an eight-bit binary number to the second device. An eight-bit binary number can produce decimal numbers from 00 to 255. There are no standards for the numbers over 127. Screens and printers often use **high bit** numbers for graphics and control purposes.

Communication Parameters

Combinations of hardware and software are used to set the communication parameters. There are a number of **parameters** that must be agreed upon before two computers can communicate using ASCII asynchronous communication (Figure 8–8). These parameters include:

1. Who will originate and who will answer
2. The baud rate
3. The **character size**
4. Parity
5. The number of stop bits
6. The use of full or half duplex.

When communicating between a central computer and a microcomputer, the usual convention is for the central computer to **answer** and for the microcomputer to be the **originator.** The computer that answers is sometimes referred to as the host, while the originator is called a terminal. Some programs limit the hardware they are used on to one role. Many programs allow the computer to answer or originate. It makes no difference which is which between microcomputers, but one microcomputer must answer and one must originate. Communication will not occur otherwise.

Baud rate is the speed of transmission during the communication of a character. Both computers in the communication process must be using the same baud rate setting. (The definition of the term ''baud rate'' has undergone changes—current usage is given.)

High bit:
The last bit in a binary number. High bit numbers are the decimal numbers that can only be created when the last bit is used.

Parameter:
A variable value. Parameters are values that must be set before communication can occur.

Character size:
The number of bits per character.

Answer:
Modern setting in asynchronous communication. One partner must answer, the other originate.

Originate:
Modern setting in asynchronous communication. One partner must originate, the other answer.

FIGURE 8–8
Sending a Character

Stop bit	Parity bit	ASCII character	Start bit
1	1	1100001	1

Ten bits are required:

The binary number 1100001 is 97 decimal and sends the letter a.

MICROS IN ACTION

Serial Communications

Gleem Paint Center's Epson HX–20 was equipped with a serial port into which could be connected a serial printer or a microcomputer such as the IBM PC.

The IBM PC, equipped with a communication program, is instructed that a communication device is sending data. The program will then capture the data and store it on the IBM PC's disk as an ASCII data file.

The inventory data needed by Gleem Paint Center can be collected and stored with minimum effort and errors.

Common baud rates for telephone communications are 110, 300, 1200, 2400, 4800, 9600 and 10,200. A baud rate of 300 means 300 bits are sent per second. Since ten bits are needed for each character (start bit, seven bits for ASCII code, parity bit, and stop bit), this results in a rate of 30 characters per second. A baud rate of 1200 means 120 characters are sent per second during communication. For most communication involving humans, the use of 300 baud is satisfactory. For large file transfers, faster baud rates are required. A twenty-page single-space report consists of approximately 3500 characters including blanks. This report would take two minutes at 300 baud and three-quarters of a minute at 1200 baud.

Parity aids in finding transmission errors. Parity may be odd, even, or none. Adding up the bits contents (0 or 1), you will get an odd or even number. Using even parity, the parity bit is adjusted so the sum of the ten bits is even. When the receiving computer finds the sum is not even, it knows a transmission error has occurred and will ask for a retransmission of the character. Parity must be matched.

In asynchronous communication the number of stop bits may be one or two. The most common is one. Communication may occur even if the number of stop bits is not matched.

Full-duplex is like telephone communications. Both parties can send or receive at the same time. **Half-duplex** is like CB or ham radio communication. One party talks, then tells the second they are finished. Each party must tell the other to "take over" when transmission is complete.

Full-duplex:
Both communication partners can send and receive at the same time.

Half-duplex:
One communication partner can send and the other receive at any given time.

Setting Up Communication Parameters

Setting up communication parameters in communication programs varies from detailed step-by-step procedures to a single-step process. In some communication programs, it is menu driven. The advantage of the step-by-step process is that you can control each parameter individually. Data Capture, a communication program, is used to illustrate this approach. PC–Talk III, another popular communication package, is used to illustrate a single-step approach. The matching task often involves some trial and error before a match is obtained.

Data Capture Setting up communication parameters in the communication program Data Capture is a menu-driven task. Figure 8–9 shows the initial screen display of this program.

FIGURE 8–9
Starting Data Capture

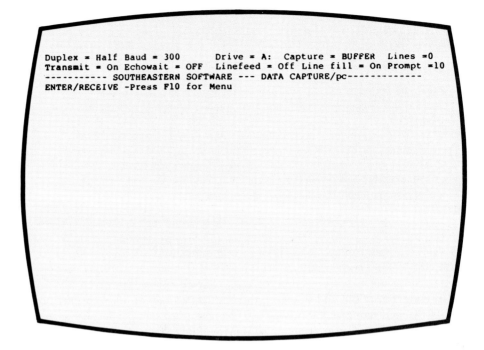

```
Duplex = Half Baud = 300      Drive = A:  Capture = BUFFER   Lines =0
Transmit = On Echowait = OFF  Linefeed = Off Line fill = On Prompt =10
---------- SOUTHEASTERN SOFTWARE --- DATA CAPTURE/pc------------
ENTER/RECEIVE -Press F10 for Menu
```

The program has built-in default values for the communication parameters. If your needs match the parameters, you will be ready to start the communication process.

When first using a program, it is important to read the information on the screen and documentation that comes with the program carefully. The only function key used by Data Capture is F10. As shown in Figure 8–9, it is the key that calls the menus where you can set the communication parameters.

Since long distance telephone calls can be expensive, it is best to check the parameter settings before proceeding. If you find it necessary to set the parameters, it will usually require five or more steps. Data Capture gives the user many controls beyond setting parameters that are menu driven in a manner similar to setting the parameters.

Figure 8–10 demonstrates some of the additional capabilities of Data Capture. For example, you may instruct the program to turn on a "C"apture Buffer to store in RAM the characters which are being sent or are received. This discussion is limited to the menu selections needed for setting the communication parameters.

PC–Talk III PC–Talk III is available for MS/PC–DOS microcomputers. It does not require you to walk through a series of menus for the setting of the communication parameters but rather does it all in one step. Figure 8–11 shows the initial screen of this program.

The help menu of PC–TALK III is examined in Figure 8–12.

Setting communication parameters is a single step. Figure 8–13 is PC–TALK III's menu for setting the communication parameters.

Communication Programs

Communication capability depends on both hardware and software. As with all other capabilities of a microcomputer, a program is needed to make things

MICROS IN ACTION

Communication Programs

Gleem Paint Center's Epson HX–20 did not require a communication program. The IBM PC needed a standard communication program to capture the data sent by the HX–20.

happen. There are many communication programs available. They are sold as individual programs or may be purchased as part of a data base, spreadsheet, or combination program package.

Programs are available for most CP/M and MS/PC–DOS microcomputers. There are three types of programs:

1. Dumb terminal programs
2. Smart terminal programs
3. Automatic originate and answer programs.

A **dumb terminal** program is one that allows the microcomputer to communicate under the supervision of a human being. When information is typed, it is sent. The information returning is displayed on the microcomputer screen.

A **smart terminal** program allows the opening of a disk file and the transfer of its contents out from the RS–232C port (uploading). It also allows the capture and storage of data received (downloading). In addition, the program can control the printer to obtain hard copy of the material sent or

Dumb terminal:
A terminal that can only communicate under the control of an individual

Smart terminal:
Terminal that can be used to transfer data files between computers.

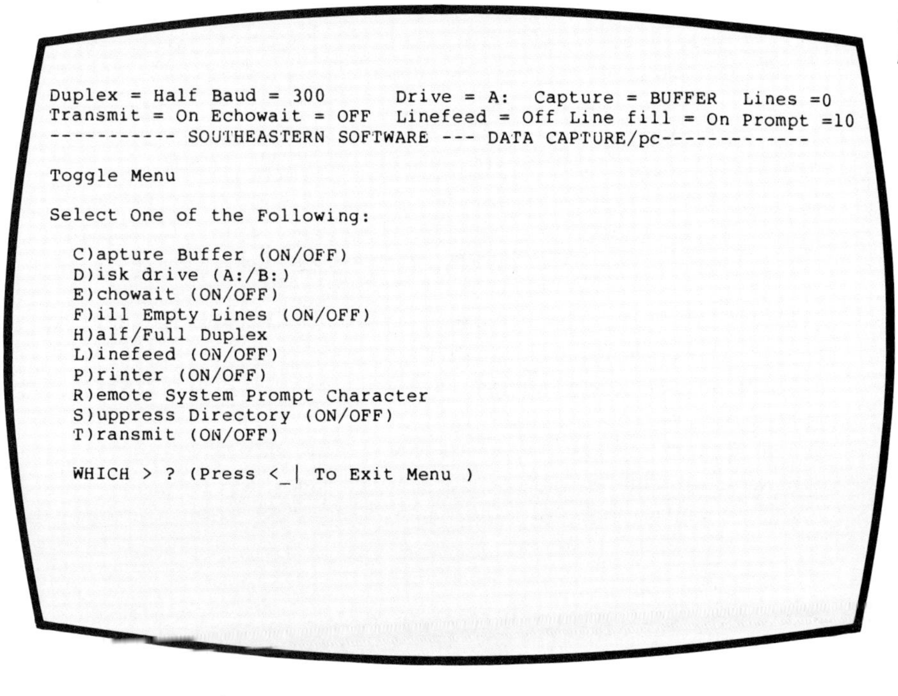

FIGURE 8–10
Additional Capabilities

```
Duplex = Half Baud = 300      Drive = A:  Capture = BUFFER  Lines =0
Transmit = On Echowait = OFF  Linefeed = Off Line fill = On Prompt =10
---------- SOUTHEASTERN SOFTWARE --- DATA CAPTURE/pc------------

Toggle Menu

Select One of the Following:

   C)apture Buffer (ON/OFF)
   D)isk drive (A:/B:)
   E)chowait (ON/OFF)
   F)ill Empty Lines (ON/OFF)
   H)alf/Full Duplex
   L)inefeed (ON/OFF)
   P)rinter (ON/OFF)
   R)emote System Prompt Character
   S)uppress Directory (ON/OFF)
   T)ransmit (ON/OFF)

   WHICH > ? (Press <_| To Exit Menu )
```

FIGURE 8–11
Starting PC–Talk III

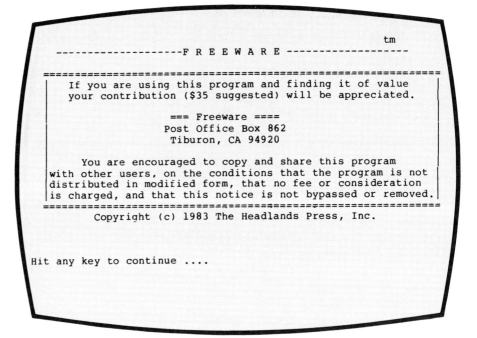

```
                                                          tm
        ----------------F R E E W A R E ----------------

   ===============================================================
   |  If you are using this program and finding it of value      |
   |  your contribution ($35 suggested) will be appreciated.     |
   |                                                             |
   |                  === Freeware ====                          |
   |                 Post Office Box 862                         |
   |                 Tiburon, CA 94920                           |
   |                                                             |
   |    You are encouraged to copy and share this program        |
   | with other users, on the conditions that the program is not |
   | distributed in modified form, that no fee or consideration  |
   | is charged, and that this notice is not bypassed or removed. |
   ===============================================================
                Copyright (c) 1983 The Headlands Press, Inc.



Hit any key to continue ....
```

received. Some microcomputer-dumb terminal combinations also allow printed output.

When combined with smart modems that can dial or answer a telephone automatically a program may instruct the microcomputer to make its own communication connection at defined times for the transfer of files. This helps take advantage of off-time telephone rates to reduce costs.

FIGURE 8–12
Help Menu

```
===Proceed ...

                       ======================================
                       |  ===PC-TALK III COMMAND SUMMARY===  |
                       ======================================
                       ||PrtSc = print screen contents       |
                       |^PrtSc = contin. printout (or^PgUp)   |
                       |Alt-R  = Receive a file (or PgDn)     |
                       |Alt-T  = Transmit a file (pr PgUp)    |
                       |transmit: pacing '=p' binary '=b'     |
                       |trans/recv:XMODEM '=x'                |
                       | Alt-V = View file   Alt-Y = delete   |
                       | Alt-D = Dialing directory            |
                       | Alt-Q = redial last number           |
                       | Alt-K = set/clear Func keys(Alt-J)   |
                       | Alt-= set/clear temp Alt keys        |
                       |Alt-E = Echo toggle Alt-M = Message   |
                       |Alt-S = Screendump Alt-C = Clearsc    |
                       | Alt-P =  communications Parameters   |
                       | Alt-F =  set program deFaults        |
                       | Alt-L =  change Logged drive         |
                       | Alt-W =  set margin Width alarm      |
                       | Alt-Z =  elapsed time/current call   |
                       | Alt-X =  exit to DOS                 |
                       |Ctrl-End = send sustained Break       |
                       ======================================

    ^PrtSc=prnt Alt-T=tran R=rec V=view D=dial E=echo M=mesg X=exit
                          <Home>=Help
```

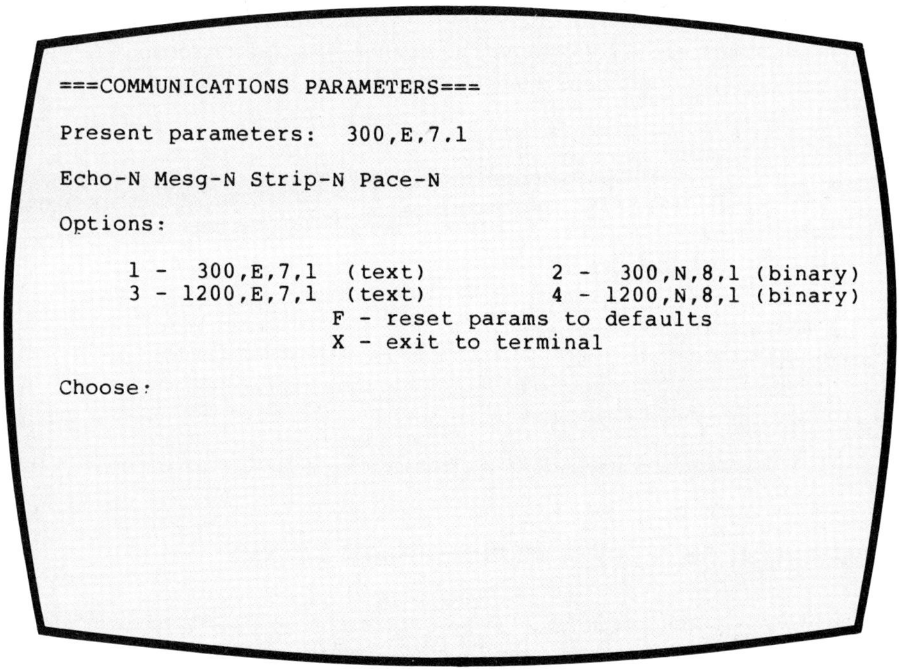

FIGURE 8–13
PC–Talk III Communication
Parameters

```
===COMMUNICATIONS PARAMETERS===

Present parameters:  300,E,7,1

Echo-N Mesg-N Strip-N Pace-N

Options:

    1 -  300,E,7,1  (text)        2 -  300,N,8,1 (binary)
    3 - 1200,E,7,1  (text)        4 - 1200,N,8,1 (binary)
                      F - reset params to defaults
                      X - exit to terminal

Choose:
```

COMMUNICATION WITH PERIPHERALS

The disk operating system is a communication controller. The microcomputer system is a communication network. Peripherals are controlled using the same codes and communication hardware that may be used to communicate between microcomputers. You may connect two microcomputers or a microcomputer and a peripheral using the same cables. There will often be slight differences in how the cables are connected.

When documenting the operation of a program, it is possible to connect a microcomputer in place of a printer and capture the data as it is printed.

USER WINDOW

IN THE STUDY HALL

A NEC laptop microcomputer and a word processor were used to write part of a term paper while in a study hall. Upon returning home, a serial RS–232C cable was connected between the laptop and an IBM PC serial port. An IBM communication program was told to capture and save the text as it was sent by a communication program in the NEC.

Off-Line Data Entry Devices

Some microcomputers have special capabilities that add to their usefulness as remote data entry devices. The relative cost of pocket, laptop, and desktop microcomputers results in an on/off-line situation similar to that of microcomputers and large central computers. The smaller, low-cost microcomputer may be used as off-line equipment relative to the desktop microcomputer.

USER WINDOW

IN THE AIRPORT

The salesperson picks up her laptop computer and types a letter while waiting in the airport. At her motel she telephones her office. The letter is transmitted to a large microcomputer with an auto-answering device for printing and mailing in the morning.

COMMUNICATION BETWEEN MICROCOMPUTER SYSTEMS

Modems, null-modems, and disks can be used to communicate between microcomputers. For example, a microcomputer can be connected to a second microcomputer using two modems and the telephone system. All communication parameters must be matched, except that one modem must be set on answer and the other on originate, and one microcomputer must be a host while the other is a terminal.

A program set in the terminal mode does not reflect code that is sent to it. A host program does. If a communication setup results in double letters being printed on screen, it is possible that the second computer is reflecting code back when it should not be. If typing information results in no characters on the screen, the computer at the other end may not be reflecting code when it should be. The duplex setting may also result in the same problem. Often there is more than one way to solve any communication mismatch.

The use of null-modem connections is common for the transfer of files between microcomputers that cannot read or write on matched disk formats and that are in the same location. This method of file transfer is slower than direct disk reading and subject to errors. Since ASCII is a seven-bit standard, control codes contained in the eight-bit may or may not be transferred correctly.

Read-Write-Format Programs

Communication, the transfer of data files from one microcomputer to another, may occur using direct disk transfer. MS/PC–DOS is one of the few disk operating systems that includes the disk format as part of its standard. Most MS/PC–DOS microcomputers can exchange disks with each other, but there are exceptions. Some microcomputers with quad-density disk drives have problems reading disks produced on microcomputers with double-density disk drives, due to slight variations from design specifications.

Disks with foreign formats may be read in one microcomputer by another with special programs. For example, programs are available for Radio Shack

TRS–80 Model I, III, and 4 microcomputers with double-density drives to read, write, and format single-sided disks using the MS/PC–DOS format. Models of Epson, Kaypro, Osborne, and other microcomputers operating under CP/M have programs available that allow the reading, writing, and formatting of disks with many different formats, including MS/PC–DOS.

The amount of time required to transfer a file using direct disk transfer programs is a little longer than to transfer a file between two disks using the same format in a given microcomputer. The transfer of files is usually without error.

Even files transferred error-free often require some editing. If you transfer an ASCII file from one microcomputer to another, you will likely not have problems. A WordStar file transferred from an Apple IIe under CP/M to the IBM PC or back will most likely transfer without error. So will a dBase II file. You will have more problems transferring a file between two different programs on the same microcomputer than between the same program on two different microcomputers.

A program written in a high-level language such as BASIC is better transferred by saving it as an ASCII file on the first microcomputer, then moving it back to machine program code after transfer. It will usually work if there are no special capabilities used on the first microcomputer that are not available on the second. BASIC programs may be written to run on a number of different microcomputers if the code selected is consistent with all machines. The transfer of machine language programs is possible, although it is unlikely they will work once transferred.

Other Special Communication Procedures

The ham radio community has been involved in microcomputers since the early days. Many "hams" were the original hardware hackers. The electronic theory and concepts of ham radio and microcomputers are closely related.

Ham operators have developed hardware and software that allow the microcomputer to produce both Morse Code and standard ASCII code, and to transmit such code by radio signals. Federal regulations limit the manner in which the microcomputer may be used for "over the air transmission" using continuous wave (CW) communications.

For international business that requires long distance transmission, ship-to-shore and ship-to-ship, the use of the microcomputer is increasing. As the capabilities increase in this area, more and more business uses will be developed.

COMPARING COMMUNICATION PROGRAMS

The features needed in a communication package are a function of the hardware used. Most communication programs will work with a variety of modems and hardware configurations. Some are designed to work with specific configurations. Some hardware configurations require specific packages. Features such as auto-dialing, auto-answering, and the maintenance of a directory require a combination of both hardware and software. See Table 8–2 for a comparison of communication software.

TABLE 8–2

Communication Software

	Crosstalk XVI Microstuf Inc.	Data Capture /PC Southeastern Software	PC–Talk III Headlands Press Inc.	Smartcom II Hayes Microcompute Products
Hardware Features				
Memory Req.	128K	128K	64K	192K
Drives Req.	1	1	1	1
General Features				
Copy Protect	No	No	No	No
Baud Rates	110–9600	110–19,200	110–9600	300, 1200, 2400
Duplex Full	x	x	x	x
Half	x	x	x	x
Auto Answer	x	x	x	x
Dialing	x	x	x	x
Re-dial	x		x	x
Keyboard	x	x	x	x
Other Features				
Menu Driven	x	x		x
Function Keys	x	x	x	
Directory	x	x	x	x
Price	$195.00	$120.00	$35.00	$245.00

SUMMARY

You have learned why microcomputer communication is important, some communication theory, the steps needed to set up, and how to operate a communication session. You have reviewed the role of some of the special communication hardware and have been introduced to the tasks performed by communication within a microcomputer system and between microcomputer systems.

The difficulties of setup and the ease of use of communication have been introduced. The key points in this chapter are:

1. Communication is the transfer of data and instructions from one computer type device to another.

2. Communication capability depends on both hardware and software.

3. The microcomputer requires a communication port for input and output to a second device.

4. A modem is a device that connects a microcomputer to a telephone. Some microcomputers have built-in modems.

5. Microcomputers may be connected with special cables for the transfer of files.

6. More than a single printer can be connected to a microcomputer with the aid of switches.

7. Knowing about communication helps the user get the most from each part of a microcomputer system and make different microcomputers work together as a system.

8. The user must understand some of the theory, know some of the terms, and be familiar with various programs to obtain the most benefit from the communication capabilities available.

9. Smart devices are at both ends of the microcomputer communication partnership.

10. The most common method of connecting two microcomputers together, or a microcomputer and a peripheral, is by serial or parallel cables.

11. Asynchronous communication requires timing when data is transmitted. Synchronous communication requires continuous timing.

12. The ASCII standard is important for the communication process.

13. Combinations of hardware and software are used to set the communication parameters.

14. Setting up communication parameters is menu driven in some communication programs.

15. The disk operating system is a communication controller.

16. Some microcomputers have special capabilities that add to their usefulness as remote data entry devices.

17. Modems, null-modems, and disks may be used to communicate between microcomputers.

18. Communication, the transfer of data files from one microcomputer to another, may occur using direct disk transfer.

19. The microcomputer can help the ham radio operator communicate.

KEY TERMS

Answer
ASCII
Asynchronous communication
Baud rate
Character size
Download
Dumb terminal
Full duplex
Half duplex
High bit

Modem
Null-modem
Originate
Parameter
Parity bit
Smart terminal
Start bit
Stop bit
Synchronous communication
Upload

REVIEW QUESTIONS

1. Identify some ports found on microcomputers.

2. What is a modem?

3. Identify the two types of modems.

4. What is a null-modem?

5. Detail the reasons why users need electronic data and instruction communication.

6. What must the user know in order to communicate using microcomputers?

7. Define microcomputer communication.

8. What is ASCII?

9. What is serial communication? What is parallel communication?

10. What is asynchronous communication? What is synchronous communication?

11. Identify the start bit, parity bit, and stop bit in asynchronous communication.

12. In asynchronous communication how many bits are needed for each character?

13. What communication parameters must be set?

14. Define these communication terms:
   a. Originate
   b. Answer
   c. Character size
   d. Full duplex
   e. Half duplex

15. What are the three types of communication programs?

16. What is downloading and uploading?

17. Why is off-line operation of microcomputers of interest to the user of microcomputers?

18. When can a microcomputer read disks with foreign formats?

DISCUSSION AND APPLICATION QUESTIONS

1. In ASCII what is the code for a blank? Identify the code numbers necessary to reproduce your name.

2. Find advertisements for communication programs in a magazine and identify what is available and what it costs.

3. Examine advertisements for modems. Identify their features and costs.

4. Find advertisements for internal and external modems. Compare the features of the two devices.

5. Identify where in your local area you would purchase special communication cables.

LABORATORY ASSIGNMENTS

1. Examine the equipment in your laboratory. Identify what communication hardware and software is available and what would be necessary to allow you to communicate between two of the microcomputers available.

2. If hardware and software are available, use two microcomputers connected with a null-modem wire to configure one to originate and one to answer. Establish communication.

3.   If hardware and software are available, use your communication program to transfer an ASCII data file from one microcomputer to another.

4.   If hardware and software are available, use your communication program to transfer an ASCII program file from one microcomputer to another. Use the program after it is transferred. Explain why the program performed as it did after transfer.

5.   If hardware, telephone line, and software are available, establish telephone communication between two microcomputers.

6.   If hardware, telephone line, and software are available, use your communication program to transfer an ASCII data file from one microcomputer to another.

7.   If hardware, telephone line, and software are available, use your communication program to transfer an ASCII program file from one microcomputer to another. Use the program after it is transferred. Explain why the program performed as it did after transfer.

SELECTED REFERENCES

Buckwalter, Jeff T. *Understanding Data Communications.* Alfred Publishing, 1983.

Flanders, Dennis. *Communications and Networking for the IBM PC.* Prentice Hall, 1983.

Glossbrenner, Alfred. *The Complete Handbook of Personal Computer Communications.* St. Martin's Press, 1983.

Kruglinski, David. *The Osborne/McGraw-Hill Guide to IBM PC Communications.* Osborne/McGraw-Hill, 1984.

Melin, Michael, and Michael Mikus. *Connections: The Micro-Communications Guidebook.* The Book Company, 1984.

Nichols, Elizabeth, Joseph Nichols, and Keith Musson. *Data Communications for Microcomputers.* McGraw-Hill, 1982.

9

GOALS

When you complete this chapter you will be able to:

Understand why microcomputer communication with central computers is important.

Understand some theory, the steps needed to set up, and how to operate a communication session.

Understand the role of some of the special communication hardware.

Name and identify the tasks performed by communication with central computers.

Understand some of the difficulties of setup and the ease of use of communication.

OUTLINE

Chapter Goals

Why You Must Learn about Communication between a Microcomputer and Central Computer

Speed
Size
Programs
Data Management
Number of Users

Communication Theory, Background, and Programs

Microcomputer Communication with Central Computers
Asynchronous or Synchronous Communication Parameters and Programs

Communication Hardware

Emulators and Interfaces

Central Computer Communication

National Data Bases
Electronic Mail
Computer Conferencing
Other Computer Data Bases and Bulletin Boards
The Microcomputer as a Remote Data Entry Device

Modems

Summary

Key Terms

Review Questions

Discussion and Application Questions

Laboratory Assignments

Selected References

COMMUNICATIONS WITH CENTRAL COMPUTERS

MICROS IN ACTION

Dean Witter is a large financial services brokerage firm owned and operated by Sears. They have offices in all major cities and in many smaller ones.

In the local offices, the professionals who advise and place orders for the public are called account executives. The account executive's potential needs for a microcomputer were identified as:

1. Communication with F.A.S.T. (Financial Action Service Terminal) system.
2. Maintenance of a client's data base.
3. Special application programs and spreadsheet analysis of client's needs.
4. Word processing.

The F.A.S.T. system is a dial-up service operated by Dean Witter for both the account executives and individual clients. Clients may access their own data files, enter into the company's research files, learn what is available, and obtain an up-to-date value at any time using their own microcomputer.

Communication is the transfer of data and instructions from one computer type device to another, and the interactive use of a larger computer using a second computer. The need for microcomputer communication with central computers exists for reasons similar to the needs of microcomputer-to-microcomputer communications. The central computer may be a microcomputer, although it is usually a large computer (**minicomputer** or **mainframe**) that has some capabilities beyond those found in a microcomputer. At times it is useful to use the microcomputer as a terminal to use the larger central computer.

The professional has a need to communicate between a microcomputer and a central computer when:

1. Data or instructions are in the microcomputer and are needed in the central computer.
2. Data or instructions are in the central computer and are needed in the local microcomputer.
3. The microcomputer is used as a terminal for a central computer.

Electronic mail is an example of the need for data transfer to a central computer and back. A memory area in the central computer is reserved for mail and messages. The sender uses a microcomputer to upload a message to the central computer. The second party checks the "mail box" to determine if any messages have been sent and, if so, downloads the message. The job of the central computer is to act as the middleman.

The lack of standards and rapid technical improvements have resulted in a slower than expected growth of **electronic mail** and other communication applications. The professional must use the same type of communication procedures that were outlined in chapter 8. The knowledge is technical, and difficult to learn and use for some individuals. The technical knowledge needed after the initial setup is completed is minimal.

The hardware needed for communication between a central computer and a microcomputer is similar to the hardware needed to communicate between

Minicomputer:
Medium-size computer, larger and more expensive than a microcomputer, but smaller than a mainframe.

Mainframe:
A large computer. Originally all computers were mainframe computers. Most require technical expertise to operate.

Electronic mail:
The transmission of letters, memos, and other messages by one microcomputer to another computer.

microcomputers. Many microcomputers come with the capability to communicate included. If not available, the addition of asynchronous communication capability to microcomputers is relatively simple and low cost.

WHY YOU MUST LEARN ABOUT COMMUNICATION
BETWEEN A MICROCOMPUTER AND CENTRAL COMPUTER

The central computer has capabilities and data storage capacity that are not available on microcomputers. Microcomputers can solve many of the problems of the user, but there are problems that may require a larger computer. Usually a large central computer is needed because of a combination of factors.

1. Speed—they are faster than microcomputers.
2. Size—they can handle files and data bases that are larger than those possible on microcomputers.
3. Programs—special programs are available only on selected central computers.
4. Data management—security and other data management tools are generally better on central computers.
5. Number of users—a central data base may service a number of users at the same time.

Speed

Because the design of large computers is different from that of microcomputers, it is difficult to make a direct comparison of the speed. The speed of a computer is a function of the speed of the central processor, the activities performed by the central processor, the operating system of the computer, as well as many other design aspects. No matter how speed is measured, the larger computers are faster and may be used where such speed is needed. Microcomputers may be used to collect data and then transfer that data to the central computer for the routine that requires the extra speed.

Size

The amount of RAM available in microcomputers has increased from 64K to over three million. In some microcomputers the additional memory can be used only for selected purposes, so the actual increase may not be as large as it may appear.

The size of on-line storage devices has increased from 50K to over 200 megabytes. The most common size of hard disks is currently 30 megabytes.

Even with these increases in internal and on-line capacity, the microcomputer still does not have as much memory available as the large central computers do. In addition, when large data bases are created, the speed of the larger central computers may be needed to handle the massive amount of data involved.

Electronic libraries (**national electronic data bases**) are available that may be called to research many different topics. Some of the available data bases are listed in Table 9–1.

National electronic data bases:
Dynamic libraries that are used by connecting a microcomputer to a telephone. Current information about economics, business, and other specialized topics is available using such data bases.

Name of Data Base	General Function
Accountant's Index	Corresponds to hard copy of the Accountant's Index.
Commerce Business Daily	U.S. Department of Commerce—corresponds to printed *Commerce Business Daily.*
CompuServe	General features including electronic mail.
Dow Jones News	Provides searcher access to *Wall Street Journal* stories, Dow Jones News Service, and *Barron's.* Dow Jones records date to 1979.
F.A.S.T. (Financial Action Service Terminal)	Financial and stock quote services.
Source	General features including electronic mail.
WESTLAW	Data base for lawyers to research legal cases.

Most data bases charge fees for joining and usage.

Electronic libraries (data bases) allow researchers to complete projects in minutes, transfer the results, and generate reports without the production of hard copy until the final report.

Using the Source Communication involves two computers. One of the most popular communication partners is the Source. The Source may be called directly or through the use of a national telephone network service, such as Telenet. Using Telenet, you must first log on to the telephone network (so you can be charged), then log on to the Source. You must make arrangements to purchase both services before you can use them (the Source will bill you for access charges).

The Source is designed to support many combinations of communication parameters. The communication parameters that work for our system on the Source are: eight-bit characters, one stop bit, no parity, and full-duplex. In addition, the Source is in the answer mode, so you must be in the originate mode. The program parameters and your modem must be set to match one of the combinations of parameters supported by the Source. Most microcomputer equipment will work with the parameters as shown, but some will need to be set differently.

Assuming you have configured the program as outlined in chapter 8 to match the Source, the next step is to dial one of the national network services and connect the telephone line to your modem.

Making the Connection (Hand-Shake) When initial contact is made, you may have some spurious characters on your screen. The inital screen should look like the one in Figure 9–1.

You must have several codes to use the system. Figures 9–2 and 9–3 illustrate the screens which require the entry of codes.

The Source is used by calling to the screen a series of menus either directly or through some other menu. The initial menu is started by typing MENU <CR>. You may go directly to any menu if you know where you are going and its name. Figure 9–4 illustrates the Source's main menu.

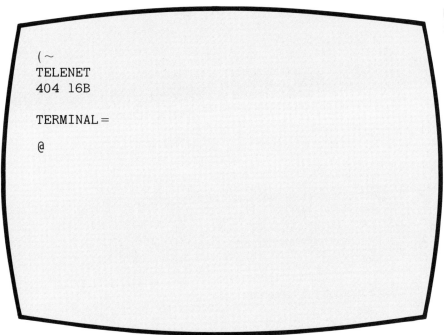

FIGURE 9–1
Starting the Source

Figure 9–5 is the Education and Careers menu while Figure 9–6 details the services available through this menu.

The Source has a help menu which may be called at almost any time. The help menu aids the user who has forgotten how to use the system. Figure 9–7 is the help menu.

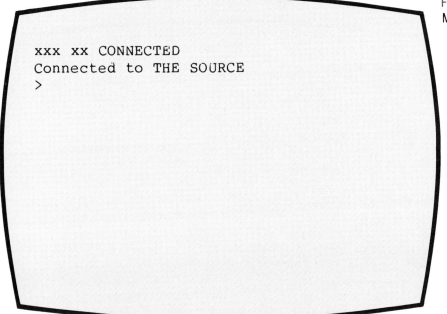

FIGURE 9–2
Making the Connection

FIGURE 9–3
Entering Your Code

```
id xxxxxx xxxxxx<CR>
TCF068 (user 18) logged in Saturday, 01 Dec 84 10:17:32.
Welcome, you are connected to THE SOURCE.
Last login Friday, 30 Nov 84 13:07:16.

(C) COPYRIGHT SOURCE TELECOMPUTING CORPORATION 1984.

THIS SYSTEM WILL NOT BE AVAILABLE FROM 4 AM
TO 6 AM (EDT) ON  12/01/84 FOR MAINTENANCE.

Pick the Heisman Trophy winner. Type
SPORTS for details.

Reader's Digest Gives You A Chance
To Earn $250. See NEW for details.

Have You Expressed Your Opinion About
The Source Business Magazine? If Not,
Type BIZDATE For Details.
-> CHAT -OFF

-> MAILCK
Your Mailbox is empty at this time.
->
```

Programs

The rule "Find the software and then select the computer" still applies when selecting a central computer service. There are many programs developed only for specific central computers that may be needed by the microcomputer user. When one of these programs is needed, the purchase of time on a central computer is a logical choice.

FIGURE 9–4
Source's Main Menu

```
THE SOURCE MAIN MENU

   1   NEWS AND REFERENCE RESOURCES
   2   BUSINESS/FINANCIAL MARKETS
   3   CATALOGUE SHOPPING
   4   HOME AND LEISURE
   5   EDUCATION AND CAREER
   6   MAIL AND COMMUNICATIONS
   7   PERSONAL COMPUTING
   8   INVESTOR SERVICES

Enter item number or HELP _
```

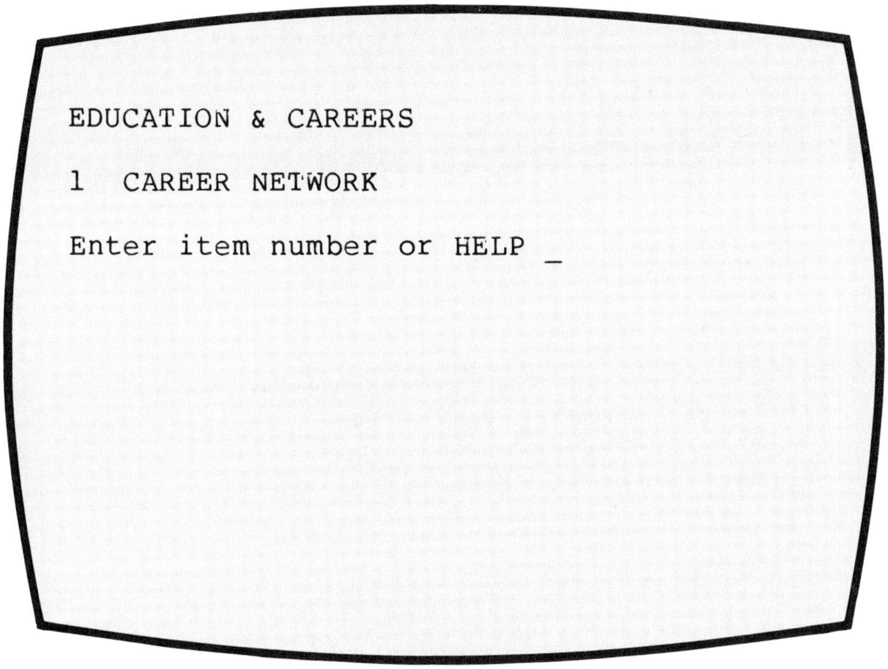

FIGURE 9–5
Making a Selection

```
EDUCATION & CAREERS

1  CAREER NETWORK

Enter item number or HELP _
```

Programs for analyzing large data sets may be limited to a particular computer due to:

1. Program size
2. Data set size
3. Computer speed.

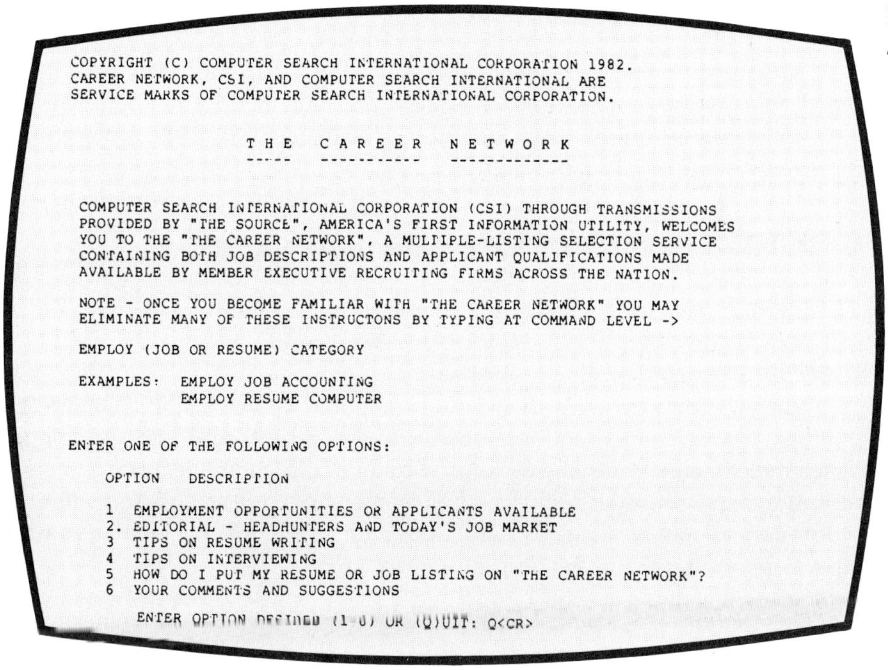

FIGURE 9–6
After the Selection

```
COPYRIGHT (C) COMPUTER SEARCH INTERNATIONAL CORPORATION 1982.
CAREER NETWORK, CSI, AND COMPUTER SEARCH INTERNATIONAL ARE
SERVICE MARKS OF COMPUTER SEARCH INTERNATIONAL CORPORATION.

              T H E   C A R E E R   N E T W O R K
              -----   -----------   -------------

COMPUTER SEARCH INTERNATIONAL CORPORATION (CSI) THROUGH TRANSMISSIONS
PROVIDED BY "THE SOURCE", AMERICA'S FIRST INFORMATION UTILITY, WELCOMES
YOU TO THE "THE CAREER NETWORK", A MULTIPLE-LISTING SELECTION SERVICE
CONTAINING BOTH JOB DESCRIPTIONS AND APPLICANT QUALIFICATIONS MADE
AVAILABLE BY MEMBER EXECUTIVE RECRUITING FIRMS ACROSS THE NATION.

NOTE - ONCE YOU BECOME FAMILIAR WITH "THE CAREER NETWORK" YOU MAY
ELIMINATE MANY OF THESE INSTRUCTONS BY TYPING AT COMMAND LEVEL ->

EMPLOY (JOB OR RESUME) CATEGORY

EXAMPLES:  EMPLOY JOB ACCOUNTING
           EMPLOY RESUME COMPUTER

ENTER ONE OF THE FOLLOWING OPTIONS:

    OPTION    DESCRIPTION

    1  EMPLOYMENT OPPORTUNITIES OR APPLICANTS AVAILABLE
    2. EDITORIAL - HEADHUNTERS AND TODAY'S JOB MARKET
    3  TIPS ON RESUME WRITING
    4  TIPS ON INTERVIEWING
    5  HOW DO I PUT MY RESUME OR JOB LISTING ON "THE CAREER NETWORK"?
    6  YOUR COMMENTS AND SUGGESTIONS

      ENTER OPTION DEFINED (1-6) OR (Q)UIT: Q<CR>
```

FIGURE 9–7
The Help Menu

```
-> HELP<CR>
BE GLAD TO!

   - STC CUSTOMER SUPPORT MAY BE REACHED VIA MAILBOX...........TCA088
       OR AT OUR TOLLFREE NUMBER...............................800-336-3330
   - FOR THE LATEST ANNOUNCEMENTS FROM THE SOURCE, TYPE........NEW
   - FOR A LISTING OF SYSTEM COMMANDS, TYPE....................HELP SYSCOM
   - FOR THE MAIN INDEX TO THE SOURCE CONTENTS, TYPE...........HELP LIBALL
   - TO ENTER THE SOURCE MAIN MENU, TYPE.......................MENU
   - FOR AN INDEX TO BUSINESS AND FINANCIAL SERVICES, TYPE.....HELP BIZDEX
   - FOR AN INDEX TO ONLINE INFORMATION ON PROGRAMMING & THE
       EDITOR, TYPE............................................HELP ADAPPR
   - FOR A LIST OF ALL HELP FILES AVAILABLE TO YOU, TYPE.......HELP LIST
->
```

Data Management

Data is a valuable asset. The security and use of data must be controlled. The protection schemes available for some microcomputer data bases are limited. In many situations, using a central computer as a central **file server** gives management tools needed to ensure such security and control needed over the company's memory, its data base.

File server:
The computer which controls the storage and retrieval of files from a common disk or hard disk when a number of computers are connected together to form a system.

Number of Users

It is difficult to separate the need for many users to access a data base from speed, size, and security factors. The large central computer or some type of network with a central file server (subject of chapter 10) is needed to perform this task.

COMMUNICATION THEORY, BACKGROUND, AND PROGRAMS

The user must understand some of the theory, know some of the terms, and be familiar with some programs to obtain the most benefit from the central computer communication capabilities available.

When communicating with a central computer, knowledge of communication parameters is important because the microcomputer user must be able to match the parameters used by the central computer. Most of the terms and concepts are the same as those discussed in chapter 8, except that most communication uses telephone lines, so only the screen of the microcomputer can be seen. Some of the things the user must know are:

1. The nature of communication between a central computer and microcomputer.

MICROS IN ACTION

Communications with a Financial Data Base

Dean Witter's F.A.S.T. system is designed to be used with a variety of microcomputers. The standard used is asynchronous using ASCII. There are no special limitations on the microcomputer equipment, modems, and prograprograms needed to communicate with the system.

2. Communication parameters (asynchronous-ASCII or synchronous-EBCDIC).
3. Communication parameters and programs.

Microcomputer Communication with Central Computers

Communication between microcomputers and central computers is the transfer of meaningful data and instructions in the form of bits. The bits may be part of a standard coding system, such as ASCII, **EBCDIC**, or the custom code of a particular system. It is possible to purchase an interface device that allows microcomputers using ASCII to communicate with a central computer using EBCDIC. These devices are called **emulators** if they are internal to the microcomputer, and interfaces if they are external. Microcomputers equipped with emulators are often joined together into a network.

When communication is between a microcomputer and a central computer, the central computer's communication parameters will usually be set, and the microcomputer will have to be adjusted to make the communication process work.

Asynchronous or Synchronous

Both asynchronous and synchronous communications are used between microcomputers and central computers. Often central computers can only communicate using synchronous communications, and interface devices are needed to convert asynchronous to synchronous and back between the two computers.

Many microcomputers produce (asynchronous) ASCII only, while most central computers produce (synchronous) EBCDIC only. Modems convert between digital and analog, change synchronous to asynchronous, and convert ASCII to EBCDIC and back.

Communication Parameters and Programs

Communication between microcomputers and central computers requires the same parameters and programs as other microcomputer communication. Asynchronous ASCII signals look the same no matter what hardware and software is used. The microcomputer user must set the parameters to match the central computer. Most central computers are set in the answer mode so the microcomputer user must set the microcomputer to originate. In most cases, the software packware package need not have the capability to answer when commu-

EBCDIC:
Extended Binary Coded Decimal Interchange Code. The standard code developed and used by IBM for its mainframe computers. It is a binary code made up of eight bits that allows 256 characters

Emulators:
A printed circuit board that fits into a microcomputer and gives it the capability to act like a special purpose terminal.

MICROS IN ACTION

Terminal Selection

Dean Witter's F.A.S.T. computer is the host. The microcomputer owned by the client or account executive is the terminal. The terminal may be either dumb or smart.

nicating with a central computer. If file transfers are not needed, the microcomputer user may need only a dumb terminal program.

COMMUNICATION HARDWARE

Most of the microcomputer hardware used for communication with central computers is the same hardware as that used for communication with other microcomputers. Some special hardware is available for special applications.

The RS–232C port is used for communication with central computers. Modems and null-modems are used in communication between microcomputers. Special printed circuit cards may be added to microcomputers to give them additional capabilities.

Emulators and Interfaces

The microcomputer may be made to work like custom devices with the addition of internal or external hardware and special software. For example, the microcomputer, plus a special printed circuit board and software, can emulate an IBM 3270. An IBM 3270 is a terminal that can be connected to an IBM mainframe computer. It has special communication and graphics capabilities.

Central computers do not do their own communicating directly. They often use **collectors** that interface with devices having special characteristics. Microcomputer manufacturers make interfaces that act like collectors. These devices are limited to specific mainframe-microcomputer combinations.

CENTRAL COMPUTER COMMUNICATION

The business problem is to determine what is best done by the microcomputer as a stand alone unit, and what is best done by the central computer.

Timesharing started with the use of large mainframe computers in the mid-1960s. The idea was to allow the user access to the central computer by way of terminals. This service allows individuals to process data in **real time,** rather than as part of a **batch run.** The original terminals were capable of operating only when connected to the central computer.

The dial-up terminal was developed for the timesharing computer. Business people quickly realized that microcomputers could act as terminals for central computers.

Collector:
An interface that collects messages from a number of devices, organizes the messages, and then forwards them to the central computer.

Real time processing:
To process data and instructions as they are transmitted to the computer. The user works interactively with the computer.

Batch run:
A scheduling system which requires computer tasks be collected and given to a central controller who then runs them as a single job batched together.

MICROS IN ACTION

Access to F.A.S.T.

Dean Witter's F.A.S.T. system is similar to other data base programs. It is available to the account executives and clients of Dean Witter only.

The economic problem is to balance the cost of on-line processing with off-line processing. The original business computers (late 1950s, early 1960s) were so expensive that great efforts were made to create and use off-line machines for sorting, printing, and other services.

The on-line/off-line problem still exists. The difference is that the off-line equipment is now a low-cost smart microcomputer. The microcomputer can do many of the tasks of a central computer at lower cost. As a professional you will have to answer the question "What is the best way to do the job: microcomputer or central computer?" Your answer will vary as the capabilities and costs of the two alternate approaches continue to change.

In addition to performing many of the tasks of the central computer and acting as a terminal for the central computer, the microcomputer may be the central computer.

USER WINDOW

Never say never in microcomputers. Three years after connecting a Model I Radio Shack as a terminal to an IBM–360, the microcomputer user was told by the system's operator it could not be done.

National Data Bases

Institutions may maintain their own data bases, use those established as commercial services (Table 9–2), or both.

The procedure for logging on, getting started, in all systems are similar to the Source. The Source was one of the first data base systems and offers over 1,200 features and programs. It is owned and operated by Reader's Digest. It offers current stock information, with custom calculation of your own portfolio, and an executive job search data base.

The Source was one of the first systems to offer electronic mail. To use this service, both senders and receivers must be members of the Source, and receivers must check their own mailbox with their own microcomputers. There is no limitation on which microcomputer is used, since the communication uses standard asynchronous ASCII. One feature of electronic mail service by the Source is the capability to send up to 200 messages at one time, to be forwarded at specific times.

TABLE 9–2

On-Line Subscription Data Bases

	CompuServe Information Service	Dow Jones News/Retrieval	EasyNet	The Source
Electronic mail	yes	yes	no	yes
Paper copy delivery	no	yes	no	yes
Teleconferencing	yes	no	no	yes
Stock quotations	yes	yes	yes	yes
Public access			yes	
Number of				
Data bases	400	38	65	70
Subject areas	1,000+	11	unlimited	11
Subscribers	270,000	235,000	not available	62,000
On-line publications	yes	yes	yes	yes
Access type				
Datapac	yes			
Durect 800			yes	
iNet			yes	
Sourcenet				yes
Telenet	yes	yes	yes	yes
Tymnet	yes	yes	yes	
Uninet	yes	yes		yes

Rates vary between $0.27 and $3.00 per minute during the day and $0.10 to $3.00 at night using a 1,200 baud modem.

CompuServe is another data base service that has been operating for a number of years. It offers services similar to those of the Source. CompuServe has electronic mail, a bulletin board, news, weather, magazines, wire services, directory, and more. News services, such as the one for commodities, are updated every twenty minutes. The cost of use during business hours is much greater than during off hours.

Dow Jones News/Retrieval System is a news and financial data base service for up-to-the-minute information on stocks and bonds. You may research a company in depth and maintain a stock portfolio for automatic update.

There are specialized data bases in law, advertising, aviation, medicine, engineering, and many other fields. You will find books listing these data bases in your library or at your local bookstore.

Electronic Mail

Electronic mail is the use of the computer to send messages through a computer network. Currently, you have the choice of electronic messaging (computer-to-computer transmission) or computer-generated mail (computer-input, terminal-output). Mail may be sent using an internal company system or through one of the commercial electronic mail carriers such as MCI, ITT, Western Union, Telex, or one of the electronic bulletin board systems.

Internal company networks may consist of a microcomputer with an auto-answer telephone modem and a communication program that can save any message received. The system is turned on after business hours, and all messages received are printed the next morning and forwarded as needed.

Some commercial electronic mail services provide a local toll-free telephone number. The user is expected to compose the letter off-line and upload it to the electronic mail service. There is usually an on-line charge to discourage on-line composition. The commercial service will save a message for downloading to the receiver's microcomputer, forward it by first-class mail, overnight mail, or hand deliver a printed copy of the message for various charges. Electronic mail is not seen as a substitution for a personal letter. It is a way to reach someone who is not available by phone, to send out mass mailings, or to get a document delivered rapidly.

Setting up to use electronic mail requires knowledge of the communication parameters and how to use the program available on your microcomputer to match the settings with the electronic mail service. EasyLink, the electronic mail service of Western Union, comes with many manuals including a training manual. The manual is well written, but the volume of material is liable to turn off all but the most determined potential user.

If your company has a central computer or a microcomputer with a modem that will automatically answer the telephone, you may set up your own electronic mail service. The ability to standardize the parameters and software used internal to an organization makes the creation of an internal electronic mail service easier than a commercial service in many circumstances.

Computer Conferencing

Computer conferencing is similar to telephone conferencing, except that microcomputers and a central computer are on both ends of the communication partnership. Many systems accept text, graphics, and voice. Using your own resources or a data base service such as the Source, you can set up a "PARTICIPATE" communication network. This allows individuals in different physical locations to "meet," using microcomputers. The advantage of this type of meeting over the telephone is that text, graphics, and voice may be transferred. If you have a microcomputer with a communication program that can capture and save what is received, you may transfer the material to your disks for future use.

Other Computer Data Bases and Bulletin Boards

There are specialized computer data bases servicing almost every industry and community. Many local retail microcomputer stores will run bulletin boards for their customers and potential customers.

Forum80 is a bulletin board found in many local communities. It was originally set up by TRS–80 microcomputer owners, but usually serves all users. You will find some business information, but mainly hobby information, in this type of bulletin board.

The Microcomputer as a Remote Data Entry Device

In the 1960s, computer systems were carefully designed to use off-line equipment for sorting and preparing data. The computer card was the popular input-output and data storage medium at that time, and there was equipment for sorting, collating, and separating decks of computer cards, depending on the need

USER WINDOW

BAR CODE READER

The supermarket clerk picks up his microcomputer with built-in bar code reader. Inventory is taken in four hours, rather than the usual twelve, with this add-on device.

The reason for off-line operation was the high cost of computer time, and the relative low cost of the off-line equipment that could do the preparation. Today, the microcomputer may be used to prepare data off-line from a mainframe computer. The best balance between the use of microcomputers and mainframes is constantly changing, as the costs of the alternatives change. Look at the use of different types of computer equipment as alternate methods of solving problems. Select the lowest cost method that does the best job for your organization.

USER WINDOW

REMOTE DATA COLLECTION

A survey is taken to determine the potential market for a product in a selected city. The data are coded and typed into a microcomputer. The microcomputer is connected to the telephone line and the data is transmitted to a central computer for addition to a data base and for analysis and evaluation.

The concept of selecting the most economical balance between on-line and off-line use of different size computers depends on the capability to transfer data, text, and other files between the computers. Communication between dumb terminals and a computer does not involve the transfer of files. Microcomputers may act as dumb or smart terminals. The capability to transfer files is one of the characteristics which differentiates dumb and smart terminals.

MODEMS

Modems come with custom features and their own programs. Most modems work with many different communication packages. Some modems come with their own software. The price is often not a measure of the features available. See Table 9–3 for a comparison of several modems.

Features	Smartlink II Business Comp. Net.	Smartmodem 1200B Hayes Microcomp.	Volksmodem 12 Anchor Automation
Speed 300	x	x	x
1200	x	x	x
Internal	x	x	
External		x	x
Duplex Full	x	x	x
Half	x	x	x
Includes Program	Yes	Yes	No
Auto answer	x	x	x
dial	x	x	x
redial		x	x
Price	$199.95	$349.00	$99.00

TABLE 9–3

Asynchronous Direct Connect Modems

SUMMARY

You have been introduced to the importance of microcomputer communication with central computers to the professional. You have learned that microcomputer-to-central-computer communication is similar to microcomputer-to-microcomputer communication.

The key points in this chapter are:

1. Communication is the transfer of data and instructions from one computer type device to another and the interactive use of a larger computer using a second computer.

2. The central computer has capabilities and data that are not available on microcomputers.

3. The professional must understand some of the theory, know some of the terms, and be familiar with some programs to obtain the most benefits from the central computer communication capabilities available.

4. Most often communication between a central computer and a microcomputer occurs over telephone lines or in a network.

5. Asynchronous (ASCII) communication is common on microcomputers while synchronous (EBCDIC) communication is common on central computers.

6. Communication between microcomputers and central computers requires the same parameters and programs as other microcomputer communication.

7. Most of the microcomputer hardware used for communication with central computers is the same hardware as that used for communication with other microcomputers. Some special hardware is available for special applications.

8. The microcomputer may be made to work like a custom device with the addition of internal or external hardware and special software.

9. The business problem is to determine what is best done by the microcomputer as a stand-alone unit, and what is best done by the central computer.

10. Institutions may maintain their own data bases or use those established as commercial services.

11. Electronic mail services are available.

12. Computer conferencing is similar to simple telephone conferencing except that microcomputers and a central computer may be on both ends of the communication partnership rather than human beings.
13. There are local data bases for use by individuals with local needs.
14. The concept of on/off-line equipment developed in the 1960s is applicable to the use of the microcomputer as an off-line data entry device for large computers.

KEY TERMS

ASCII	File server
Asynchronous	Interface
Collector	Mainframe computer
EBCDIC	Minicomputer
Electronic mail	National electronic data base
Emulators	Synchronous

REVIEW QUESTIONS

1. What are mainframe and minicomputers?

2. When does the microcomputer user need to communicate between a microcomputer and a central computer?

3. Identify one reason why electronic mail has been slow to grow.

4. Define electronic mail.

5. Why does the microcomputer user need a large central computer?

6. What is a national electronic data base?

7. What is Telenet? How is a data base such as the Source contacted using Telenet?

8. What is on the Source's main menu?

9. Identify and explain the following key terms:
   a. ASCII
   b. EBCDIC
   c. Emulators
   d. Interfaces

10. What is asynchronous and synchronous communication?

11.

11. How is communication organized in central computers?

12. Identify some of the services offered by CompuServe.

13. What is required to set up electronic mail?

1. Why is ASCII a key concept in both microcomputer-to-microcomputer and microcomputer-to-central computer communication?

2. Examine some microcomputer magazines and report on the type of modems now being advertised and their costs.

3. Contact some electronic mail services and report on the nature of the services being offered and their cost.

4. If your central computer has a mailbox service, find out about it and report on its operation.

5. From magazines and other sources find out about emulators and collectors. Report on their capabilities, costs, and availability.

6. Contact a national data base and report on its services and the cost of these services.

To perform communication laboratory assignments, your microcomputer needs to be equipped with a modem or a null-modem. You must have the correct communication software, and the communication partner identified must be available.

1. Use your microcomputer to communicate with the university's central computer. Report on the problems and initial log-on screens. What communication parameters were used?

2. Use your microcomputer to communicate with a local data base. Report on the problems and initial log-on screens. What communication parameters were used?

3. Use your microcomputer to communicate with a national data base. Report on the problems and initial log-on screens. What communication parameters were used?

4. Send a text file created on your microcomputer to a different brand microcomputer.

Cameron, Janet. "Electronic Mail Gallops into the Future," *Computerworld on Communications,* November 1984, vol. 1, no. 1, p. 71.
Campbell, Joe. *The RS–232 Solution.* Sybex Books, 1984.
Edelhart, Mike, and Davies Owen. *OMNI Online Database Directory.* Collier Books, Macmillan Publishing Company, 1983.

Glossbrenner, Alfred. *The Complete Handbook of Personal Computer Communications.* St. Martin's Press, 1983.

Lesko, Matthew. "Low-Cost On-Line Databases," *Byte,* pp. 167, 168, 171, 172, 174.

Schwaderer, David. *Digital Communications Programming on the IBM PC.* John Wiley and Sons, 1984.

10

GOALS

When you complete this chapter you will be able to:

Understand why local area networks are important.

Understand some of the theory of local area networks.

Understand the role of some of the special local area network hardware.

Understand some of the difficulties of setup and the ease of use of local area networks.

OUTLINE

LOCAL AREA NETWORKS

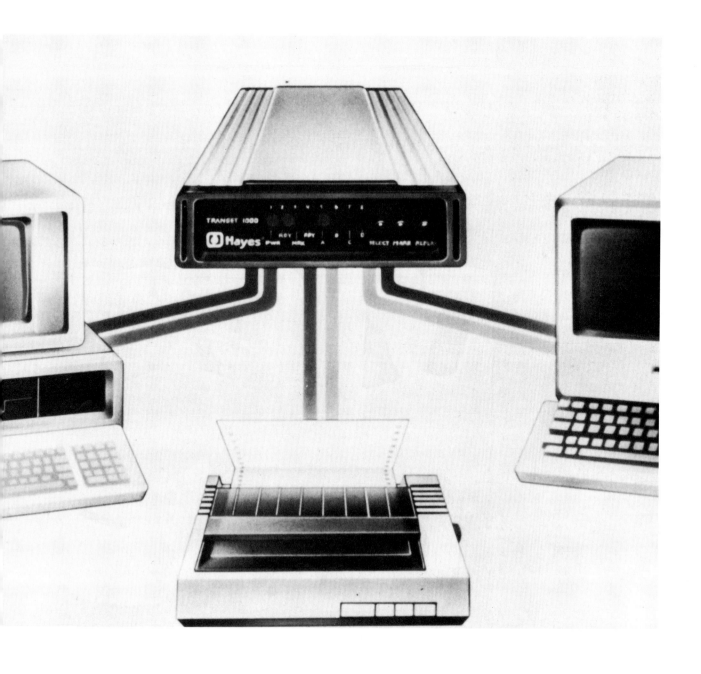

MICROS IN ACTION

Burnett-Wilson General Contractors of Mobile, Alabama, has fourteen full-time employees, of which six are superintendents or project managers. Up to fifty subcontractors may be active at any given time. As general contractors they are responsible for the supervision of all their jobs and the subcontractors.

After an exhaustive study they identified their microcomputer needs as:
■ Cost control–job costing
■ General ledger
■ Accounts payable
■ Accounts receivable.

Because a number of jobs needed to be done at one time, it was estimated that two to four data entry stations would be constantly in operation.

LAN:

Local Area Networks. A series of microcomputers connected together sharing peripherals, files, and programs.

A local area network (**LAN**) allows a company to tie a series of microcomputers together to form a system for the purpose of sharing peripherals, files, and programs. The cost of expensive peripherals, such as letter quality printers, may be spread among a number of users rather than carried by a single user.

The most basic network is one that uses a mechanical or electronic switching device to connect microcomputers and peripherals together. The connection of microcomputers to peripherals form networks. These networks are considered a limited case only. Figure 10–1 illustrates a local area network of microcomputers in operation.

FIGURE 10–1
A Local Area Network

It is often necessary for several individuals to use the same file. By having a network, all users can get to the files. The latest version or update is always available and there is no need to transfer disks among individuals. The LAN accomplishes the communication objective of making data available to several users at different locations.

LANs allow a single copy of a program to be used by many individuals. The program may be stored in a central area along with the common data files. When needed, the program is called up.

The large central computer has long been used as the core of networks for the sharing of data, programs, and peripherals. A network of microcomputers may be used in place of a central computer in situations in which the speed, programs, and other special capabilities of the larger computer are not needed. The current interest in LANs is due to the drop in the cost of networks, programs, terminals, wiring, and all other aspects of networks. Technical improvements and cost reductions are making LAN a solution for many more problems.

Because the technology is new, there is no single accepted LAN standard. For example, the type of cable used varies from twisted wire pairs such as those in telephone wires to the use of fiber-optic cables. Often many different types of cables, including telephone lines, will be combined in a single network.

The three aspects of a LAN are:

1. Physical transmission media and transmission techniques.
2. LAN topology (logical arrangement of stations).
3. Access methods.

WHY YOU MUST LEARN ABOUT LANS

LANs mean cost savings in equipment, better control of data files, and the sharing of expensive programs. LANs are needed in situations in which sharing must occur. Small businesses may need only personal computers that work alone. As an organization grows, however, and more individuals use microcomputers, sharing may be the best alternative for company growth.

In large corporations there is a need for both stand-alone work stations and coordination between individual microcomputer users. Data management and security are important in situations in which a number of users need to use and update the same data file constantly.

In small companies where cash is short, the sharing of peripherals may be the most important reason for a LAN. In larger companies, the sharing of data and program files may be more important.

RELATED CONCEPTS AND BACKGROUND

Networking is part of the growth of technology that is occurring in many aspects of microcomputers. A precondition for the general use of microcomputer-based local area networks was the availability of microcomputers with speed adequate enough to perform more than one thing at a time, that is, with the capability for **multi-tasking.**

Multi-tasking:
The capability of the microcomputer to perform more than one task at the same time.

Multi-use:
Microcomputers and programs
that allow more than one use
to share the same
microprocessors.

A special type of network may be created by using the microcomputer's capability for **multi-use.** In a multi-user environment, all users share the same microprocessor. This means the system need only have dumb terminals, but many use both smart and dumb terminals. Standard RS–232C, asynchronous serial communication may be used in this type of network.

The capability for multi-using is part of the hardware and operating system. It is not found in all microcomputers. Software is available that adds this capability in some microcomputers.

Multi-using is not a solution to all problems. If only one person uses a microcomputer, or if the microcomputer used does not have to share data bases, multi-using may not be needed.

The cost of this feature, relative to the cost of operating two stand-alone microcomputers, is in a state of change. For small offices, a central microcomputer with a limited number of terminals may be an economical solution to computer usage in the future. The terminals often will not have all the capabilities of the stand-alone microcomputer. The operation of a terminal in a network is similar to the operation of a microcomputer, except that data and instructions may be sent and received from other work stations in the network.

Central file server
(program):
Program that controls the
access to files by individual
work stations in a LAN.

A **central file server** program which makes a microcomputer into a central file server is often used in a local area network to control the access of individual work stations to the files stored in the "large" central storage device (hard disk). The central file server handles problems that occur when several users are trying to update a file at the same time. The central file server is often designed to handle the problem of file security, keeping selected users from using specified files.

It is possible to connect a series of microcomputers together with the addition of hardware and software that allow the sharing of data and instructions between them.

The control, such as limiting users, that management may exercise with central file servers approaches that of a large central computer. Data management of central data files is critical in many business situations.

Local area networks may be stand-alone networks or part of a larger system. You may have several different types of networks tied together with an interface device, and then, through another interface device, tied into a large central computer. The objective of networks is to carry out the concept of on-/off-line balancing of costs and benefits from different devices.

The central data storage device may be a hard disk with 10 megabytes of memory or more. Generally, LANs are designed for computers to communicate within an organization, using direct-wire connections with special interface devices for communication across telephone lines. When a LAN uses telephone lines, the operator will encounter many of the security problems of the timesharing mini and mainframe computer operator.

There are some copyright problems yet to be solved in the sharing of commercial programs. The technical developments in local area networks have progressed faster than the legal and moral solutions to the use of software on more than one microcomputer.

Some multi-user networks are created by the addition of a program to a microcomputer system. Most local area networks are combinations of hardware and software that must be matched to create the network.

MICROS IN ACTION

Setting up a Network

Burnett-Wilson General Contractors selected a twisted-wire paired network because the distances between terminals were limited, and the maximum number of terminals was not expected to exceed four.

PHYSICAL TRANSMISSION MEDIA

There are four popular cables used for connecting networks. Cost limitations, performance, and speed determine the best selection. The microcomputer is connected to a local area network through a port. This port may be built-in or created with the addition of a special purpose printed circuit board to the microcomputer.

There are four popular types of cable used for microcomputer networks in addition to the standard serial and parallel cables already discussed. They are:

1.   Twisted-pair wire cable
2.   Baseband coaxial cable
3.   Broadband coaxial cable
4.   Broadband optical-fiber.

The lines used to connect telephones, called twisted-pairs, can be used for networks. Networks using this type of wire are often designed around a central switching station. Generally this type of network is the least expensive, has the lowest speed (approximately 1Mbps—one million bytes per second), and is limited in the distance data can be sent to approximately 200 feet.

Baseband coaxial cable networks are medium speed, between 1Mpbs and 10Mpbs, depending on the physical type of cable. This type of cable is used by PC Net and Ethernet (two popular commercial networks). A baseband coaxial cable is similar to cable television wiring. The baseband is limited to allowing one terminal or microcomputer to transmit at a time. The single bus can handle only a single user at a time. Distances are limited to a few thousand feet without the use of repeaters. A repeater is a device similar to an amplifier that inputs a weak electrical impulse, then forwards a stronger impulse. The installation cost of baseband coaxial cable is generally higher than that of twisted-wire pairs or broadband cabling.

Broadband coaxial cable can handle many transmissions at one time, even different kinds of transmissions. Speeds of from 1Mbps to 10Mbps in each of up to 30 channel pairs are common. (For communication, a channel pair is needed to transmit information in both directions.) Optical-fiber cable is becoming more popular for broadband applications. Broadband cable can extend for miles with the use of inexpensive amplifiers.

A system built around one type of cable is easy to control and understand. Hybrid systems requiring a mixture of cables, interfaces, collectors, and telephone lines can become complex and technical.

LAN TOPOLOGY

The arrangement of stations relative to each other and relative to a central file server fall into some simple classifications. LANs are often perceived to be a central communications network among individuals and machines in a local office. LANs require flexibility in adding and changing hardware devices to keep the system current as technological changes occur. A LAN may need to be interfaced with mainframes or other LANs. Some popular **LAN topology** configurations include **central switching stations, communication buses, communication rings or circles,** and **point-to-point communication** (see Figure 10–2).

ACCESS METHODS

Access methods determine how stations communicate with the other physical parts of the network. The availability of a LAN depends on the existence of an operating system that can control a number of units. UNIX and UNIX derivatives have been the principal operating system supporting LANs in the past. MS/PC–DOS 3.1 is also capable of operating a LAN.

The **access method** is the scheme used by the operating system to control the individual work stations' right to transmit. Access control is either centralized or distributed. In a centralized system, a central file server checks on the activities of all stations and controls the transmissions. In a distributed system, each station participates in controlling the LAN.

The access control techniques include:

1. CSMA/CD
2. Token-passing

CSMA/CD (Carrier Sense Multiple Access/Collision Detect) operates similar to a party-line telephone system. The line is checked by the work stations program to see if it is being used. If it is not, transmission proceeds. All stations are able to read the messages sent, and must have software to check and see if the message is addressed to them. There is no central control microcomputer because the control is exercised by the individual stations. Ethernet was one of the first systems to use this approach to networking.

Token-passing is a common method of transmission control when a circle network is used. Each station checks to see if a given transmission is for them and, if it is not, passes the message along to the next station.

LAN topology:
The relative physical and logical arrangement of stations in the network.

Central switching station:
The central microcomputer connected to a series of stations in a LAN.

Communication bus:
A LAN layout around a bus which serves as a channel of communication.

Communication ring or circle:
Layout of LAN where the stations are connected in a ring or circle.

Point-to-point LAN:
Layout of LAN topology where each station is connected directly to other stations.

Access method:
The scheme used by the operating system to control the communication between work stations in a LAN.

FIGURE 10–2 LAN Topology

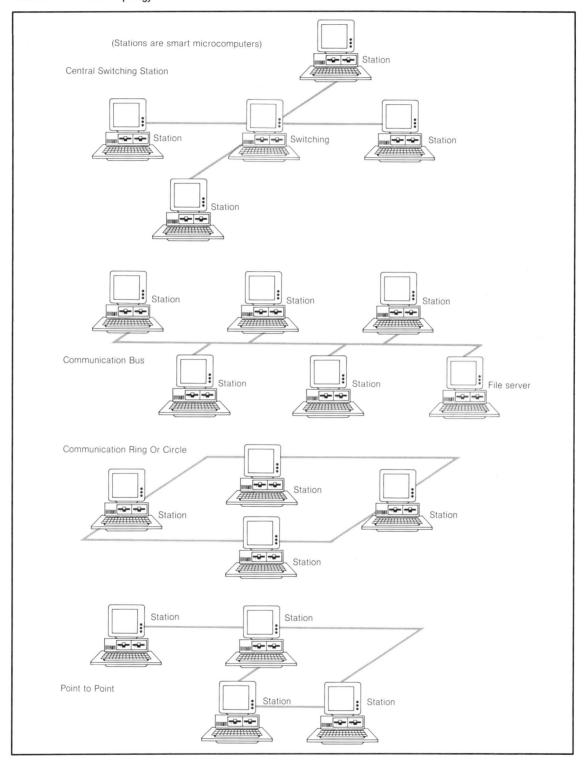

TABLE 10–1
Local Area Networks

	Omninet Corvus Systems	Davong MultiLink Davong Systems	Easinet Esprit Systems	PC Network IBM
Architecture Features				
Topology	Bus	Star	Ring	Bus
Cable	Twisted Pair	Coaxial Baseband	Twisted Pair	Coaxial Broadband
Data Rates MMbps	1.0	2.5	1.0	2.0
Access Method	CSMA/CD	Token Passing	Token Passing	CSMA/CD
Interface (gateway to mainframe)	Yes	Yes	No	Yes
Software Features				
File Locking	Yes	Yes	No	Yes
Record Locking	Yes	Yes	No	Yes
Electronic Mail	Yes	Yes	No	Yes
Remote Access	No	No	No	Yes
Capacities Features				
Maximum stations	63	255	254	72*
Maximum cable length	1,000 feet	2,000 feet	500 feet	2,000 feet**

*Additional stations with special cables.
** Longer distance with special cables.

Broadband coaxial systems use modems to control the frequencies of transmissions. A modem is needed to translate the microcomputer transmission to a special frequency and back. More than a single user may transmit at one time because modems divide the cable into channels.

Networks may be created with a variety of cables and with the addition of telephone connections. A central problem in creating such a network is the timing of each cable subsystem. A large file being transferred over one of the slower links can create bottlenecks that can tie up the entire system. The creation, maintenance, and organization of networks are tasks that often require engineering skills.

The data management needs of an organization may determine the type of local area network which may even dictate the selection of a large central computer rather than a microcomputer system. Capabilities such as securing (locking) files and records from individual users is important. These capabilities are built into some local area network systems.

COMPARING LANS

The number of varieties of local area networks is growing. The number of local area networks available has increased as the capability of microcomputers has grown. Some of the more popular ones are shown in Table 10–1.

SUMMARY

You have been introduced to the use of local area networks to solve the business problem of communication between microcomputer users. The key points to remember are:

1. Local area networks can increase the productivity of the business user.
2. LANs means cost savings in equipment, better control of data files, and the sharing of programs.
3. Networking is part of the growth of technology that is occurring in many aspects of microcomputers.
4. There are four popular cables used for connecting networks. Cost limitations, performance, and speed determine the best selection.
5. The arrangement of stations relative to each other and relative to a central file server falls into some simple classifications.

KEY TERMS

Access method   File server
Bus   LAN
Central file server (program)   LAN topology
Central switching station   Multi-tasking
Communication bus   Multi-user
Communication ring   Point-to-point

REVIEW QUESTIONS

1. What is a local area network?

2. What are the three aspects of LANs?

3. What is multi-tasking? Why is it of interest when establishing a LAN?

4. What is multi-user?

5. What is a central file server program?

6. What are the four types of cables used for microcomputers networks?

7. What is LAN topology?

8. Identify the layout of a central switching station, communication bus, communication ring or circle, and point-to-point communications.

9. What is a LAN access method? Which two are reviewed in the text?

DISCUSSION AND APPLICATION QUESTIONS

1. Examine magazines and other sources for articles about the legal aspects of sharing programs on microcomputers in a network.

2. Examine the license agreement that comes with one or more pieces of software. What is the significance of these agreements to LAN operations?

3. Investigate the present methods of controlling the access of individual work stations to a given data record to prevent or allow more than a single individual to update a file at the same time.

4. If possible, tour a local area network and report on its operation. Identify the type(s) of cables used and the topology.

5. Interview a business person who has set up a LAN. Report on the problems involved with such a setup.

6. Interview a professional who has used electronic mail. Report on the interview.

LABORATORY ASSIGNMENTS

1. If a local area network is available, use one of the work stations to load a program from your work station's on-line memory and recall a data file from one of the other stations or central file server. Update and use the data file. Transfer it back to a second station or central file server using a new filespec.

2. If a local area network is available, use one of the work stations to load a program from one of the other stations or central file server. Use the program.

SELECTED REFERENCES

Allegretti, Enzo V. *Understanding and Using Symphony.* West Publishing Company, 1987.

Varnon, M. S. *Developing and Using Office Applications with AppleWorks.* West Publishing Company, 1987.

Watterson, Karen L. *Understanding and Using FRAMEWORK.* West Publishing Company, 1986.

11

GOALS

When you complete this chapter you will be able to:

Identify the need for programs to integrate data files.

List some of the reasons for integrating program operations.

Specify the need to hide the complexity of the disk operating system.

List some of the capabilities that may be added to the operating system.

Review the operations and some of the advantages of transfer programs.

Identify some of the ways RAM-resident software is used.

Critique the procedure to use integrated software.

List how operating shells are used.

OUTLINE

Chapter Goals

Why You Must Know about Integrated Data Files and Operations

Data File Transfer Software

RAM–Resident Software

Integrated and Modular Software

Operating System Shells

Comparing Integrated Programs

Comparing Operating Shells

Summary

Key Terms

Review Questions

Discussion and Application Questions

Laboratory Assignments

Selected References

THE INTEGRATION OF
OPERATIONS AND DATA FILES

MICROS IN ACTION

Smart Integrated Systems, Inc., is a system integrator selling software, hardware, consulting services, custom programs, and hardware maintenance services. A part of their consulting time is spent moving data files between applications and moving data files between computers or teaching firms to do so themselves.

SIS helps clients decide between:
- A series of independent programs.
- Integrated programs.
- System shells.

They have purchased and developed a number of specialized data and software transfer programs for firms that use independent programs.

Much of the personal productivity increase obtained from using the microcomputer is due to the general application programs that were reviewed in earlier chapters:

1. Word processing
2. Electronic spreadsheets
3. Data base management
4. Graphics (standard charts)
5. Communication.

Your personal microcomputer productivity may be increased by the capability to move data between programs and to integrate the operation of different types of programs. Your organization's microcomputer productivity may be increased by using a common data base and integrating the operation of such special application programs as:

1. Membership lists
2. Customer lists
3. General ledger
4. Inventory control
5. Accounts receivable
6. Accounts payable.

Programs and hardware systems that you have studied that integrate the use of microcomputers include:

1. The disk operating system
2. Programs that communicate between computers
3. Programs that transfer files between computers
4. Data base management programs
5. LANs.

Some additional solutions to the transfer of data and operational integration include:

Data file transfer software: Programs designed to read data in the format produced by one program and change it to a format needed by a second program.

1. **Data file transfer software** (between programs)

2. RAM-resident programs for integrating
        Data
        Operations
3. **Integrated and modular software**
        General application programs
        Specific application programs
4. **Operating system shells.**

Integrating programs have four general objectives:

1. To integrate data files for more than one application.
2. To integrate operations.
3. To hide the complexities of the disk operating system.
4. Add capabilities to the operating system.

There are multi-tasking programs that allow the user to have several windows open on the screen, with an individual application program running in each window at the same time. Data available in a program operating in any window may be transferred to a program operating in any other window.

Data transfer between applications may be performed by:

- DOS
- Word processors
- Spreadsheet programs
- Data base programs
- File transfer programs
- Integrated and modular programs
- RAM-resident programs
- Disk operating system shells.

The best solution depends on the number of times such a transfer is required, the disk operating system, the specific program used, the programs available, and the data file structure used (Table 11–1).

WHY YOU MUST KNOW ABOUT INTEGRATED DATA FILES AND OPERATIONS

The combination of data files and application program and system operation may make you more productive. As the number of programs used expands, transferring data

Integrated software: Programs that combine one or more microcomputer general or specific application programs.

Modular software: Programs sold in individual modules that can be put together to form a system. The user has the option of purchasing only those modules desired.

Operating system shells: Programs that take over the disk operating system and add such capabilities as multi-tasking and file transfer between two programs operating concurrently.

TABLE 11–1
Objectives by Software Type

Type of Package	Data Integration	Program Integration	DOS Simplification	Add Capabilities
Data file transfer	x	some		x
RAM-resident				
Data	x	some		x
Operation	some	x		x
Integrated & modular	x	x		x
Operating system shells	x	x	x	x

between programs and integrating the operation of programs become more important. It is frustrating to reenter data that is already in the computer. As the volume of data increases, reentry becomes more difficult and time consuming.

The first time many users encounter the need to move data between programs may be when the output of a spreadsheet or data base program is needed in a word processing text file for the preparation of a report. This capability is often available by using the operating system in combination with spreadsheet or data base programs. The transfer method, although effective, is not efficient.

The steps in most systems to move a spreadsheet display to a word processing program are:

1. Load the spreadsheet program.
2. Load the data file.
3. Print an ASCII (.PRN) file in the spreadsheet program.
4. Exit the spreadsheet program.
5. Use the operating system to add the spreadsheet print file to a word processing ASCII file.
6. Load the word processing program.
7. Load the file created in step 5.

The software discussed in this chapter makes the transfer of both text and graphics between program applications easier (Table 11–2).

The effort and time needed to learn a new program or routine can be reduced if the design and organization of the new routines are similar to one already learned. Each application in an integrated and modular program looks similar to the other applications and are relatively easier to learn than a series of different packages.

RAM-resident and integrated programs may provide routines that are often needed, even in the middle of another task. For example, when creating a word processing document, you may find the need to perform calculations. It is frustrating to have to use a pocket calculator when the full power of a microcomputer is available. RAM-resident programs allow you to move a calculator routine onto the screen in front of the word processing program, perform the needed calculations, and then return to the word processor exactly where you left it.

Programs such as Framework and Microsoft Windows hide the complexities of the disk operating system, add capabilities, and often make it easier to learn to perform many tasks. These programs include routines to move data

TABLE 11–2
The Capability to
Transfer Data and Programs

Type of Program	Method of Solution
Data file transfer software	Changing file formats.
RAM-resident	On-line utilities.
Integrated & modular	Uses same format.
System shell	Allows both programs to operate at the same time and provides a method of moving between programs.

files and to operate more than a single program at one time, even in an operating system without this capability.

The transfer of data files between the same program on two different microcomputers, even ones using different operating systems, may be easier than the transfer of data files between two programs on the same microcomputer. Usually, programs operating on different systems use a consistent method of file storage, while different programs on the same microcomputer use unique methods of file storage.

In organizations with central computers, a common transfer cycle is often used (Figure 11–1). The data must be constantly transferred in and out of the common data base to get the updates from other sources and to aid management in maintaining the control needed in some situations. If the central computer is a microcomputer central file server, the format conversion may be a conversion from the central data base format to one needed by the application program. If the central file server is a mainframe, the conversion may include a conversion in and out of ASCII.

DATA FILE TRANSFER SOFTWARE

Programs are needed to change the format created by one program so the data may be used in a different program. You should already know that there are many different types of data files used on a microcomputer. Among them are:

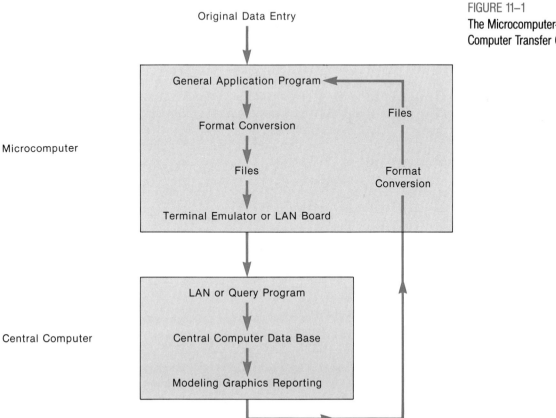

FIGURE 11–1
The Microcomputer–to–Central
Computer Transfer Cycle

MICROS IN ACTION

Transferring Output to Word Processors

Smart Integrated Systems, Inc., has found that their clients often need to use the output of accounting and spreadsheet programs in word processing programs for report generation. They also find many clients have a number of word processing programs and must be able to transfer files between them. SIS tries to limit a client's selection of programs so that transfer is easy.

1. ASCII files
2. DIF, data interchange format files
3. Near ASCII files
4. Special custom files (some using all eight bits)
5. SYLK, symbolic link files
6. Graphics data files.

With the exception of some special custom files and graphics data files, the standard code used in each file is available from manuals or user groups. You can purchase programs that transfer material between these files. Some application programs include routines to transfer files between formats.

Custom and graphics files often use an eight-bit code rather than the seven-bit ASCII code. If data is contained in the "high" bit, these files cannot be converted to ASCII because of data loss. The files using eight-bit codes contain numbers from 000 to 255 and are called binary files.

It is often easier to transfer data into a word processor text file than into a spreadsheet, data base, or graphics program file. Spreadsheet and data base files contain labels, formulas, and numbers, while text files contain text and numbers. Transferring formulas into a spreadsheet, data base, or graphics file is difficult unless you are using a DIF or SYLK type format or if you have a transfer utility.

The transfer of graphic files is also difficult due to the current lack of standards in this area. The trend is to develop standards, and it may be possible to import and export graphics files in the future. Current graphics transfer is performed using the screen display.

It is common for many programs to come with their own conversion software. Figure 11–2 illustrates the Lotus TRANS.COM program for converting files. The number of such transfer utilities is increasing. For example, SuperCalc4 has the capability of reading and writing Lotus files.

RAM–RESIDENT SOFTWARE

RAM-resident software may be purchased that adds a variety of capabilities and makes them readily available to the user. RAM-resident programs give you the capability of stopping what you are doing and calling up a second program to perform some necessary function.

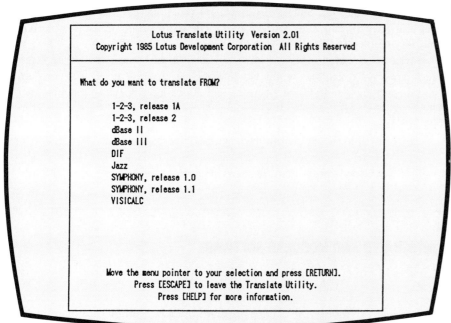

FIGURE 11–2
Lotus Transfer Program

Checking the time or date, making calculations, looking up a telephone number, and writing a note are examples of the type of utilities added. Table 11–3 provides a list of some RAM-resident programs and some of their characteristics.

A common method of transferring graphics between applications is to capture a screen display. A program must be RAM resident to perform this

Common Feature	Enermerge	Fancy Fonts	Frieze	Home Base	MYDESK	Poly-Windows	Sidekick	Spot-light
ASCII table							x	
Autodialer				x	x		x	
Calculator				x	x	x	x	x
Calendar						x	x	x
Cut/paste				x				
Data base				x	x			
Data transfer				x				
DOS control				x			x	
Game						x		
Merge Graphics								
into text	x							
into editor			x					
Merge text							x	
Notepad				x	x	x	x	x
Printer control	x	x						
Rolodex				x			x	x
Screen capture								
Graphics	x		x					
Text							x	

TABLE 11–3
RAM–Resident Programs

task. Many programs, such as Enermerge and Fancy Fonts, stand between an application program and your printer. These programs make it possible to merge graphics and produce special fonts.

RAM-resident programs may conflict with one another and application programs. For example, when Fancy Fonts or Enermerge is loaded, certain codes cannot be sent to the printer. The codes have special meanings to the RAM-resident programs and are captured, rather than being passed through to the printer.

It is possible to jam a computer with combinations of RAM-resident programs. You will learn which programs work with each other, and which do not. If you have more than two RAM-resident programs, it is difficult to forecast how they will work together without trying them.

INTEGRATED AND MODULAR SOFTWARE

Routines may be purchased as an integrated package or one at a time as a series of modules. Program sets created by one organization may be controlled to make the transfer of data between routines easy. These programs may be designed to operate using similar menus and operating procedures, so the user has an easier time using the software.

Modular programs are sold one routine at a time. You may purchase the word processor and then add the spreadsheet or data base at some future date when you have a need for it. Modules are operated from a menu or loaded from the disk operating system. Each module is called as needed. Upon instruction from the user, the program returns to the menu for the next module.

You can purchase a word processor and operating shells, among other programs, to transfer Lotus into an integrated program. Some of the additional programs are sold by Lotus, others by independent vendors.

Integrated programs (Figures 11–3 and 11–4) are purchased as a unit and usually operate from a common menu. Some integrated programs, such as Symphony, have windows (Figure 11–5) in which different parts of the program may be executed at the same time, and between which data may be transferred.

Most programs that combine:

1. Word processing
2. Spreadsheet
3. Data base
4. Graphics
5. Communications

are integrated, rather than modular. These programs often have one powerful foundation unit, such as a spreadsheet. The other capabilities are built around the foundation capability. Integrated programs were one of the first to have the capability of combining text and graphics. Some integrated programs contain additional capabilities, such as a slide presentation procedure. This is the exception rather than the rule.

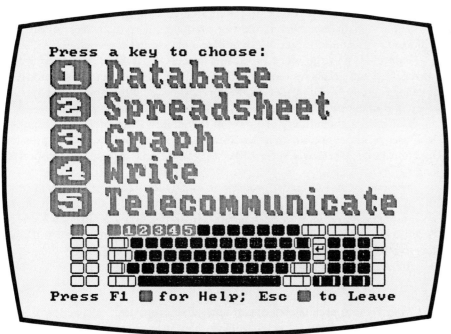

FIGURE 11–3
Ability First Menu

The advantages of integrated programs include:

1. A single entry may change results in all applications.
2. Cost of program is less than sum of its parts.
3. Training needs are reduced.
4. Support costs are reduced.

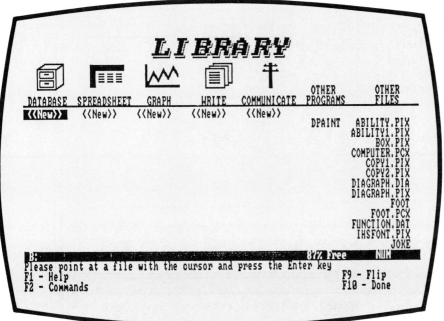

FIGURE 11–4
Ability Main Menu

When creating a report with graphics based on a spreadsheet evaluation, the single update capability is most convenient to have. It saves effort and reduces errors due to forgetting to update a part of the presentation.

Figure 11–6 is the word processing screen of Ability. Text as well as a spreadsheet and graph are included. If the value under the cursor is changed, it is changed in the word processor, the spreadsheet, and the graph. The spreadsheet and graph display in the word processor is updated.

Including a spreadsheet or graph in the Ability word processor is simple. The user positions the cursor at the future location of the insert and, pressing function key F2, selects a spreadsheet or graph, types its name, then presses enter.

The cost of an integrated program is usually less than the cost of all of its modules. For new computer users, the reduced cost and training needs make an integrated program a good selection. In some instances, users who need only two or three modules of an integrated program will find that it still costs less to purchase the integrated package.

Some of the disadvantages of integrated programs include:

1. They require large amounts of RAM.
2. They require greater speed than individual programs.
3. Individual applications may not have the power of stand-alone programs.

FIGURE 11–5   Lotus Symphony Windows

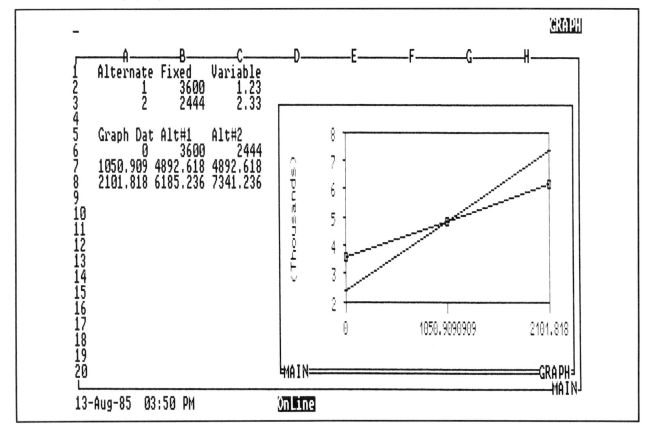

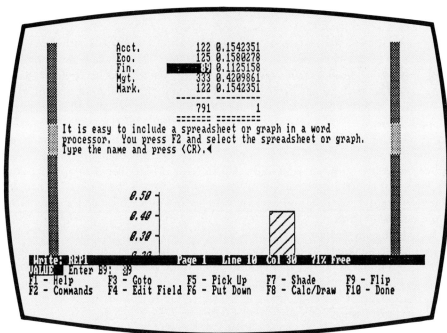

FIGURE 11–6
Ability Word Processor

The cost of RAM has reached a level where it is not critical. Most users are well advised to purchase RAM in the quantity needed by integrated programs. With a few exceptions, the speeds of today's microcomputers are adequate to support an integrated program. Some integrated programs require turbo boards and math co-processors to bring their performance up to acceptable levels. The need to display a combination of text and graphics often requires the greater speed.

Individual modules often do not have the power of stand-alone programs. The power of peripherals (specifically, printers) has increased. Word processors need extensive controls to obtain the features available in these printers. Often the controls are available in stand-alone word processors and not in integrated programs.

Integrated and modular software are available for such special applications as:

1. General ledger
2. Job costing
3. Project control
4. Time management
5. Billing/accounts receivables
6. Accounts payable
7. School administration
8. Banking applications.

Some packages combine both general and special applications. Many available software products use general application programs as their base. Accounting, real estate, and statistical templates may be purchased for popular spreadsheet programs, making them ready to solve specific applications and giving the business user a starting point for custom applications.

OPERATING SYSTEM SHELLS

Operating system shells are integrating programs that have been created to hide the complexities of the disk operating system and to add features. There have been a number of attempts to develop shells around operating systems that make them easier to use. The early shells were aimed at making the operating system user friendly, rather than trying to integrate operations or data files between applications.

The shells available today not only control the capabilities of the operating system, but also add some of their own capabilities in a manner similar to the overlay utility programs and allow the transfer of data between applications. Often, the utility programs cannot be operated at the same time as an operating system overlay program because they fight with each other for control of the microcomputer.

Among the features added by many operating system overlay programs are multi-tasking and windows. Concurrent operation of word processing, data base, and graphics is possible in some shells. Some shells use windows allowing the operation of more than one program to be viewed at one time. Text may be transferred between windows in a manner similar to moving blocks of text in word processing.

COMPARING INTEGRATED PROGRAMS

Integrated programs have a mix of capabilities depending on which modules are selected. Some of the features of a selected group of integrated programs are compared in Table 11–4.

TABLE 11–4
Comparing Integrated Programs

General Features	Ability	Enable	Framework II	IBM Personal Decision Series	Smart Software Systems	Symphony
Memory required	196K	256K	384K	256K	256K	384K
Maximum memory used	640K	640K	640K	640K	640K	with expansion board 3Mb
Hard disk subdirectories	yes	yes	yes	yes	yes	yes
Program backup limits	none	none	yes	yes	none	yes
Modules						
Spreadsheet	yes	yes	yes	yes	yes	yes
Data management	yes	yes	yes	yes	yes	yes
Word processing	yes	yes	yes	yes	yes	yes
Graphics	yes	yes	yes	yes	yes	yes
Communication	yes	yes	yes	yes	yes	yes
Presentation	yes					
Data Formats						
ASCII	x	x	x	x	x	
dBase II		x	x	x	x	x
DIF		x	x	x		x
WordStar			x		x	x
1–2–3	import	x	x	x	x	x

General Features	DESQ-view	GEM Desktop	Microsoft Windows
Memory required	150K	150K	200K
Maximum memory used	640K	640K	640K
Disk space installed	500K	500K	1460K
Number of files on disk	56	25	93
Type of display	ASCII	Bit-map	Bit-map
Color	yes	EGA only	yes
Windows	Overlap	Overlap	Tiled
Cut & Paste	yes	yes	yes
Utilities			
Alarm	yes	clock	clock
Appointment	yes		
Calendar	yes		yes
Calculator			yes
Cardfile		yes	yes
Clipboard			yes
Macro	yes		
Notepad			yes
Print Spooler		yes	yes
Terminal			yes

TABLE 11–5
Comparing Operating Shells

COMPARING OPERATING SHELLS

Operating shells perform many of the same functions as integrated programs. Table 11–5 compares general features and utilities of a number of these shells.

SUMMARY

The task of managing data on a microcomputer goes beyond the capabilities of the disk operating system. The programs discussed in this chapter give you a number of additional routines to use. The key points in this chapter include:

1. There are a number of software packages available to aid the user in integrating operations, data files, and improving disk operations.
2. The combination of data files, application program, and system operation may make the user more productive.
3. Programs are needed to change the format created by one program so its data may be used in a different program.
4. RAM-resident software makes a variety of capabilities readily available to the user.
5. Routines may be purchased as an integrated package or one at a time, as a series of modules.
6. Programs have been created to hide the complexities of the disk operating system and to add to its features.

KEY TERMS

Data file transfer software
Integrated software
Modular software

RAM-resident software
Operating system shell

REVIEW QUESTIONS

1. What programs give the user the initial increase in personal productivity?

2. Name programs studied in earlier chapters that integrate the use of microcomputers.

3. Name some additional programs that integrate the use of the microcomputer.

4. Identify the similarity and difference in the following terms:

   ■ Data file transfer software between programs.
   ■ Modular software.
   ■ RAM-resident software.
   ■ Integrated software.
   ■ Operating system shells.

5. What are the three objectives of integrating software?

6. When is the first time a user usually encounters the need to transfer material between programs?

7. What steps are needed on most systems to move material from a spread-sheet program to a word processing program?

8. Describe the microcomputer-to-central-computer transfer cycle.

9. Identify some different types of data files.

10. What basic capability do RAM resident programs offer the user?

11. Are all RAM resident programs compatible with each other?

12. What are the advantages of integrated software programs?

13. What are the disadvantages of integrated software programs?

14. What are operating system shells?

DISCUSSION AND APPLICATION QUESTIONS

1. Examine microcomputer magazine advertisements for data file transfer software between programs. What programs are available, how much do they cost, and what features do they have?

2. Examine microcomputer magazine advertisements for modular software. What programs are available, how much do they cost, and what features do they have?

3. Examine microcomputer magazine advertisements for integrated software. What programs are available, how much do they cost, and what features do they have?

4. Examine microcomputer magazine advertisements for overlay utility software. What programs are available, how much do they cost, and what features do they have?

5.   Examine microcomputer magazine advertisements for system overlay software. What programs are available, how much do they cost, and what features do they have?

LABORATORY ASSIGNMENTS

1.   With the programs available in your laboratory, determine the number of ways you can transfer data files between programs. Use as many of these methods as possible to move data files. Report on the results.

2.   If available in your laboratory, use a modular program set and an integrated program set to solve the problems outlined in the earlier chapters of this text and report on the difference between these programs.

3.   If available, use a utility program and report on its features.

4.   If available, use a system utility program and report on its features.

SELECTED REFERENCES

Bell, Don. *The DIF File.* Prentice-Hall, 1983.

Clark, Roger E. *Executive SuperCalc 3.* Addison-Wesley, 1984.

Cobb, David, and Geoffrey LeBlond. *Using 1–2–3.* Que Corporation, 1983.

Ewing, David P. *Using Lotus Symphony.* Que Corporation, 1984.

Graff, Lois. *Financial Analysis with Lotus 1–2–3.* Prentice-Hall, 1984.

Harris, David. *Lotus 1–2–3 Mastery w/Disk.* Prentice-Hall, 1984.

Harrison, Bill. *Framework: An Introduction.* Ashton-Tate, 1984.

Howard, Mary L. *Understanding and Using Microsoft BASIC/IBM PC BASIC.* West Publishing Company, 1987.

Miller, David. *IBM Data Files—A Basic Tutorial.* Prentice-Hall, 1983.

"New Solutions to the Micro-to-Mainframe Puzzle." *Business Computer Systems,* April 1985, pp. 42, 46–48.

12

HOW TO SELECT SOFTWARE AND MICROCOMPUTERS

MICROS IN ACTION

Flautt and Mann Properties, Inc., of Memphis, Tennessee, is a large motel/restaurant investment and management firm. They own and manage properties in the southeastern part of the United States between Florida and Texas. Over the years Flautt and Mann Properties, Inc., have developed a number of evaluation procedures for the selection and evaluation of properties. They specialize in purchasing properties that have the potential for growth under their special management style.

The microcomputer can save dollars when it is carefully selected to fill specific needs. The microcomputer concepts and applications learned in earlier chapters must be integrated with the needs of a user. The microcomputer is a low-cost method of solving problems. It can solve problems when it is fitted for, and accepted into, your overall system. You must learn how to identify which of your needs might be solved with microcomputers.

You have computer options in addition to microcomputers. Some of these options can better satisfy specific needs.

WHY YOU MUST KNOW YOUR NEEDS

You must analyze your situation to determine your needs before purchasing a microcomputer to fill them. You are in a position to determine your current and potential needs now and in the future, and to identify where a microcomputer system may be used to meet these needs. To prepare yourself to perform a microcomputer analysis, your background should combine:

1. Microcomputer training
2. Business and professional training
3. Experience in an organization.

A microcomputer purchase requires a detailed plan and analysis, which is your job.

Home versus Professional Needs

Selecting a microcomputer system for home use involves the same considerations as selecting one for professional use. The key issues include the current and future needs of:

- All family members
- For compatibility with school
- For compatibility with work.

In an organization there may be a microcomputer manager who can help organize and evaluate the needs of the institution. (You may be the micro manager.) At home, you must perform the job of the micro manager and identify the needs of the entire family for microcomputer equipment.

MICROS IN ACTION

Flautt and Mann Properties, Inc., feel that a large part of their success is due to their management. They have a team of men and women who are capable of developing an idea, setting an objective, making a plan, evaluating the potential of the plan, and implementing the plan to obtain the results wanted.

Home resources are limited in the amount of available software, the level of computer training of each family member, and the dollars available for the investment.

Shareware

One low-cost method to obtain software is to use public domain and shareware programs. Public domain and shareware programs are available through computer clubs, your public library, computer communication networks, friends, and commercial firms that sell the software for the value of the distribution charge (between $3 and $5 per disk). The new owners of shareware programs are asked to send a donation of between $25 and $100 to the holder of copyright if they find the program useful. Users of public domain software are not expected to pay.

Shareware programs do not have the same capabilities of commercial programs. In most cases, the capability of shareware programs is less than commercial programs. Some shareware programs are limited-capability demonstration parts of commercial programs, some are more powerful than commercial programs.

Generally, the public domain–shareware program does not have support. If you have a problem, you are on your own. Only if you become a registered owner, i.e., pay the $25 to $100 purchase fee, can you expect any support.

Included among shareware programs are word processors, font generators, spreadsheet, data base, graphics (business and drawing), communications, games, training, mathematical, and statistics programs. You may operate a system using shareware programs only.

PLANNING AND ANALYSIS

The steps in analyzing the need for software and a microcomputer are the idea, the objective, the plan, the analysis, and the installation. The steps to determine the need for a microcomputer are:

1. An IDEA (dream).
2. An OBJECTIVE that is measurable, feasible, and achievable within a time limit.
3. The PLAN, with priorities and phases.
   IDENTIFICATION of where you are.
   Identification of LIMITATIONS, constraints.

4. ANALYSIS and the decision to go ahead or stop.
5. IMPLEMENTATION of the plan—usually, running old and new systems in parallel.

Idea

Idea:
Recognition of a need or opportunity.

A problem or opportunity emerges from an idea. A human being must evaluate all the facts available and come up with an idea. The idea is the recognition that there may be a problem or opportunity in need of study. The idea precedes all other steps because it is the recognition of need.

Brainstorming sessions, a good night's sleep, a passing sight, or the occurrence of a problem might trigger the idea. Only people can create ideas or dreams. One of these ideas might be using a program and microcomputers to solve some of your problems.

Objective

Objective:
A goal that is feasible, measurable, has a time limit, has recognized limitations, and has a plan for its accomplishment.

For an idea to become an objective, it needs to have several characteristics:

1. It must be feasible.
2. It must be measurable.
3. It must have a time limit.
4. Its limitations must be recognized.

Feasibility A feasible objective is one that can be accomplished. It is meaningless to dream of earning $10 million this year if you are starting at a base of $1,000. It is better to set realistic objectives and then to modify the goals as the organization's capabilities grow.

No software/computer combination can do everything. Some of the considerations when selecting software are:

1. Capabilities
   a. Simple to learn and use.
   b. Power to produce results.
2. Compatibility with a specified user group.
3. Availability of (national and local) support.
4. Market penetration.
5. Look and feel.
6. Price.

Often a package that is easy to learn and use does not have the power to perform the complex tasks needed for a particular application. The new user must decide to purchase either the ease of learning or the capability to obtain the results needed.

There is a lower limit to the price of any software/hardware system. For example, your organization requires a new word processor and microcomputer system with

1. 640K of RAM.
2. A 20Megabyte hard disk.

3.   A 360K floppy disk.
4.   MS/PC–DOS.
5.   A high-resolution card and color graphics.
6.   A color monitor.

With a budget of $300, purchasing this equipment would not be a feasible objective. No matter how hard and long you worked, the objective could not be realized, unless you purchased a stolen microcomputer system or the current price level dropped.

Measurable If you cannot measure the completion of a goal, there is no way to tell if you have achieved it. To be rich is meaningless. To earn a million dollars is a measurable objective that can be accomplished.

The goal "To improve the operation of this office" does not mean anything and cannot be measured. The word improve does not have a precise meaning. If there is a 2 percent increase in the output of the office, is this an improvement? If the lighting is replaced and the employees find the office an easier place to work, is this an improvement? If a microcomputer with a word processing program is purchased to replace a typewriter, is this an improvement? A restatement of the objective as "To increase the output letters by 20 percent with no increase in personnel" gives the manager a goal that can be measured.

Time Limit A time limit means a task must be completed by a specified date. If an objective does not have a time limit, you can never fail to reach it. For example, "To computerize your organization some day" is a dream, while "To replace 90 percent of the typewriters being used with microcomputers in the next twelve months" is an objective, if it is feasible.

Other Limitations

Examples of limitations are:

1.   The availability of support for a program.
2.   The availability of repair facilities for a microcomputer.
3.   The need to transfer files within a user group.
4.   The desire to match the look and feel of a program with ones used for other purposes.
5.   The need to have a specific capability.
6.   Limited number of trained persons.
7.   The availability of cash or credit.
8.   Floor space or storage room.
9.   Legal and moral constraints.

Limitations are restrictions that inhibit the ability to make decisions. With the exception of legal and moral constraints, limitations may exist only in the short run. Software support may be needed only during the initial learning period. Trained people can be hired, cash can be obtained, floor space can be rented or purchased.

Your need for software capabilities changes over time. When daisy wheel printers were the only letter quality printers available, word processors only needed to control these printers. When laser printers became available, word processors needed to be changed to include the codes needed for laser output. Generally, laser printer codes are longer and use more characters than daisy printer codes.

You may wish to purchase a software-microcomputer system, but if you do not have the cash or credit to make the purchase, you will have to delay your purchase until the limitation can be eliminated. The time limit is what makes limits real in any given decision-making situation.

Plan

Plan:
A series of steps detailing what must be done to move from where you are to where you want to go.

A plan details how to get from where you are to where you want to go. If the objective is to replace ten typists/typewriters with three typists/word processors, then a plan could be:

1. Management evaluation: Ms. Mai Tran will determine the cost of using typewriters and the cost of using word processors. She will develop a plan of action and report to the manager's committee on June 3. A decision will be made to complete the project or stop it.
2. Operations: Mr. Andy Simbasolv will determine which word processor to select. He will report on:
    a. The most popular program used by other local users
    b. Local support
    c. Capabilities of alternate packages including:
        (1) Training programs
        (2) Ease of learning
        (3) Ease of use
        (4) Capabilities to control the printer selected
3. Accounting: Ms. Carla Juarez will determine if cash or credit is available to complete the project and report to the manager's committee on July 6. The manager's committee will decide on the project's status.
4. Purchasing: Ms. Freda Flippo will
    a. Write the final specifications with the aid of Ms. Mai Tran and Mr. Simbasolv by June 30
    b. Select vendor by July 23
    c. Place order for delivery on September 12
5. Personnel: Mr. Steven Lombard will
    a. Determine personnel transfers by September 5
    b. Determine training needs by September 5
    c. Set up and organize training program by September 12
    d. Report on any problem relative to the relocation of people by January 1
6. Supervision: Ms. Betty Schilling will
    a. Supervise the installation and training with the aid of the Personnel Department
    b. Report on level of performance October 1, November 1, and December 1
7. Final analysis of project by manager's committee on January 1.

Levels It is common to have several levels to a plan. Different levels in an organization are responsible for different types of decisions. Each level in the overall plan may have a detailed plan of its own.

A single step in a plan for a high-level manager may result in a long series of detailed activities for a lower-level manager. A set of microcomputer purchasing specifications may be detailed and complex.

Care should be taken in regard to the level at which a decision is made. If a word processor is to be used by two different departments, the decision maker should be in control of both units. One answer to controlling software and hardware decisions among groups is to appoint a micro manager to manage an organization's microcomputer software and hardware. Among other things micro managers evaluate software, determine training needs, provide training, control the introduction of updates, and help provide hardware maintenance as needed.

Milestones Milestones are simply steps on the way to the completion of a plan. They are used to aid staying on course. If a milestone is missed, you must investigate to see why and how to get the project back on plan.

A milestone in the installation of a microcomputer system may be the completion of a training program. If the program is not completed at the time specified, you know the process is not proceeding according to plan and action is needed.

Identification of Options An option represents a choice that you can make. One of the objectives of this book is to help you learn what microcomputers can do. With this knowledge you have a collection of solutions. Now it is necessary to match the problems with candidate solutions.

The general application programs covered give the microcomputer capabilities for word processing, electronic spreadsheets, data base management, graphics, and communications. Most organizations have some applications for all these capabilities.

Figure 12–1 is a word processing checklist. Many important considerations for word processing selection are listed. This checklist should be customized for your needs. You may also develop similar checklists for spreadsheets, data base, graphics, and other packages.

If a single package is to be used by a variety of user groups, there may have to be some compromises made. For example, capability may require the casual user to learn a more complex package because the everyday (power) users need the package for the printer being used.

The importance of each item on the word processing checklist depends on your application. If you have a laser printer, you will need a word processor that can produce the codes needed to control it. Some user groups will need more spelling and thesaurus aids. Footnote capability will be needed by other groups.

The user must select from among many good application programs. Most will produce better results and improve performance over a manual approach. Selecting the best word processor, spreadsheet, or any other package from among good options is a difficult task. You must identify your needs exactly and study the capabilities of a number of programs to make such a selection.

Custom programs cover accounting, production management, project management, quality control, real estate management, and almost any other topic you might require. Details, needs, and opportunities are known only to you. The task of matching needs with solutions often falls on you.

Special application software has a "single" use. Accounting programs can produce general ledgers, control accounts payable or receivables, or perform some other specific function.

The form shown in Figure 12–2 is a good starting place to begin your thinking about a purchase of a microcomputer. This form forces you to identify those activities where the microcomputer is to be used. The form identifies the problems the microcomputer can solve.

Included on the form in Figure 12–2 is a place to indicate the timing of the computing application. Microcomputers are not difficult to use, but they do take time to learn. You cannot install all the capabilities of the microcomputer

FIGURE 12–1
Word Processor Selection
Checklist

Word Processor Checklist

Name _____ Date _____

Department _____

Organization _____

Street _____

City _____

State _____ Zip _____

Package: _____

Overall Objective: _____

User Groups: _____

Frequency of Use: _____

Knowledge of DOS: _____

Knowledge of Word Processing: _____

Knowledge of Other Packages: _____

Need to Transfer to Other Packages: _____

Printer Control: _____

Need for Desktop Publishing: _____

Support Needs:

Spelling	_____	Thesaurus	_____
Outline	_____	Math	_____
Multi-documents	_____	Proportional Spacing	_____
Multi-columns	_____	Printer ( )	_____
Hyphenation	_____	Footnotes	_____
Network	_____	Path (hard disk)	_____

overnight. You must allow for learning and adjustment time. The form forces you to identify the beginning and ending time of each application. These are milestones in the task of introducing the microcomputer into your organization.

The form is designed with a thirty-six month planning horizon. The field of microcomputers is changing so fast that a longer planning horizon is not recommended. If the low cost of microcomputer applications cannot be justified in less than three years, you may not need one.

Another advantage of a time plan is that it allows you to determine whether you need to purchase all your equipment at the beginning. The cost of microcomputer hardware is steadily decreasing; at least, the capabilities that may be purchased are increasing while the price remains constant. A piece of equipment should not be purchased until it is needed.

The microcomputer may be the correct computer for many applications, but acquiring microcomputers is not the only answer. You may hire a service bureau to perform computerized tasks for you. Many banks offer accounting services. If you have no interest in having your own computer, or if your needs are limited, this may be an answer for you. The cost of service bureaus includes the labor for operating the computer as well as an overhead cost for the equipment.

Detailing the Plan A plan starts with an idea and the identification of the problems to be solved. The exact equipment needed in the initial purchase, needed in six months, in a year, etc., can then be identified. For example, if you use word processing, a daisy wheel printer is usually required immediately. If you add graphics after six months, a dot matrix printer or printer plotter may be purchased then. The price and capabilities of dot matrix printers can be expected to change over six months.

The layout of potential needs is shown in Figure 12–3.

It is easy to identify when a microcomputer application begins to be used. It is more difficult to identify when the training period is over and the technique is being used. The basics of word processing may be learned in an hour. Users may never learn to use all the capabilities of the word processor. They

Microcomputer Purchase Checklist

Name .... Date ......
Department ....
Organization ....
Street ....
City ....
State ...... Zip ....
Overall Objective

Microcomputer Applications	Start	6 Months	12 Months	24 Months	36 Months
1					
2					
3					
4					
5					
6					

FIGURE 12–2
Microcomputer Purchase Checklist

FIGURE 12–3
The Planning of
Microcomputer Needs

Microcomputer Applications	Start	Identify the beginning and ending			
		6 Months	12 Months	24 Months	36 Months
1. Word Process .	...Start...	.. Comp ..	....	....	....
2. Graphics	...Start...	....	.. Comp ..	....	....
3. Spreadsheets ..	....	...Start...	....	.. Comp ..	....
4. Data base	....	...Start...	....	....	.. Comp ..
5.	....	....	....	....	....
6.	....	....	....	....	....

may never need all the capabilities. The measure of completeness is a function of the application and is left to you as the manager.

The plan for applications helps us determine our hardware and software needs. To do word processing, you need a microcomputer with one or two disk drives, a word processing program, a daisy wheel printer, and the cables necessary to connect the units together. Table 12–1 outlines the software-hardware needed by the system. Some later needs will make the earlier purchases obsolete. You will have to decide whether it pays to purchase the wide carriage printer originally to avoid the later need for a third printer.

When a 20Megabyte hard disk is purchased for the data base program, the second disk drive will be of little value. You may want to purchase the hard disk drive initially rather than wait until it is needed. Using the information in a table such as Table 12–1 can help you develop an intelligent plan.

Capacity Planning The maximum amount of RAM needed is usually a function of the software program that uses the largest amount and the RAM needed for a RAM disk or spooler. A RAM disk is a part of RAM that acts like a disk drive. RAM drives avoid slow and sometimes noisy disk I/O. They are like regular disk drives, but all information is lost when the power is shut off.

A spooler enables simple microcomputer multi-tasking. A segment of RAM is set aside to hold information sent to the printer. The data is placed in the spooler at a rate faster than any printer can operate. Once all the data is

TABLE 12–1   The Milestones of Your Plan

Microcomputer Needs	Start	6 Months	12 Months	24 Months	36 Months
Microcomputer	x				
Furniture	x				
Single Disk Drive	x				
Second Disk Drive	x				
Daisy Wheel Printer	x				
Cables	x				
Word Processor Prog.	x				
Dot Matrix Printer		x(80 Column)			
Printer Switch/Cables		x			
Graphics Program		x			
Dot Matrix Printer			x(132 or 200+ Column)		
Spreadsheet Program		x			
Data Base Program		x			
Hard Disk 20Megabytes				x	

stored in the spooler, the microcomputer is free to be used for another purpose. The printer continues to produce output as the microcomputer is used.

Spreadsheet, data base, graphics, and integrated programs tend to use the most RAM. Programs designed for CP/M, TRS–DOS, Apple DOS, and other eight-bit systems are designed to operate within the limitations of these systems, that is, usually 64K of RAM. MS/PC–DOS programs often use up to 256K of RAM or more, because of added program features.

To estimate the size of RAM requires that you identify specific programs that perform each of the capabilities you need. Since RAM cost is low, we recommend you buy more than you need initially. As your skill in using the microcomputer grows, you will find that you need more memory.

A hard disk drive adds speed and storage capacity to a microcomputer system. The speed is convenient to have for many different program applications. The storage capacity allows flexibility when many applications are needed on short notice, and when a data base system is established.

Data bases for inventory control, personnel, customer identification, credit, club membership, and data analysis may require large amounts of memory. There are ways you can estimate the amount of storage needed.

In the data base discussion in chapter 7, you learned what a field, record, and file are. Capacity planning starts with determining the size of a record, then estimating the number of records needed. Growth estimates are added, and the size is rounded off to the next largest hard disk system available. It is usually more cost effective to purchase more storage than you need initially than to add additional storage by replacing one hard disk drive system with another at some future time.

Another factor that will affect the selection of a hard disk drive is how it is organized. There are ways to partition the hard disk between different applications and different operating systems used on the same microcomputer.

It is useful to develop checklists for your needs. Figures 12–4 and 12–5 are two lists to use as starting points.

Vendor Selection The price of a microcomputer is only one of the factors upon which to base the selection of a microcomputer. A business selling in a local market must make some of its purchases in the local market. You cannot expect business professionals to buy from you unless you give them the opportunity to sell to you.

A microcomputer, once installed, rapidly becomes an important part of your operational needs. The ability of your vendor to train, repair, service, and upgrade your microcomputer is important. A loss of several days' work for equipment repair may be costly in terms of lost time and effort and inconvenience.

You may purchase different types of service plans from many vendors. You may have on-site service, carry-in service, or risk just paying for service as needed. Remember, a microcomputer is like any other piece of equipment;

Application #

RAM
On-Line Storage
Printer(s)

FIGURE 12–4
Factors to Be Sized Checklist

USER WINDOW

THE VALUE OF LOCAL CONTACTS

The insurance salesman brags to a local microcomputer salesperson that his area insurance company purchased a microcomputer through its home office. The insurance man claims the price of the unit was better than the local market could offer.

The insurance salesman then talks about making an appointment to talk about insurance. The computer salesperson says, "I'm sorry, I already bought through my home office."

when used by a large number of individuals, it will require more maintenance than the same unit operated by a single user.

Training takes time and costs dollars. Training needs include start-up expenses and personnel replacement and retraining. When additional capabilities are added, you will again need more training. You must evaluate the ability of a vendor to provide such training, and what the cost is expected to be. A retail store may provide introductory-level training for new programs, but little more. Further training from an additional source or a hired consultant is often necessary.

FIGURE 12–5

Factors to Be Specified Checklist

Application #

Monitor Type
  Color
  Monochrome
Printer Type
  Dot matrix
  Daisy wheel
  Laser
  Ink jet
  Plotter
Special Boards
  Graphics
  Communication
  Speech recognition
  Speech synthesis
  Special interfaces
  Additional memory
  Network
Other Devices
  Mouse
  Joy sticks
  Koala pad
  Paddles
  Bar code reader
  Digitizer pad
  Touch sensitive screen

Many individuals learn how to use a program by reading the documentation. If you do not have the time or background to understand the documentation, you should consider hiring someone to help.

USER WINDOW

THE UNWRITTEN INSTRUCTION

The microcomputer user carefully read the instructions on how to transfer the program from a single-density to a double-density disk. Each instruction was carried out exactly as written.

After the transfer was complete, the single-density disk was placed in drive A, and the double-density disk in drive B. The program never worked correctly.

The documentation did not tell the user to place the master single density disk in a safe place and use the double-density disk as the operating program. One documentation error made it impossible for this user to get the program running.

Some firms with centralized purchasing procedures often prepare a bid request form when purchasing equipment. A bid request is part of the computer use and purchase plan. You must know what your microcomputer is to do before its configuration can be determined. Whether you prepare a formal bid request or not, you should identify the required capabilities of your system.

If you have a problem and do not wish to spend the time finding out how to solve it, it is often advisable to hire a consultant to do the job for you. Developing microcomputer specifications is a time-consuming task. You or an associate must spend the time to learn your microcomputer needs, or you must spend your dollars hiring an outsider to do the job. If you spend neither the time nor money doing the job right, you are likely to make costly errors by purchasing the wrong equipment. A good, reputable vendor may also be able to help.

Analysis

The analysis of alternative methods is based on the productivity of an organization, office, or individual. The productivity is output divided by input, the equation is:

$$\text{Productivity} = \frac{\text{Output}}{\text{Input}}$$

You must identify and measure the input and output.

Input Input includes all the factors of production:

1. Land (raw materials)
2. Labor (the women and men who do the work)

Analysis:
Comparison of alternate management actions.

Productivity:
Output divided by input.

3. Capital (the dollars and equipment that the dollars may purchase; software and hardware)
4. The enterprise (management and other aspects of the organization).

The substitution principle of the factors of production says if one factor becomes expensive, it should be replaced by another factor so the lowest cost balance is maintained. In a like manner, if one factor becomes less expensive, it should replace the other factors.

Microcomputers with application programs are a part of the capital factor. The capital factor as applied to microcomputers is decreasing. As the capabilities of microcomputers and the effectiveness of their programs improve, the cost of using this equipment decreases.

You have learned what a microcomputer can do.

Output Output is the goods and services produced by a company. The output of each company, office, or individual is a function of the job that must be done. You are in a good position to determine what this output is.

Each person or work station in an organization adds to the overall objective by producing some contribution. Figure 12–6 shows the possible priority of some objectives in a local car dealership.

Simply writing down the objectives and output of specific positions brings to light some possible uses for microcomputers.

Measuring Input and Output Dollars and time are the most common measurements for input (factors of production). Each of the input factors must be identified and then measured.

Output measurement involves counting. In general, for a specific output you must:

1. Count the amount of material or power used.
2. Count the number of hours of labor used.
3. Count the number of capital dollars or amount of hours of capital equipment used.
4. Count the dollar and time costs of management input.

The key word is "count." There is no substitution for hard work and counting. After counting you must record the results. Table 12–2 shows a "Work Sampling" report used to measure the labor activities in a typing group.

FIGURE 12–6
Hierarchy of Some Objectives

Level	Objective
Business enterprise	To make a profit
Sales department	To sell vehicles
Individual salesperson	To sell vehicles
	To set up and maintain a data base of all contacts.
Secretary	To produce contracts, letters, and other documents.
	To set up and maintain a data base of all buyers.
Repair and maintenance	

Once the input has been measured, the output must be measured. The output of a typing group might be documents. If the mix of large documents (contracts) and small documents (letters) is constant, then just counting documents may be satisfactory. If the mix changes, then a more detailed measure of output is needed. When the study is complete, you will have a productivity equation:

$$\text{Productivity} = \frac{\text{Documents}}{\text{Power and supplies} + \text{labor hours} + \text{equipment cost} + \text{management costs}}$$

Finding a combined measure of input is difficult and often not necessary. If the cost of power, supplies (including land), and management does not change, you need not be concerned about measuring them.

When replacing a typist-typewriter with a typist-microcomputer/word processor, you need to be concerned with labor hours input, equipment costs, and document output. The objective is to compare the productivity of the old method with the productivity of the new method to determine if the investment in the microcomputer system is justified.

Justifying a Microcomputer There are a number of investment justification techniques. Among them are:

1. Break-even analysis
2. Payback period analysis
3. Present worth analysis.

All techniques depend on the measurements made in determining productivity. The break-even and payback period analyses are simple and will be covered. Present worth analysis is better but requires a background in finance. An ideal method of solving break-even, payback, and present worth problems is with the use of an electronic spreadsheet and microcomputer graphics.

Break-even Analysis The objective of break-even analysis is to determine the number of units of output when the total cost of one method is equal to the total cost of another method.

Assume one method is using a typist with typewriter, the other is a typist with word processor, and that the cost and time data are as shown in Figure 12–7.

Activity	Percent of observations
Talking on phone	20%
Typing	65%
Talking to individuals	10%
Out of area	7%
Other	3%
	100%

TABLE 12–2

Work Sampling Report on a Typing Group

MICROS IN ACTION

Flautt and Mann Properties, Inc., uses a number of different evaluation and analysis methods including break-even, gross multipliers, and calculations of average daily rates combined with occupancy ratios in the case of motel and hotel investments. These simpler techniques are used as the initial pass to determine if it pays to spend additional time and effort making a detailed period-by-period income and expense analysis.

The analysis procedures apply to the purchase of investment properties, the bidding on management service contracts, and the investment in equipment including trucks and microcomputers.

The increased output of the word processor is often due to its editing capability, especially when doing corrections for second and third drafts. It is assumed that the document would be typed once and two additional edited copies produced.

The break-even equation is:

$$\text{Break-even} = \frac{\begin{array}{c}\text{Capital cost} \quad \text{Capital cost}\\ \text{new method} - \text{old method}\end{array}}{\begin{array}{c}\text{Old cost} - \text{New cost}\\ \text{per unit} \quad \text{per unit}\end{array}} = \frac{\$3,000 - \$0.00}{1.95 - 0.96 \text{ documents}} = 3,030.3030$$

The break-even equation may be used to compare any two alternatives. You may replace new method by method # 1 and old method by method # 2 in the formula.

It may also be used to compare a revenue with a total cost. The revenue is considered an alternative with no capital cost in the formula.

This means that it is more economical to use the typewriter until 3,030 documents are produced. Above 3,030 the word processor becomes more economical.

Payback Period A payback period analysis is a break-even analysis with the scale in terms of time rather than in pieces. Assuming that enough work exists to keep the typist/word processing system operating at full speed, the output per day would be 8.3 times 8 or 66.4 pages per day. Dividing 3,030 by 66.4 yields a result of approximately 46 days for the payback period.

FIGURE 12–7
Break-even Analysis

	Typist with typewriter	*Typist with word processor*
New Investment	None	$3,000
Pages per hour	4.1	8.3
At $8/hour cost per page	$1.95	$0.96

Estimates based on 45-character-per-minute average including the time required to load and unload the typewriter, 10 characters per line, and 66 lines per page. The result is 14.7 minutes per page or 4.1 pages per hour.

The word processing cost per page assumes one original and two copies. The time to correct and print a copy is 25 percent of the time to create an original. The result is 7.252 minutes per page or 8.3 pages per hour.

The mathematical results tell us that if full output is maintained for 46 days, then it pays to purchase the microcomputer with a word processor.

Using Spreadsheets and Graphics The break-even and payback analysis may be performed using a spreadsheet and graphics program. Figure 12–8 is a Lotus 1–2–3 spreadsheet with formulas to solve this program. The total cost at break-even for the two alternatives should be equal. The spreadsheet shows the values to be typewriter = 5909.090, and word processor = 5909.090.

Figures 12–9 and 12–10 are graphical analyses of the problem produced on Lotus 1–2–3. The differences between these two graphs are the labels and specification of the X scale.

Both graphs tell the same story. The total cost of the old method (use of typewriters) is less than the total cost of word processors until the break-even point (3,030 documents) or the end of the payback period (46 days).

Current versus Future Demand In an actual study you will be concerned with how to administrate the introduction of the new equipment. If you cur-

	A	B	C	D	E	F
1	BREAK.wks					
2			Breakeven and Payback Analysis			
3						
4						
5	Alternative			Fixed Cost		Variable Cost
6	Typewriter			0		1.96
7	Word Processor			3000		0.96
8						
9	Breakeven			3030.303		
10						
11	Payback Period			45.63709		
12						
13	For Graph:					
14	Pieces	Days		Typewriter		Word Processor
15	0	0		0		3000
16	3030	46		5909.090		5909.090
17	6061	91		11818.18		8818.181
18						
19						

Cell	Formula
C9	(C6-C7)/(E7-E6)
C11	+C9/66.4
E15	+C7
A16	+C9
A17	+2*C9
B16	+C9/66.4
B17	+A17/66.4
C15	+$C$6+$F$6*A15
C16	+$C$6+$E$6*A16
C17	+$C$6+$E$6*A17
E15	+$C$7+$E$7*A15
E16	+$C$7+$E$7*A16
E17	+$C$7+$E$7*A17

FIGURE 12–8
Lotus 1–2–3 Analysis of Break-even and Payback

FIGURE 12–9
Graph of Break-even Analysis

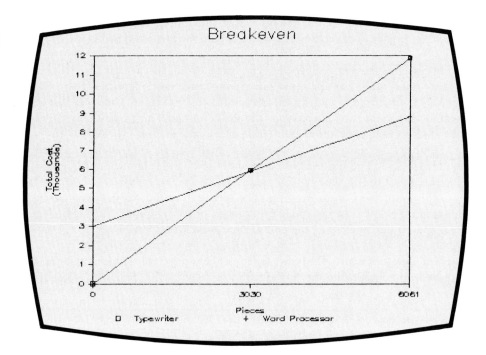

rently have three typists, it may be necessary to lay off two of them in order to justify the word processor. If you expect growth in the demand for documents, you may be able to introduce the new equipment without any layoffs by simply not hiring additional people as the growth occurs.

FIGURE 12–10
Graph of Payback Analysis

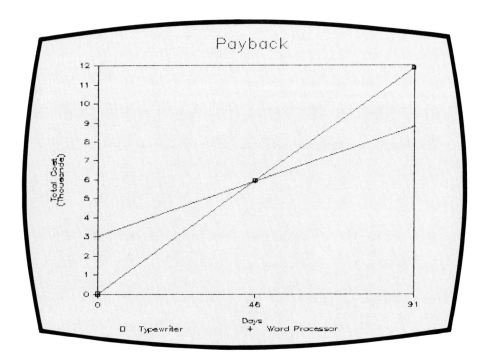

Implementation

The last step is implementation. The plan details the steps to be followed in the implementation. The decision to go ahead is management's. The reports of accomplishments are returned to management.

Implementation: Putting a method or microcomputer to work in a company.

SUMMARY

A microcomputer is an investment and must be justified using the same methods used to justify all other investments. You have learned how to identify the needs for a microcomputer and how they are justified. You have seen how the knowledge gained in earlier chapters must be used to help identify and develop specifications for a microcomputer system.

The key points in this chapter are:

1. Microcomputer systems save dollars only if they are carefully selected to fill specific need(s).
2. You should analyze the organization to determine its needs before purchasing a microcomputer to fill those needs.
3. All planning and analysis start with an idea.
4. The objective is an idea with a plan detailing how it may be accomplished.
5. A plan identifies the steps necessary to complete a defined objective.
6. You should justify the purchase of a microcomputer with careful analysis.
7. The final test of a microcomputer is its installation into the organization.

KEY TERMS

Analysis	Objective
Idea	Plan
Implementation	Productivity

REVIEW QUESTIONS

1. Why is the user who has had a course in microcomputers in a good position to evaluate microcomputer acquisition?

2. What are the steps in the analysis of a microcomputer application?

3. What is an idea?

4. What is an objective? What does an idea need to become an objective?

5. What are some of the limitations you may expect to be imposed on a decision?

6. What is a plan?

7. What are milestones?

8. Identify a computer option to microcomputer ownership.

9. What is productivity?

10. What is meant by "capacity planning"?

11. What are some ancillary costs to be considered when purchasing new software?

12. What is an analysis?

13. What are the factors of production?

14. What is output?

15. How is output measured?

16. Name three commonly used investment analysis techniques and identify the objective of one.

17. Detail and explain the break-even formula.

18. What is the last step in the purchase of a microcomputer?

DISCUSSION AND APPLICATION QUESTIONS

1. Use the forms developed in this chapter to configure a system for your remaining college years.

2. Develop a short outline of the needs for microcomputers in your school. Use the forms in this chapter to configure a system.

3. If you are working, configure a system through the idea, objective, and planning steps.

4. Study the needs of your religious organization and configure a system for them.

5. Start with Figure 12–1 detailing the factors to consider when using a word processor and add some ideas of your own.

6. Use Figure 12–1 to develop checklists for selecting:
   a. Spreadsheet programs
   b. Data base programs
   c. Graphics programs
   d. Communication programs
   e. Integrated programs
   f. Integrating programs.

LABORATORY ASSIGNMENTS

1. There are two microcomputer systems being considered. The purchase prices and operating costs are given below:

Purchase Price	Cost Per Document
$3,600	$1.23
2,444	2.33

a. Determine the break-even point by calculator or the use of an electronic spreadsheet program.
b. Draw the break-even chart by microcomputer or manually.
c. If the yearly volume in document output is 1500, what is the payback period?

SELECTED REFERENCES

Cohn, Jules A., and Catherine S. McKinney. *How to Microcomputerize Your Business.* Spectrum Book, Prentice-Hall, 1983.

Barden, William, Jr. *How to Buy & Use Minicomputers & Microcomputers.* Howard W. Sams & Co., Inc., 1976.

Dologite, D. G. *Using Small Business Computers.* Prentice-Hall, 1984.

Harold, Fred G. *Introduction to Computers.* West Publishing Company, 1984.

Hicks, James O. *Management Information Systems—A User Perspective.* West Publishing Company, 1984.

Mandell, Steven L. *Computers and Data Processing Today with BASIC.* West Publishing Company, 1983.

Varnon, M. S. *Developing and Using Office Application with AppleWorks.* West Publishing Company, 1987.

Veit, Stanley S. *Using Microcomputers in Business.* Hayden Book Company, 1983.

Zimmerman, Steven M., and Leo M. Conrad. *Business Applications for the IBM Personal Computer.* Brady Publishing Company, 1983.

Zimmerman, Steven M., Leo M. Conrad, and Donald R. Smith. *Business Applications for the Apple II & IIe under CP/M.* Brady Publishing Company, 1985.

THE HISTORY OF MICROCOMPUTERS TIME LINE

Phase 1   Pre-microprocessor: Before the development of the Intel 4004 chip.

Before 1800—Abacus.

1800–1850 Charles Babbage, analytical engine design.

1851–1900 Allan Marquand, electric logic machine.
  Herman Hollerith, tabulating/sorting machine.

1901–1925 The Computing-Tabulating-Recording Company became International Business Machines (IBM).

1926–1940 Benjamin Burack, first electric logic machine.
  John V. Atanasoff and Clifford Berry use vacuum tubes as switching units; Iowa State College, in Ames, Iowa, develops the "ABC" or the Atanasoff-Berry Computer. The first electronic computer.

1941–1950 John Mauchley and J. Presper Eckert, Jr., proposed an electronic analyzer to develop ballistic tables for the U.S. Army.
  John Mauchley, J. Presper Eckert, Jr., and John Von Neumann build ENIAC, the first all-electronic digital computer.
  The transistor was developed at Bell Laboratories.
  Mark I computer—Automatic Sequence Controlled Computer—built by Dr. Howard Aiken at Harvard University under an IBM grant.
  Concept of stored program developed.

1951–1955 UNIVAC 1—First commercial computer to become operational.
  IBM planned production of fifty model 650 computers; over one thousand were sold.
  FORTRAN (FORmula TRANslator) computer language developed.

1956–1960 COBOL (COmmon Business Oriented Language) computer language developed under the leadership of Grace Hopper.

1961–1965 President John F. Kennedy dreams of space flight and creates NASA, National Aeronautics and Space Administration.
  BASIC (Beginners All-purpose Symbolic Instruction Code) developed in 1964 at Dartmouth College by John Kemeny and Thomas Kurtz under a National Science Foundation grant.
  Operating systems developed.

Phase 2   Hardware and Operating System Development: The development of the microcomputer hardware and operating system; computer clubs and creation of the basic hardware.

1966–1970 Intel received commission to produce integrated circuits (ICs) for calculators.
  Intel built microprocessor 4004 with Ted Hoff, Stan Mazer, Robert Noyce, and Federico Faggin as the project team.

1971 Intel developed 8008 microprocessor.

1972 Gary Kildall wrote PL/1, the first programming language for Intel's 4004.

1974 Intel 8080 developed.

Microcomputer disk operating system, CP/M, developed by John Torode and Gary Kildall.

1975 The MITS Altair—the first microcomputer in kit form based on the 8080 microprocessor—went on sale.

Bill Gates developed MicroSoft BASIC for Altair.

Many computer clubs started across the nation.

Dick Heiser opened The Computer Store, the first retail computer store in Los Angeles.

1976 IMSAI started shipping first computers.

World Altair Computer Conference held (first microcomputer conference).

Apple I demonstrated by Stephen Wozniak.

CP/M (Control Program/Microcomputer)—disk operating system for MITS Altair—went on sale.

Michael Shrayer developed Electric Pencil, the first word processor for microcomputers.

Phase 3   Software Development: The commercial programs needed by the business professional were developed.

1977 Computerland opened its first franchise in Morristown, New Jersey.

Apple introduced Apple II.

Commodore introduced PET computer.

Tandy-Radio Shack introduced TRS-80 Model I microcomputer.

1978 Apple added disk drives.

1979 TRS-80 Model II introduced by Tandy.

The word processing program WordStar released by MicroPro.

VisiCalc, the first electronic spreadsheet, produced by Personal Software.

Source—national data base for electronic mail and other information services—was started.

CompuServe opened its computer for information services, electronic mail, etc., for microcomputer users.

1980 Hewlett-Packard released HP-85.

MicroSoft developed PC-DOS, the operating system for IBM PC.

Dow Jones News/Retrieval Service opened to Apple computer users.

First LAN, local area networks, available.

Phase 4   Business Use: The use of the microcomputer by business professionals without computer training or background.

1981 Osborne Computer Corporation introduced Osborne 1 with packaged software.

Xerox released 8010 Star and 820 computers.

IBM introduced the IBM PC personal computer.

1982 Apple III introduced.

1983 IBM introduced PC Jr.

Osborne Computer filed for reorganization.

DEC introduced the Rainbow personal computer.

Apple introduced the Macintosh.

1984 IBM PC AT introduced.

AT&T entered microcomputer market after divestiture.

Laser printers introduced for microcomputers.

1985 IBM PC Jr. production discontinued.

AT&T introduced the UNIX-PC, a multi-using, multi-tasking personal computer with network capability.

Many firms introduced local area networks.

Methods developed to increase the amount of internal memory using special hardware and software systems.

1986 IBM introduced the PC-RT based on a reduced instruction set (RIS) technology.

Apple released the Macintosh Plus.

COMPAQ unveiled its Portable II line, built around the Intel 80286 microprocessor.

Access, COMPAQ, and Kaypro led in the introduction of microcomputers using the 32-bit Intel 80386 microprocessor.

Hyundai, a Korean firm, entered the American mass market with a PC based on the Intel 8088 microprocessor.

Software development continued to create better desktop publishing capabilities for Macintosh and IBM PC compatibles.

1987 COMPAQ released its Portable III (80286) line of computers.

Apple released open architecture Macintosh with the capability of operating under MS-DOS.

Versions of UNIX and other operating systems released for Intel 80286 and 80386.

MicroSoft and Bell Laboratories announce development of a version of UNIX for 80386.

TYPES OF INDEX ORGANIZATION

The schemes used for indexing include:

1. Binary search methods
   a. B-Tree
   b. Inverted B-Tree
   c. Modified B-Tree
2. Hashed
3. Index entry
4. Inverted file (keyed)
5. Sequential
6. ISAM-Index sequential access method
7. Key words
8. Pointer.

The binary search technique works only on data that is in sequence. It is a technique for locating an item by continuously dividing the file into groups by two. This is a simple but effective method for making a rapid search for data in a file. The B-Tree, inverted B-Tree, and modified B-Tree are variations of the binary search concept.

Hashing is most commonly used in multi-user data base systems. Hashing uses a **nonlinear** rather than **linear algorithm** for storing data in and retrieving it quickly from a data base.

An index entry is an individual line or item of data contained in an index. It is similar to an entry in a dictionary.

An inverted file is a file indexed on characteristics. All individuals on the scout master list who are trained have a marker to indicate the level of training. A key number is maintained to tell the system the meaning of the code used.

A sequential or **ordered file** is one where the data has been ordered. Such sorting is slow but necessary for binary searching. When it is necessary to sort on more than one field, individual indexes for each field are often more effective. This is referred to as ISAM, index sequential access method. The recordrecords may then be left in random order.

Key words are used to retrieve data from libraries and other data bases. A set of key words for searching is entered. The key word list of each record is searched. When a complete match is made, the record is flagged. Key word search is often combined with some other indexing scheme.

The pointer method is a table look-up technique that permits each data set to be stored with a pointer pointing to a list of associated data.

Linear:
A straight line. Nonlinear is a mathematical relationship that is not a straight line.

Algorithm:
A sequence of mathematical rules used to obtain a desired result.

Nonlinear algorithm:
A sequence of mathematical rules based on nonlinear mathematical relationships for obtaining a desired result, the rapid storing and retrieving of data in a multi-user data base.

Ordered file:
A file stored in the data base in numeric, alphabetic, or ASCII code number order relative to a specific field.

CASES

CASE #1

William Barton is setting up a real estate office for himself and two sales associates. Among other things needed in the office is a copy machine.

The estimated number of copies is between a low of 500 and a high of 2000 per month. The options include:

1. Using a machine down the hall.
2. Purchasing a low-speed cartridge copier.
3. Purchasing a high-speed copier.

The secretary's wage is $8.50 per hour. Figures 1–1 and 1–2 list some of the detailed cost and performance information.

Alternative	Purchase Price	Single Copy Time	Monthly Recommended Capacity
Down the hall	0	38 seconds	no limit
Low speed unit	1,300	10 seconds	1,000
High speed unit	3,000	7 seconds	15,000

Figure 1–1
Purchase Price and Performance

The time required to produce a single copy on the machine down the hall is 38 seconds. This includes the walking time, and the amount of time required to produce a copy.

Down the hall	Paper	Cartridge	Toner	Developer	Drum
Cost	0.15				
Copies	each				
Low speed unit					
Cost	8.00	60.00			
Copies	500	2500			
High speed unit					
Cost	8.00		25.00	26.00	90.00
Copies	500		5000	10000	20000

Figure 1–2
Operating Cost

The low-speed unit requires a cartridge that includes the toner, developer, and drum maintenance cost. There are no additional costs other than paper. The high-speed unit does not use a cartridge but requires a toner, developer, and drum maintenance cost.

The power cost for operating each machine is approximately $0.50 per day. All calculations are to be based on 1,000 copies per month and an assumption of single copies being made.

Assignment

Make an analysis of the cost of each alternative. Use a break-even and payback analysis to compare the different methods. Use a spreadsheet to make the analysis and produce the graphics. Use a word processor to prepare a letter or memo detailing the results obtained and make a recommendation. on which alternative is better and why.

Examine the costs carefully. What would happen if the monthly volume estimate was 500 copies, 1,500 copies, or 3,000 copies? Assume that one cartridge copier will handle the 1,500 copies per month, but two are needed for 3,000 per month. The reason for the second machine is that maintenance costs become excessive when the monthly volume increases to 3,000.

CASE #2

An analysis of the selling price of hard disk systems with tape backup resulted in the data shown in Figure 2–1.

You are employed by a firm that is marketing hard disk drives for microcomputers. Because of your background in microcomputers you have been asked to prepare a report on what is a hard disk drive, what is a tape backup, and who might possibly be customers for microcomputers with these types of on-line storage systems.

You must prepare message(s) for the:

Stockholders
Management Groups
  ■ Central Management
  ■ Marketing department.

All messages must contain three paragraphs. The objective of each paragraph is:

1. To identify what is a hard disk, tape backup.
2. To identify the need for and use of tape backup.
3. To To identify potential users of these systems.

Data Capacity Megabytes	Prices (in dollars)
7.9	3290
10	2795, 3995, 3599, 2995, 3295
11	3135
12	2895
15	4345
16	4295, 4595, 3275, 3990
16.6	3790
20	4495, 4695, 4099, 3759, 3799, 2995, 3995, 3295
21	3195, 4290
25.3	4290
32	4395, 5700
33	5245, 5390
33.5	3995
35	6350, 5595, 5745, 4995
40	5699
41	5995, 6295
41.8	5890
42	5899
43	4995, 6090
43.5	5400
45	1495, 1595
56	7950
57	6699
60	7895
65.6	6590
67	6995, 7295, 7499
70	7495
71.3	6400
75	8995
81	7090
91.8	7990
92	8390
119	10950
141	9290
150	10900
160	10995
238	17450
441	15900

Figure 2–1
A Data Set

Assignment #2

Your task is to organize the data for presentation to management as a table and as a graph. You must determine what information is needed by management and how the data is best organized to provide this information. A memo is to be prepared for management detailing your results.

You will be expected to use pie charts, bar charts, line, and XY charts to help analyze the data.

CASE #3

Juanita Anderson, president of T-P Manufacturing Co., Inc., (T-P Mfg. Co.), founded the company in 1982. The company began business with limited capital. Although they have enjoyed a profit in the last three years, they constantly found themselves short of the working capital needed to purchase raw materials such as canvas, rope, and other supplies, as well as wages.

Currently, T-P Mfg. Co. produces four tent styles in two weights. The tents are 1, 2, 4, and 8-person models. The canvas weights are 10 and 12 ounces. All canvas is flame resistant as per current government regulations.

The tents are marketed through mail order houses, local retail dealers, and selected youth organizations. All retail dealers sell the tents under the brand name T-P. Mail order houses use house brand names, and the youth groups sell the tents under their own names.

During the first four years of the company's history, sales have been 65% to mail order outlets, 25% to retail stores, and 10% to youth groups.

The company has been contacted by a large retail discount chain about supplying them with tents. The volume (20,000 per year) required by this discount chain is equal to twice the current volume. No change in tent design or mix of sizes is expected. However, manufacturing procedures will have to be automated and the number of employees, the in-process inventory, and the investment in raw material inventory are expected to double.

Assignment #1

You must prepare message(s) for the:

- Stockholders
- Management
- Employees
- Local bank that provides short term funds.

All messages must contain three paragraphs. The objective of each paragraph is:

1. To identify the opportunity and to communicate to all concerned that no decision has been made.
2. To outline the steps of the decision making process.
3. To tell each specific department what has to be done.

Assignment #2

Your task is to organize the current sales, revenues, and costs data into a spreadsheet format for the first four years of operation. The final value needed is the gross profit per year. The initial analysis is to be performed assuming no tax obligation.

The average prices paid by the three types of buyers are shown in Figure 3–1.

	Year			
	1982	*1983*	*1984*	*1985*
Ten Oz.				
Number of Units				
Sales by Type				
1-Person	900	1241	1544	1466
2-Person	1217	1402	1744	1656
4-Person	633	1149	1430	1357
8-Person	260	560	697	662
Price per Unit by Year				
1-Person	20.75	22.83	25.11	27.62
2-Person	31.36	35.12	39.33	44.05
4-Person	38.78	43.43	48.64	54.48
8-Person	72.72	79.99	87.99	96.79
Twelve Oz.				
Number of Units				
Sales by Type				
1-Person	200	655	706	645
2-Person	652	740	797	728
4-Person	534	606	653	596
8-Person	486	296	318	291
Price per Unit by Year				
1-Person	23.25	25.58	28.14	30.95
2-Person	36.87	41.29	46.24	51.79
4-Person	43.96	49.24	55.15	61.77
8-Person	89.30	98.23	108.05	118.86

Figure 3–1

Average Prices Paid by Buyers

In Figure 3–1 you will find the sales volume and selling price per unit for both the 10 and 12 ounce fabrics for the four types of tents. You will need to combine the information in Figure 3–1 to determine the revenue earned by T-P Mfg. Co. for each fabric type during the time period given.

The direct manufacturing costs depend on the type of tent being manufactured and the fabric used. In a 1-person tent 3.5 yards of canvas, 4 yards of line, 12 grommets, and a yard of belting for tie downs are needed. The material cost is determined by the cost per yard times the amount of canvas needed. The cost for a 10-oz. 1-person tent was $6.72 in 1982 and it increased to $8.94 by 1984. The material costs other than canvas started at $2.76 in 1982 and increased to $3.67 by 1984. In a 2-person tent 4.5 yards, in a 4-person tent 6 yards, and in an 8-person tent 12 yards are required.

The tent is manufactured by laborers working exclusively on piecework. Under a piecework payment scale the employee receives no dollars except on the number of units produced. The employer does not have to maintain a fixed payroll for employees under this payment plan.

The labor cost for a 1-person tent, regardless of fabric, was $4.81 in 1982 and increased to $6.40 by 1984.

The raw material shipping costs represent the allocated costs of shipping to each tent type. This cost started at $0.12 in 1982 and increased to $0.15 by 1984. These costs are shown in Figure 3–2.

Figure 3–2

Cost of Tent Manufacturing

Costs	Year			
	1982	*1983*	*1984*	*1985*
Direct Cost 10 Oz.				
1-Person				
10 oz. canvas	6.72	7.39	8.13	8.94
Other material	2.76	3.04	3.34	3.67
Direct labor	4.81	5.29	5.82	6.40
Raw mat'l ship	0.12	0.13	0.14	0.15
2-Person				
10 oz. canvas	8.64	9.50	10.45	11.50
Other material	3.54	3.89	4.28	4.71
Direct labor	5.61	6.17	6.79	7.47
Raw mat'l ship	0.13	0.14	0.15	0.17
4-Person				
10 oz. canvas	11.52	12.67	13.94	15.33
Other material	3.87	4.26	4.69	5.16
Direct labor	6.55	7.21	7.93	8.72
Raw mat'l ship	0.22	0.24	0.26	0.29
8-Person				
10 oz. canvas	23.04	25.34	27.87	30.66
Other material	4.21	4.63	5.09	5.60
Direct labor	7.05	7.76	8.54	9.39
Raw mat'l ship	0.33	0.36	0.40	0.44
Direct Cost 12 Oz.				
1-Person				
12 oz. canvas	8.44	9.28	10.21	11.23
Other material	2.76	3.04	3.34	3.67
Direct labor	4.81	5.29	5.82	6.40
Raw mat'l ship	0.14	0.15	0.17	0.19
2-Person				
12 oz. canvas	10.85	11.94	13.13	14.44
Other material	4.45	4.90	5.39	5.93
Direct labor	5.61	6.17	6.79	7.47
Raw mat'l ship	0.16	0.18	0.20	0.22
4-Person				
12 oz. canvas	14.46	15.91	17.50	19.25
Other material	3.87	4.26	4.69	5.16
Direct labor	6.55	7.21	7.93	8.72
Raw mat'l ship	0.24	0.26	0.29	0.32
8-Person				
12 oz. canvas	28.92	31.81	34.99	38.49
Other material	4.21	4.63	5.09	5.60
Direct labor	7.05	7.76	8.54	9.39
Raw mat'l ship	0.41	0.45	0.50	0.55

In addition to direct costs, T-P Mfg. Co. incurs a number of indirect costs. The factory overhead costs include the cost of rent, maintenance of the building, and supervision costs, among others. The administrative overhead costs include salaries for the corporation managers and office employees, supplies, and similar items. The utilities costs are for heat, light, phone, and water. The interest expense is for payments on the loans for working capital currently outstanding. The insurance expense is for workman's compensation, product liability, and fire, theft, and other liability. These costs are shown in Figure 3–3.

Costs	Year			
	1982	1983	1984	1985
Factory overhead	30000	33000	36300	39930
Adm overhead	32000	34560	37325	40311
Utilities	13000	14300	15730	17303
Interest exp	5000	5000	5000	5000
Insurance	5430	6082	6811	7629

Figure 3–3
Indirect Costs

T-P Mfg. Co. has some additional selling and distribution costs in the form of selling and advertising expenses. These costs include visits to individual retail outlets, phone calls, radio, newspaper, and TV ads. The costs are shown in Figure 3–4.

Costs	Year			
	1982	1983	1984	1985
Selling expense	9792.94	13924.54	18266.93	19025.56
Adv exp.	5875.76	8354.72	10960.16	11415.33

Figure 3–4
Selling and Distribution Costs

With the information in Figures 3–1 through 3–4 you will be able to make an analysis of the profit performance of T-P Mfg. Co. over the past four years.

Assignment #3

You are an expert (accountant, computer, financial, personal, management, etc.) hired to help T-P Mfg. Co. solve its growth problems. Your job is to identify the most critical problem in your area of expertise, identify the current position of T-P Mfg., identify the goals they should set, develop a plan to accomplish the goals, and determine what information is needed to solve the problem.

A memo is to be prepared for the president detailing your opinion on what is T-P Mfg. Co.'s most critical problem.

1. Expansion needs: Equipment
2. Expansion needs: Marketing team
3. Expansion needs: Plant square footage
4. Expansion needs: Personnel (management, shop supervision, shop floor)
5. Expansion needs: Training
6. Expansion needs: Financial
7. Expansion needs: Inventory plan
8. Expansion needs: Accounting system
9. Expansion needs: Microcomputers
10. Determine price of company if sold
11. Investigate question: Should company expand?

THE IMPORTANCE OF SOFTWARE DOCUMENTATION

Laura B. Ruff
Mary K. Weitzer

There is an old saying which teachers are fond of quoting. It goes as follows, "Give me a fish and you have fed me for a day, teach me to fish and you have fed me for a lifetime." That quote came to mind as we were writing this piece on documentation research. Most software comes with some sort of written directions commonly referred to as documentation. Learning to use documentation is the key to realizing the capabilities and power of the accompanying software. Much documentation, however, is written by technical people using technical terms and can be rather intimidating, especially to the novice. But with a table of contents, an index, some of the pages in between, and a good measure of determination and fortitude, even the beginner can learn a software package by correctly using the documentation.

Unfortunately, some people never learn to use the documentation. Employers are dismayed to find that an employee who is trained in the use of one software package often cannot transfer that knowledge to another software package without additional training. It seems that many employees depend on learning a package from someone else and never learn to look things up for themselves. Several problems ensue from this lack of independence. This type of employee never learns to solve the unexpected problems that can arise when using software and never develops the tools needed to learn more about either the package currently being used, an update of that same package, or even a totally new package. Of course, in this rapidly changing field, new packages and updates of old packages are facts of life with which all microcomputer users must deal.

Another problem results from not using the documentation. A user can learn only so much at any training session or in any course. Initially, a user is content with just the simplest functions of the software as opposed to the alternative of doing the tasks manually. Over a period of time, the novice becomes more comfortable with the software and starts looking for ways to increase productivity by doing the same tasks more efficiently and by adding applications that formerly were accomplished manually. "I wonder if I could do that with my software . . ." many times can be answered affirmatively simply by referring to the documentation.

It is easy to say that a user should "simply" read the documentation. For the first time user, however, this can be a frustrating experience. Documentation has become easier to read, better organized and more error free than it has been in the past. With anything new, though, there is a need to learn how to use this source of reference efficiently. The more often a person uses documentation, the more proficient that person will become at interpreting any type of software manual. Most software documentation does have several things in common. In order to gain microcomputing independence, look for the following items in software documentation. Happy fishing!

LICENSING INFORMATION

The licensing agreement will be of most immediate concern to you. Find out what the copyright will allow—how many backup copies (if any) are permitted? Is the software licensed to the user for use on any machine or licensed for use on only one machine? Can the software be used by more than one user at one time or by only one user without exception, or used by a variety of users as long as only the one copy is in use at any one time? The licensing agreement is usually fully visible before you even remove the wrapping. The terms of the agreement should be carefully followed.

As part of the licensing agreement, you will usually find a user registration card that will register you as a user of the software with the software publisher. Some software publishers issue a serial number for each package sold. If it is your responsibility, be sure to fill out the registration immediately and mail it to the publisher so that you will be entitled to receive any technical support, update information, or newsletters that may be provided to registered users.

PACKAGING

Documentation can be found in all shapes, weights, and forms. It may be contained in one or more three-ring binders, spiral bound book(s), a single sheet of paper, or simply as part of the program disk. If the documentation is in hardcopy form, one of the first things you will want to do when you open your documentation is to find out how the documentation is organized. If it is bound as one manual, does the manual have divider tabs? If there are two or more books that make up the documentation, which one should be examined first? Which one will be used most often? Sometimes when there is more than one book included as the documentation, there will be one manual for the novice microcomputer user (usually in tutorial form), one for day-to-day reference, one for the more technical or less frequently used functions, and so on. There may be separate quick reference cards and/or a keyboard layout chart or template. If you happen to be the first person to use the software you will find that the disks themselves will be somewhere within the documentation package. After you have examined the documentation as described here, you will be ready to more closely peruse its contents.

TABLE OF CONTENTS

A good Table of Contents will give you the first picture of the software and its functions. This section would be one of the first referral areas with which you would want to become familiar. The Table of Contents will help you to find out if the documentation has the other sections we are mentioning here and help you to discover any other special features and aids that may be available within the documentation.

INTRODUCTION (OR "READ ME FIRST")

All good software will offer some sort of introductory section that will explain the overall capabilities of the package, what tutorial materials are included with the software (if any), and possibly the hardware requirements of the software package. Even before you purchase a software package, this section of the documentation is a good guide to help you decide whether the software is appropriate for your applications. Usually documentation is available for examination before you purchase it at a retail computer software store. If so, you can check the hardware requirements so you will know if your machine has enough memory to support the software, for instance, or if a hard disk is required, or if your printer is supported by the software. Through the use of documentation at the point of purchase, you are already taking a step towards independence by not having to rely solely on what a sales representative tells you. You can read it for yourself.

If you are in a situation where you are responsible for selecting software, you definitely want to check the clarity and completeness of the documentation. The documentation is an important feature to consider when purchasing software. The Table of Contents and Introduction are good places to begin your evaluation. In addition to the documentation manual that comes with the software, check to see what other types of training aids, such as a tutorial disk or sample data disk, may be available for the software. Such training aids are excellent for the first time user, especially if used in conjunction with the documentation.

In a new software package, the actual program disks may come to you in a nice shrink-wrapped package. These disks must be "set-up," "installed" or in some way prepared to be used on your microcomputer system. Each package must be set up differently and even the same package may need to be prepared differently depending on the configuration of your machine. These directions are usually found in the introductory section of the documentation. If the information that you think should be found in the Introduction is not there, just check the Table of Contents to find out where the information is located. The warranty information is likely to be in this section as well as the license agreement. The number of backup copies (if any) of a program will be stated in the license agreement as well as the policy on updates.

Other information you might look for in the introductory sections includes an explanation of the keyboard layout that defines all keys as they will be used with the specific software, an explanation of the cursor movement keys and edit keys, descriptions of the screen layouts, an explanation of the help function, if available, and so on.

ADDRESS AND PHONE FOR TECHNICAL SUPPORT (HELP)

Another important part of the introductory information should include the address and phone number that can be used for technical support or at least some information regarding the software publisher's user assistance services. Most companies offer at least short term phone assistance that can later be extended for a fee. Others will offer free technical support indefinitely. What type of technical support is available for the software you are using or plan to buy? If you read the documentation you will find the answer.

REFERENCE SECTIONS

The most frequently used sections of the documentation will be those containing the actual description of how to use the capabilities and functions of the software. The number of reference sections contained within the documentation will directly depend upon the complexity of the software program and possibly the structure of the documentation layout. Become familiar with the arrangement of the reference sections. Are they arranged according to functions? Are they alphabetically arranged? Those two arrangements seem to be the most popular and logical but logic does not always seem to be the criterion for arrangement. The time you take to investigate and to become familiar with the reference section(s) will be time well spent.

SUMMARY SECTIONS

Much of the software documentation offers summary or quick reference sections that become increasingly helpful as you gain expertise. These sections will serve as a "tickler" to remind you of the procedures that you have already learned and used.

APPENDIXES

As with all other sections described in this appendix, the information found in the Appendixes will vary from software package to software package. In general, however, you might look for information on the error messages that are used by the program, printer configuration information (how to set up the program so that it works with your printer), printer codes (so that you can send special messages to the printer), explanation of menus used within the program, glossary of terminology, shortcuts for the advanced user (even software publishers realize that a lot of the knowledge acquired while using one type of software package can be transferred to make learning a different software package easier), and so on.

GLOSSARY

Some documentation includes a Glossary, which is an alphabetical listing of terms along with their definitions. Some of the terminology and definitions may be specific to the particular software package while others are more general terms that are not software specific. The Glossary is usually located right before the Index.

INDEX

The alphabetically arranged Index found in most documentation can help you find more detailed information than is contained in the Table of Contents. You can find the page number for an explanation of specific procedures, functions, capabilities and so forth. If you know that the software is capable of performing a function, you might check the Glossary to find out what term is used for the specific function and then look up the page number for a description of the function in the Index. Just taking the time to slowly go through the Index can reward you with quite a bit of information about a software package and its capabilities.

GLOSSARY

Absolute reference (spreadsheet): The indication of where specific data are found in a fixed column/row location. When cells are moved or copied absolute references do not change. 148

Access method: The scheme used by the operating system to control communication between work stations in a LAN. 292

Acoustical coupler modem: A modem that connects directly to the telephone system using acoustical cups to hold the telephone. 246

Analog devices: Devices used to monitor real-world conditions such as temperature, sound, and movement. These devices use continuous voltage rather than the binary coding system of the microcomputer. 250

Analysis: Comparison of alternate management actions. 327

ANSI: Standards defining the acceptable statements in BASIC and other programming languages are maintained by ANSI, American National Standards Institute. 25

Answer: Modem setting in asynchronous communication. One partner must answer, the other originate. 254

Apple–DOS: Disk operating system used on Apple computers. 83

Application programs: A program designed to perform a specific function. 4

Architecture: The design of the microcomputer. How the parts are put together. Also called design architecture. 35

ASCII: American Standard Code for Information Interchange. This is a seven-bit binary code. Numbers from 00 to 127 can be produced with a seven-bit binary number. The decimal number 90 is 1011010. Each number in ASCII

stands for a character or control instruction. 82, 250, 275

ASM: CP/M Utility used to create a machine language file from assembly language code. 85

Assembly language: A language that is close to machine language and easily converted using a special program called an assembler. 25

Asynchronous communication: Communication that requires timing only when a bit is being transmitted. 252, 275

Artificial Intelligence: The art and science of making computers behave in a manner resembling intelligent human behavior. 11

Attribute: A particular characteristic of interest about an entity. 177

Backup: A copy of a disk or file. 69

BAK: Extender used to indicate a file is a backup file. 81

BAS: Extender used to indicate a file is a BASIC program file. 81

Baseband coaxial cable: Similar to television cable, for medium-speed local area networks. Can handle one transmission at a time. 291

BASIC: Beginners All-purpose Symbolic Instructional Code. 25

Batch run: A scheduling system which requires computer tasks be collected and given to a central controller who then runs them as a single job-batched together. 276

Baud rate: Usually refers to the transmission rate. 1200 baud means 120 characters per second. 246

Binary file: Programs stored in machine language form. A binary file may be directly executed by the microcomputer. 82

Binary number: A number consisting of 0 and 1. Each 0 or 1 is a bit. The decimal numbers 0 to

126 require 7 bits. To add the decimal numbers 127 to 255 require the 8th bit. 82

Binary search: For ordered records. An item is located by continuously dividing the file into groups by two.

Bit: A binary digit. The microcomputer uses a binary number system consisting of 0 and 1. A bit is a 0 or a 1. 37

Bit map: Picture represented by dots, digitizing. 212

Block: A collection of characters with beginning and ending markers that must be entered by the user. 100

Boards: See cards. 15, 40

Booting: Starting the system. 39

Boot strap: Program that starts the system. 39

Breakeven analysis: An evaluation technique that calculates the amount of output when the total cost of one method is the same as the total cost of a second method. 329

Briefcase microcomputer: A microcomputer that fits in a briefcase and/or may be used on an individual lap. 17

Broadband coaxial cable: Cable that may handle many transmissions at one time for local area networks. 291

Bubble memory: A memory device that uses no power. Uses a thin magnetic recording film that looks like bubbles. 40

Bus: Pathway or channel for data and instruction between hardware devices. 84

Business graphics: Pictorial representation of business data. 194

Business graphics programs: Programs with the capability of producing bar charts, pie charts, line type graphs. 7

Byte: A sequence of binary digits taken as a unit. Eight binary digits per byte microcomputers are currently the most common. Seven or eight bits are used to create characters. 37

C: A microcomputer and computer language that uses structured programming and can perform many tasks that would normally require the use of assembly language. 26

CAD: Computer aided design. 8

CADD: Computer aided design and drafting. 8

CAE: Computer aided engineering. 8

Cards: Flat pieces of material with printed circuits and electronic components to add special capabilities to the microcomputer. Often called PC (Printed Circuit) boards. 15, 40

CAT: The name of the directory in (Apple) PRO-DOS. See DIR. 74

CATALOG: The name of the directory in Apple-DOS. See DIR. 74

Cells: Column (vertical division) and row (horizontal division) location on screen and in spreadsheets. 5, 129

Central file server (program): Program that controls the access to files by individual work stations in a LAN. 290

Central switching station: The central microcomputer connected to a series of stations in a LAN. 292

Centronics connection: The name of the standard parallel connector. Centronic was the first printer company to make this connection popular. 75

Character size: The number of bits per character byte. 254

CMOS: Memory that uses little power, complementary metal oxide semiconductor. 40

COBOL: COmmon Business Oriented Language. A mainframe computer language that is available on microcomputers. 26

Code: The use of symbols or numbers to represent letters, numbers, or special meanings. 25, 82

Cold boot: Starting the system from the beginning when the system is first turned on. 70

Collector: An interface that collects messages from a number of devices, organizes the messages, and then forwards them to the central computer. 276

Column: Vertical division of screen and spreadsheet. 5, 129

COM files: Files in machine language ready to operate on a specific microcomputer. 81

Communication Bus (Layout of LAN): A LAN layout around a bus which serves as a channel for communication. 292

Communication program: A program that allows computers to communicate with each other. 4

Communication ring or circle: Layout of LAN where the stations are connected in a ring or circle. 292

Compatibility: Capability of microcomputers to work together as a system and to exchange physical parts. 34

Compiler: A translator program that takes near English code and translates it into a set of machine language codes all at one time. 25

Composite monitor: Type of color monitor. 44

Compressed mode: Printer that produces small letters to increase the characters per line of output. 45

Condensed mode: See compressed mode. 45

Configuration: Matching the hardware, software, and operating systems settings so that all the parts work and communicate with all the other parts of a system. 34

Conventions: The standard and accepted abbreviations, symbols, and their meanings for users of microcomputers. 70

Copy (block): To duplicate an image of a block at a new location (in word processing). 111

Copy protected (program): Programs sold with a limit placed on the number of copies a user may produce. 54

CP/M: Operating system, Control Program/Microcomputer. One of the first operating systems developed for microcomputers. 25

CPU: Central processing unit. 13

CRT: Cathode ray tube, screen, monitor. 13

CSMA/CD: Carrier Sense Multiple Access/Collision Detect, a communication system that operates like a telephone party line. 292

Cursor: A symbol on the monitor that indicates where text will be typed. The cursor is often a line (_) or a box. It may be steady or blinking. 104

Data: Facts that have been collected, organized, and stored.

Data base: A collection of data stored in your microcomputer, that is used for a variety of purposes. 5, 164

Data base management programs: Programs designed to store, update, and retrieve business data. These programs are not limited to any particular type of application. 164

Data file transfer software: Programs designed to read data in the format produced by one program and change it to a format needed by a second program. 300

DDT: CP/M Utility used to debug an assembly language file. 85

Debug: To remove errors from a program. 85

Default drive: The disk drive from which data and programs are read unless the microcomputer is instructed otherwise. The default drive is the logged drive if no additional instructions are given. 55, 71

Delete: An instruction to remove a character, block, or file. When characters are removed, the text closes up. 104

Desktop microcomputer: A microcomputer that has the greatest capabilities, most expansion room, and requires a part of a desk for its work area. 18

DIF: Data interchange format. An ASCII file in a specific format developed for VisiCalc used for both spreadsheet and data file interchange. 182

Digitize: To convert a picture or other data to numbers, that are then recorded in the microcomputer. 196

DIP: Dual Inline Package, housing to hold a chip or other items to printed circuit board. 41

DIP switches: A series of toggle switches built into a DIP, that are mounted on a pc-board. The switches are used for system configuration. 41

DIR: Directory. Instruction that tells what files are on a storage media. Name used in CP/M, TRS–DOS, and MS–DOS. 73

Direct-connect modem: A modem that connects directly to the telephone system using telephone line. 246

Disk: An eight inch or 5¼ inch flat, round piece of plastic coated with magnetic material and placed in a protective cover. The disk is used to record microcomputer programs and data. 52

Document assembly programs: Programs that create documents from prerecorded paragraphs. 5

Documentation: Narrative supplied with programs to help the user operate the software. 4

DOS: Disk operating system. See operating system. 68

Dot matrix printer: Printer that produces characters using dots rather than whole letters. 45

Download: To transfer a file from another computer into yours. 187, 257

DSDD: Double sided and double density disk drive. 55

DSS, Decision Support Systems: An integrated management information and planning system. 11

Dumb terminal: Terminal that communicates only under the control of an individual. 257

EBCDIC: Extended Binary Coded Decimal Interchange Code. The standard code developed and used by IBM for its mainframe computers.

It is a binary code made up of eight-bits that allows 256 characters. 275

ED: CP/M utility used to edit a file. 85

Editing: Making corrections to spreadsheets, word processor, and other files.

Electronic mail: The transmission of letters, memos, and other messages by one microcomputer to another computer. 268

Electronic spreadsheet: See spreadsheet programs. 129

Emulators: A printer circuit board that fits into a microcomputer and gives it the capability to act like a special purpose terminal. 275

End user: An individual who uses a computer to increase his/her personal productivity in solving problems. 5

Engineering/scientific graphics: Includes CAD, computer aided design; CAM, computer aided manufacturing; CADD, computer aided design and drafting. 6

Entity: Something that has separate and distinct existence. 176

EOF: End of file. A code placed at the end of a file to indicate the end has been reached. 73

EPROM: Erasable programmable read only memory chips. This type of chip makes it easy for individuals to produce custom programs. 39

Erase: To remove a block. 111

Esc.: Key found in the upper left of most keyboards. Used as a control type key. 81

Extra capabilities: State of the art features. 13

Facts: Something that exists and must be taken into consideration. 172

Families: Groups of microcomputers that use the same or similar microprocessor and the same or similar operating system. These groups have similar capabilities. 68

Field: A unit of data about an attribute of an entity. 177

File: A collection of related material. May be data or programs or both. 68, 171

File maintenance: The entering and updating of data in a data base. 173

File management programs: Programs designed to store, update, and retrieve business data. These programs are limited to managing simple files with narrow objectives. 5, 179

File management-report generators: See File management programs. 179

File server: The computer that controls the storage and retrieval of files from a common disk or hard disk when a number of computers are connected together to form a system. 274

Filename: Name given to a data or program file. 81

Filespec: Includes name of disk drive, colon, path (if any), filename, decimal point, and extender. 81

Floppy disk drive: Data storage devices; stores data, programs and other computer files. 14

Font: A style of letter or character such as Italic, Courier, or Prestige. 97

Footprint: The amount of space taken on a desk by a microcomputer. 18

Format: Defines how code is saved on a disk. It also defines how characters are placed on a piece of paper and how the characters are displayed on the screen. 77

FORMAT: Instruction used to tell the microcomputer to prepare a disk for use. Magnetic marks are made on the media to identify tracks and sectors where data is to be stored. 77

Formula: Rules defining the relationship (outcome) between numbers used in the spreadsheet. Electronic spreadsheet formulas often use cell references as variables. 129

FORTH: FOurTH generation language. A microcomputer language used for business, scientific, process control, and robotics. Contains a resident assembly language. 26

FORTRAN: FORmula TRANslator. A mainframe computer language now available on microcomputers. Used for engineering and science application. 26

Free format data bases: Data bases that combine different forms of data entry including text, lists, tables, charts, and graphs. 173

Full-duplex: Both communication partners can send and receive at the same time. 255

Full-featured microcomputer: A microcomputer system that includes most of the accessories available at a given time. 13

Function key: Keys found on the left side of the IBM PC keyboard, or the top of some look-alikes that send custom instructions to the microcomputers. In some programs the user may define the instructions sent by the function keys. 100

Functions (operating system): Routines built into the operating system. These routines provide the user with the capability to perform needed tasks. Functions are loaded into RAM with the operating system and remain there. 68

Functions of management: Planning (including goal setting), organizing, directing, and controlling. 175

Gigabyte: One billion bytes, 1,000,000,000 or 10 ^ 9. 56

Graphics: Pictorial representation of data. 194

Hacker: An individual working alone who developed both the hardware and software of the microcomputer. A person who may or may not be trained for the task (hobbyist). 19

Half-duplex: One communication partner can send and the other receive at any given time. 255

Hard copy: Text printed on paper. 5

Hard disk drive: Data storage devices, may be fixed or removable. Stores data, programs, and other computer files. 14

Hardware: The part of the microcomputer you can see and feel. 13

Hex: Hexadecimal. A Hex file is a file stored using numbers based on 16 digits. 85

Hierarchical data bases: A data base organized from the top down. 179

Hierarchical files: A file structure consisting of a top sown organization. Files are organized in what is often referred to as a tree structure. Some operating systems allow sophisticated security to be established for hierarchical files. 73

Hierarchy: Classification or grading of a group or set from high to low. 23

High bit: The last bit in a binary number. High bit numbers are the decimal numbers that can only be created when the last bit is used. The decimal numbers 00 to 126 may be created by seven-bit binary numbers. The addition of the eighth-bit allows the creation of decimal numbers 127 to 255. 254

High-level language: A computer language near English. 25

Idea: Recognition of a need or opportunity. 318

IEEE–488: Port specification. Used for laboratory type devices. 75

Implementation: Putting a method or microcomputer to work in a company. 333

Index hole: Hole on disk and diskette used to index the reading operating in some operating systems. 54

Indexing: The manner in which a program orders the records in a file. 174

Information: Data that has been processed and recalled from a data base in an organized manner. 172

Ink-Jet printers: Printers that use jets of ink to produce characters. 47

Input: see I/O 16

Input (factors of production): The factors of production, land, labor, capital, and the business enterprise used to produced goods and services. 327

Input devices: Devices connected to the microcomputer through which data and instructions are entered. 13, 41

Insert: When a word is typed into existing text, the text that follows it moves over to make room. 104

Instruction set: Instructions built into the computer. The instruction set is contained in the microprocessor. 82

Integrated programs: Programs that combine the capabilities of two or more general or specific application programs. 4, 301

Interface: A common boundary between independent systems; in the field of microcomputers the connection between two parts of the system; the programs and hardware that make it possible for two parts of the microcomputer system or two computers to work together. 276

Interpreter: A program that translates a line of near English code into machine language, executes the line of code, translates the next line, etc. until all instructions have been completed. 25

I/O: Input and output devices or methods. 16

Justified: Lining up of type on a page or in a cell. Left justified means lined up evenly on the left side of page or cell, while right justified means lined up on the right. 138

K: see kilobyte. 39

Kilobyte: 1024 bytes, or 2 ^ 10. 39

Knowledge: The assignment of meaning to information by a human being. 172

Labels: Words identifying columns, rows, or overall titles. 128

LAN: Local Area Networks. A series of microcomputers connected together sharing peripherals, files, and programs. 288

LAN topology: The relative physical and logical arrangement of stations in the network. Types include central switching station, communication bus, communication ring, and point-to-point. 292

Language: See programming language. 5

Laptop microcomputer: A microcomputer that fits in a briefcase and/or may be used on an individuals lap. 19

Laser printer: Printers that use technology similar to that of some copying machines. They produce quality results at relatively high speeds. 46

LCD: Liquid crystal display microcomputer output device. 44

Letter quality printer: Printers that use thimbles, balls, daisy wheels, or other impact devices. 46

Limitations: Restrictions on the decision making process. 319

Linear: Relating to a straight line. Nonlinear is a mathematical relationship that is not related to a straight line.

Load: To transfer a file from an on-line storage media into the RAM of a computer so it can be used. 68

LOAD: CP/M utility used to convert Hex files to COM files. 85

Logged drive: The disk drive from which data and programs are read. 71

LOGO: A microcomputer educational language that uses graphics for programming. 26

Low-level language: A computer language near machine language. 25

Machine language: A formal system of signs and symbols including rules for their use that convey instructions to a computer. 25

Macros: Custom routines which substitute a few keystrokes for many. They may be created by the user and saved on disk as routines that are recalled with a few keystrokes when needed in spreadsheets or similar programs. 152

Magnetic tape: Data storage media. 14

Mainframe: A large computer. Originally all computers were mainframe computers. Most require technical expertise to operate. 268

Master disk: Disk upon which data or programs are stored for safekeeping. A copy of the master disk is made to be used as the working disk. 57

Mathematical operators: Symbol that indicates a mathematical process such as addition $(+)$, subtraction $(-)$, multiplication $(*)$ division $(/)$, and raising to a power $(^)$. 143

Measurable: An activity or item which can be measured. If a goal cannot be measured there is no way of knowing when the goal has been accomplished. 319

Megabyte: One million bytes. 40

Menu: A list of microcomputer actions displayed on the screen from which the user selects the one wanted. 84

Microprocessor: An integrated circuit on a silicon chip usually less than two inches long and a half inch wide that, contains the arithmetic, logic, control, and memory units. The remaining hardware supports this chip. 15, 37

Milestones: Steps on the way to the completion of a plan. 321

Minicomputer: Medium-size computer, larger and more expensive than a microcomputer, but smaller than a mainframe. 268

Modem: A device to connect the microcomputer to the telephone. It changes binary codes to sound for telephone transmission and then back again. 246

Modular software: Programs sold in individual modules that can be put together to form a system. The user has the option of purchasing only those modules desired. 301

Monitor: see CRT, VDT. 14

Monochrome monitor: A green, amber, or black and white monitor. 44

Mother board: A printed circuit board or card containing the microprocessor, computer memory, and selected controller circuits to direct the signals that are received from external connectors. 35

Move: To relocate a block. 111

MOVECPM: CP/M utility used to relocate the system to make room for special programs. 85

MS/PC–DOS: Microsoft disk operating system; personal computer disk operating system used on the IBM PC and look-alike family of microcomputer. 25

Multi-tasking: The capability of the microcomputer to perform more than one task at the same time. 40, 289

Multi-user: Microcomputers and programs that allow more than one user to share the same microprocessor. 40, 290

Multi-user data bases: A data base program that allows more than a single user access at the same time. 179

National electronic data bases: Dynamic libraries that are used by connecting a microcomputer to a telephone. Current information about economics, business, and other specialized topics are available using such data base. 269

Near ASCII file: A file that uses the ASCII codes, has some additional control codes, and may be edited to an ASCII file without excessive effort. 115

Network data base: A hierarchical data base that allows for multiple relationships among levels. 182

Non-procedural language: A programming language that does not require programming techniques to be used. It allows the user to send instructions to the computer in English-like statements. 173

Null-modem: Device that makes the computer behave as if it is connected to a telephone to allow communication between computers. 247

Numbers: Mathematical values, business data. 128

Objective: A business goal that is feasible, measurable, has a time limit, has recognized limitations, and has a plan for its accomplishment. 318

OCR: Optical Character Reader. 42

On/off-line: The operation of computer equipment at the same time as other equipment under the control of the microprocessor (on-line). Independent operation is called off-line. 49

On-line devices: Devices connected electronically through controller circuits. They may or may not be physically part of the microcomputer. 14

On-line storage devices: Devices available to the microcomputer through communication cables. 49

On-line storage media: Material used to store microcomputer files. 50

Operating system: The program that directs the flow of data among the parts of the microcomputer, the user, and application programs, often called the disk operating system (DOS or OS). 4, 68

Operating system shells: Integrating programs that have been created to hide the complexities of the disk operating system and to add features. 310

Operational compatibility: The capability of microcomputers to work together as a system. 57

Originate: Modem setting in asynchronous communication. One partner must originate, the other answer. 254

Output (business): The goods and services produced by a company. 328

Output devices: A device connected to the microcomputer through which data and instructions are communicated to the user or other devices. 14, 44

Overflow (cell): More characters are entered than the cell can contain. The additional characters appear in the next cell. (See also Truncated.) 137

Overlay utility software: Programs that provide selected routines to the user at all times. 292

Overwrite: When a character is typed, it replaces the character formerly at the location of the cursor. 104

Parallel communication port: Connection to communicate over a number of "parallel" wires at the same time. 40

Parameter: A variable value. Parameters are values that must be set before communication can occur. 254

Parity bit: The error checking bit. 252

Pascal: A simple and structured microcomputer language for general use. 26

Path: Used on a hard disk divided into subdirectory to locate a file. 75

Payback period: The amount of time until the total cost of one method is the same as a second method. 330

PC–boards: See cards. 15, 40

PC–DOS: See MS/PC–DOS. 25

Peripheral: A device such as a printer, bar code reader, or modem connected to a microcomputer to give it special capabilities. 18

Physical compatibility: The capability to exchange physical parts with other microcomputers. 40

PIP: CP/M utility, Peripheral Interchange Program, used to transfer files from one diskette to another. 85

Pixels: The dots on a microcomputer's screen used to create numbers, graphics, and other characters (letters, numbers, and symbols). 44, 194

Plan: A series of steps detailing what must be done to move a business from where it is to where management has decided it is to go. 320

Plotter printer: Printer that uses lines to create graphic type output. 48

Pocket microcomputer: Computer small enough to fit in a pocket. 19

Point-to-point LAN: Layout of LAN topology where each station is connected directly to other stations. 292

Portable microcomputers: Often refers to transportables, and at other times to all computers smaller than transportables. 18

Ports: Outlets or connections that allow the microcomputer to communicate with peripherals and other computers. 75

Precedence (Math): The order in which mathematical operations are executed. The standard order is parentheses, power, multiplication and division, and addition and subtraction. 144

Print spooler: A program that sets aside part of the RAM or disk to receive text to be sent to the printer. 117

Printer controllers: Programs or routines that take a text file and produce a hard copy. 114

Productivity: Output divided by input. 327

Programming language: A language used by programmers to create, store, recall, and edit instructions to computers. 7

Programs: See Software. 4

PROM: Programmable read only memory chips. 39

Proportional spacing: Allows for differences in letter size to make the document look like typeset material. 115

Protected cell: A cell that has been protected from change by the spreadsheet designer. It is good practice to "protect" the cells with labels when a standard form is created. 141

RAM: Random access memory. Memory used for data and program storage by the user. The user can read and write data in RAM. 16, 39

RAM resident software: Programs that remain in RAM and may be called up at any time, there-by allowing ancillary functions to be performed, and then return to the original work without having to exit or restart. 304

Range (spreadsheet): The identification of the cells in a spreadsheet by the specification of the cell in the upper left position and the cell in the lower right position. 141

Raster graphics: Graphics using a bit map. 196

Real time processing: To process data and instructions as they are transmitted to the computer. The user works interactively with the computer. 276

Record: A collection of facts about an entity. 176

Relational data bases: A data base with the capability to combine the data from a series of records that have a field with a matching relationship. 179, 180

Relative reference (spreadsheet): The indication of where specific data are found in terms of a fixed number of columns and rows from the cell where the data are needed. When cells are moved or copied the relative references are changed to maintain their relative position. 148

Report generation: The creation of a formatted report to output information from the data base. 173

Resolution: The sharpness of the image produced by a monitor. 44

RGB: Type of color monitor (red, green, blue) for microcomputers. 44

Right justification: When the text is lined up evenly on the right margin. 108

ROM: Read Only Memory. Memory with instructions (programs) needed when operating the microcomputer. The user cannot write data into ROM. Sometimes called firmware. 16, 39

Rotation hole: Hole in the middle of disk. 54

Routine: A part of a program that performs specific tasks. 68

Row: Horizontal division of screen and spreadsheet. 5, 129

RS–232, RS–232C: The standard serial port for input and output communication with peripherals and other computers. 75

RS–422: A serial port. 75

Screen: See CRT, VDT. 16

Scroll: Text is moved up or down to display text that cannot be shown on the monitor at one time. 104

Sector (of disk): A division of a track on a disk. 52

Sequential search: A search of a file starting at the beginning and examining each record in turn seeking a particular record. 174

Serial communication port: Connection to communicate sending one bit after another in series. 40

Smart terminal: Terminal that can be used to transfer data files between computers. 257

Software: Programs, instructions that tell the microcomputer how to perform. 4

Spreadsheet: A method for organizing, calculating, and presenting financial, statistical, and other business data for managerial decision making. 128

Spreadsheet programs: Programs used for calculation (formula oriented) and presentation. 4

SSDD: Single-sided and double-density diskette or disk drive. 55

SSSD: Single-sided and single-density diskette or disk drive. 55

Stand-alone: Programs that operate independently of other programs. 40

Start bit: The bit (in asynchronous communication) that tells the second microcomputer a character is being sent. 252

STAT: CP/M Utility used to check the status of disks and system. 85

Stop bit: The bit (in asynchronous communication) that tells the second microcomputer the character is complete. 252

String: A character or characters. Strings may be one or more characters in length. 108

SYLK: Symbolic Link. An ASCII file is a specific format developed for MultiLink used for both spreadsheet and data file interchange. 182

Synchronous communication: Communication that requires continuous timing. 252

Syntax: The manner in that code must be put together for the computer to understand, including spelling. 25

SYSGEN: CP/M utility used to generate a CP/M operating system on a new diskette. 85

Template: A spreadsheet or other model saved on disk to be recalled into a spreadsheet or other program as a pattern for future applications. Templates may be purchased on disk or copied out of books for many business applications. 149

Terminal: A computer work station, input/output device. It may consist of a keyboard and a monitor or be a microcomputer. 76

Text: Characters found on paper, on the screen, or stored in a microcomputer text file. Text may be a letter or manuscript length book. 94

Text editor: A program that makes possible creating, changing, storage, and retrieval of text in the file. 103

Text file: A computer file that contains words and characters. Such files are commonly created during word processing. 94

Thermal printers: Printers that use a heating element to make a letter or character on either heat-sensitive paper or regular paper with a heat-sensitive ribbon. 47

Time limit: A date or time of day by which a task must be completed. 319

Timesharing: More than one terminal may be connected to and operated at one time on the same computer. 76

Token-passing: Transmission control system when a circle is used. Each station checks to see if a transmission is for them, and if it is not, passes it along to the next station. 292

Track (of disk): A magnetic circle on a disk for storing data. 52

Transportable microcomputers: Microcomputers that are packaged with most of the features of a desktop, including a monitor. 18

TRS–DOS: Tandy Radio Shack disk operating system used in various forms on the many Radio Shack microcomputers. 25

Truncated (cell): More characters are entered than the cell can contain. The additional characters are cut off at the end of the cell. 137

Twisted-pairs: Telephone wires used for some local area networks. 291

UNIX: The multi-user operating system of AT&T. 25

Upload: To transfer a file from your computer or terminal to another computer. 187, 257

User friendly: Microcomputers and programs that are easy to use. 4

Utilities: Programs that support the operation of the operating system by adding capabilities. 23, 68

Variable: A quantity that may assume any one of a set of values. There are two types of variables: Independent—variables that change by themselves, such as time; Dependent—variables that depend on a second variable(s), such as sales per month, that depend on the month of the year. 201

VDT: Video display tube. 16

Warm boot: Starting the system from the beginning when the system is already operating. 70

What if?: The investigation of economic and business consequences assuming that changes in business decisions are to be made, and the conditions under that the decisions are made. 133

Windowing: The capability to divide a monitor into parts. In each part a different task or program may be operated. 76

Word processing program: A program designed to aid an individual in the creation, editing, printing, storing and retrieving of text. 4, 94

Word size: Microcomputers commonly process 8, 16, and 32 bits at one time. A 16 bit microcomputer may process two eight-bit bytes (characters) at one time. The overall speed of a microcomputer is a function of the number of bits per word, word size. In microcomputer communication the bits per character is also referred to as word size. 37

Word wrap: The moving of the last word in a line to the next line when there is no room between margins. 101

Write protect notch: Notch on disk that is covered to make write only on five and one quarter diskette and uncovered on eight inch disk. 53

⟨**CR**⟩: Press the return or enter keys. 69

^ n: ^ Means press the control key at the same time as n, where n is another key. 81

Index

Registered Trademarks—Continued

Chapter Opening Photos

Chapter 1 Courtesy of Hewlett-Packard Company, Chapter 2 Courtesy of International Business Machines Corporation, Chapter 3 Courtesy of AT&T Information Systems, Chapter 4 Courtesy of International Business Machines Corporation, Chapter 5 Courtesy of International Business Machines Corporation, Chapter 7 Chorus Data Systems, a manufacturer of image acquisition and data management products for P.C.'s, Chapter 8 Courtesy of Radio Shack, a division of Tandy Corporation, Chapter 9 Courtesy of Radio Shack, a division of Tandy Corporation, Chapter 10 Courtesy of Hayes Microcomputer Products, Inc., Chapter 11 Courtesy of Hewlett-Packard Company, Chapter 12 Courtesy of International Business Machines Corporation

Intext Photo Credits

Fig. 1–1 Courtesy of Hewlett-Packard Company, Fig. 1–4 Princeton Graphic Systems, An Intelligent Systems Company, Fig. 1–5 Micro Technology, Inc., Fig. 1–6 Princeton Graphic Systems, An Intelligent Systems Company, Fig. 1–7 MicroTouch Systems, Inc., Fig. 1–8 Courtesy of Hewlett-Packard Company, Fig. 1–10 Courtesy of International Business Machines Corporation, Fig. 1–11 Courtesy of Compaq Computer Corporation, Fig. 1–12 Courtesy of Hewlett-Packard Company, Fig. 1–14 Princeton Graphic Systems, An Intelligent Systems Company, Fig. 1–15 Courtesy of Interface, Inc., Fig. 1–16 Courtesy of Interface, Inc., Fig. 1–17 Courtesy of AT&T Information Systems, Fig. 1–18 Courtesy of Hewlett-Packard Company, Fig. 1–19 Courtesy of Epson America, Fig. 1–20 Courtesy of Radio Shack, a division of Tandy Corporation, Fig. 2–1 Courtesy of NEC Information Systems, Inc., Fig. 2–2 Micron Technology Systems Group, Boise, Idaho, Fig. 2–6 Courtesy of International Business Machines Corporations, Fig. 2–7 Courtesy of the Voice Connection, Irvine, California, Fig. 2–8 (a) Courtesy of Apple Computer, Inc., (b) Courtesy of Koala Technologies Corp., (c) Courtesy FTG Data Systems, (d) Courtesy of Hewlett-Packard Company, Fig. 2–9 Courtesy of NEC Information Systems, Inc., Fig. 2–10 Courtesy of NEC Information Systems, Inc., Fig. 2–11 Courtesy of NEC Information Systems, Inc., Fig. 2–12 Courtesy of Hewlett-Packard Company, Fig. 2–13 Courtesy of Hewlett-Packard Company, Fig. 2–14 Courtesy of Hewlett-Packard Company, Fig. 2–15 Courtesy of NEC Information Systems, Inc., Fig. 2–16 Courtesy of Epson America, Fig. 2–17 Courtesy of NEC Information Systems, Inc., Fig. 2–18 Courtesy of Radio Shack, a division of Tandy Corporation, Fig. 2–21 Courtesy of Apple Computer, Inc., Fig. 2–22 Courtesy of International Business Machines Corporation, Fig. 3–3 Courtesy of NEC Information Systems, Inc., Fig. 8–2 Courtesy of Radio Shack, a division of Tandy Corporation, Fig. 8–3 Courtesy of Radio Shack, a division of Tandy Corporation, Fig. 8–4 Courtesy of Radio Shack, a division of Tandy Corporation, Fig. 10–1 Courtesy of Hewlett-Packard Company